WAR AND OTHER MEANS

VIOLENCE AND POWER IN HOUAÏLOU (NEW CALEDONIA)

WAR AND OTHER MEANS

VIOLENCE AND POWER IN HOUAÏLOU (NEW CALEDONIA)

MICHEL NAEPELS

PRESS

STATE, SOCIETY AND GOVERNANCE IN MELANESIA SERIES

Published by ANU Press
The Australian National University
Acton ACT 2601, Australia
Email: anupress@anu.edu.au
This title is also available online at press.anu.edu.au

National Library of Australia Cataloguing-in-Publication entry

Creator: Naepels, Michel, author.

Title: War and other means : violence and power in Houaïlou (New Caledonia) / Michel Naepels ; Rachel Gomme, translator.

ISBN: 9781760461539 (paperback) 9781760461546 (ebook)

Series: State, society and governance in Melanesia.

Notes: Translation of: Conjurer la guerre: Violence et pouvoir à Houaïlou (Nouvelle-Calédonie).

Subjects: Political violence--New Caledonia--Houaïlou.
Violence--New Caledonia--Houaïlou.
Kanaka (New Caledonian people)
Kanaka (New Caledonian people)--Politics and government.
Kanaka (New Caledonian people)--Government relations.
Minorities--Government policy--New Caledonia--Houaïlou.
Houaïlou (New Caledonia)--Ethnic relations.
Houaïlou (New Caledonia)--Politics and government.

Other Creators/Contributors:
Gomme, Rachel, translator.

All rights reserved. No part of this publication may be reproduced, stored in a retrieval system or transmitted in any form or by any means, electronic, mechanical, photocopying or otherwise, without the prior permission of the publisher.

Cover design and layout by ANU Press. Cover photograph from Deborah Adam flic.kr/p/W3Ww8W.

This edition © 2017 ANU Press

French original edition © 2013, *Conjurer la guerre. Violence et pouvoir à Houaïlou (Nouvelle-Calédonie)*, Éditions de l'École des hautes études en sciences sociales ISBN 978-2-7132-2376-1

The translation was carried out with the financial support of Institut de Recherche Interdisciplinaire sur les enjeux sociaux, the laboratory of excellence Tepsis carried by the EHESS, bearing the reference ANR-11-LABX-0067, and Fondation Maison des Sciences de l'Homme.

For Ulysse and Isidore

Contents

List of figures and tables............................... ix
Acknowledgements xi
Introduction 1
1. Lineage Rivalry and Colonial Control: The Dynamics
   of War in a Globalised Space 9
2. Objects of War 71
3. The Chiefdoms within the Colonial Order 111
4. Post-*indigénat* Mobilisations..........................161
5. The Subjectivity of Violent Action 207
6. The Construction and Fiction of Consensus 235
Conclusion..281
References..287

List of figures and tables

Figure 1. Detail of map showing 'the dwelling of George Wright' (1876)........................... 18

Figure 2. Extract from the genealogy of the Néjâ family........... 63

Figure 3. 'Néporo lineage'.................................. 65

Table 1. Chronological and genealogical relationships between some of the individuals referred to in this text.............. 99

Table 2. Mobilisation for the First World War, by district......... 119

Table 3. Mobilisation for the colonial war in Koné and Hienghène.................................. 123

Figure 4. Award of decorations in April 1918: 'The stage'......... 128

Figure 5. Award of decorations in April 1918: 'The frenzied *pilou*'.. 128

Table 4. Principal categories and results of 1911 census in Houaïlou... 133

Figure 6. Plan of the partial leper colony of Kananu............. 150

Figure 7. The Mandaoué chiefdom in the *Livre du centenaire*, 1953.. 170

Figure 8. Genealogical identification of some of the accused related to high chief Apupia in 1955..................... 182

Acknowledgements

I would not have been able to conduct the research presented in this book had it not been for my post as researcher at the Centre National de la Recherche Scientifique (National Center for Scientific Research, CNRS) and the École des hautes études en sciences sociales (School for Advanced Studies in the Social Sciences, EHESS), in three successive laboratories: the SHADYC (Sociology, History and Anthropology of Cultural Dynamics, now the Norbert Elias Center), GTMS (Genesis and Transformation of Social Worlds) and IRIS (Institute for Interdisciplinary Research on Social Issues). In addition to their support, I received grants for my fieldwork in New Caledonia from ORSTOM (Office of Overseas Scientific and Technical Research), LACITO (Languages and Civilisations with Oral Traditions, CNRS), ITSO research group (Identities and Changes in Oceanian Societies, CNRS), CORDET (Co-ordinating Committee for Research in Overseas Departments and Territories, Ministry of Overseas Departments and Territories), the ESK program (Study of Kanak Societies, Ministry of Culture), the Anthropological Heritage Mission (Ministry of Culture), NCESC research group (New Caledonia: Contemporary Social Issues, CNRS), and the ANR (National Research Agency) program 'Transformation of wars'.

Many scholars offered encouragement, support and criticism. I am especially grateful to Jean Bazin, my thesis supervisor, and Patrick Williams, my postdoctoral supervisor. Meeting Alban Bensa and Jean-Claude Rivierre was also of crucial importance. I owe much to the work and discussions conducted in the CNRS research group 'New Caledonia: Contemporary Social Issues'. The work of Christine Demmer, Isabelle Merle, Adrian Muckle, Hélène Nicolas, Marie Salaün and Benoît Trépied were particularly valuable sources of reflection in my attempt to articulate different historical scales. I owe special thanks to Christine Hamelin and Christine Salomon, with whom I have been able to share my doubts and my difficulties since 1991, and whose works are an essential source of inspiration. I am also grateful to Dorothée Dussy, Isabelle Grangaud and Bernard Vienne. Étienne Balibar and Yves Duroux made decisive contributions to the writing of this book. Finally, I am grateful to Julie Biro for her invaluable reading of earlier versions of this text and for her consistent encouragement and support.

In New Caledonia, my work benefited from my interactions with a number of institutions, particularly the Agence pour le développement de la culture kanake (Kanak Cultural Development Agency), the Agence pour le développement rural et l'aménagement foncier (Rural Development and Land Planning Agency), and the Archives of New Caledonia. Above all, I remember the faces of my Kanak interlocutors – those singular combinations of marginality, power and powerlessness, of knowledge and ignorance, of truth and morality, of kindness and harshness, which initially constitute what I understand as 'Houaïlou'; some of them are cited in the text. I had the good fortune to build lasting warm and even close relationships with a number of people, especially Narcisse and Marie Kaviyöibanu; Maurice and Suzanne Mèèvâ and their children Édouard, Yvonne, Charley, Natacha, Viviane, Paul, Fabrice, Jeanne and Ludovic; Louis and Josyane Mapou; Willy Bwérhéxéu; Yvon Mârâhëë; Georges Mandaoué; and Joseph Wéma Nirikani; without forgetting Jean-Luc Karé, who was killed in Houaïlou as I was reading the proofs for this book. My debt to them is incalculable.

Huge thanks to Françoise, Étienne and Jeanne Balibar; Karin and Adam Biro; Annette Ungewitter and Fabien Von Nagel, as well as the Fondation des Treilles where I spent a study period in June 2007: they provided me with the best possible conditions for writing the various chapters of this text. Lastly, Rachel Gomme, the translator of the book, and Justine Molony, the copyeditor, did wonderful work: I am enormously grateful to them.

Introduction

They say that they foster disorder in all its forms. Confusion troubles violent debates disarray upsets disturbances incoherences irregularities divergences complications disagreements discords clashes polemics discussions contentions brawls dispute conflicts routs débâcles cataclysms disturbances quarrels agitation turbulence conflagrations chaos anarchy.

Monique Wittig, *Les Guérillères*, translated by David Le Vay, Urbana and Chicago: University of Illinois Press, 2007, p. 93.

A political anthropology of civil conflict

This book analyses the conventions of the use of violence in managing a wide range of conflicts, in a colonial and subsequently a postcolonial context, taking occasions of resorting to violence, segmentary disputes and internal wars as a central theme, and a lens through which to analyse social relations in Houaïlou, New Caledonia. In short, as Michel Foucault suggested, I want to ask: 'Can war serve as a useful tool for analysing relations of power?' (Foucault 2003, p. 18). Through this approach, I hope to make visible a set of rationales for action deployed by the inhabitants of this region, the historical context of the problems they face and the categories of analysis that can be used to describe them. Examining social relations through the lens of conflict and segmentarity should thus make it possible to counter 'an implicit definition of anthropology that identifies it *de facto* with a suspension of the political' (Loraux 2006, p. 50). Nicole Loraux demonstrates how productive this approach can be in her article 'Ares in the family', a theme to which she returns in *The Divided City*, where she develops her analysis of *stásis*, 'internecine war installed in the heart of the city' (p. 35).

In his 1976 lectures at the Collège de France, Foucault argues, in opposition to juridical discourse, which is based on the sovereignty of the ruler and the subject's obligation of obedience, that there is a need to make space for a non-state discourse that reintroduces the complexity of real actions, confrontation and the defence of the rights and interests of the individual. Taking into account actual practices in conflict situations, investigating the detail of mechanisms, taking as a starting point power relations in all their diversity, their heterogeneity, their historicity and their complexity – in other words, as far as this study is concerned, taking seriously the statements of my Kanak interlocutors, whose discourse is always circumstanced, contextualised, and bound up with the relationship between the speaker and his interlocutors, means that the study needs to be firmly embedded within the field of empirical human sciences.[1] It also implies that politics needs to be thought within the spaces of autonomy that each individual strives to construct in the set of social situations s/he encounters, rather than purely within institutions. The key is to reintroduce the discourse of violence and contingency into our analysis of social relations:[2]

> Explaining things from below also means explaining them in terms of what is most confused, most obscure, most disorderly and most subject to chance, because what is being put forward as a principle for the interpretation of society and its visible order is the confusion of violence, passions, hatreds, rages, resentments and bitterness; it is the obscurity of contingencies and all the minor incidents that bring about defeats and ensure victories. This discourse is essentially asking the elliptical god of battles to explain the long days of order, labor, peace and justice. (Foucault 2003, p. 54)

Such a perspective, Foucault tells us, 'develops completely within the historical dimension' (p. 55). My analysis, which continually links the description of spaces of political action to their historical context, will take this path.

In addressing 'conflict', my intention here is in no way to advance a specific theory of the nature of violence or the conflictual character of social relations, but rather to examine a number of social situations that have a political dimension, and show similarity in their combination of collective mobilisation and the use of physical violence. 'Violence',

---

1   Foucault 2003, p. 40.
2   Foucault 2003, pp. 53–54.

as I propose to interpret it, is thus not an ontological category – a tragic figure of the impoverished human condition – rather, it constitutes a heuristic lever through which to approach social relations in both their singularity and their ordinariness.³ Foucault, describing the new historico-political discourse that emerged in the late 17th and early 18th centuries, sums up one of its features thus: 'War has not been averted' (Foucault 2003, p. 50); in the view of the authors he goes on to consider, particularly Boulainvilliers, war continues under the ostensible rule of law. The present work similarly evokes the dual sense of the multiple meanings contained in the French word *'conjuration'*.⁴ This seems to me an apt description of the Kanak social and political relations on which I seek to shed light here. Starting from the first sense, that of calling forth, I shall attempt to understand the place given to physical violence in social relations in Houaïlou, and to what extent local conflicts prompt interventions aimed at preventing them from degenerating, averting war and controlling violence. But drawing on the second sense, that of banishing, I shall counter this juridico-philosophical perspective, based on sovereignty, the chiefdom, contractualisation and the ordering of collectively inhabited spaces, which is also that of Kanak public ceremonial discourse, with an oppositional reading that places emphasis on the historical and political dimensions of social reality. It will be understood that one can conjure war as conspirators, as rebels, as bandits and by preparing war in secret, as the *Conspiracy of the Comte de Fiesque* showed.⁵ There is in fact an extensive Ajië⁶ lexicon relating to secrets, dirty tricks and ambushes. In short, while conflicts can be 'shut into the pot' (*uxöwî*), compensated, settled and forgotten in order to better restore the social contract, following the Greek model of amnesty, there are contrary means – transmission of knowledge being one – of fanning 'the fire under the pot'⁷ in the dark, in the home rather than in front of others, maintaining a private hatred alongside public politeness: 'For the universal principle of reciprocity that

---

3 Naepels 2006a. See Collins 2008; Nassiet 2011.
4 In the original French title, *Conjurer la Guerre*, the word *'conjurer'* connotes both the sense of 'conjuring up, summoning, plotting' and that of 'conjuring away, averting, banishing' [trans.].
5 *La conjuration du Comte Jean-Louis de Fiesque* (*The Conspiracy of Count Jean-Louis de Fiesque*) (1665), in Cardinal de Retz, *Œuvres* (*Complete Works*), Paris, Gallimard (1984), pp. 1–50. Translated from the Italian by the young Cardinal of Retz, this account relates to the history of Genoa in the 16th century.
6 In this book I use the spelling Ajië for the name of the language spoken in Houaïlou, as proposed by Aramiou, Euritéin and Kavivioro (2001) and Lercari (2002).
7 To adopt René Guiart's phrase (2001).

applies to barter and gifts also applies to revenge' (Sofsky 2003, p. 195). And in effect, in New Caledonia a degree of accumulation of obligations and debts can be observed as much in violence as in exchange.

In this book I present a series of cross-sections through the colonial and postcolonial history of Houaïlou, an analysis of some historical moments and particular structures of power, which I have sought to reconstitute in their full density by depicting the interlocking contexts in which political action is played out. I focus particularly on two interconnected domains. Firstly, I examine practices of war, the forms and conventions of the use of physical violence, and the changes in these from the mid-19th century to the present day. Secondly, I strive to describe the social forms of mobilisation, the modes of constitution of collectives, particularly around institutions, that are sometimes treated as self-evident, such as the chiefdom and the council of elders, but also around forms that are more obviously historically contingent, such as ceremonial collectives or political parties. These two dimensions are linked on a number of levels: some inhabitants of Houaïlou were able to mobilise for the purpose of exercising physical violence, constituting ad hoc collectives (for example, during the pre-colonial or colonial wars analysed in the first three chapters, or at the height of the independence struggle described in Chapter 5); in other cases, mobilisations aimed at bringing order to villages' communal spaces led indirectly to violent action being taken (for example, in the context of the changes in governance structures that followed the ending of the *indigénat*,[8] in the 1950s, and since the 1990s, following the 'events' of the 1980s;[9] these periods are addressed in chapters 4 and 6 respectively). Focusing on the forms of physical violence, the efforts made to avoid it and the modalities by which it is instrumentalised leads me to touch on certain forms of subjectivation, whose complexity I have attempted to convey.

---

8   The French colonial system of indirect rule exercised via indigenous rulers, organisations and officials. It was governed by the Code de l'Indigénat [trans.].
9   Disturbances and acts of violence (including hostage-taking) that followed the adoption of a series of statutes [trans.].

INTRODUCTION

Political anthropology, colonial and postcolonial history

In his essay 'Three concepts of politics', Étienne Balibar puts forward an analysis of the articulation between social relations, conceived as the pre-existing conditions of any political action, and power relations, conceived as constitutive at the scale of micropolitical strategies. It is at the intersection of these two dimensions, he suggests, that effects of subjectivation can be articulated:

> Subjectivation is the collective individualization which occurs at the point where change changes, where 'things begin to change differently' – that is to say, wherever the *tendency* immanent in the system of historical conditions finds itself affected from within by the action of an equally immanent *counter-tendency*. (Balibar 2002, p. 13)

My argument is organised around the central thread of analysing episodes or scenes that take place precisely at such unresolved moments of change, where the modalities of government of the self and of others are rearticulated. These are as follows: the repressive operation conducted by the French military in 1856 (examined in Chapter 1), a further military operation conducted in 1867 in the Houaïlou valley (Chapter 2), the appointment of four paramount chiefs in the territory of Houaïlou municipality[10] in 1912 (Chapter 3), a witch-hunt conducted in the latter part of 1955 (Chapter 4), the period of the 'events' at the time of the mass independence movement between 1984 and 1988 (Chapter 5), and finally the situation during the early 2000s (Chapter 6). By focusing on such moments I am able to give an account of what can be known about subjective experiences, moral sentiments, and modalities of work on the self through ecstasy, rage, exaltation and laughter. These moments, and the scenes of violence that unfold within them, thus constitute my point of entry in attempting to understand social relations and modes of political thinking that may not have a distinct temporal demarcation. While the various chapters follow a roughly chronological sequence, I have sought to embed different timescales within them, by combining the description of scenes that show political actors in action at a particular moment with broader movements. Thus I have chosen discord, division,

---

10 '*Commune*': administrative district in France and French colonies [trans.].

disputes, violence and compromise primarily as guiding threads or levers, in both my field research and my analysis, to understand the rationales for action of the inhabitants of Houaïlou.

The nature of the violence described in the successive chapters of this book clearly reveals the fact that the history of Houaïlou, like that of New Caledonia as a whole, has for more than a century and a half been tied to developments in French colonisation. Choosing a local scale of analysis thus makes it possible to reflect on the concrete methods through which colonial governance is operated; I focus particularly on the invention, import or adaptation of repressive techniques used in Houaïlou that are closely linked to the French colonial experience in Algeria. This approach also makes it possible to reflect on colonial and postcolonial history without reducing it purely to the coloniser/colonised binary, but at the same time without losing sight of the dissymmetry of their respective positions in war and conflict. Indeed, the moments of violence that I shall analyse take on different meanings depending on the perspective from which they are viewed; colonial and postcolonial situations cannot be reduced to a great divide between two types of actors, and the forms of action that unfold within them cannot always be easily categorised according to a binary logic. Some moves towards partial decolonisation can thus be viewed as recolonisation, and instances of resistance or collaboration as constructions of internal relations of inequality. At the level of my analysis, politics can only be understood in the framework of a contextualised history.

Poetics and pragmatics

This book is thus consciously situated within a broad movement of historicisation of anthropological knowledge, and seeks to contribute to reflection on the relations between history and anthropology.[11] Hence it will be understood that it also constitutes an attempt to write an action-centred anthropology, in a resolutely pragmatic mode.[12] The text is articulated around a detailed description of episodes of violence (from the repressive operations of the 19th century to contemporary village conflicts, via the 'events' linked to the Kanak independence movement between 1984 and 1988). While it is organised chronologically, it strives

---

11 Naepels 2010a.
12 I give a detailed account of the epistemological bases of my method in Naepels 2011.

to draw out thematic resonances between the different chapters, without falling into a form of causal demonstration or a culturalist claim that Kanak violence is in any way specific. Descriptions of particular social situations allow us to analyse the interweaving of various different contexts within a given situation, to reveal the various rhythms and to show how a particular place is altered by the currents that flow through it. This close description thus offers scope for broadening the view both spatially and temporally. The fact that an idiographic investigation of a present or past situation implies the invention of a praxeography (as Jean Bazin put it), a cartography of possible actions,[13] in other words, essentially a writing, constitutes an example of what Claude Imbert refers to in 'Le cadastre des savoirs', as one of the most important epistemic shifts contributed by the social sciences in recent years: 'Were we to borrow from ethnography, focusing on a "micro-history", the anticipated advantage is not an excess of concrete detail, but rather to offer scope for other perspectives on the real, at the cost of a different intelligence' (Imbert 2005, p. 257).

In my view, this pragmatic, non-causalist perspective is the best way to reveal the practical inventiveness, ingenuity and the intelligence and reflexivity of the actors (here Kanaks) involved in political (here conflictual) relations. Thus, following the themes of mobilisation, the chiefdom, war and witchcraft enables me to reveal the historicity of these social realities without thereby engaging in establishing the causes of evolving dynamics. These themes emerge as a series of contrapuntal lines, while the combination of various temporalities in each chapter reveals the harmonics of personal investments within each of the social situations considered.

In terms of empirical materials, my approach requires me to point out the difficulties inherent in the articulation between oral and archival sources. In order to understand what the characters in my story are doing, we must constantly ask how the testimonies were gathered, what were the positions of my interlocutors and what was the position of those in the past who produced the written documents and archival sources. If we assume that, empirically speaking, we can sometimes know what such and such a person is saying in certain circumstances, but cannot have access to what they are thinking, the support of detailed history and linguistic anthropology are indispensable. In my view, if we hold to this critical

---

13 Bazin 2003.

nominalism, much more can be drawn out of the collected historical and ethnographic documents than if we seek to integrate them in their entirety with generalising considerations that are both elevated and hypothetical. My aim is therefore not to offer explanations of the social facts observed, but rather to articulate a question (that of the relationship between conflict, violence and power) with a particular way of describing reality. Ultimately, I have attempted to look at the history of Houaïlou differently, through the interlocking, collating and the heterogeneity of the documents cited and their registers of analysis. My descriptive journey through a series of moments in the history of Houaïlou leads me to return several times to the same places, the same hamlets, and to meet the same family names several times over. These echoes are deliberate, a way of revealing the historical thickness of the subjective experiences of my Kanak informers. But it will be understood that at the same time, this text does not aspire to be exhaustive or complete. I am fully aware that I know only some aspects of the reality of which I speak, and only a small part of the events that make up social life in Houaïlou. There are many other ways of telling this story.

1
Lineage Rivalry and Colonial Control: The Dynamics of War in a Globalised Space

> One might suggest an elementary subaltern principle of historiography: that no assertion of an imperialist discipline can be received as an event of colonial history without the ethnographic investigation of its practice. We cannot equate colonial history simply with the history of the colonizers. It remains to be known how the disciplines of the colonial state are culturally sabotaged.
>
> Marshall Sahlins, 'Goodbye to *Tristes Tropes*: Ethnography in the Context of Modern World History', 1993, pp. 485–86.

I open my argument with an account I was given in Houaïlou in 1995 by Narcisse Kaviyöibanu, who had himself heard it from Gilbert Népörö, his mother's husband:

> I'll tell you a story, it was when the Canala chiefdoms formed an alliance with the Whites ... In their history, the Néjâ and the Népörö [Houaïlou chiefdoms] were the seniors, and the others in Canala, the Bwaxéa and their families, were the juniors, the ones who come after ... When they formed an alliance with the Whites, the first thing they did, they decided they had to neutralise the people of Houaïlou. Because they wanted to be above both the chiefdoms in Houaïlou. So, what they did was, they sent a [European] ship to go and neutralise the two chiefs in Houaïlou.
>
> The ship sailed from Canala, it entered the Parawiè channel, and when it entered the channel ... there are lookouts in the chiefdom, and the lookout at the harbour, that night when he was asleep, he had a dream. In his dream,

he saw a shark coming towards him, and then it came up onto the beach, then it struck like that with its tail ... then it says: 'Are you awake or asleep?' Then the old man answers: 'No, I'm awake.' The shark says: 'Quick, go and blow the *tutu* [conch], because there's a ship coming into the harbour with people from Canala on board, they're coming to kill the two chiefs.'

...

He runs from Parawiè to Warai ... there's a ford between Parawiè and then Warai ... he crossed that ford, he went up the other side onto the ridge ... and there he blew the conch. Usually people know, it's a signal that's understood, when the *tutu* sounds there, it means that there are people coming into the harbour down below. So when he blew, straightaway the warriors guarding the harbour ran to their pirogues, and they got into the pirogue, they went to the harbour with spells, they cast spells. The spells they cast made fog, so they called up the fog; that meant that when the ship entered the Houaïlou channel, they couldn't see anything, it was all covered in mist. And the pirogues came, they arrived, they came alongside the ship, they boarded and then they killed the people on board, the people from Canala and the Whites who were there. And then they took the bodies, and then they made an oven over there, there where the Nékwé church is, there's a big oven behind the chapel, they cooked all the people. When they finished cooking them, they took [the bodies] down to the house of Félix, the Népörö elder, and they cut them into portions. When they finished cutting them up there, they went down to the house of my two younger brothers [the two sons of Gilbert Népörö], to the house called Ka-öi, the Ka-öi alley, that means the place where people eat, and they ate them there in the alley, they ate the people from Canala and the Whites who came. (Narcisse Kaviyöibanu, extract from interview, September 1995)

I shall have occasion to address this text on several levels including anthropophagy, representations of ancestrality and the powers of action (here called 'spells') pertaining to it and the local forms of ceremonial apportionment. In this first chapter, I propose first to explore what can be known of the political meaning of war and the evolution of the chiefdoms in the region of Houaïlou during the second half of the 19th century, particularly but not exclusively on the basis of a close and critical reading of colonial sources on colonial wars. I shall therefore trace the appearance of Houaïlou in writings, accounts and French 'sources', at the time of the first repressive operation conducted there in 1856. The use of the term 'repression', and even of the name 'Houaïlou', derives from an entirely Eurocentric perspective, a strongly biased view of the local social situation. For what took place at that time and became memorialised as a significant date in 'local' history – a repressive operation carried out in 1856[1] – is also embedded, on a variety of levels, in multiple series of events and Kanak discourses of which those newly arrived from Europe were entirely unaware, and of which today we can only have a very partial perception. The Europeans who wrote reports, memoirs, letters or notes about what was happening in the Houaïlou region were entering *in media res*, into a multiplicity of Kanak and Oceanian histories; they themselves were embedded in a global history of trade (which involved, among other things, the search for sandalwood, gold, nickel and other minerals in New Caledonia) and the development of European imperialisms. While I make no claim to opening out the enormous complexity of these histories and this flow, I would, nevertheless, like to try to reconstitute one part of it.

The French takeover of New Caledonia on 24 September 1853 was ratified by several chiefs, in central Grande Terre, on the east coast, and in Kwawa and Canala – but not in Houaïlou. Who were these 'chiefs'? Which families did they belong to? What was their understanding of a document written in a language they did not know, which used concepts of sovereignty peculiar to Western nation-states? What meaning could they give to the cross they inscribed at the bottom of this document? Greg Dening has explored the convoluted meanings of takeover in the case of Tahiti,[2] and a number of discussions have subjected the Treaty of Waitangi in New Zealand to similar analysis;[3] we can, then, safely posit that misunderstanding was the constitutive register of the colonial relations thus instituted. Be that as it may, at the time of taking possession, the French had had no contact with the Kanaks living in the territory now designated as Houaïlou, and controlled absolutely no part of it. Previously, from 1843 onwards, French Catholic missionaries had taken up residence in Balade, and then in other places in the north of Grande Terre (Touho and Wagap), during the course of sojourns marked by a series of crises and expulsions. The colonial power's state control of Grande Terre at the time of 'taking possession' was in truth limited to Nouméa and the surrounding area (and that not without difficulty: wars continued in the Nouméa region throughout the 1850s),[4] to the Catholic missions in the north, and to a few isolated points of contact on the coasts (made during the military circumnavigation of the islands).

---

1   See Dousset-Leenhardt 1970; Saussol 1979.
2   Dening 1996.
3   Kawharu 1989.
4   Dussy 2000 and 2012; Dauphiné 1995.

1847–55: Sandalwood traders, 'Houaïlou' and the Oceanian world-system

Contact through trade and war

Dorothy Shineberg has demonstrated the importance of the links established in the second half of the 1840s throughout Grande Terre by sandalwood collectors, mainly British and Australian, particularly during the sandalwood rush of 1846–49.[5] Examination of the logs of a number of the ships involved[6] reveals that they wove a network of commercial and military relationships with the Kanak inhabitants of Houaïlou well before the French did so: there was certainly contact in August–September 1849 (*Eleanor*, Captain Edward Woodin, in 'Whalo'), between 27 April and 7 June 1851 (*Eleanor*, Woodin, in 'Wylow'), and on 24 January 1854 (*Louisa*, Captain Beresford, in 'Wilo').[7] In Houaïlou these were trading relations. The *Louisa*'s log of 24 January 1854 reports the ship's sojourn in 'Wilo', where she arrived at six o'clock the previous evening:

> Daylight turned to clear away the Boats ready for lowering, 2 hands employed repairing the Jib, at 9 lowered the Boat and proceeded up the river in search of sandalwood and shells, Noon fine and cleared NNE. P.M. Steady Breeze and clear, at 4 returned with the Boat with no wood. Bought 8 shells for 1 musket, at 6 hoisted up the boats. At 8 set the watch, night light, breeze and cloudy at 4 am hove short and got under weigh and proceeded down the coast. (Beresford 1853–54, 24–25 January 1854)

A recently collected account refers to a similar commercial relationship:

> Old Baudoux[8] told me about when the first rifle arrived in Houaïlou. In the olden days, there was a boat that was going round Caledonia looking for sandalwood. It stopped to take some down in Nérhô lands, at Warai. The sailors asked them for their war weapons, spears and axes;[9] they gave them to them. Another day, the captain came, he asked them for their war

---

5   Shineberg 1967.
6   Woodin 1846–53; Beresford 1853–54.
7   While Philip Vigors sailed past 'Wylow' and probably made land in Poro bay ('Red Harbour') on 20 October 1850.
8   I shall return later to the figure of Georges Baudoux, surveyor in Houaïlou and New Caledonian writer (see Chapter 2). It is noteworthy that the Kanak 'oral' tradition can on occasion pass through the mediation of a colonist.
9   The fact that exchange could involve not only natural goods, like sandalwood and shells, but also ethnographic curiosities, particularly weapons, is a point to which I shall return (Chapter 2).

weapons, they gave them to him. In return he gave them a rifle. Then, by the sea, he taught them to shoot. They learned to shoot. (Euritéin 1990, p. 9; my translation)

These relations can probably be traced back even further than 1849. For example, the as yet unpublished manuscript by William Diaper reveals that he was present in Houaïlou in mid-1848.[10] Shineberg also reports that Woodin in his two ships, the *Eleanor* and the *Spy*, explored all the rivers of the east coast in 1846–47 in search of sandalwood, and left a number of men at different points along the coast to collect the precious timber.[11] It was during this exploration that a skirmish took place between some Kanaks from Houaïlou and the sandalwood collectors:

> Thursday, 25th November [1847]. – Arrived on the east coast of Caledonia, anchored in a bay, where the brig *Spy*, Captain Whyte, was lying, found that the party I had left on shore and the crew of the brig *Spy* had had a desperate encounter with the natives, in which five of the crew of the *Spy* were severely wounded; fortunately no one killed. From the best information I could obtain, nine or ten of the natives were killed, and a great many wounded, as several of them applied to me to extract the balls out of their arms and legs. It appears that this encounter arose from the jealousy of the Wiloian tribe against my friends, (natives), caused, I suppose, by my friends getting rich in trade. The Wiloans are a very numerous tribe, and have great influence for many miles along the east coast. I am of opinion that great provocation had been given by some of my party, who remained on shore. (Woodin 1850, p. 298)

Unfortunately, the *Eleanor*'s log for this period of November 1847 is missing from the State of Tasmania archives,[12] and I was unable to locate the log of the *Spy*; there is nothing to indicate that it was preserved in any archive collection. Nevertheless, it seems to me very likely that this episode recounted by Woodin can be identified with one of the 14 armed incidents between Europeans and the inhabitants of the New Hebrides, New Caledonia and the Loyalty Islands between 1841 and 1848, which John Erskine, captain of the British warship HMS *Havannah*, listed in a letter written from on board in October 1849. Erskine's criticism of the lack of discipline and provocations by the sandalwood collectors in this text testifies both to a degree of understanding of the indigenous people

---

10 I await William W. Emilsen's forthcoming edition with great interest.
11 Shineberg 1967, p. 75.
12 The log held in the Crowther collection covers the periods April 1846 – June 1847 and March 1848 – August 1853.

on the part of a liberal officer, and to his sense of order, as a representative of the British state: his criticism of the anarchic nature of the sandalwood collectors' individual initiatives is not unmarked by distinct class prejudice.

> All kinds of excesses have been committed by the undisciplined crews, who always carry arms, and are but too ready to make use of them. It is not surprising that the natives of the different islands (anxious though they are to traffic with Europeans) consider themselves justified in taking every advantage of men who treat them in such a manner. During the last few years, accordingly, constant disputes, attended with loss of life on both sides, have taken place. [A list follows, including:] 10. An expedition undertaken by the boats of the barque 'Spy' of Hobart Town, up the river Kanela, in New Caledonia; one man wounded, and many natives said to have been killed. (Erskine 1851, pp. 235–36)

It seems plausible that these two converging texts relate to the same event: in this reading, some of the members of the *Spy*'s crew who had been left in Canala, and Kanaks with whom they were in contact, were attacked in late 1847 by warriors from 'Wilo'. Woodin's article in the *Nautical Magazine* of May 1850 represents the first published reference to the inhabitants of this region, which was to become 'Houaïlou'.

Contacts between sandalwood collectors and Kanaks seem to have been even more extensive in the neighbouring language area, or *xârâcùù* (around Canala), where it appears that dozens or even hundreds of rifles were exchanged;[13] this contributed to the development of wars and the emergence of a single dominant chiefdom that took control in Nakéty and Kwawa, with the support of whites. According to Nicholas Thomas,[14] trade with Europeans contributed throughout the Pacific region to the increasing pre-eminence of chiefdoms or families living in the coastal zones over those in the interior. It should be added that Shineberg, in her article 'Guns and Men in Melanesia', demonstrates that the social and political significance of the introduction of firearms should not be overstated on the technical level, since the firearms used in the Pacific in the mid-19th century were sometimes less effective than indigenous weapons. Two comparative advantages of firearms are often highlighted: their capacity to kill at close range and the psychological effect of the noise, smoke and powder flash. But this picture should be balanced against the slow and difficult process of reloading, the frequency of misfiring, and the powder's sensitivity to damp,

---

13   Dauphiné 1990a.
14   Thomas 1989a.

particularly problematic in a tropical maritime zone. Technical progress only began to alter this situation in the latter half of the 1860s.[15] Following Shineberg's argument, Kerry Howe shows that:

> The assumption that firearms had a devastating effect when introduced into hostilities in the Pacific is not supported by events on the Loyalty Islands. There, Europeans and their technology did not change the tactics and techniques of warfare as long as it lasted and, in particular, firearms were responsible for killing only a small proportion of those who died in the fighting. (Howe 1974, p. 38)

Marshall Sahlins made a similar point in relation to Fiji: 'it was not European muskets that historically made Fijian chiefs powerful so much as the chiefs that made muskets historically powerful' (Sahlins 1993, p. 22).

In any case, the sandalwood trade in the central area of the coast developed out of Canala, and may thus have contributed to the 'jealousy' (Woodin 1850, p. 298) of the people of Houaïlou, by shifting the political and economic balance of relations between these neighbouring areas. The attack on the *Spy*'s crew could then be understood against a background of tensions between Houaïlou and Canala.

The name 'Houaïlou'

The uncertain origin of the name 'Houaïlou' has been pointed out more than once:[16] the region's inhabitants tend rather to make reference to their linguistic identity, speaking of the *Ajië* area. The name 'Houaïlou' is not found in any of the earliest written sources available on this region. The great bay and anchorage situated between Kanala-Kanela-Canala and Kwawa-Kouaoua (in the south-east) and Tiwaka-Wagap-Suaka (in the north-west) are referred to by the following terms: 'Whalo' (Woodin, log of the *Eleanor*, 1849); 'the Wiloian tribe', 'the Wiloans' (Woodin 1850); 'Wylow' (Vigors 1850); 'Wylow' (Woodin, log of the *Eleanor*, 1851); 'Wilo' (Beresford, log of the *Louisa*, 1854); 'Ouaïlo' (Foucher 1988); 'Wuaïlo' (Testard 1856, cited in Pannetrat 1993); 'Waïlou' (Le Bris 1856); 'Wuaïlo' (Pannetrat 1993); 'Uailo' (Poupinel 1857); 'Wailu' (Laurent 1857); 'Vaïlu' (Du Bouzet 1858); 'Waïllo' (Grimoult 1859); 'Uaïlu' (Montrouzier 1862); and 'Uaïlo', 'Waïlo' (Vieillard and Deplanche 1863). It happens

---

15   Shineberg 1971.
16   Jacqueline de La Fontinelle, papers presented on 2 November and 18 December 1990 at Inalco, cited in Naepels 1998.

that the most sheltered anchorage in the Houaïlou region, particularly for deep-draught ships like those used by the sandalwood traders, lay at the entrance to the bay known today as Lebris Bay, and is often (but not exclusively) associated with the Nérhô clan,[17] in the immediate vicinity of what were the two coastal hamlets of Bailöö and Bwawi, near the mouth of the river Tü.

> When you look at the bay there and you look at the coast, it's the most accessible point, that's where it's a bit calmer, you see. And then in relation to Parawiè, to explain, in Parawiè it's difficult to get in because of the fringing reef there, but there at Bailöö, it's really open to navigation, it's quite accessible to navigation. And then if the people coming in were afraid … I mean, the space down there, you've got a view over a big space, the space is clear, strategically, it's a [very suitable] place. (Jean-Jacques Ayawa, extract from interview, July 2006)

Thus Bailöö is a place known locally as having been an anchorage or a landing for Polynesian pirogues coming from Ouvéa. It seems reasonable to hypothesise that the names 'Wilo', 'Wylow', 'Waïlo', 'Wuaïlo' [Wailöö] are a corruption or an approximation of Bailöö.[18] As the sphere of reference of this toponym was extended in the sandalwood traders' accounts, by the middle of the 19th century the name encompassed the whole of the coastal region around the anchorage, including the delta or mouth of the main river of Houaïlou and that of Néawa. It was only through a subsequent corruption in French texts that the term 'Houaïlou' appeared, initially referring only to the coastal region and never used as a name to designate the whole of the present-day territory of the district. It was thus through this anchorage, used in earlier times and concurrently by other Oceanian migrants, that the sandalwood traders inserted themselves into an Oceanian system of political–commercial and, as we shall see, matrimonial exchange, as it was manifested in the Ajië area.

---

17 This clan is mentioned in the text by Nissol Euritéin, cited above in connection with the sandalwood trade and the exchange of weapons.

18 Or, conversely, that the name 'Bailöö' used today evolved from the older 'Wailöö'. Constructing hypotheses on the basis of what Anglophones, and subsequently Francophones, grasped of the complex phonology of New Caledonian Kanak languages is obviously problematic. We may nevertheless note that for the first syllable the English 'wi' or 'wy' and the French 'ouaï', 'wuaï', 'uai' and 'wai' incontestably give [wai]; and for the second syllable the English 'lo' or 'low' transcribes a long, open 'o' sound (as in the English 'willow' or 'halo'), which corresponds to the French 'lo' but certainly not the phoneme 'ou' [u]. Wailöö thus seems to me the best transcription of what is recorded by these various early notations.

There are several texts reporting migrations from Polynesia (particularly from Wallis, Samoa and Tonga) to Ouvéa and Grande Terre during the 18th century.[19] It seems legitimate in this respect to speak of an 'Oceanian world-system' (to adopt Immanuel Wallerstein's concept),[20] returning us to the key insight in Epeli Hau'ofa's essay 'Our Sea of Islands', that the pre-colonial Pacific Ocean unified a network rather than isolating islands.[21] Bwawi and Bailöö represented important nodes in this network.

George Wright, first European in Houaïlou, and the Néjâ chiefdom

James Paddon, the most active of the sandalwood traders during the 1850s, set up trading stations at which the sandalwood was gathered and prepared in the interval between calls by the collecting ship, in various locations on the east coast. One of these was the large station in Canala; another was established in Houaïlou around 1855.[22] The settling of a sandalwood trader, in the person of the English sailor George Wright, thus constitutes, to the best of my knowledge, the earliest lasting European presence in Houaïlou. Jean Cacot, himself the son of a Houaïlou colonist, wrote in his 'Notes sur Houaïlou' ['Notes on Houaïlou']:

> Of the earliest Whites to arrive in Houaïlou, the first was Captain Wright, who commanded a sandalwood ship belonging to Paddon. It was shipwrecked at the mouth of the Houaïlou river, and the crew swam to shore and was welcomed by the ancestors of Mindia [a member of the Néjâ family]. The 16 sailors rejoined Paddon on Nou island, and Captain Wright remained with this tribe on the coast, where he married a member of the Chief's family. (Cacot 1985, p. 41)

Patrick O'Reilly also mentions Wright in his biographical note on Thomas Wright:

> Born of an English father, Georges [sic] Wright, former captain in the merchant navy, settled in Houaïlou towards 1855 (?). His mother was the daughter of a Houaïlou chief named Fonwiwé. He [Thomas Wright, the son] had three sisters and a brother, John. (O'Reilly 1953, pp. 410–11)

---

19 Rochas 1862; Jouan 1865; Priday 1950; Hollyman 1959; Guiart 1963.
20 Wallerstein 1980, 1983 and 1984.
21 Hau'ofa 2008.
22 Knoblauch 1903 and 1988, p. 46.

In fact, the earliest map of the Houaïlou coast (drawn by the surveyor Martin between 1874 and 1877) shows the precise location of 'the dwelling of George Wright' on the Houaïlou delta, close to the mouth of the Néawa, not far from 'Pèta, village of the Aïe chief (present-day village)' and 'Ouapo' [Wâpwê] – in other words, in the space now shared between the European village of Houaïlou and the autonomous reserve of Lèwèö-Parawiè, which made up the zone under the direct control of the Néjâ chefferie (Figure 1).

Figure 1. Detail of map showing 'the dwelling of George Wright' (1876)

Source: Topographic Services Archive, Department of Infrastructure, Topography and Land Transport, Map 30A 003R.

1. LINEAGE RIVALRY AND COLONIAL CONTROL

The civil register for the district of Houaïlou shows that George Wright had several children: Thomas (born in 1868), Sarah (1869), Ruth Anne (1871), Nancy (1875), Mercy (1877) and John Powers (born in 1880). Notes in the margin show his date of birth as 1827 and indicate that his registered professions were farmer, merchant and trader. I have so far been unable to identify George Wright's Kanak companion, Bawiri[23] or Pûwiri,[24] and do not know to which lineage she belonged. However, statements gathered by the Protestant missionary Philippe Rey-Lescure do tell us that John Wright (George's younger son) married a woman from the Göwémëu family:

> Later, Kapea said to Samoa: 'Father, I think we are going to see John Rayek (Wright)'. This was an Englishman in Neuio, a Protestant, he had married a woman of the Gouemeu family. (Rey-Lescure 1967, pp. 87–88)

This Göwémëu lineage seems to have brought together individuals of Samoan origin who had come via Ouvéa,[25] or from Ouvéa itself, around the Néjâ chiefdom; this is also suggested by the fact that its totem is the shark[26] (whose role we have noted in the account cited at the start this chapter, in the war between the inhabitants of Houaïlou and Europeans in alliance with Canala Kanaks). It is not impossible that the Göwémëu, by virtue of this fact, bore the role of administrators of the chiefdom's external contacts on the seaward side – and hence with the newly arrived sandalwood traders.

---

23 In the civil register, Baououi or Baouioui or Baouinoui.
24 In the civil register, Pouwini or Pouwiri. The consonant 'f' does not occur in the Ajië language, and thus her name cannot be Fonwiwé, contrary to O'Reilly's 1953 report.
25 Pillon 2001, p. 184.
26 Pillon 2001, p. 189; Guiart 1949, 1953 and 1963, p. 618. William Diaper also mentions Ouvéa speakers living in Chief Wanga's area.

October 1855 – March 1856: Gold prospectors, Canala and the European world-system

Martin Pannetrat and his companions

It was into this setting that at least 11, and more probably 15 'colonists', travelling directly from Sydney and led by Martin Pannetrat, arrived in Canala in October 1855.[27] The arrival of this cosmopolitan group (one German, Ferdinand Knoblauch; one Sardinian; one Swiss and a number of French men)[28] in New Caledonia resulted from a phenomenon of global significance:[29] the gold rush.[30] 'Gold fever' prompted major migrations to California and Mexico from 1849, and to Australia in 1851.[31] During the same period, the first half of the 1850s, the sandalwood trade declined owing to a shortage of available sailors, since the workforce had moved on to searching for gold. The French takeover of New Caledonia aroused a degree of interest among prospectors, who anticipated the possibility of major mineral resources: in February 1855, a letter from governor Joseph Du Bouzet reported a fruitless visit by gold prospectors who had travelled from Australia to New Caledonia without result.[32]

The new arrivals from Canala came as a direct result of this gold fever. A number of French people, mainly working-class individuals disappointed by the way the second Republic had developed,[33] left France for San Francisco.[34] In this passage from *The Eighteenth Brumaire of Louis Bonaparte*, Karl Marx, while commenting ironically on Bonaparte and his government, testifies to the Californian interests of a proportion of the proletariat:[35]

---

27 The first figure is cited by Laurent (1857), the second by Le Bris (1856).
28 According to Pannetrat (1993).
29 For a comparable example, see Clifford 1997.
30 Le Bris 1988.
31 Blainey 1963.
32 Gold was discovered in New Caledonia in 1862, however, in the far north of Grande Terre.
33 The French republican government between the revolution of 1848 and the 1851 coup by Louis Napoléon (Napoleon III) [trans.].
34 Le Bris 1999.
35 It was through reading Le Bris (1999) that I was led to this passage.

1. LINEAGE RIVALRY AND COLONIAL CONTROL

> On December 20, Pascal Duprat interpellated the Minister of the Interior on the 'Goldbar Lottery' … Seven million tickets, a franc a piece, and the profit ostensibly destined to the shipping of Parisian vagabonds to California. Golden dreams were to displace the Socialist dreams of the Parisian proletariat; the tempting prospect of a prize was to displace the doctrinal right to labor. Of course, the workingmen of Paris did not recognize in the lustre of the California gold bars the lack-lustre francs that had been wheedled out of their pockets. In the main, however, the scheme was an unmitigated swindle. The vagabonds, who meant to open California gold mines without taking the pains to leave Paris, were Bonaparte himself and his Round Table of desperate insolvents. (Marx 2005, pp. 53–54)

On 9 September 1850, California became part of the United States of America, following the conclusion of the Treaty of Guadalupe Hidalgo of February 1848, under which Mexico ceded Alta California, Texas and New Mexico (while Baja California, Chihuahua and Sonora remained Mexican). At this point, the English speakers in California turned on the foreign, Spanish- and French-speaking prospectors, forcing them to pay a tax on any gold they found. Following this measure, and the ensuing discontent, the Count of Raousset-Boulbon attempted, with a handful of French people, to create a new independent colony in the Mexican province of Sonora: he landed there twice, in 1852 with 250 armed men and, again, in 1854. He was taken prisoner and executed in 1854.[36] Pannetrat was a close associate of the count; he claimed to own the latter's rifle, and acted as the executor of his will.[37] It is worth dwelling a moment on the figure of Raousset-Boulbon: he constitutes an entirely remarkable example of the reformist colonial entrepreneur, who settled in Algeria in 1845 and owned property in Mitidja:

> who turns out to be a fervent colonist because he is a quite radical reformer, concerned to improve the lot of the poor and the labouring classes in France … It was thus that this republican, particularly concerned to work towards improving the living and working conditions of workers, linked the social question to the colonial question (Le Cour Grandmaison 2005, pp. 303–05).[38]

---

36 Le Bris 1998; González de Reufels 2003.
37 Moreover, Lachapelle's tribute to the Count of Raousset-Boulbon (1859) includes poems by Pannetrat.
38 See Raousset-Boulbon 1848.

Following the failure of the second expedition to Sonora in 1854, Martin Pannetrat returned to San Francisco before leaving for Sydney, whence he set sail for New Caledonia and then, accompanied by Knoblauch, journeyed on foot from Canala to Nouméa and back, principally to inform the colonial authorities of the group's arrival. These working-class men, 'these colonists, recruited mainly in the poor districts of Paris, from among weavers, shop-boys and printers' apprentices' (Laurent 1857), 'indigent artisans' (Le Bris 1856), 'painter and decorator … joiner-engineer … tanner' (Pannetrat 1993), initially set up in Canala as farmers: they grew 'cotton, sugarcane, tobacco and vegetables' (Laurent 1857). Some of them, however, were impatient to find the gold that they had come to seek: a few months after they arrived, seven of them decided to set out for the north of Grande Terre, on 1 March 1856.

The ambush of the gold prospectors

Six of them were never seen again; the fate of the seventh is disputed. The received account of this episode claims that the first six were killed and eaten in Houaïlou, while the seventh remained a prisoner for a while, employed in maintaining firearms, before escaping.[39] The sources relating to this episode are, however, highly problematic: let us consider the first accounts of the ambush. Anatole Bouquet de la Grye, a naval hydrographer who had settled in New Caledonia in 1855, offers an account that was not published until 1891:

> Their journey was not long; as soon as they had left the territory of Kanala and entered the mountains, Kanaks from another tribe set fire to the hut where they were sleeping one night, and killed them with axes as they crawled out. (Bouquet de la Grye 1891, p. 16)

Émile Foucher, a naval adjutant, who arrived in Nouméa in May 1856 on board *La Bayonnaise* (a vessel to which we shall return), reported:

> They went first to Ouaïlo, where they were well received by the natives; for a few days they advanced into the interior, digging holes in various places. The natives followed them in a friendly fashion, and soon the colonists thought they had nothing to fear from them. They were moreover armed with rifles and revolvers, and were all determined men. Trust was their downfall, for the Kanaks had long been planning an attack, and were waiting for a suitable moment to execute it without exposing themselves

---

39 Dousset-Leenhardt 1970; Saussol 1979.

to danger. Finally one day, after an extremely taxing march, the colonists arrived at a place that was very difficult to cross. Burdened with their packs, which they had not yet resolved to entrust to the natives, they struggled to walk on. The natives offered to take on some of their baggage: their scheme duly succeeded; it consisted of three or four of them gathering around each defenceless colonist and, when a shout gave the signal, attacking all of them at once.

Several Kanaks therefore approached each colonist to take some of his baggage, and at the point when each of these unfortunate individuals was occupied in passing it over, a shout went up and six colonists fell at the same time, mortally wounded by blows from axes and clubs.

The seventh was only slightly wounded; he was not finished off, thanks to the intervention of a chief who kept him to make him a servant tasked with maintaining and repairing a few firearms. (Foucher 1988, pp. 123–24)[40]

Father Poupinel, procurer for Oceanian missions in Sydney, wrote during his voyage between Nouméa and Sydney on the same ship, *La Bayonnaise*, in 1857:

Our poor unfortunates fell into the hands of a tribe in the interior, where six of them were killed and eaten. The last, armed with a revolver, defended himself bravely and was taken under the protection of a chief, saving him from death. (Poupinel 1857)[41]

We also have two identifications of the geographical location, the origins of which are unknown, in the account by Ulysse de la Haütière (a naval officer who, in November 1863, became chief clerk to the government, secretary of the colony's council of administration, librarian and conservator of the colony's archives), published in 1869:

It was in the village of Boughoat,[42] that six Europeans, who had departed from Kanala, searching for gold-bearing lands, were massacred and eaten, in the month of March 1856. The tragedy occurred in the village of Atoumoa, on the right bank of the Ouaïlou river. (de la Haütière 1869, pp. 56 and 104)

'Boughoat' and 'Atoumoa' do not obviously point to any toponyms known today in the zone referred to by de la Haütière, apart perhaps from Bwéwa.

---

40   The account given by Legrand (1893) is drawn directly from Foucher's text.
41   I am grateful to Bronwen Douglas for alerting me to this reference.
42   Six nautical miles (around 11 kilometres) up the Houaïlou river.

How can we know what happened? And what was known at the time, between March and July 1856, when the fate of the expedition was determined? Unless it is entirely fictitious, which is not impossible, the account of the ambush, with the detail of its three contradictory versions (fire in the hut, or crossing difficult terrain?) has only two possible origins, since there were only two categories of eyewitness to the events: the Kanaks who were responsible, who did not confide in Europeans, and the prisoner who escaped murder – but I have found no trace of any account he might have given. Moreover, anything he may have said is highly compromised, since published accounts of his story report that he went mad (see inset).

> **'Abribat, having lost his wits, could give no information'**
>
> 'After two months, he contrived to escape and took refuge with our missionaries in Uagap.'[1] (Poupinel 1857)
>
> 'The one who was saved remained struck by the terror he had experienced and his intellectual faculties suffered. We learned of this massacre from missionaries who made approaches to the chief to urge him to release this colonist. The chief lived in the interior, but nevertheless quite close to the west coast. In 1857, this colonist managed to escape.' (Foucher 1988, p. 124)
>
> 'The seventh was kept prisoner a long time and was later saved by an English coaster, alas without happy outcome, for his reason had been deranged and the government of the time sent him to France.' (Knoblauch 1988, p. 48)
>
> 'A…, taking advantage of a dark night, fled, and having wandered for two days and two nights, prey to the torments of hunger, in constant fear, met one of the many Englishmen who had settled on the Caledonian coast at this time:[2] the latter, seized by pity, took him to Ouagap, where there was already a Marist missionary station. But so many moral and physical shocks had weakened the unfortunate man's brain: when he was questioned, on arrival in Ouagap, it was evident that he had lost his wits. Since then A… has roamed Caledonia, living at the expense of the tribes he visits, and respected by all.'[3] (de la Haütière 1869, p. 105)
>
> 'One of our unfortunate compatriots, who was their prisoner for three months (Mr Napoléon Abribat) says that he suffered almost constantly from hunger, although they never omitted to give him his share, and often served him a double portion, because they saw him wasting away.'[4] (Rochas 1862, p. 145)
>
> 'This man finally succeeded in escaping during the night, and after wandering for two days, arrived in a tribe where he met an English adventurer who led him, after two further days' walk, to the Catholic mission in Ouagap. Abribat, having lost his wits, could give no information.' (Anonymous 1988, p. 289)

1. It should nevertheless be noted that there is no mention of the event in Marist publications, except for Poupinel's letter itself [Michel Naepels].
2. There is no way to know for sure, but could this have been George Wright? [Michel Naepels]
3. According to de la Haütière, he was seen in Kanala in 1866.
4. According to Rochas, he had been adopted by a chief who was keen to take advantage of his assumed skill in repairing firearms. This man, who had escaped the massacre of his six companions who, like him, were searching for gold and found only death, finally managed to escape.

So where did the news of the disappearance of the prospectors and the account of the ambush come from? I believe that these accounts come first from Kanak intermediaries who were in contact with Martin Pannetrat, the leader of the group of proletarian settlers in Canala. In fact, Pannetrat learned of the disappearance of his former comrades from a Canala Kanak, and informed the French authorities. A version of his account ('A letter from a friend in San Francisco'[43]) was published in the *Journal du Havre* newspaper in May 1857:

> A few days later, the Indian[44] Marah came to me looking sad, and told me: 'Your white men were killed and eaten in Wuaïlo by Aliki Wangâ's tribe.'[45]
>
> …
>
> By dint of prayers and presens [*sic*], after four days I assembled three men who offered to brave all the dangers and go to seek information. They left by sea, in canoes, and returned only eight days later; their report only confirmed that of Marah; six Whites had been killed and eaten; the description of the seventh, whom they themselves had known in Kanala, was so exact that I could make no mistake about him: he had been spared. The good fortune of this lucky individual derived from the fact that he had been offered as a gift to a tribe in the interior, who are keeping him prisoner. His name is Apollon Abribat, of Sainte-Croix, in the department[46] of Ariège. (Pannetrat 1993, pp. 31–32)

Some Canala Kanaks, like 'Marah', thus acted as mediators. We need to examine their position in order to understand the account they gave to the French, both because they had chosen to welcome the latter in Canala, and because they were free to identify the guilty and the enemy as they chose, in line with their own interests.

---

43 This title refers to his time in California as a gold prospector.
44 'Indian' meaning native, again referring back to Pannetrat's Californian experience.
45 *Aliki* is a Polynesian (Futunian) term usually translated as 'chief', and used in interactions between Europeans and Kanaks since the time of James Cook.
46 French administrative region [trans.].

10 July 1856: War

Colonial war and the terrorist tools of empire

Martin Pannetrat informed the colonial authorities in Nouméa about this ambush. Until 1860, New Caledonia was administered by the Établissements français d'Océanie (French Oceanian Administrations) (whose head office was in Tahiti): the joint military governor travelled between the two locations (a journey of some 4,500 kilometres, made by sail). Joseph Du Bouzet held this post from January 1855 to October 1858. In his absence from the territory of New Caledonia (notably from June 1855 to May 1857) there were two individuals who stood in for colonial authority: the senior commander of New Caledonia (É. Le Bris from May 1856 to May 1859), and the special commander for New Caledonia, who headed the general service (Jules Testard from January 1855 to December 1858).[47] At the time that they received Pannetrat's message, their military manpower was small, their control over the territory limited and their presence was already being contested in the Nouméa area. Moreover, at that point, the soldiers had not yet mentioned the prisoner: Testard wrote to Pannetrat in April 1856: 'I cannot contemplate waging war on Wuaïlo, since there are no longer any lives to be saved' (cited by Pannetrat 1993, p. 32); and, in August, Le Bris writes: 'A few days after they left, those who had stayed in Kanala learned from natives of their comrades' sad end, they had been murdered and eaten by a tribe not far away' (Le Bris 1856). They therefore waited for reinforcements, expected with the impending arrival of the sloop *La Bayonnaise* (a large ship bearing cannon with a 1,000-metre range) and its soldiers.

The policy then espoused demonstrates that the French military were convinced of the necessity of bloody reprisal. Le Bris sums up the principles motivating his action thus: 'I therefore resolved to give them a lesson that would remain in the tribal memory [of the Houaïlou tribe responsible], and would have an impact that could only be favourable to our position in the midst of these savage tribes' (Le Bris 1856). It was imperative to demonstrate to the colonised that they would never have the upper hand. This was a terrorist policy in the true sense of the word, one that aimed to inspire terror in order to assert sovereignty; it recalls Michel Foucault's reading of public execution under the French Ancien Régime:

---

47 See Savoie 1922.

Its aim is not so much to re-establish a balance as to bring into play, at its extreme point, the dissymmetry between the subject who has dared to violate the law and the all-powerful sovereign who displays his strength … The ceremony of punishment, then, is an exercise of 'terror' … What had hitherto maintained this practice of torture was not an economy of example, in the sense in which it was to be understood at the time of the *ideologues* (that the representation of the penalty should be greater than the interest of the crime), but a policy of terror: to make everyone aware, through the body of the criminal, of the unrestrained presence of the sovereign. The public execution did not re-establish justice; it reactivated power. (Foucault 1995, pp. 48–49)

Testard also writes: 'The revenge may be delayed, but it will be taken if I am granted permission, and I shall make it as terrible as I can' (Testard 1856, cited in Pannetrat 1993, p. 32); and Le Bris notes 'the principle that against savages, all action must be firm and fearsome' (Le Bris 1856). The justification given for the repressive operation conducted against the inhabitants of Houaïlou was summed up most clearly by Laurent, the captain of *La Prévoyante*, who arrived in Nouméa in October 1855:

The truth cannot be overstated, that any hostile demonstration on our part that is not fully followed through, any expedition that results only in making the natives flee into the forests, burning huts that will be rebuilt the following day, or cutting down a few isolated coconut palms, will have entirely missed its target, increasing the boldness of the savages and completely discrediting us in their eyes. It pains me to say so, but if a decision is made to punish, the punishment must be complete and must leave a lasting memory: a single incidence will suffice. (Laurent 1857)

The second singular aspect of the colonial war, which also testifies to the circulation of models of colonial government,[48] was the reliance on local auxiliaries (in this case, originating from Canala). 'It was very important that we had natives with us in fighting our enemies on the island; it was simply an application of the policy that is the order of the day in Africa'[49] (Pannetrat 1993, p. 36). Thus, according to Pannetrat, for the operation against Houaïlou, 'more than four hundred savages' (p. 37) were mobilised. This reinforcement served a dual purpose: both military – it helped to facilitate victory (given that the French knew nothing of

---

[48] Partly because officers circulated between various colonial locations, but more generally because the conventions of state violence were taught as theory and tested in practice, their application was not restricted to colonial regions and occasionally extended into metropolitan France: see Maspéro 1995; Le Cour Grandmaison 2005; Dewerpe 2006.
[49] In the French colonial vocabulary of 1856, this means in Algeria.

the terrain, since they had never been to Houaïlou, their numbers were limited, and the superiority of their weapons only relative, particularly at close range)[50] – and 'pedagogical' (that is to say, terrorist), since the violence inflicted also made an impression on the auxiliaries. Le Bris acknowledges this in his report to the ministry, though he magnifies his own part in the proceedings: 'Rather in order to generate spectators who would also benefit from the lesson than to recruit auxiliaries, I allowed a hundred or so warriors from Kanala to accompany us in their pirogues.' The Kanak fighters (400, or 100, auxiliaries) should be set beside the 20 soldiers or the 'sixty men' (Le Bris 1856) on board *La Bayonnaise* at that moment. As Bouda Etemad writes in his analysis of the technologies of European imperialism: 'In the final analysis, the white coloniser won the colonial wars thanks to better organisational abilities and the adaptation of his fighting techniques, but also to the liberal use of indigenous recruits' (Etemad 2007, p. 78). Although the term 'auxiliary' was incorporated into colonial vocabulary, here it was not a legal concept or a status. The second half of the 19th century was precisely the period when the legal framework of the colonies was being progressively put in place; during this period concepts had not yet become fixed and were often rather vague. Sometimes a legal framework existed for the employment of these backup troops – a native company was formed in 1857 in the Nouméa region – but usually not. Whether denoting official status or not, the term formed part of a deprecatory mindset in which these fighters were a subcategory of the category 'native': in the colonial wars, the terms used were almost always 'rebels' and 'auxiliaries', rarely 'enemies' or 'allies'.

We have a number of primary sources on the repressive operation itself: the report by Le Bris and Pannetrat's letter, written in the months following the event, and the memoirs of Knoblauch. Pannetrat and Knoblauch both participated in the operation, backing up the soldiers. We also have many historical secondary sources, for example a letter from Poupinel (who was transported to Sydney on *La Bayonnaise* by Le Bris shortly afterwards), and the recollections of Foucher. The operation consisted of a cannonade, the landing of troops, the pursuit and murder of the inhabitants, and destruction of property. Here is Poupinel's summary:

---

50 I have already referred to Shineberg's analysis on this point. To quote Bouda Etemad: 'At least until the end of the nineteenth century, the colonisers' victory did not stem from their technical superiority' (2007, p. 75).

La Bayonnaise left with a company of marines, under the command of Captain Testard. The inhabitants of Uailo did not know what the ship's intentions towards them were, and as they had no suspicion and were gathered in large numbers, there could have been real carnage. But as the whaleboats moved towards the shore to land the troops, several cannon shots sowed terror among the savages, who scattered and fled as fast as they could. Our soldiers set off in pursuit of the fugitives, and killed a number of them at a river crossing. There was no reason to follow the Kanaks across their mountains, where they run and climb like mountain goats, and which offer them inaccessible hideaways. During this time, our native allies from Kanala were burning huts, destroying plantations, knocking down coconut palms, and were very joyful, because there was much to eat. These wretches did worse: they fished out the bodies of those who had been killed and withdrew to an islet to eat them, despite the vigilance exercised at the behest of Captain Testard. (Poupinel 1857)

Le Bris gives a total of 30 dead, compounded by the destruction of plantations and pirogues:

> Their losses must have amounted to about thirty men. An unprecedented number in any Caledonian war. Adding to this the destruction of their plantations, their pirogues, in a word of all their means of subsistence, there is reason to hope that they will in the future refrain from cruelty like that of which they were guilty. (Le Bris 1856)

Pannetrat quotes three villages destroyed (including those of 'Aliki Wanga' and 'Aliki Ykà', his 'vassal'), and 50 dead: 'We had burned three villages and killed about fifty of the enemy, when our soldiers' bugle call sounded the retreat once more' (Pannetrat 1993, p. 37). Clearly recognisable here is the theory of total war developed for the conquest of Algeria by the French officers Thomas Bugeaud, and subsequently Louis de La Moricière, from as early as 1840: the practice of the 'razzia' [raid], the destruction of crops and pasture[51] that, in Lucien de Montagnac's view, constitutes an entire 'system of destruction of all their means of existence' (cited in Maspéro 1995, p. 194).

> [In Algeria], the French decided to alter their methods of warfare and considerably increase the size of their forces. From 1840 on, the military leaders (La Moricière, Bugeaud) recommended the 'razzia' or raiding technique. 'The Arabs', said Bugeaud, 'must be prevented from planting, harvesting or grazing without our permission'. This technique, which

---

51 See Maspéro 1995, pp. 177–79.

postulated that the coloniser was fighting, not 'against an enemy army, but against an enemy people', degenerated into a method of systematic devastation. The correspondence of the French officers gives an idea of this methodical sacking: 'We lay waste, we burn, we pillage, we destroy houses and trees. Battles, few to none.' (Etemad 2007, p. 76)

In Houaïlou in 1856 there was much fighting and also extensive destruction.

The Kanak war

The meaning of this 'repressive' operation must have been hard to fathom for its victims: it took place on 10 July 1856, more than four months after the disappearance of the prospectors, and on the coast, whereas a range of later sources point to the killings having taken place in locations at least 10 kilometres from the coast: in 1869 de la Haütière speaks of a place situated 11 kilometres up the Houaïlou valley, Émile Foucher describes the prisoner being held by a chief living 'nevertheless quite close to the west coast' (Foucher 1988, p. 124), the paramount chief Joël Mèèjâ, in an account collected by Bernard Brou in the mid-1970s, locates the event near Poya (Nérá or Gwapâ[52]), and Jean Guiart 'in the upper Houaïlou valley' (Guiart 2004, p. 94). Further evidence in support of this theory emerges from the record by Knoblauch, who participated directly in the repressive operation: 'The "collective murder" followed by anthropophagy of the six colonists was committed *perhaps much further away than Houaïlou* but the chiefs of these regions were ashamed and disconcerted because they recognised the wrongs, the crimes perpetrated on their lands' (Knoblauch 1988, p. 49, my emphasis).

We must therefore resolutely distance ourselves from the viewpoint of French sources on this aggressive violence that was deemed a 'repressive' operation: there is no reason to believe that any of the Kanak actors involved made the justificatory link established by the military between the disappearance of the gold prospectors on the one hand, and the devastation of coastal villages and massacre of some of their inhabitants on the other. In this respect, the French accounts, however diverse (written by colonists, missionaries, soldiers) are a pure artefact relative to what was played out between the Kanaks of Houaïlou and Canala in this war, and to the temporality peculiar to these relations. Here we should

---

52   Brou 1988, pp. 119, 266.

recall the conflict that probably took place in 1847 between the 'Wilo tribe' and some of the crew of the sandalwood ship *Spy*, assisted by their 'native friends' from 'Kanela'. We do not have a detailed chronology of these earlier relations. While there is no doubt that the French military instrumentalised their Kanak auxiliaries for the benefit of their imperialist drive, there is every reason to believe that the Canala Kanaks themselves steered the French military action in line with their own political interests, if not exactly co-directing it.

As we have seen, the people of Canala, through the intermediary of the man named 'Marah', identified those 'guilty' of the murder of the gold prospectors and guided the French soldiers to the villages they wished to 'punish'. We may even hazard, if we are to believe Le Bris, that they might first have fanned the anger of the French to guarantee their engagement, by transmitting or inventing 'words of threat and challenge':

> The tribe of Waïlou, which is the name of the guilty tribe, not seeing anyone seeking revenge for their unfortunate victims, eventually stopped believing in the arrival of a warship, with which some of their neighbours, more aware of our means of repression, had tried to frighten them. Proud of their temporary impunity, the chiefs of this tribe dared to utter words of threat and challenge against us, should we set foot on their territory. I therefore resolved to teach them a lesson that would remain in the tribal memory and would have an impact that could only be favourable to our position amidst these savage tribes. (Le Bris 1856)

The repressive operation seems also to have been a Kanak war, through the application of Oceanian practices of war. The destruction of crops and coconut palms was not inspired purely by the Algerian razzia: there is widespread evidence of it in the anthropology of the South Pacific, as there is of anthropophagy (there is no proof of the abduction of women in this attack in July 1856, but we shall encounter examples below).

A note on anthropophagy

Following William Arens, some authors argue that anthropophagy is not a historically documented fact, but rather a colonialist cliché designed to cast the colonised as savages, to attribute to them an intolerable violence, in order to justify the policies of repression and colonisation (while masking their own violence). Arens condemns the 'double standard' (Arens 1979, p. 21) whereby accounts of European cannibalism are subjected to harsh criticism, contrasting with the positivist acceptance of all accounts of non-European cannibalism. He presents case studies of famous incidences from the anthropological literature. After deconstructing Hans Staden's 'testimony' about the Tupinamba, Arens examines and criticises a case attesting forms of anthropophagy among the Kanak people – the testimony of the Rarotongian evangelist Ta'unga – pointing out two particular internal contradictions in his account: 'If the natives of New Caledonia ate everyone, from distant enemy to close kin, then how did Ta'unga escape this fate?' (Arens 1979, p. 33); and how could he report a conversation between a father and son about a victim to be devoured, yet be unable to intervene because he did not know enough of their language?[53] We should note that these two arguments are not entirely unanswerable: we have no sociological account of Ta'unga's local social relations that would allow us to understand what support there was for his presence; and we can also imagine him having a stumbling linguistic capacity that would enable him to understand without giving him the means to speak, and to have a passive understanding of the language. But more broadly, it is the generalised suspicion with which Arens concludes that has been most contested, and which led Pierre Vidal-Naquet to compare the logic of his argument with that of Holocaust denier Robert Faurisson.[54]

The debate was subsequently reignited in an unexpected development of the bitter dispute between Gananath Obeyesekere and Marshall Sahlins. In a study on Fiji Obeyesekere, while not categorically denying the practice of anthropophagy, whether ritual or alimentary, nevertheless argued that the vast majority of cases of alleged cannibalism reported in European accounts (by sailors, missionaries and soldiers) are fantasy, and that a number of anthropological analyses (notably that of Sahlins) make the mistake of relying on these accounts wholly uncritically.[55] While it is based on a similar principle, his analysis is certainly more sophisticated than that of Arens.[56] His demonstration using the case of Fiji centres on a critique of the account by John Jackson, alias Cannibal Jack, alias William Diaper, who we have already encountered as the first sandalwood trader to have left an account of his time in Houaïlou.[57] Sahlins responded by reasserting the importance of cross-verifying sources, pointing to

---
53 Arens 1979, pp. 34–35.
54 Vidal-Naquet 1992; see also Lévi-Strauss 2016.
55 Obeyesekere 1998. He develops this argument in his 2005 book.
56 Arens wrote a glowing review of Obeyesekere's book (Arens 2006).
57 See Diapea 1928 and 1999; Diaper 1951; Erskine 1853.

the multiple testimonies of anthropophagy in Fiji, and the necessity of examining the entire body of such accounts: the fact that one of them is unreliable does not mean that they are all delusional.[58]

Arens' position has been defended more convincingly by historian Alice Bullard in the case of New Caledonia: 'The legend of Kanak cannibalism … took on a determining role in colonial culture' (Bullard 2000, p. 173).[59] Indeed, until the mid-20th century, there was widespread use of the trope of cannibalism to stigmatise the Kanaks as savage, from the Kanak cannibal village exhibited at the Paris Colonial Exposition in 1931[60] to *Cannibal Island*, the American book offered as an introduction to New Caledonia when it served as a support base during the war in the Pacific.[61] Isabelle Merle has demonstrated the weaknesses in this analysis.[62] More surprisingly perhaps, Jean Guiart has recently come over to this position, asserting that Kanak anthropophagy was extremely limited in scale and ritual in nature: 'Cannibalism has never been proven in New Caledonia … The only verifiable historical accounts speak of the ingestion of part of the heart of an enemy during war, by the war leader alone' (Guiart 1998, p. 124).

Unless we are to give up on any possibility of writing about the past, it is difficult to discard a number of historical testimonies,[63] and particularly to brush away the multitude of accounts passed down in the oral tradition, with the claim that the Kanaks themselves have internalised the missionaries' prejudices (during the contemporary period), or the assertion that they used these accounts to frighten Europeans (in the 19th century). For the Kanaks readily offer accounts of anthropophagy in their tales of old wars, like the one cited at the beginning of this chapter.[64] Maurice Leenhardt himself brought together examples 'recorded in the present-day conversation of the natives' in his dictionary of the Ajië language (Leenhardt 1935, p. v.): I shall cite two. In the article on 'Wenena' [*wênénââ*] (heart):

---

58 Sahlins 2003.
59 See also Bullard 1998.
60 Dauphiné 1998.
61 Priday 1944.
62 Merle 2005.
63 For example Moncelon 1885, p. 363–64.
64 See also the articles by Bensa and Goromido, 1996, 1997 and 1998.

> *Na pè wenena xie ma ara ma oi ro nemè re wanii ere, O kamo re ye oro go ye oi unu a wenena xie* (He took his heart, cooked it and ate it before all of them, saying: whoever flees, I will eat his heart as I eat this one). (Leenhardt 1935, p. 353)

In the article on 'Kamosari' [*kâmöyaari*] (servant): '*Na ki oi kamo kere e, nè oi dexa boè kamosari* (If he eats a relative, he will eat a woman from the younger generation)' (Leenhardt 1935, p. 131). Moreover, Leenhardt repeatedly associates anthropophagy with greed, on the basis of a statement by Bwêêyöuu Ërijiyi, one of his clerical pupils (see Chapter 2), which describes the season when the guaiacum trees are in blossom as the best time to consume human flesh:[65] '*Na moke mii na mù nedaa ne ke dè rhère I kamo* (The guaiacum is yellow – flowering – it is the day when man is really fat, the season of murders or raiding sorties for anthropophagous purposes)' (Leenhardt 1935, p. 261).

Rather than pursuing this reflection on an abstract level, I shall return to the material available on the events of 1856, cited above. The vast majority of authors assert that the gold prospectors who disappeared were eaten: this was a prejudice – not based on any evidence or investigation – that effectively justified a particularly harsh repression. They were 'murdered and eaten' (Le Bris 1856), 'massacred and eaten' (de la Haütière 1869), 'killed and eaten' (Poupinel 1856); in the same letter Poupinel describes 'a horrible scene of cannibalism'. But, as we have seen, the information did not derive from any eyewitness, and was no doubt rooted partly in the strong hold it had on the Europeans' imagination. But we should not forget that the original account came via the Canala Kanaks: 'Your white men were killed and eaten', Marah is alleged to have said, if we are to believe Pannetrat (1993, p. 31). One thing is certain: the French colonists' firm belief that they were dealing with anthropophagi removed the need for any real investigation of the alleged facts.

By contrast, a number of those who participated in the repressive operation in July 1856 left direct testimonies of these events. Pannetrat reports a scene of anthropophagy that he claims to have witnessed himself, carried out by Canala auxiliaries on the night before they disembarked:

> One of the chiefs, Romoneko, said to me in a low voice that they were eating four or five prisoners who had been captured on the coast a few hours earlier. I shall not describe the scene in question. Hundreds of black

---

65 Quoted in Leenhardt 1930, p. 95; 1935, p. 190; 1937a, p. 151.

bodies slipping like shadows through the trees, the light of the fires, the corpses that were cut up, the cries, the dances, all of this together was enough to strike terror in the heart of even the most battle-hardened man. (1993, p. 37)

He goes on to describe the collection of limbs of victims in Houaïlou (for the purposes of consuming them) during the conflict:

I had just hit an enemy who was swimming across the river with a rifle shot. It took one of our Kanala men only moments to seize the corpse, drag it through the mud, place it in the bottom of the canoe, cover it with banana leaves and return to the fray, looking as if butter would not melt in his mouth. I later found out that he had collected three other bodies in the same way. (1993, p. 38)

This scene is reported by Pannetrat's contemporaries Foucher and Popinel, who did not witness it directly, but were in direct contact with the soldiers who participated in the operation:

In the evening, we noticed that a small pirogue that we imagined was full of taros or yams, covered with many banana leaves, seemed to be an object of particular attention among some of the Kanala men, who asked permission to go and spend the night on a nearby islet.

This seeming suspicious, we went to look at the pirogue and found a hundred or so arms and legs of natives who had been killed, which the Kanala men had brought, covering them with grass and banana leaves to make them look like taro and yams.

We towed the pirogue out into the open water and threw the contents into the water. (Foucher 1988, pp. 125–26)

They went to recover the bodies of those who had been killed and withdrew to an islet to eat them, despite the vigilance of Mr Testard. (Poupinel 1857)

These texts have to be read with the vigilance demanded by critical discourse analysis: while we can have no way of knowing the fate of the bodies of the six gold prospectors who disappeared, the written and oral documents available do seem to confirm that, in the mid-19th century, anthropophagy formed part of the register of action in war.

1857–78: The alliance with the French and the auxiliaries' investment

The violence of the massacre of 10 July 1856 in the coastal zone of Houaïlou had long-term consequences for relations between the chiefdoms of this zone and the French colonial authorities. In order to understand the contemporary situation in New Caledonia, it is important to note that the chiefdoms in this region were in large part shaped by their military relations with the Europeans, and subsequently by the rules and practices associated with 'native peoples' status'.[66] The concept of 'chief' should not, therefore, be construed as an ahistoric, purely taxonomical category, assuming continuity from the pre-colonial period to the present.

Following the devastation caused by the operation conducted by *La Bayonnaise*, its colonial troops and its allies from Canala, the Kanaks in the coastal zone of Houaïlou sought to build contractual relations of alliance with the French through exchange, in all possible ways: with the French missionaries in Wagap, with the colonists and administrators in Canala, using both Oceanian and European exchange goods (respectively a small tapa or bark cloth, and a penny acquired from the sandalwood traders):

> After that day, the people of Uailo were struck by terror, they ever thought they saw the great ship arriving, and they had not dared to come down from their eyries to rebuild their huts and restore their plantations. Finally they sent to Kanala to ask if the great ship would return and exterminate them; the reply came that if they were good, no harm would be done to them; at this, the chief sent a deputation to our fathers in Uapag with quite unusual gifts, a small tapa and a penny; they went to ask for missionaries, because they wanted to be the ally, the friend of the French. It was thus in these circumstances that *La Bayonnaise* recently set off once more for Uailo: the inhabitants were not greatly reassured. The chief was summoned and admonished: a pardon was granted, and peace concluded to the great satisfaction of this tribe, who came to rebuild their huts and once again requested missionaries. (Poupinel 1857)

---

66   Code de l'indigénat: the system of colonial government adopted in 1881 and imposed throughout French colonies from 1887 until 1947, subjecting indigenous people and immigrant labourers to forced labour, curfews, requisitioning and capitation taxes, among other conditions [trans.]. See Merle 1995; Bensa 2000.

At the same time, as Poupinel's account indicates, the French political hold over Houaïlou and the 'pacification' of this zone – which, as we shall see, in no way signified the absence of war – was reinforced by visits from a number of ships in 1857, with Du Bouzet on the *Styx* and Le Bris on *La Bayonnaise*.

> In Vaïlu the tribe previously punished by *La Bayonnaise* for having participated in the massacre of Mr Pannetrat's companions, the Natives are calm, last year they were permitted to rebuild their villages. This is one of the most beautiful and most populated parts of New Caledonia. They offered Captain Le Bris land for the colonists, but as the population is large there is little space available. (Du Bouzet 1858)

It is worth noting that the name of Le Bris is today inscribed in the landscape and toponymy of Houaïlou: 'Lebris Bay', previously known as 'Lebris Harbour' (*Moniteur*, 30 August 1863), is the name of the gulf enclosed by the Mévéxô (or Mwâxa) peninsula or Cap Bocage, and the shore running from Ba to Nékwé and Warai: 'That is Lebris Bay, named after a navy captain, you know his history, he's the one who came with those militia, to destroy all our villages' (Guy Mèbwèdè, extract from interview, July 2006).

The alliance thus concluded had lasting effects: in the years afterwards, men from Houaïlou were recruited as auxiliaries in their turn, in 1863–64 against Kanaks from Ponérihouen (in the north), under the leadership of chief 'Ai'; in 1867 and 1868 against Kanaks from the upper Houaïlou and Bourail valleys (in the west), under the leadership of chiefs 'Ai', 'Kambo' and 'Ica'; in 1878 against inhabitants of Poya (in the north-west), under the leadership of chiefs 'Peuh-Peuh' and 'Dimagué'; and finally in 1917, against the inhabitants of the far north (especially in Koné and Hienghène), under the leadership of chiefs 'Mindia' and 'Mandaoué'. In addition, they supplied 'volunteers' in the two world wars, and policemen and orderlies for Nouméa.

1863–64: The recognition of Ai on the coast

Paradoxically, the military operations of the 1860s in which auxiliaries and chiefs from Houaïlou were involved are more difficult to describe than that of 1856. This is because there are fewer sources available and they become standardised, partly because, as French political control became more established, correspondence with the government ministry responsible grew less frequent; similarly, with the increase in the French military and administrative presence, officers – who tend to make up the majority of those writing testimonies – were less systematically involved in all operations. The expansion of the administration also included the establishment of the *Moniteur de la Nouvelle-Calédonia* (*New Caledonia Monitor*), which became virtually the only source on the history of this period. Classic historiography refers extensively to it, usually uncritically.[67] Rather than repeating these easily accessible accounts, I would like to emphasise the link between the mobilisation of auxiliaries and the administrative recognition of chiefdoms, and to highlight a number of points.

The French military authorities based in Napoléonville – the name given to Canala at that time – visited Houaïlou and Ponérihouen twice in early 1864. The purpose of the first visit, from 25 to 27 January, was to create an impression; the second, from 28 March to 5 April, was a repressive operation. The local stakes involved in the conflicts that arose in the coastal zone between Houaïlou and Ponérihouen in 1863–64, between inhabitants and chiefs from Ponérihouen and those from Monéo, are related in particularly obscure and anecdotal form in the *Moniteur de Nouvelle-Calédonie*: 'There are constantly new versions of the story in the struggle between the chiefs of Panariva and of Monéo, which we reported in a recent issue' (*Moniteur*, 4 October 1863). The context in which the chiefdoms of Houaïlou became involved in this conflict located further north is also unclear. We are never told the primary source of the information given, nor how reliably the circumstances are reported. The military were themselves aware that they knew very little about the local issues:

> The commanders of two posts on the east coast [Wagap and Napoléonville] constantly reported new conflicts between tribes. The almost insurmountable difficulty they had in communicating with all these places prevented them from finding out the precise truth … [On 25 January 1864] Lieutenant Carrey, captain of *La Gazelle*, landed straightway and questioned the colonists; but there, as subsequently in the bay of Monéo, he was unable to decipher the motives for the wars we have mentioned. Some claimed they were instigated by Catholics; others that abduction of women and above all the desire to eat human flesh were the pretext for a war which has continued almost since time immemorial

---

67   Dousset-Leenhardt 1970 and 1976; Saussol 1979; Dauphiné 1989.

between the two bays. With a caution that can easily be understood, each colonist holds back a part of the whole truth about the chief of the territory in which he is resident. (*Moniteur*, 1 May 1864)

The reasoning behind the repressive action, on the other hand, is clear: 'In January [1864], the schooner *La Gazelle* was sent to the east coast to try to pacify the natives and make them understand their duties toward the colonial authorities' (*Moniteur*, 1 May 1864). In March–April, the repressive operation was undertaken 'in order once again to settle differences between the natives and to provide effective protection for our colonists' (*Moniteur*, 1 May 1864). The aim was both to put an end to (real or presumed) cases of physical violence, murder and anthropophagy in conflicts between Kanaks, and to protect 'our colonists' property' (the phrase is used twice in the *Moniteur de la Nouvelle-Calédonie* on 1 May 1864), which had been destroyed or threatened in September 1863 and February 1864. The confirmation, in late March 1864, that these two principles of civil peace and respect for colonisation had been violated was the immediate trigger for the military operation in early April:

> Information obtained on his visit to Houaïlou having confirmed that the tribe of Monéo, notwithstanding its promises, had destroyed the plantations of the people of Nékoué and that the tribe of Mou, by means of harassment, had forced the colonists Peter Grundy and Lecaille to leave their homestead. (*Moniteur*, 8 May 1864)

Local interventions by the French were always backed up by an appeal to 'chiefs' and by the mobilisation of auxiliary troops. Thus, on 25 January 1864, the schooner *La Gazelle* 'anchored in Houaïlou, with on board, in addition to the infantry detachment, the chiefs Gélima and Kaké, from Kanala, and the native Sandoli, as interpreter'. It was the military operation itself that most directly involved the warriors from Houaïlou:

> On 28 March, 20 men of the naval Infantry and 12 people of Kanala, under the command of Sub-lieutenant Scellos, left Napoléonville on the schooner *L'Étoile*, captained by Leleizour, and disembarked that evening in Houaïlou. The following day 150 volunteers from this area, of Nékoué, and from Houaraye and Ba, joined them and all journeyed towards Monéo, while the *Étoile* sailed close to shore … On 3 April … at three o'clock, the soldiers entered the encampment after having fought a thousand men for ten hours, killed or injured about sixty of them, and destroyed more than 600 huts. As we have already noted, the auxiliaries took charge of destroying the plantations. (*Moniteur*, 8 May 1864)

The operation also left a number of auxiliaries wounded: 'From Houaïlou, 8 natives; from Nékoué, 3 natives; from Houaraye, 1 native' (*Moniteur*, 1 May 1864).

In considering the Kanak involvement in this operation, a number of features need to be highlighted: on the one hand, it was once again mediated through relations between the chiefdoms on the Houaïlou coast (Houaïlou strictly speaking at that time designating the region of Lèwëö, where the sandalwood trader George Wright had settled and which was becoming an administrative centre, as were Warai, Nékwé and Ba), and those of Canala (the chiefs 'Gélima' (Nôme) and 'Kaké' (Bwaxéa) are mentioned). On the other, we have a system of events that all tend in the same direction: the man identified by the *Moniteur de la Nouvelle-Calédonie* as the chief of Houaïlou was seeking full recognition from the French colonial authorities. Here are a few salient moments: in August 1863, the chief of 'Ouaïlou' participated, alongside other chiefs and native workers, in the Emperor's Day celebrations that took place in Nouméa (*Moniteur*, 23 August 1863). This chief seems to have had difficulty in establishing his authority locally: '[The population of Houaïlou] previously had a single chief, who died two or three years ago … The subaltern chiefs of Nékoué, Houaraye, Bâ and others liberated themselves by separating from the heir of the paramount chief; since then, this region has resounded with war cries' (*Moniteur*, 1 May 1864). In November 1863 and February 1864, the latter appealed to the military base in Napoléonville, receiving ceremonial recognition in January 1864, before supplying auxiliaries in mass numbers in March–April 1864:

> [In November 1863] the commander of the post at Napoléonville received an emissary from Aï, the heir of the paramount aliki [chief] of Houaïlou, who requested our intervention to put an end to the constantly revived hostilities between populations now resistant to his authority.
>
> …
>
> [On 26 January 1864], before troops and sailors in battle formation on the coast, proceedings were opened with a bugle call, and Captain Carrey, in the presence of chiefs and natives from the various tribes of Houaïlou, declared, in the name of the Government, that Aï, the heir of the former chief, was recognised as supreme chief of the whole of the territory lying between Cap Kouha and Cap Bocage. Taking advantage of the assembled numbers, he informed them they were ordered to end the war with Monéo: the chiefs agreed and promised him that they would treat the Whites with friendship, that they would in the future bring any

dispute before the commander of the post in Napoléonville, and that they would prevent their people from engaging in acts of anthropophagy … The schooner weighed anchor, announcing that a ship would come soon to verify whether these promises were being kept. Returning then to Port-de-France, it also took the chiefs Ica, from Houaraye, Kamb'bo, from Nékoué, Polind'do, from Bouéhoua who, on the advice of the captain, were coming to present themselves in submission to the Governor.

…

On 21 February [1864], the death of the chief of Pounérihouen triggered renewed hostilities targeted particularly at the property of our colonists, who were not spared death threats. On this occasion, the chief of Houaïlou reiterated his appeal for assistance from the base at Napoléonville. (*Moniteur*, 1 May 1864)

It thus emerges that chief Ai was successful in his attempt to win recognition from the French military of his pre-eminence over the other chiefdoms on the coast between Wagap and Canala.

1867–68: Control over the valley

Similarly, the colonial wars that took place in the region of Houaïlou and Bourail in 1867–68 can be seen as a translation of the extension of the colonisers' political control, by means of recognition and unwavering support granted to a few individuals who were able to supply substantial numbers of auxiliaries, and the quest by the latter for a degree of ascendancy in the local social context, derived through military support received from the French and their auxiliaries.

In 1867, a conflict appears to have arisen among the chiefdoms on the Houaïlou coast (Lèwèö-Houaïlou, Warai, Nékwé) that had allied themselves with the French in 1864:

At the beginning of 1867, the people of Nécoué, taking up a dispute over the possession of a woman that arose between Cazaouimans, junior chief of Houaïlou, and Ica, chief of Houarail, and led by Djannou, brother of their chief Cambo, who was absent, attacked the natives of Houarail; the latter were supported by their friends and neighbours from Houaïlou. Sub-lieutenant Marchal, sent by Captain Garin, restored order on the coast and reconciled the enemies; and in order to teach them a lesson, Ica was interned for one month in Canala, and Cazaouimans for six months in Nouméa. (*Moniteur*, 2 August 1868)

The end of 1867 was marked by a large-scale military operation conducted across the Houaïlou valley and its tributaries. We have today no way of confirming or refuting the accounts produced by colonists and auxiliary chiefs that justified the use of force. But we may note that the violence employed followed the same conventions as in the preceding military operations, in terms of justification (reacting to violence between Kanaks, particularly when auxiliary chiefs were involved; protecting colonists) and practice (relying on auxiliary troops, destroying residences and crops).

> On 2 December [1867], at two o'clock in the afternoon, the small detachment disembarked at Houarail, on the property of Mr Pichard, where the colonists were gathered ready to defend themselves. Chiefs Aï, Ica and Cambo, under the command of Mr Marchal, arrived shortly afterwards and gave the following report:
>
> Since the month of February 1867, chief Polinda of Bouéoua had been defending himself against Catamouino, chief of Méa, who had been joined over the year by people from several other villages, including those of Houinbé and Bouin-oué. In November 1867, chief Ponindo of Bouin-oué sought to form a coalition with the aim of expelling the natives from the Houaïlou coast and, they say, killing the Whites who had settled on the shores of Lebris Bay.
>
> …
>
> The Bouin-oué burned a number of huts in Houaïlou and Houarail, prompting the Europeans to take refuge in Mr Pichard's boat.
>
> …
>
> On the evening of the day they disembarked, at eleven o'clock, our contingent from Canala, accompanied by the tribes of Houarail, Houaïlou and Nécoué, made their way to Bouéoua; close to this point lies the village of Bouin-oué, which was attacked from three sides, the fourth not having been attacked owing to a delay in the march led by chief Polinda, who had been charged with resonsibility for this side.
>
> …
>
> While Ica's and Cambo's men pursued them, Bouin-oué was delivered to the flames; at the same time, the people of Houaïlou, led by junior chief Cazaouimans, who had returned to nobler sentiments, mounted a vigorous attack and destroyed Nindié, which lies at the foot of a hill topped by a huge rock that contains deep caves, with two very fine peaks pointing heavenwards. Seven of the inhabitants of this village were killed. (*Moniteur*, 2 August 1868)

The inhabitants of Mèaa and the Houaïlou valley, forced by the repressive operation to flee to the west coast and threatened by French soldiers accompanied by Aï's, Ica's and Cambo's warriors, seem to have taken refuge in the upper valleys of Bourail, among Kanaks identified as members of the 'Houin tribe', or among the mountain Houin also known as 'Honrôés': 'The governor had the villages of Bouin-oué, Nindié, Houinbé, Méa, etc. burned. The Houaïlou from the interior were sheltered among the Honrôés' (*Moniteur*, 30 August and 6 September 1868). The French perception of the events at Bourail in 1868 is entirely shaped by the plan to bring the coastal auxiliary chiefdoms of Houaïlou, Canala and Bourail into conflict with the chiefdoms that were resistant to French presence in the mountains, in the middle Houaïlou valley, in Mèaa and in the upper valleys of Bourail. Thus the murder in Bourail of freed prisoner Bridon 'by men of the tribe of Houin' was attributed to their desire to win the release of Dialicouyo, 'one of the most influential instigators of the insurrection' (*Moniteur*, 2 August 1868), 'the uncle of Ponindo, chief of Bouin-oué' (*Moniteur*, 2 August 1868), 'imprisoned in the Penitentiary on Île Nou for 6 months' (*Moniteur*, 9 August 1868). Similarly, the attack on the Kanaks of Nékou, who were allied with the French, was attributed to people from the mountains (Houaïlou, Bourail, Mèaa); the repression was therefore – according to the logic of this system – led by auxiliaries from the coast, the Kaké (Bwaxéa, from Canala) and Houaïlou.

In addition to the description and interpretation they offer of a series of events, the articles in the *Moniteur* also testify to the increasingly marked intention to identify places and proper names as accurately as possible, and to set them in a one-to-one relationship wherever possible. Thus the following were identified:

> The tribes of Houaïlou (chief Aï), of Houarail (chief Ica) and of Nécoué (chief Cambo) … Behind the village of Nécoué lies that of Bouéoua, chief Polinda. Further upstream, in the direction of Bourail, lay the villages of Bouin-Oué (chief Ponindo), Nindié (chief …), Houinbé (chief Nécha), Crouin or Houin (chief …), etc.; on the left, near mounts Couaoua and Page, lived the people of Méa (chief Catamouino), of whom the people of Canala have often had cause to complain, even after the Napoléonville post was established. (*Moniteur*, 2 August 1868)

These identifications are to be sure approximate, based on indications given by the auxiliaries themselves. The transcription of the Ajië language, in particular, varies widely, and the Kanaks are identified only by their given name, with no reference to their lineage name or clan. At that time, toponyms were localised without any kind of mapping. There is evidence of this in the great confusion that surrounds two 'chiefs' who appear in the accounts of 1867–68 in the following form: chief Polinda, of Bouéoua, allied with the French, is mentioned as being in conflict with chief Ponindo, of Bouin-Oué or Bouen-Oué, an enemy of the French. Given that, as we learned above, the former's 'delay' allowed the latter to escape capture by the French, there are clearly grounds for questioning the dualist reading of social relations put forward by the military, in terms of friends or enemies. Moreover, to add to the confusion, the latter was finally identified as 'Polinda (not Ponindo) of Bouin-oué' at the time of his 'submission', which took the form of allowing two of his children to go to school in Canala.[68] But, regardless of these vagaries, this project formed part of a pragmatic will to knowledge aiming towards political control of the territory.

1878: On the side of the victors – coast and upper valleys

The great colonial war of 1878–79, which directly involved almost half the territory of Grande Terre, confirmed the alliance between the chiefdoms of Houaïlou and the French colonial authorities, to the great advantage of both sides. With a more detailed reading, some important mechanisms can be identified. Initially, when the Kanak war broke out in the south of Grande Terre, the administration sought to stabilise its alliances by intervening to settle an internal conflict in the coastal zone of Houaïlou-Ponérihouen:

> In the beautiful and prosperous valley of Monéo ... two tribes were in conflict, one led by chief Segou and the other led by chief Tehen. The tribe of Tehen, reinforced by men from the tribe of Cambo, attacked the tribe of Segou and took away four women of this tribe. Chief Segou ... therefore went to complain to military supervisor Hory, who was stationed at Houaïlou. Hory, with the support of chief Peuh-Peuh, of the tribe of Malvino, and warriors from Poulvano, organised ... an expedition against Tehen and Cambo ... These two chiefs and eight of their warriors were arrested and transferred to Canala, where they were put in prison.

---

68   *Moniteur*, 30 August and 6 September 1868.

The others managed to escape and some of them took refuge in Bâ Bay (or Lebris Bay), on the land of the colonist Moncelon, who refused to give them up. (Dousset-Leenhardt 1976, p. 101)[69]

These relationships were further stabilised by reinforcing the French military presence, at a time when no sign of hostility towards the French had been observed in this part of Grande Terre:

> On 28 June Captain Merlaud, commander of the 7th naval infantry company, landed at Houaïlou to reinforce the garrison. (Bierman 1992, p. 522)

When the French mobilised further auxiliary troops on the west coast, as the hostilities increasingly spread northwards, the Houaïlou tribes were mobilised mainly through the alliance that some of them had with Canala, which had already played a part in the earlier military operations. Particularly noteworthy is the mediating role played by 'Sandouli', who had previously acted as intermediary between Canala and Houaïlou in 1864:

> [In early September 1878] the tribes of Houaïlou sent to Mr Servan, in Canala, fifty warriors under the command of the war chief Dimagué. [… On 14/9 in Oua-Tom] the Kanaks of Houaïlou were under the orders of Dimagué and Sandouli. (*Moniteur*, 25 September 1878)

In contrast to the specifically targeted actions of 1856 and 1864, the military operations in which Houaïlou auxiliaries participated in 1878 made systematic use of a practice that had already been employed in the Houaïlou valley in 1867, though its use in the colonies dates much further back: this was the mobile column, which accompanied the razzia in Algeria from the 1840s onwards. These were units usually composed of an officer, between 10 and 40 French soldiers, and from 100 to 500 Kanak auxiliaries, who marched for several days at a time to kill presumed enemies, destroy their means of subsistence, and take women and children prisoner. Father Hillereau, a missionary at Bourail who fled to Ourail (La

---

69   The source of this information is a copy of supervisor Hory's letter of 20 June 1878 to the governor and the director of the interior, Houaïlou, Centre de documentation sur l'Océanie (Centre for Documentation on Oceania) 2, 67. Since the Centre's collection, created by Jean Guiart when he was director of the musée de l'Homme (Museum of Mankind) in Paris, has been lost, I was unable to find the letter in question, and can only base my conclusions on the summary given by Roselène Dousset-Leenhardt. Confirmation is, however, found in a report from the *Moniteur*: '[In early August 1878] the dispute between the tribes of Monéo, which had given rise to armed attacks between natives, was referred to the council of the paramount chiefs of Canala' (*Moniteur*, 4 September 1878).

Foa) when the war became too intense in his mission area, offers a succinct summary of this mode of operation: 'An expeditionary column leaves from one place or another and goes man-hunting!' (Hillereau 1878). Clearly, the auxiliary troops had a degree of autonomy in these sorties. On occasion, mainly on the west coast, these mobile columns were reinforced by other representatives of the social landscape of the colony: colonists, Algerian Kabyles (members of the tribe of El Mokrani who had been deported from Algeria following their rebellion against the colonial authorities), and transported convicts sentenced to hard labour (especially people who had participated in the Paris Commune of 1870–71). Extensive participation by Houaïlou auxiliaries in actions against groups hostile to the French presence in Bourail and Poya was a typical feature of local social life throughout the period from September 1878 to late February 1879:

> Captain Merlaud, who left from Houaïlou on the 16th [September 1878] with twenty soldiers and two hundred allied Kanaks, returned on the afternoon of the 22nd. (*Moniteur*, 25 September 1878)

> [On 7 November 1878] two hundred Kanaks, led by Peuh-Peuh, from Houaïlou, Toroboro and Ni, asked to march against Ninday and Hiro, and left with 40 soldiers under the command of Mr Rochel. (*Moniteur*, 13 November 1878)[70]

There is an excellent description of the way these mobile columns operated in the account of what, from the point of view of the colonisers, constituted the Houaïlou auxiliaries' greatest military feat during this period, the taking in November 1878 of the rocks of Adio, in the upper Poya, following a failed first attempt in October.

> On the 25th [October] Captain Merlaud departed from Houaïlou, with 30 soldiers and 200 Kanaks from the allied tribes, for Naïgon, an Adio village. (*Moniteur*, 30 October 1878)

> On the 25th, Captain Merlaud, who had departed from Houaïlou, camped at Nérin. At noon on the following day he attacked the Ningou who were perched up in the rocks. The Houaïlou war chief, Dimagué, with his warriors, launched an attack on the Adio. He was supported by fifteen soldiers under the command of Mr Monniot, but he was unable to penetrate into the cave enclosure, which is enclosed by a strong wooden gate. The auxiliaries killed three rebels and wounded many more. In the

---

70   For other examples of such involvement, see also the *Moniteur de la Nouvelle-Calédonie* of 9 October 1878, 18 December 1878 and 26 February 1879, as well as the 'Rapport sur les opérations militaires (Report on Military Operations)' for the period 22 November – December 1878.

battle five of them were wounded, one by a gunshot and the others by stones. The soldiers also killed or wounded a number of rebels. The enemy kept up their resistance until nightfall.

[On 27 October] the Houaïlou burned the villages of Nego and Gorodni, and chased a number of rebels armed with rifles. Dimagué himself killed chief Malambru, who had delivered the first axe blow to Mavimoin, the chief of Nékliaï, on the day of the massacre at the Houdaille farm. (*Moniteur*, 6 November 1878)

On the 22nd [November], Colonel Wendling went to the Adio rocks. They had been removed on the 21st by Captain Merlaud and the Houaïlou Kanaks. Five rebels were killed. Five women and a rifle were taken. Three soldiers and twelve auxiliaries were slightly wounded by stone shrapnel. One auxiliary received a spear in his right arm. Wendling's column and that of Captain Merlaud, who joined forces on the 22nd in the territory of the Ningous, continued to search the caves: two men were killed and twelve prisoners taken, including two children. The auxiliaries from Ni, Koné and Houaïlou completed the destruction of the Ningous' huts and crops. The columns spent the night at the Houdaille outpost. On the following day, the 23rd, they … searched the whole of Poya, with the Kanak auxiliaries. Chief Dimagué, from Houaïlou, who had stayed with the Ningous, killed two rebels and two women. The Kanak contingents then returned to their tribes.

On the 26th, Merlaud's column returned to Houaïlou. (*Moniteur*, 27 November 1878)

Another new aspect of the conventions of use of force during the repression of 1878–79 was that auxiliaries were encouraged to bring back the decapitated heads of their victims:

On 16 October [1878] around fifty Houaïlou who had been sent on reconnaissance at the request of chiefs Peuh-Peuh and Dimagué brought back the heads of two insurgents, that of Kaoumorani from Greater Nékou and that of Kapourani from Lesser Nékou, these two rebels having been killed in the valley of the tribe of Bouiro. On the 21st some allies from Monéo and Ponérihouen who had been sent to the Adio lands on reconnaissance returned with the heads of three rebels they had killed at Ouari, near Panemat. ('Rapport sur les opérations militaires' for the period 28 September – 24 October 1878)[71]

---

71 See also the *Moniteur de la Nouvelle-Calédonie* of 23 October 1878 for a further example.

This practice also emerged directly from the modes of colonial government established in Algeria, and was accompanied by a bounty paid to the auxiliaries for each head or pair of ears cut off.[72] The auxiliaries' booty also included captured women and children:

> A reconnaissance mission conducted by Houaïlou auxiliaries towards Ninday brought back 3 women and 6 children as prisoners. (*Moniteur*, 20 November 1878)

> On the 14th [December], Houaïlou auxiliaries brought to Bourail by Captain Merlaud, and led by Dimagué, killed three rebels and took 23 prisoners, women and children, in the environs of Ouanho and Néra. ('Rapport sur les opérations militaires' for the period 22 November – 22 December 1878)[73]

The administrative sources, in the form of reports in the *Moniteur*, are notably silent on the women and children, who appear only passively, as booty or cause of conflict, and generically, without individual identity. It is only by searching elsewhere, in the missionaries' correspondence and in the margins of the few Kanak sources we have on the war, that we find some traces of their modes of engagement in, or against, the war. There is, for example, a striking contrast between the presentation of one particular fact in two reports, one administrative and one from a missionary (Father Lecouteur, a missionary at Bourail):

> Two dozen Kanaks from Houaïlou who remained behind ... took a woman from Nékou. (*Moniteur*, 16 October 1878)

> [On 15 October] the woman Catherine, a Christian Kanak lawfully married to a native of La Conception was given to one of the chiefs of Houaïlou. This Catherine led the life of a prostitute. I warned Commander Chausson, but Catherine had already left for Houaïlou. (Lecouteur, cited in Cornet 2000, p. 174)

The authorities' tolerance of the abduction of women is confirmed by the testimony of Léon Moncelon:

---

72 See Maspéro 1995, p. 339.
73 See also the *Moniteur de la Nouvelle-Calédonie* of 18 December 1878, and the 'Rapport sur les opérations militaires' for 16 January – 5 February 1879 for further examples.

> Following the events of 1878, the authorities left the women captured on the west coast to the attentions of the Kanak auxiliaries from the east coast, who shared them out and treated them like their other women. (Moncelon 1886, p. 367)[74]

Bronwen Douglas has shown that women's role as mediators in war, in famine and in situations of depopulation, can be read in these documents.[75] Hillereau's letter testifies to this mediating function, particularly in relation to the missionaries: 'Many enemies were killed and the native women also say that wounds and diseases have led to still more deaths' (Hillereau 1878).

It is in fact in the context of a serious demographic crisis that the choice made by Kanak actors either to attack European colonists in 1878, or to become auxiliaries of colonisation, needs to be situated. There is unfortunately very little information on the history of the general material conditions (climate, demographics, economy) of these political events. The question of the extent of Kanak depopulation during the century following the first contact with Europeans (that is, with James Cook and his crew in 1774, in the north of Grande Terre), and still more in the years following the French takeover, is therefore highly disputed.[76] According to the lowest estimate,[77] the Kanak population fell by more than 40 per cent; Christophe Sand, on the other hand, has put forward a number of arguments suggesting a much higher figure for the reduction in the Kanak population over the 19th century. Whatever the case, it is likely that the gender ratio was at this time seriously unbalanced, to the disadvantage of women. We might surmise that the ravages of new diseases were interpreted locally as the result of powers of attack wielded by local actors. On the level of global economic dynamics, Mike Davis has shown that the great famines and political uprisings that occurred simultaneously in several tropical regions throughout the world in 1877–78 can be explained in terms of a particularly strong El Niño, combined with methods of managing the crisis that were extremely deleterious to colonised populations.[78] He cites

---

74 Léon Moncelon also picked up a young Kanak man, Gayouman, 'who was one of the Kanak rebels from the west coast', who was less than eight years old in 1878, and who he presented as a live specimen at the meeting of the Société d'anthropologie de Paris (Paris Anthropology Society) on 7 May 1885 – by which time Moncelon had become the senior delegate for New Caledonia to the Conseil supérieur des colonies (Supreme Council for the Colonies).
75 Douglas 1998.
76 Rallu 1990; Kasarhérou 1991; Shineberg 1983; Sand 1995; see Rivers 1922.
77 Rallu 1990.
78 Davis 2001.

New Caledonia as a specific example. Among the 'cruel ordeals that the colony has suffered', Hillereau does indeed mention 'locusts, drought' (Hillereau 1879).[79] It is only by resituating the Kanak rebellion in the context of the demographic and economic crisis the Kanaks were then suffering, exacerbated by the increasing European control over land, that we can gain a sense of the numbers of victims of the repression (2,000 in Grande Terre?) – amounting, even in the most conservative estimate, to over 5 per cent of the population of Grande Terre in less than a year.

> If peace and security depended only on our own military forces, years might pass before the country was habitable. Fortunately they come to us of their own accord, driven by hunger and deprivation of all kinds. Harried, hunted each day, though they cannot be caught, seeing their camps destroyed, their plantations ravaged, the coconut palms cut down in many places, the natives have entered a period of the most dire poverty. Those who are less involved in the revolt, who still hope to escape punishment, have no trouble in surrendering completely, once they are assured their lives will be spared. (Hillereau 1879)

As we have seen, much more is known about the military operations of 1878–79 than that of 1868. This abundance of sources, for example the reports published in the *Moniteur*[80] (the main historiographic source on the subject), is due to the importance of this information in the administrative and military management of the crisis, given its wide geographical spread and, particularly, in coordinating the repressive operation at a time when more and more Europeans were settling all over Grande Terre. The quality and number of reports obtained by Nouméa and published in the *Moniteur* are due above all to the communication network that had recently been established in New Caledonia through telegraphy, one of the instruments of imperial control. Hence, the local news and reports of operations were edited by none other than Charles Lemire, the head of the telegraph service, who had overseen its installation between 1874 and 1875. Even more than the *chassepot*,[81] the telegraph and the mobile column emerge as the significant innovations in the repression of 1878–79.

---

79 See Saussol 1979 on this point.
80 Dousset-Leenhardt 1976; Latham 1978; Cornet 2000.
81 A breechloading rifle used by the French army from 1866 onwards; there is limited evidence of its usefulness in the repression, since most of the Kanak victims were killed by Kanak auxiliaries.

1. LINEAGE RIVALRY AND COLONIAL CONTROL

The specific contextual factors determining Kanak actors' choice of whether or not to act are obviously much more difficult to establish than the general background. It can, notwithstanding, be stated with certainty that the crude dualism of the military sources (the Kanaks are either auxiliaries or rebels, over whom 'chiefs' are deemed to have uncontested authority) masks a much greater social complexity. The undifferentiated mass of the fighters, on both the auxiliaries' and the rebels' side, is particularly difficult to identify, to localise, and therefore to analyse. To recall Hillereau's hypothesis: 'perhaps entire tribes have been drawn into the insurrectionary movement against their will' (Hillereau 1879). In the same letter, he cites the complex position of 'Naounou', a Kanak from Bourail, 'allegedly the war chief most feared and most terrifying in the eyes of the people of Bourail', who went over to the side of the French.

Still more telling is the example of how the Houaïlou auxiliaries protected the tribe of Ni, in the upper Bourail valley, and directed the war toward the Kanak villages on the Bourail coast. There are various accounts of this episode, with a number of different protagonists. The oldest known version, written up about 1919, appears in the notebooks of Bwêèyööu Ërijiyi:

> In some ceremonies in Bourail, Ni and Bwiru, yams are added to the pile of foodstuffs for the Mèyikwéö and the Bwéwé. They are a reminder of how the lands of Ni, Kikwé, Bwiru and Ayarhe were saved during the war of 1878, when Ni was changed to Nédi. The French wanted to attack Ni and the commanding officer was looking at a map of the regions that were at war. An elder from Mèyikwéo, of the name of Pienô Unayi Ëribwa, then whispered to Pepe Bwéwé Gwâê that he should tell the commanding officer that this was not the land of Ni, but Nédi. And the commanding officer asked where is it? – Down below, by the sea. And Ni was saved! This yam bears witness. (Ërijiyi in Aramiou and Euritéin 2003, pp. 11–12, my translation)

It is worth noting in passing that this text helps to identify the lineage of 'Peuh-Peuh', one of the two principal 'war chiefs' of the Houaïlou auxiliaries in 1878 (the other being 'Dimagué').

The military operations conducted by the Houaïlou auxiliaries in 1864, 1867–68 and 1878–79 incorporate elements that some of them or their families had suffered as victims in 1856. Viewed in retrospect, some of the actions of a group of Houaïlou Kanaks, confirmed by various sources, form a system that defines a general trend of political approach:

we can thus say that, in the alliance with the French between 1857 and 1879, there was a negative interest, resulting from the colonial and repressive terror; there was also a positive interest in continually seizing opportunities to win greater freedom, more room to manoeuvre and more power by maintaining the alliance with the French colonial authorities, allowing them to eliminate adversaries, capture women and children, and hence to reinforce local chiefdoms. I do not suggest a deliberate strategic calculation but, in retrospect, it is possible to reconstitute a sort of guiding orientation, as well as noting that this re-reading is also offered by our informants themselves. The point I make here is simply a descriptive and analytical choice, rather than imputing belief or establishing causality. Thus the action can be considered on a register that is not psychological: we need only adopt Elizabeth Anscombe's analytical rule as our methodology – intention, in a nutshell, is what people do.[82]

My point, then, is not to claim that all the inhabitants of the coast and valleys of Houaïlou became wholehearted supporters of colonisation, but rather firstly that some of the individuals perceived by the French as 'chiefs' committed themselves decisively, in increasing numbers, to colonisation, and secondly, that the cost of publicly expressing a different opinion, of hostility towards Europeans or the auxiliary chiefs, became increasingly high between 1856 and 1879. In this sense, the various colonial wars conducted with or against the people of Houaïlou can be viewed as so many stages in the construction of increasing French control over the territory of New Caledonia. But these were also local conflicts, in which the stakes for the fighters themselves remain largely unknown to us. And we must hypothesise that there were many forms of abstention, of playing off both sides and of distancing themselves from their role that have left not the smallest trace in the colonial archives.

1875–81: Local control and globalisation

The colonists of Lebris Bay

While I have focused on the relationship between war, the capacity to mobilise fighters and the political recognition (accompanied by means of coercion) obtained by auxiliary chiefs from the colonial administration,

---

82 Anscombe 2002 [1957].

it should immediately be added that the period from 1856 to 1879 in Houaïlou was not only one of confrontation or agreement between Kanak warriors and the French military: it was also the period when the first colonists began to settle there. There are indications of this even in the accounts of repressive operations; for example, in March 1864, the colonist Guillaume Maradhour, who had settled in Lebris Bay, offered soldiers from Napoléonville (Canala) a hut for storing supplies and munitions, and the means to install a military outpost near to 'the little village of Néha, which is part of Nékoué, at the mouth of the Bâ Bay (Lebris Bay)' (*Moniteur*, 8 May 1864). In the same year, a delegation that was prospecting around Grande Terre on board the ship *Fulton*, to investigate the possibilities for immigration of settlers from Réunion who were suffering from a serious economic crisis, devised a plan to settle in Houaïlou: 'The town could be built at the back of Le Bris harbour, with houses and public buildings in the valleys, on the very gentle slopes of Cap Bocage and of the coastal plain, from the Rock to the harbour mouth' (*Moniteur*, 6 November 1864). And, in effect, this part of the coast, from Ba to Warai, was where the first colonists settled, including settlers from Réunion, who were known in New Caledonia at that time as the Bourbonnais.[83] Thus the colonist Pichard, who in December 1867 offered shelter on his boat to colonists from Lebris Bay who felt threatened by the conflicts on the coast, was a Bourbonnais, as was Léon Moncelon, who intervened in the conflicts of June 1878.[84] It is also known that the Kabar family, who arrived in New Caledonia in 1868 and introduced lychees to Houaïlou, settled in the lower reaches of the principal river of Houaïlou.

Settlement, however, remained an individual affair during the 1860s, limited to the coastal zone and close to the centre of a very rudimentary administrative network. This was still a frontier situation: the first colonists had to negotiate their positions just as the sandalwood traders had had to – though with the additional support, as we have seen, of the intermittent but formidable presence of the French military, supported by their Kanak auxiliaries.

---

83   From 'l'île Bourbon', the former colonial name for Réunion [trans.].
84   'I even had the good fortune to save the skin of *Aouënda*, when he was about to be executed by mistake, in *Kanala*, following the gruesome events of 1878' (Moncelon 1887, p. 270).

The second globalisation of Houaïlou

The opening of the Bel-Air mine in the lower Houaïlou valley in 1875,[85] very close to the delta and the Néjâ chiefdom that was based there, therefore altered the situation considerably. It led to a clear statement of the state's hold over Houaïlou, in terms of both territorial control and local social organisation. Here are some of the key dates leading up to this takeover: in 1876, operations are undertaken to demarcate and limit the Kanak lands.[86] In June 1879 New Caledonia is divided into five administrative regions; the third with Houaïlou as its administrative centre, and Jules Moriceau as administrator. In July of the same year, a number of municipal committees are established, including that of Houaïlou; the first electoral registers are drawn up in 1881, in preparation for the first elections to this committee.

The link between demarcation of lands and the development of mining was explicitly stated in the deliberations of the colonial Privy Council[87] of 4 and 6 March 1876, which laid down the principles for delimiting native reserves:

> The discovery of mines, the extension of cattle-rearing, exposed the New Caledonians [Kanaks] to daily invasions; the best way to ensure they are protected from this is by defining their territory. This operation, which is essential in order to reassure a population that is of interest to us, will also make it possible to determine the country's land resources, so that the administration can have greater freedom in making them available for colonisation. (Privy Council of 4 and 6 March 1876)

The Privy Council's discussion ended with a question about mines:

> Mr Marchand asks what will be the situation of the tribe thus demarcated in relation to the miners? The head of the Estates Service replies that, in this respect, the property of the tribe shall be held under the same conditions as individually owned properties. Moreover, where mines are discovered, the demarcation may if necessary be modified, and compensation given. (4 and 6 March 1876)

---

85 Thompson 2000, p. 83.
86 See Dauphiné 1987, 1989.
87 Consultative and jurisdictional body that existed in some French colonies [trans.].

1. LINEAGE RIVALRY AND COLONIAL CONTROL

To complete this account of the link between mining exploration and demarcation of Kanak lands, we may note that the next item on the agenda for this session of the Privy Council is the 'presentation of a draft decree on mines'. It tells us notably that the first boundaries were drawn not throughout New Caledonia, but only in Houaïlou, Canala and Nakéty: these were precisely the areas with chiefdoms that had good relations with the administration, and where the first nickel mines had recently been opened (John Higginson's Bel-Air mine in Houaïlou, and Jean Louis Hubert Hanckar's Boa-Kaine mine in Canala).

Cartography is the immediate corollary of the demarcation of reserves and mining development, unless the reverse is the case: the first maps we have of Houaïlou were made by the surveyor Martin between 1874 and 1877; these were precisely detailed for the coastal zone (which, as we have noted constitutes, on one side of the main valley, by Lebris Bay, the colonists' main area of settlement and, on the other side of the river, the principal mining zone). Here cartography did not primarily serve for the purposes of war; it was moreover of little use during the repressive operations of 1878. Like telegraphy, however, it was a key tool of imperial governance, because it made it possible to identify the various components of the colony: 'Questions are urgent and demand a solution. Space for natives, space for Europeans, justice for all. With everyone in his place, said Governor de Pritzbuer, the ship stays on course' (Privy Council of 4 and 6 March 1876).

Following the glut of nickel caused by the introduction of New Caledonian ore onto the European market, the mining crash of 1876 and the failure of the Bank of New Caledonia (also known as the 'Banque Marchand'), which financed mining investment, mining at Bel-Air was halted. It was resumed, however, when Higginson and Hanckar founded the Société Le Nickel (Le Nickel company, SLN) in 1880; André Marchand, who we encountered above intervening in the Privy Council's discussions on boundaries, then became secretary to the company's board of directors, and subsequently its director from 1889 to 1904. As he had when the Bel-Air mine first opened, Higginson summoned a workforce from the New Hebrides and those individuals were the victims of 'human flesh contracts'. We know of this mainly through the remarkable research of Dorothy Shineberg.[88] This labour force was recruited under extremely

---

88 Shineberg 1999; see also Jolly 1987.

violent conditions, of which we learn mainly because of the diplomatic incident caused by recruitment for the Bel-Air mine: in the wake of the violent forced recruitment conducted in the New Hebrides by Mr Madézo (captain of the *Aurora*), which was accompanied by a murder at Api and various assaults, New Hebrideans killed a number of Europeans in revenge when the next ship arrived. This led to the Australian government lodging a complaint with the French Ministry of Foreign Affairs, reported the following year in articles in *The Times* and through the protest by French senator Victor Schoelcher, with the result that the French minister for the navy and the colonies asked the governor of New Caledonia, Amédée Courbet, to set up a commission of inquiry, which heard 80 witnesses and submitted its report in December 1880. The commission determined that 'recruitment of New Hebrideans is frequently conducted through threats, ruses or surprise', that none had come of their own free will, that 'almost all these Kanaks[89] [were] put on shore in Houaïlou to work in the mining industry', the *Aurora* having arrived there on 23 August 1880 ('Affaire des navires *Aurora* et *Lala*').[90]

The conditions of recruitment can be discerned between the lines of the summary of the register of births, marriages and deaths (civil register) in Houaïlou: four New Hebrideans aged 17, 18, 22 and 30 (Keloï, Halülo, Boulleouari and Mahaïte) are recorded as having died on board the *Aurora* in August 1880; five others, aged 17, 18, 25, 30 and 45, died at the Bel-Air mine in September 1880 (Sangaratta, Boulelli, Ousin Moili, Mansiou and Couit); two more, aged 17 and 50, died in October (Veounon and Tauli); and a 13-year-old child (Paccarou) died in November. Other deaths of New Hebrideans had been recorded between June 1876 and April 1878, during the first period of operation of Bel-Air, and the deaths continued through 1881 and 1882. It is reasonable to assume that the *Aurora* affair was a major factor in the decision by the Ministry of the Navy and the Colonies, in June 1882, to forbid recruitment of workers in the New Hebrides.[91]

---

89 In the 19th century this term, derived from the Polynesian (Hawaiian) word *kanaka*, meaning 'human being', was used for all Melanesians from New Caledonia to New Guinea – in this case denoting the New Hebrideans.
90 The records of the commission of inquiry's sessions give details of the methods of constraint used; see 'Affaire de l'*Aurora*'.
91 Thompson 2000, p. 263.

1. LINEAGE RIVALRY AND COLONIAL CONTROL

Following the exploitation of sandalwood in the triangular trade between Australia, China and New Caledonia during the 1840s, the late 1870s effectively constitutes a second globalisation of Houaïlou through the extraction of nickel destined for Europe, the importation of contract labour for the purposes of this mining, and the expropriation of land to enable the immigration of European colonists.[92] The very fact that Houaïlou was presented at the international Universal Exposition in Paris in 1878 testifies to this recent situating of the region in a world that was no longer limited to Oceanian networks:

> In Houaïlou, major nickel mines, the principal one being the Bel-Air mine (yield 15 to 17%). Houaïlou municipality was incorporated in 1874. Fine coffee, rice, manioc, pineapple and banana plantations, etc. As throughout the island, coconut palms are abundant; they are used to make oil and copra, used widely in fine soap-making. Sponges of mediocre quality, and trepang or sea cucumber, have been harvested. (*Exposition universelle internationale de 1878*, pp. 310–11)

By this time, the name 'Houaïlou' had stabilised around the European administrative and economic centre (although the territory of the municipality had not yet been clearly defined). The description Charles Lemire gives of the village and the Bel-Air mine is particularly illuminating about the changes brought by this mining globalisation in the lower Houaïlou valley:

> Most of the miners engaged in this mining are English, or rather Australian; ships take on the ore at Houaïlou, bound for Nouméa. These large ships anchor at outer anchorage. Only small boats can come up the *Boama* [the main river of Houaïlou] at high tide. On the beach there are nickel depots, and a number of stores or warehouses much better provisioned and constructed than those in Canala. It is only a short distance to the centre of Houaïlou, where all the dwellings are strung out along the right bank of the river. First there is the residence of the head of the third district. There is a native police station, a telegraph office and the post office, a well appointed hotel, with restaurant and very well supplied shops; finally, the buildings of the Bel-Air mine (drying kilns, wharves, warehouses, stores, offices, dwellings, outhouses and stables, cattle paddocks). The huts of office employees and labourers are grouped together here. Water pipes serve these buildings, which are linked to the mine by a 3-kilometre mule track. An hour's walk up the mountain, we come to the freed prisoners' village. On the right are the villages of free

---

92   Merle 1995.

> individuals and the English people's neat houses. Opposite are the forge, the warehouse and the main entrance to the tunnels. This mine, which was opened in 1875, employs white and 80 black workers, many of them from the New Hebrides. (Lemire 1884, pp. 181–82)

This description makes clear the way in which the categorisation of individuals (English and Australians, free and emancipated, Black and White, native and New Hebridean) and the spatialisation of the differences thus constructed contribute to the establishment of a system of segregation. We may add that the absence, or the minimal presence, of Kanaks from Houaïlou in the mine is probably due to the fact that the mine owners did not have the powers of coercion over them that they had over the New Hebrideans, and that the people of Houaïlou had little interest in becoming part of the proletariat. Thus the status of Houaïlou around 1878 was paradoxical: while European settlement remained concentrated around the coastal zone and the lower reaches of the principal valley, the social system as a whole was marked by the deployment of tools of empire that took over the local population and set them in a globalised colonial space, in the midst of spatial and ethnic categorisations that defined and limited their possibilities of action. Bouda Etemad's analysis sheds light on this development: 'During [the] last great act of modern colonisation, the white conqueror did indeed lay railway lines and erect telegraph poles at the same time he was establishing his hold over the space and the people' (Etemad 2007, p. 80). In New Caledonia, plans for a railway were short-lived, and never involved Houaïlou. Between 1856 and 1881, the situation thus shifted from a fairly minimal colonial hold over local social organisation, supported by military control (based on the association of the gunboat, the razzia and the call for auxiliaries), to the institution of territorial and administrative control in order to enable expropriation of land, and mining (through the telegraph, demarcation of lands, cartography, and the introduction of municipal and regional committees). Roads, running into the interior, came shortly after, in order to roll out this system of control. The 'Houaïlou' that emerged at this point was less a place than the result of this colonial process of localisation and enclosure, categorisation and subordination.

Subsequently, these systems of control and segregation became more rigidified, through the introduction of the Code de l'Indigénat in 1887,[93] the internment of Kanaks that ensued,[94] and then the policy followed by governor Paul Feillet. The auxiliaries' liberty and Kanaks' freedom of movement largely disappeared at this time.

Wars and the constitution of 'chiefdoms': A rereading of colonial sources

At this point, I would like to complicate the picture of the participation of a certain number of men from Houaïlou among the auxiliary troops by changing perspective, and also by drawing on some new sources. By focusing on the figure of the 'chiefs' referred to in the colonial documents cited above,[95] I enter into a prosopographic history of particular individuals and particular families. Through them, I aim of course to grasp the social structures more generally, and to make clearer the solid reasoning behind the Kanaks' actions. But I should like first to emphasise two points. Firstly, this reading, based on a critique of sources, sets up a mechanism of authority whose analytical coherence, it must be borne in mind, only has the status of a hypothesis. I have stressed elsewhere the divergence of versions of history that can be gathered through ethnographic research, the link between this divergence and contemporary social conflicts, the difficulty of collecting these versions, and the margin of uncertainty in an enquiry that is, by its very nature, endless.[96] I shall try to leave as much space as possible for doubt and silence, the incompleteness of the enquiry, while noting that my propositions here are not only potentially but necessarily subject to future revision. One way I make my hypothesis available to critique is by publishing the documents themselves on which I base my propositions, whereas in the discipline of anthropology, silence as to sources and authoritative discourse are more often the rule. Secondly, it is crucial to note above all the violence inherent not only in reducing divergence and fragmentation, but simply in breaching the private nature of these local versions of history. While I never quote statements that my informants have asked me not to quote, or which I understand might

---

93   Merle 2002 and 2004.
94   Muckle 2010.
95   See Bensa 2000.
96   Naepels 2000a.

disrupt contemporary social relations,[97] the dynamic of understanding that I am attempting to introduce partially contradicts the social logic of forgetting that Wolfgang Sofsky showed to be so important in *Violence: Terrorism, Genocide, War*, where he points to the catastrophic potential of remembrance:

> A society that never forgot anything would be intolerable. If human beings were not so made that most of what they experience disappears from their minds forever, they would be bound to an endless chain of the balancing of accounts, setbacks and retribution. They would be entirely occupied to the last with paying each other back for their actions. (Sofsky 2003, p. 215)

This remark seems to me highly pertinent to the Kanak case, where the polemical dimension of historical knowledge is easily mobilised.

Wanga: The Néjâ chiefdom

I begin with the case of the Houaïlou chiefs who were victims of the 1856 repression, 'Aliki Wangâ' and 'Aliki Ykà', as they are called in Martin Pannetrat's account, as I seek to articulate participation in colonial wars with local political strategies. In order to do this, we need to overcome an enormous problem of identification in colonial sources: as I have already noted, these do not give clan names, and are barely aware of the phonological subtleties of the Kanak languages. Moreover, the Kanak practice of having several personal names, and reusing given names within the same clan after a gap of a few generations, adds problems of identification that ethnographic investigation can nevertheless be of some help in resolving.

The first example is that of chief Wanga. Apart from Pannetrat's text, the only occasion I have found where his name appears is in William Diaper's unpublished manuscript on his stay in New Caledonia; he calls the chief with whom he spent several weeks in 1848, in the coastal zone of the right bank of Houaïlou (the place now known as Lèwèö or Néwèö), by this name. We may also note that this given name, Wanga, is currently borne by a resident of the same place, whose family name in the civic register is 'Mindia'. Finally, and convincingly, the name Wanga appears

---

97 Similarly, I use several kinds of anonymity (for the speaker or the names of individuals or places described by her/him) in all cases where I believe the mention of proper names might be harmful to individuals involved in the social situation described. See Naepels 2011, pp. 61–62.

1. LINEAGE RIVALRY AND COLONIAL CONTROL

in a manuscript notebook written by the missionary Maurice Leenhardt, which I was able to photocopy at the house of Geneviève Leenhardt, his daughter-in-law, and in which Leenhardt establishes the genealogy of the family of the paramount chief Mindia. Leenhardt himself describes this genealogical volume in a letter to his parents:

> I therefore went to Néouéo. I sought for three weeks to engage Mindia, who is so difficult to meet with, about his family, and each Friday I went to spend a long morning with him, in the house of the *nata* [Kanak evangelist] in Néouéo. The first time, it was difficult to get him to unbend, as he told me that we Whites are too stupid to understand their family relationships, and we *missis* [missionaries] too concerned for their souls to be interested in their obscure fleshly bonds. Through a few questions, I was able to lead him to the heart of the matter. On the second Friday, he had prepared a little sheet which he brought, after keeping me waiting for an hour. This time he was waiting for me at the *nata*'s house, and had written four large pages, inspired by the genealogy in Matthew, X begat Y, Y begat Z. We have 7 and 8 generations, and all the descendants who died when the Whites settled in the centre can clearly be seen. It is so striking that it seems a crime. I shall go again next Friday to complete the task, but my real aim was to draw this poor Mindia closer in. I have not yet succeeded … this goodhearted and poor, duplicitous and sincere Mindia. (Leenhardt, Lettre à ses parents, 29 January 1914)

This genealogy was taken up by Jean Guiart in a report for the Institut français d'Océanie (French Institute for Oceania),[98] and then again in his thesis, published in 1963. I am extracting part of it in my turn and filling in some elements on the basis of a reading of the manuscript. Kanak historical and mythical accounts cannot, however, be analysed independently of the political situation in which they are articulated,[99] given that there are so often competing and sometimes contradictory versions of the same local histories, even if they take exaggeratedly metaphorical form. Similarly, we cannot take a positivist approach to the genealogy collected by Leenhardt as forms of written knowledge based on the materialisation and decontextualisation of data, the genealogical table, like the entry in the land register, constitute procedures for establishing a legitimacy that is very different from the present-day production of a local consensus.[100] Maurice Leenhardt, a Protestant missionary heavily

---

98 Guiart 1955.
99 Bensa and Rivierre 1988.
100 See Goody 1977; Backouche and Naepels 2009.

involved in the life of Houaïlou, was not entirely independent of these lineage conflicts and there is little doubt that, through him, some Kanaks also sought forms of social recognition.

It emerges not only that this genealogy allows Wanga to be identified as a member of the Néjâ clan, and more precisely of the Wâpwé lineage descended from the ancestor Nemwanô, but also that it enables us to link together a large number of individuals whose names appear in the colonial sources I have cited in this first chapter, devoted to their involvement in auxiliary forces. Thus, in addition to Wanga, the following names are found:

- Ai, who appears in the *Moniteur* of 1 May 1864 because of the appeal he made to French officers in Napoléonville in November 1863; the latter recognised him as 'supreme chief of all the land between Cap Kouha and Cap Bocage' in January 1864. He continues to supply auxiliaries in 1864 and 1867–68. His name also appears on the first map of Houaïlou, in the village of 'Pèta, village of chief Aïe' (see Figure 1). He is mentioned in Lemire's 1877 text as the 'late chief Hai' (Lemire 1877, p. 170) and then as 'Hai, who died some years ago' (Lemire 1884, p. 179). On 4 September 1914, Leenhardt records statements by Mèèjâ about his father Ai, which testify to the colonial alliance concluded by the latter: 'My father told me that of all countries only France loves natives, everything good we have comes from France' (Leenhardt, Journal, 4 September 1914).

- Kayövimwâ, who appears under the name 'Cazaouimans, junior chief of Houaïlou', condemned to six months' internment in Nouméa in 1867 for a conflict with 'Ica, chief of Houarail'; subsequently he leads part of the repressive operation in the Houaïlou valley in late 1867 (*Moniteur*, 2 August 1868).

- Jëmaxé, son of Wanga. He appears under the name 'chief Simagué' (Lemire 1877, p. 170), but mostly as 'Dimagué', an auxiliary in 1878, who was the principal Houaïlou chief recognised during the repression of 1878–79.[101] It was for this reason that the dispatch of 21 December 1878 proposed him 'for the award of a gold medal first class with a stipend of 100 francs per year' ('Rapport sur les opérations militaires', p. 315).

---

101 See Amouroux and Place 1881.

1. LINEAGE RIVALRY AND COLONIAL CONTROL

- And, finally, Mèèjâ (Mindia). To my knowledge, his name appears in a text published for the first time in the second edition of Léon Gauharou's *Géographie*,[102] which mentions 'Houaïlou, chief Mindja' (Gauharou 1892, p. 77). More particularly, he was recognised as the paramount chief of all Houaïlou in 1897, at the time of the reform of the Native Affairs Service, headed by Paul Feillet until 1912, when four districts were created (see Chapter 3). Close to the Feillet administration and to Leenhardt, a supplier of auxiliaries in 1917 and of infantrymen for the First World War (including his son Apupia), he was the first Kanak from New Caledonia to receive the French Legion of Honour medal.[103]

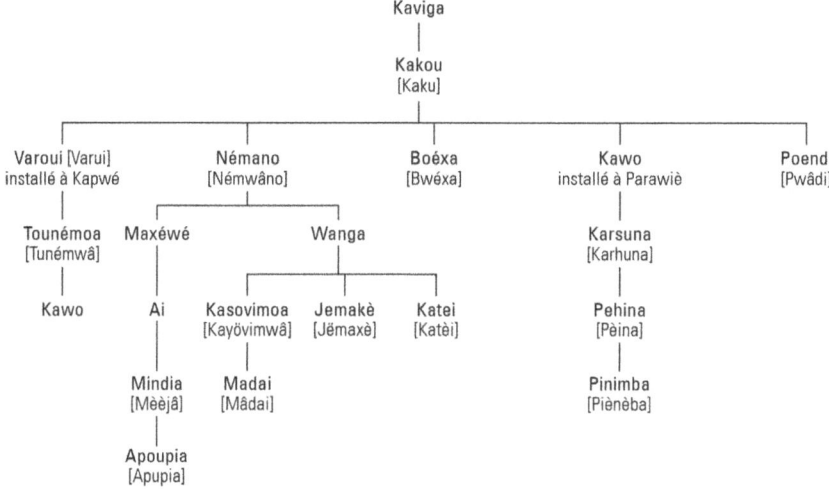

Figure 2. Extract from the genealogy of the Néjâ family
Source: Author's research, from information collected by Maurice Leenhardt in 1914.

Thus, after the terrible destruction wrought on their village in 1856, Ai, Kayövimwâ, Jëmaxè and then Mèèjâ won unquestionable recognition and support from the French administration by resolutely integrating themselves, generation after generation, in the French colonial system. This integration was not without its tensions, particularly in the case of Mèèjâ (see Chapter 3). Nevertheless, it enabled this Wâpwé branch of the

---

102 The official candidate in the elections for the first delegate from New Caledonia to the Conseil supérieur des colonies (Supreme Council for the Colonies) (O'Reilly 1953, p. 184), Gauharou was beaten by Léon Moncelon, the Houaïlou colonist whose career I outlined above.
103 Leenhardt and Vasseur 1987.

Néjâ clan to considerably increase its influence and its capacity for coercion of others. In Leenhardt's genealogy, it is remarkable that their recognition by the French is accompanied by elimination of the elder line (of Varui) – which nonetheless continues to exist up until today.[104] Guiart, partly on the basis of data from Leenhardt's study, asserts that this elder branch was chased out of Houaïlou before returning:

> The elder branch, of Varui, perhaps because of misconduct, and in any case because their offspring came much later, lost the chiefdom to the descendants of Nemwano. The Varui had to leave and go to Nemwano, south of Kapwe, and then moved on to Wa, Kwawa, Mea, until they were recalled and returned to Kapwe (Bwayo), after a stay in Wa. (Guiart 1955, p. 5)

One might then surmise that, in the clan's internal conflicts of legitimacy for the chiefdom, the arrival of the Europeans allowed the younger members to marginalise the elder. This proposition must, however, remain hypothetical, and we should avoid the temptation to attach the legitimist self-evidence of right of primogeniture to a pre-colonial social situation that may have been more complex.

Ika: The Népörö chiefdom

The second chief mentioned in the repressive operation of 1856, 'Ykà', can be identified by the same means: we know that he was chief of Warai (his name has already appeared in accounts of the repressive operations of 1864 and 1868). A list of names of chiefs identified by colonial sources in this village, and in the neighbouring village of Nékwé, can be compiled, and compared with another genealogy drawn up by Maurice Leenhardt, that of the chiefdom of Népörö, which I found in the same notebook as the lineage of the Néjâ.[105]

---

104 Today, in the civil register, the junior branches bear the family name 'Mindia', from the forename of the late 19th-century paramount chief Mèèjâ, while the senior branch bears the name 'Nédia', from the name of the Néjâ clan.

105 I present a more detailed analysis of this genealogy in Naepels 2010b.

1. LINEAGE RIVALRY AND COLONIAL CONTROL

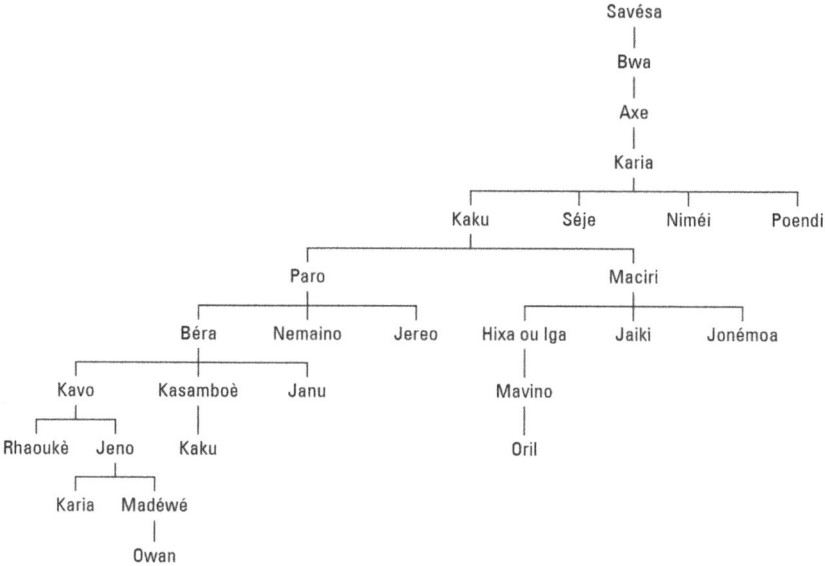

Figure 3. 'Néporo lineage'
Source: Author's research, after Maurice Leenhardt, n.d. (c. 1914–26). In 1914, Maurice Leenhardt stated that he had reconstituted the genealogy of the paramount chief Mèèjâ Néjâ. In 1915 his students began to edit his notebooks. The year 1926 marks the end of his third mission to New Caledonia, which was probably also a research visit to gather material for his three monographs for the Institut d'ethnologie (French Institute of Ethnology).

On the basis of this genealogy, we can identify a number of individuals mentioned in colonial sources, and read the competition between the two branches of the Népörö family, descended from Parö and Mwâciri, the two sons of the ancestor Kaku, to obtain recognition from the French. On the Warai side we can recognise chief Ika (correct linguistic transcription) Népörö (Ykà, Hixa, Ica, Iga (all forms found in colonial sources)) who, in addition to being named as one of the targets of the 1856 operation, appears several times in the colonial sources. In January 1864, 'Ica, of Houaraye', performs an 'act of submission' to the governor in Nouméa (*Moniteur*, 1 May 1864). In 1868, following 'one month's internment in Canala' (*Moniteur*, 2 August 1868), he participates in the repression aimed at eliminating the refugees from the valley who had settled in Bourail. He is succeeded as chief of Warai by 'Mavino', who is recognised in the deeds of demarcation of lands,[106] according to Charles Lemire: 'Tribe of Ouraye, chief Mavino' (Lemire 1877, pp. 170 and 309; Lemire 1884, p. 180), and Léon Gauharou: 'Mavino (between the rivers of Houaïlou and Dû)' (Gauharou 1882). It is therefore not surprising to see him recognised as one of the chiefs of the third arrondissement, 'Ouarai, chief Mavino', at the Privy Council session of 12 November 1886.

On the other side of the Tü river, in the neighbouring hamlet of Nékwé, 'Kamb'bo of Nékoué', Kavo Népörö, also performs an 'act of submission' to the governor (*Moniteur*, 1 May 1864). He participates as an auxiliary in the colonial wars of 1864 and 1868. He is recognised as chief in the principal administrative documents of the late 19th century.[107] Lemire also identifies him as chief: 'Tribe of Nékoué, chief Kambo' (Lemire 1877, p. 170; Lemire 1884, p. 180), or 'Cambo' (Lemire 1877, p. 309 and 1884, p. 179), as does Gauharou, who mentions 'Kambo, in Nékoué (left bank of the Dû)' (1882). He also seems to have been an intimate of Léon Moncelon, who mentions 'chief Cambo, of Houaïlou, whom I have had the honour of receiving often at my table' (Moncelon 1885, p. 363). This recognition is ratified when his name is included among the chiefs of the third arrondissement at the Privy Council session of 12 November 1886 ('Nékoué, chief Cambo'). The identification of 'Cambo' with the Kavo in Leenhardt's genealogy is confirmed by two additional mentions: the *Moniteur* of 2 August 1868 refers to 'Djannou, brother of Cambo', while Lemire speaks of 'Kaïamboé', 'brother and deputy to Cambo' (Lemire 1884, p. 179). These are certainly Kayabwé and Janu, the two brothers of Kavo in Leenhardt's genealogy. Similarly Gauharou, in the second edition of his *Géographie*, mentions 'Dionon' as the chief of Nékoué; this is Kavo's younger son Jénô.

Although they participated together as auxiliaries in the colonial wars, the chiefs of Nékwé and Warai seem to have had a relationship of open hostility: 'At the beginning of 1867, people of Nécoué ... led by Djannou, the brother of Cambo ... attacked the natives of Houarail' (*Moniteur*, 2 August 1868). We may therefore surmise that, in their participation in the auxiliary troops,

---

106 'Ouraye, chief Mavino' (*Bulletin officiel de Nouvelle-Calédonie* (*Official Bulletin of New Caledonia*), decree no. 211 of 17 May 1876 relating to the boundaries laid down in the decree of 6 March 1876) and 'Tribe of Ouraye, chiefs Mavino and Maou (*Bulletin officiel de Nouvelle-Calédonie*, decree no. 375 of 17 November 1876 relating to the demarcation of the Kanak tribes of Houaïlou, Canala and Nakéry).
107 During the demarcation of lands in 1876 – the official records of which mention 'Nékoué, chief Combo' (*Bulletin officiel de Nouvelle-Calédonie*, decree no. 211, 17 November 1876) and the 'tribe of Nékoué, chief Cambo' (*Bulletin officiel de Nouvelle-Calédonie*, decree no. 375, 17 November 1876).

their position was not so much one of alliance within the auxiliary forces, as one of competition for recognition from the colonial authorities. One remark by Moncelon suggests that this hostility might have emerged from a dispute over legitimacy and inheritance: 'The father Mahou shared the great chiefdom of Houaïlou among all his sons, and Kambo, *his adopted son*, received the chiefdom of Nékouè' (Moncelon 1886, p. 366, original emphasis).

Finally, when the great chiefdom of Houaïlou was divided into four districts in 1912 (see Chapter 3) it was Jénô's son 'Mandaoué' (or 'Madéwé') who was named chief of the district, confirming his administrative pre-eminence over the branch of the family settled in Warai (the descendants of 'Maciri'), but also over the senior branch of his own lineage (the descendants of 'Rhaoukè'). These forms of recognition thus testify to the same segmentary relationships that we have seen in operation in the relations of the Néjâ chiefdom with the administration: among all the families living in the coastal zone, the numerous 'chiefs' mentioned in colonial sources come from only two families, Néjâ and Népörö; and both the dominance established by some lineages over their seniors (in both cases) and the rivalry between collateral branches (in the case of the Népörö family) are evident. Jean Guiart, for example, describes 'the internecine disputes aroused by competition for prestige and authority, and hence by the junior line's challenge to the senior line. Examples are the Varui or Nejè Gwê è, in Neweo, replaced by the Nejè Gowe; the Neporo Gowe in Nekwé, who took the place of the Neporo Gwé' (Guiart 1987, p. 176). In the engagement with the French a doubly segmentary practice develops: the quest for pre-eminence of one clan over the others, and, within this clan, of one or several lineages over the other lineages. This strategy made use of the French presence to inscribe relations of power operative at the time in law.

Models of the chiefdom

In order to gain deeper understanding of the position of the Néjâ and Népörö families, we may consider the wars that had, a few generations earlier, at the time of their ancestors Kaku Néjâ and Kaku Népörö, brought these clans into conflict with a number of families in the Houaïlou valley in what is generally known as the war of Néajië or Nindiah.[108] It is interesting

---

108 I have collected several accounts of the origins of this war. Through identification of the two Kakus, the genealogies of the two families (Figures 2 and 3) indicate that it took place during the second half of the 18th century.

to speculate to what extent the repressive operation of 1867 might have furnished the Néjâ and Népörö families with an opportunity to settle the scores of this pre-colonial conflict. As colonisation progressed from the coast towards the interior of the island, the French administration recognised other chiefs, but the pre-eminence of the coastal chiefdoms was assured. Mèèjâ had four wives, from different parts of Houaïlou: this illustrates both the desire of these women's families to ally themselves with a chiefdom with connections to the European power, and Mèèjâ's quest to reinforce the dominance he was establishing with the Europeans, through matrimonial alliances (see Chapter 2).

All the evidence I gathered from interviews during my research indicates that the Néjâ and Népörö chiefdoms are agnatically related. For example, the two Kakus are always described as being related by blood (conventionally) and agnatically, in short as classificatory brothers. More broadly, the Néjâ and Népörö clans are said to be related, and to have moved around the land together before they separated in the lower valley or coastal zone of Houaïlou. This helps us to understand why Martin Pannetrat used the concept of 'vassal' to translate what the people of Canala told him in defining the relationship between 'Aliki Wangâ' Néjâ and 'Aliki Ykà' Népörö. The feudal vocabulary, widely used by the French in their early descriptions of Kanak 'tribes', testifies here to the fact that the Népörö were considered by many local people to be junior to the Néjâ. A comparable relationship, of virtual consanguinity, is sometimes identified in the relations between these two families and the coastal chiefdoms of Canala.

I should like to add one final remark to broaden out the question of the form of pre-colonial chiefdoms. Some of my informants mentioned the fact that these families, or some of their founding ancestors, came from Polynesia, probably Samoa, passing via Ouvéa and possibly via Canala: 'The Népörö, the Népörö family, they're guys who come from Samoa' (extract from interview, September 2002); 'the first of the Mwâdéwé who arrived here came from Samoa, they're Samoans (extract from interview, June 2006); 'Because in the 17th century, you see, my clan took in some of the first people to migrate from Polynesia ... the Néjâ and the Népörö' (extract from interview, July 2006). Two remarks may be added: firstly, the name of the primary ancestor of the Népörö in the genealogy compiled by Maurice Leenhardt (see Figure 3), Savésa, sounds Polynesian, even Samoan; secondly, I have already noted that many sources report migrations from Polynesia to

Ouvéa and Grande Terre during the 18th century.[109] Jean Guiart writes of 'people from Samoa who came to Ouvéa with the migration of the people of Wallis, who journeyed on to Parawiè, on the Wailu coast. The members of this group know one another, and maintain relations between Teuta, on Uvea, and Parawiè' (Guiart 1953, p. 95). The relationships between families in Houaïlou (such as the Néjâ and Népörö), Canala (particularly the Bwaxéa) and Ouvéa, into which both the sandalwood traders and the French military inserted themselves, thus offer evidence of the complexity of pre-colonial social dynamics. In the light of this analysis, let us return to the text with which this chapter began:

> In their history, the Néjâ and the Népörö were the seniors, and the others in Canala, the Bwaxéa and their spouses were the junior ones, they come after … When they formed an alliance with the Whites, the first thing they did, they decided they had to neutralise the people of Houaïlou. Because they wanted to be above the two chiefdoms in Houaïlou. So, what they did was, they sent a [European] ship to go and neutralise the two chiefs in Houaïlou.

Such hypotheses are clearly highly conjectural. They are, nevertheless, illuminating in terms of how we are to understand the historicity of the chiefdom form. One of my Kanak informants, for example, spoke of the coastal Néjâ and Népörö chiefdoms as holding a different conception of the chiefdom, distinct from that of the strongly independent small chiefdoms of Grande Terre; a more territorial chiefdom, more akin to a state, which hence found a reflection of its conception of chiefly dominance in the apparatus of the French state. One thing seems certain: the territorial aspect of the chiefdom was reinforced under the influence of the colonial model and through the recruitment of auxiliaries.

***

This first chapter has centred on the description of a repressive operation conducted in Houaïlou in 1856. In order to understand it, we need not only to assess the reliability of the documents available to us, but also to set it in the context of the changes in the contacts between Europeans and the Kanaks of Houaïlou from 1847 (with the sandalwood traders) to 1881 (the end of the first mapping of Houaïlou and the importation

---

109 With all due reservations as to the reliability of legitimising dynastic genealogies, it is worth noting that, if we go by the genealogies of the Néjâ and the Népörö compiled by Leenhardt, we can estimate the date of birth of the two Kakus, who lived in Houaïlou, to be around 1760, and that of Savésa (whose date of birth and place of residence are unknown, to say nothing of whether he actually existed) a century earlier.

of New Hebridean contract labourers for the mine). This has led me to present a brief history of the thinking behind repression and the military techniques used (razzia, mobile column, recruitment of auxiliaries), and also to reflect on the tools of imperial control (cartography, demarcation of land boundaries, telegraphy, the press, the administrative apparatus, law), and finally to understand how Houaïlou is defined by flows that are at once political and commercial, whether within Oceania or linked to the European trade in sandalwood, gold and nickel. I have also shown how the imperial relationships with Algeria, Bourbon Island (Réunion) and the New Hebrides played a part in the transformation of this remote part of the east coast of Grande Terre. Finally, I have sought to shift the perspective on this event in 1856 in order to show that the colonial war was also a Kanak war, to give a sense of the reasons for the auxiliaries' involvement, and to understand the lineage strategies at play in the military relationships between some chiefdoms and the French colonial authorities. In order to do this, I have made substantial use of genealogical sources. In this way the analysis of the 'chiefdoms' laid out here extends from the mid-17th century (the probable date of Polynesian migrations to Houaïlou) to the very end of the 19th century (with the administrative recognition and reconfiguration of the chiefdoms, to which I shall return).

The investigation I have undertaken here is incomplete – being based essentially on colonial sources, which I have begun to cross-reference with Kanak accounts – but it seems to me sufficient to show how important it is for anthropology to understand its categories and its objects, such as the 'chiefdom', within a historical process, particularly in colonial situations. 'Houaïlou' is a result of the intersection, in a highly unstable period, between movements, exchanges and conflicts bound up with the fluid functioning of the Oceanian world-system in the mid-19th century (Houaïlou–Canala–Ouvéa, but also the relations of Samoa and Tonga, and perhaps Fiji, with New Caledonia) and the movements, exchanges and conflicts linked to the expansion of the European world-system, in the competition between imperialisms (commercial, political and religious) – in which New Caledonia, all things considered, plays a marginal role. 'Houaïlou' is the new name, created between 1865 and 1875, of this globalised space. The inventiveness and opportunism of all involved is deployed here in ways that can only be very partially grasped; the blind spots of the 'sources' are particularly striking as regards all the subaltern positions (women, children, subjects of the chiefdom) and some which are not ('holders of the land' or 'founding guardians of the land').

2
Objects of War

> Near us sits the young English scientist who is to enlist for the war in fourth months' time ... Recently he, Laffay and I used a rare magic stone to cast a spell against the Kaiser. Let us hope that this will bear fruit ...
> Maurice Leenhardt, Lettre à ses parents, 11 December 1914

I propose to continue this investigation of the conventions of the use of violence in Houaïlou by introducing a second thread of analysis, opening the way to a deeper understanding of the wars and repressive operations that took place there during the 19th century. To this end, I move away for a moment from the written sources dating from the earliest days of colonisation of Grande Terre, to focus on material drawn from the interviews I conducted on local modes of preparation for war.

War stones

Mourners and propitiatory stones

In the accounts of war I gathered during my research in the Houaïlou region, a key role is played by a symbolic device – a propitiatory mechanism – that is absent from the old European texts examined in Chapter 1. These present-day accounts ascribe the efficacy of the warriors of the past to a number of procedures for purification and propitiation. I should like to focus particularly on two forms of propitiation for war.

Several inhabitants of the Houaïlou valley make reference to a process of selection and propitiation using a cooking pot. The first notable feature of the two interview extracts cited below is that they ascribe success in war to the power of the ancestors. The second is that this scene is set within a broader landscape of invocations in the smoke or steam from a cooking pot, a common method of communicating with the ancestors.

> Down there, there's the lizard. This lizard will come and will spit blood into the pot ... in the sacred place ... What will they do the other heads of the other huts? They will come, they will dip arrows, slingshots; this one will dip his arrow, this other one will dip his slingshot, I'll do the same ... Then [when] war [comes], when there are enemies on the other side ... all the fighters are with me, they have already dipped in my pot, because I dipped the blood ... Then we will hit the target every time, like crack shooters. That's for sure, there won't be any bullets wasted. We won't ever miss, because it is the *bâö* [ancestral power] that is fighting. (Extract from interview, May 1991)

> In this pot, they put medicines ... and then they set it to boil. And before they go to war, all the men line up like this, then each one comes with his spear, and he plunges it in, and he takes [it] out. If the drops that fall from the spear are drops of water, he is eliminated automatically. He can't go to war. The next one who comes, who comes after, [if] blood drips from his spear, he is kept on. (Extract from interview, July 1995)

The second, much more widespread practice of propitiation described by contemporary informants is the use of war stones (*panyaö* or *pè-paa*), which are believed to bring the best chance of success: 'The title of war chief is always bestowed on someone who also holds ... the war stone' (Raphaël Wéma Nééè, extract from interview, August 1993). Their efficacy is held to be specifically dependent on certain rules of use: 'There are rituals to be carried out, there are things to do with the revelations that were made at the moment when it was given' (Narcisse Kaviyöibanu, extract from interview, July 1995). These stones are unique, specific to particular families and are named. Another account describes a process of selecting warriors using a war stone very similar to that described above with the cooking pot:

> Like us the XX, we have a pebble that is held by the Y family and the Z, it's a hole like that, it's a stone but it has a hole. Before they leave for war, people who are going to go to war, they come with their spear, and then they're going to put it in the hole like this. When they take the spear out, when there is blood on the end of the spear, that one can go off to war,

but if it comes out and there is no blood, he has to stay at home. So that means that if there are fifteen who have blood, those ones will go to war, they will all come back. And stones like that when they start, it's the soul of a fellow who is skilled. (Extract from interview, 1993)

The negative obverse of this warrior power in war is the constant urge to war that some of these stones are believed to stimulate. Several of those that embody the ambivalence of the desire to kill are therefore known as Katââyèi, literally 'weeping all the time', because of their thirst for blood. An account of another stone describes this phenomenon:

> This war stone, there was nobody who could stand up to it, every time people struck a blow, it produced victims. So in the end, they were all the time moving from place to place, because of this war stone. And every time they attacked a tribe, a country. Well, they were forced to in fact, because this war stone, it had to be fed, and it had to be fed with blood. So every time it was fed, there was peace for a few years, one year, two years … Every time the stone started to get hungry, then the stone wept … and then they had to kill, they had to kill more enemies to feed the stone, or else the stone would turn against the clan, it might eat the guardian of the stone. So that's why they moved about during the different phases of their moving. (Extract from interview, July 1993)

The accounts that follow, which also offer evidence of contemporary experience of contact with such objects, describe how the war stone was effectively 'fed' by the blood of a victim:

> For example, me, I've seen some, you know, out of all the stones we have … My father took me to a place where there are small bushes … But it's frightening when you go in, you don't go in there just like that, there are herbs you have to take, and then you have to blow each time you take a step forward … So he took me up to that place, and there there is the skull of some of my ancestors, people who were very strong, very powerful. And then there among these skulls, tiny little pebbles, then there were stones that were underneath … My father told me to hold one, I held it in my hand, I looked at it, but it was heavy … And then next to it, there's a little stone the shape of a slingshot stone, smaller, but it looks like a slingshot stone. And that's the stone they used to take when they went to war, and they put it in a little pouch.[1] Then when they killed someone, they would dip it in his blood. So that's what fed the mother

---

1 The Ajië word used here is *mwaawè*, a term to which I shall return (see below, note 8).

[the principal war stone]. They came back from war and they touched the mother with the stone and the mother sucked out the person's blood. (Extract from interview, July 1995)

These stones, they always have to be fed with blood. And it cries like a baby. Me, I've heard these stones with my own ears, we had one at home. Where we stayed. Just before X died, for example, the stone cried all through the house. It cried several evenings before the old man died. Because there are places where there are these stones. And people for example who make medicines [who use powers of attack in sorcery], when they hold these things, they have to be killing people all the time, or else the stone eats them afterwards. Very often you hear that in the stories, the legends the elders tell, the people who held the stone, they always had to feed them, they always had to be massacring people. (Extract from interview, July 1995)

So the other day we talked about *panyaö*. Well they're the ones who are the guardians, of the *panyaö*, of a pebble this size. There's a hollow that's red, it's the blood there is inside, but when they go to pick up the peelings, I told you about that the other day, they will put them in, they will pack down [crush] with a piece of bone, and then, you know, they will call your name [addressing the interviewer]: 'Michel, you will die little by little.' And that's how it is, every week they will do that, and you will catch a disease, you'll start to cough, and then you'll go down, down, down, until you die, you know. (Extract from interview, July 1995)

These war stones form part of the larger set of propitiatory stones; notable among these are horticultural stones (especially yam stones, *pè-mëu*, and taro stones, *pè-mwa*, which are believed to make the corresponding crops more productive, or their cultivation easier, and stones that summon rain, *pè-kwa*) and seduction stones.[2]

Accounts of the origin of these propitiatory stones take a characteristic form. They describe the capture of the spirit (*ko*) of a person who has died, who is revered for his personal prowess (military, agricultural or other) and the transformation of it into a propitiatory stone through the action of a mourner (*âvii*). In the past, when a person of importance died, his body was rolled in a mat and laid on a platform (*néyapè*) in a tree – it is said, a banyan. A mourner (*âvii*), usually represented as a junior member of the deceased's family, would keep watch over the body. Steeped in

---

2   Stones whose form resembles male or female genitals: 'The aphrodisiac stones are also figure-stones, feared on account of the immediate privileges they confer, during festivals, on the individual whose sadistic imagination has become excited through seeing or touching them' (Leenhardt 1909a, p. 294).

black dye from the candlenut tree (*tâi*),³ and obeying a certain number of prescribed restrictions, he would pour water over the body to accelerate the process of decomposition. He was also responsible for ensuring that the deceased's skull was not stolen by any enemies who might have wanted to appropriate it and thus capture the spirit (*ko*).

> The *âvii* is someone who does not bathe [does not wash], who does not have relations with women [especially sexual relations], who lives alone and is in communication with the afterlife, you see. And for example his food mustn't be contaminated by women's hands … Well, that's in the sense of a dead person, but the *âvii* is also the person who transforms the dead person's spirit into a war stone, a taro stone, a yam stone. (Narcisse Kaviyöibanu, extract from interview, July 1993)

The term *âvii* seems to be derived from the verbal suffix *–vii*, denoting the idea of breaking, rupturing, detaching, separating, which confirms the liminal character of the mourner. The transformation of the spirit into stone passes through a number of stages: the dead person's spirit appears to the mourner in material form, for example in the form of an animal. The mourner catches it (sometimes after a fight or a spiritual test), and immerses it in the water of a river, from which it emerges in the form of a propitiatory stone:

> The *âvii* keep watch over their dead, after the third day or the fourth day, the spirit of the [dead] person comes to disturb the body, the human person. He feels something like an animal or a lizard …, and then him, he catches it and that's it, it becomes a stone, and it's immersed in the water. You immerse it in water and it becomes a stone, either a taro stone … or a rain stone, that makes rain … I wanted to tell you that because my grandfather told me … His grandfather's skull⁴ is up there among X's stones. Then him, he told me: 'I kept watch for my grandfather, then when his spirit came into the body [the corpse], yes the spirit came up like that, it's like a wind.' … He caught it, it's a lizard that fell from the cliff, it's a big cliff, at least 20 metres, without a scratch, even into the stones. Then down below, there is water, there's the river, he went to dip the lizard in. But when he dipped it in the water, the lizard there became a stone pebble. You see, then after when it was finished, it's a war stone for us the Y family, that's it … I tell you that because it was my grandfather who told me, you see, he told me about [mourning] his grandfather who he went to keep watch over there on the other side. (Extract from interview, August 1993)

---

3   *Aleurites moluccana*, a tree of the family Euphorbiaceae.
4   In other words, the skull of the speaker's great-great-grandfather.

Another interviewee emphasised the agonistic aspect of the reputed interaction between the mourner and the spirit of the dead person:

> [The *âvii*] doesn't keep watch over all the dead, he only watches over the [prestigious] dead people, like a spear thrower or a slingshot thrower, or a cultivator of yam or taro. He will come, he will lie down with the dead person, the *âvii*, he will come and lie down alongside the dead person. On the third day, according to them, the spirit of the dead person will come out of him to leave, and that's when he will catch it, and they will fight … And finally, it's him [the mourner] who overcomes it [the spirit of the dead person], and it will become a pebble. And that pebble, it's for planting yams, and when you go to plant yams, you take the yam and you touch the stone like that there, then you go to plant, then it will produce big yams. Or if the fellow was a warrior, you take your spear and you touch the pebble before you go off to war, or the slingshot stone, and the spear or the slingshot stone will never fall on the ground, it will always hit its target. (Guynemer Karé, extract from interview, August 1993)

One final text adds a further dimension to these descriptions of the origin of propitiatory stones in the capture of the spirit of prestigious dead people – that of transmission of a practical knowledge. The acquisition of a stone is said to be accompanied by communication of medicinal herbs and sometimes of invocations that are required to ensure full efficacy of the propitiatory mechanism:

> Me, I give some examples, the house where I lived in X. Well, that was my *âvii* place, that was where my ancestors lived. And there the one who is *âvii* [mourner] brought the dead person's body and then kept watch over it. And then often it was in five days … and there he will see the spirit of the dead person arriving, you know, then thanks to the power of the weapons he has, he will catch the dead person's spirit. And at that point, there will be a fight between him and the dead person's spirit. So it's a challenge in fact to challenge the courage of the one who is *âvii*, and it will transform itself into all kinds of animals, it will try to frighten him. Until the point when the other proves he is not frightened. At that point, the spirit says to him: 'You have won.' And he catches the spirit, he immerses it in the water, and when it comes into contact with the water, the spirit becomes a stone. But before it becomes a stone, it tells him secrets … like how he can communicate with it. And to get into contact with it, it will teach him the herb or the tree that will be used for communicating. I'll give you an example, if it's a taro stone, say you want me to make the taro grow, you will bring your cutting, you'll touch the stone, but you will, for example, chew the leaves of a particular tree, you'll place them this way or that way, you know. That's the language, you see,

so it's a code. So that one, he learns the code at that moment, he puts the soul in the water, so the soul becomes a stone. If it's for taro, the stone has the shape of a taro, if its for yam, it takes the shape of a yam, if it's a war stone, it will have the shape of a war stone for spear, slingshot or axe. (Extract from interview, July 1993)

This set of accounts poses a problem of temporality: they refer practices or representations in an ahistorical and abstract way to a specific cultural identity, rather than a clearly defined social situation.[5] I personally have never seen anyone make use of a propitiatory stone, but this obviously does not prove they are no longer used at all.[6] Several of the interviews quoted mention present-day experience of these accounts, through the relationship some of my interviewees describe with ancestors' skulls or stones. It has been definitively established, however, that this process of mourning and this treatment of the dead body are no longer practised, particularly since the conversion of the inhabitants of Houaïlou to Christianity during the first half of the 20th century. Likewise, mourners (*âvii*) disappeared nearly a century ago.

1918: 'Jopaipi'

It is worth pointing out that these various tales – which hence cannot be considered descriptions of current practice, despite the fact that they were collected in the 1990s – broadly converge with what Maurice Leenhardt wrote on this issue. In one of his very first published scientific articles, during his first mission leave in 1909, he already describes propitiatory stones:

> This stone may be found by chance, but it is often revealed to the Kanak by an ancestor who visits him while he is asleep and tells him that he has left a stone with a particular property for him in such and such a place. At dawn the Kanak will go to find this precious stone.
>
> The value of the figure-stone depends less on how closely it resembles the desired object than on its origins, the way it was revealed, and whatever tradition it may inherit. (Leenhardt 1909a, pp. 292 and 295)

---

5   Thus illustrating what Jean Bazin has called an 'ethnographic explanation' (Bazin 1996, 2000a, 2000b).
6   There are reports of war stones being used during the 'events' of the 1980s.

This is an interesting point at which to return to a classic of New Caledonian anthropology, written by Bwêêyöuu Ërijiyi in 1918, translated and published by Leenhardt under the title 'Jopaipi' in his 1932 *Documents Néo-Calédoniens*, and on which Leenhardt commented several times. This text describes a variant of the process of acquiring a war stone that I considered above:

> Jööpwaipi was given a herb [*deewi*] when he was in a second state [*vinyêê*][7] at Népèru. He had gone to seek the spirit of a long-dead ancestor of the Mèyikwéö family, by the name of Rhabwê. He had a band of beaten bark [*mwaawè*][8] around his wrist so he could look for the spirit, and catch it so that it could become a *panyaö* war stone. For there was a war at that time, a war between the Mèaa and the Mèyikwéö. This is how he entered the ecstatic state. He went to the place where the ancestors are invoked [*ka-mwârö*] at nightfall and sat in the deepest darkness. He was overtaken by a feeling of disorientation as if he was drunk, then he was in a second state and he flew; he didn't feel as if he was walking any more, but his heart kept hold of a little strength and was thinking. When he was close to the place of invocation of the ancestors [*ka-mwârö*], watching over the pot he was boiling, he saw the spirit of the ancestor he was seeking. Immediately, crouching, bent over so the spirit wouldn't see him, he jumped on it and seized it. And the two thrashed about; but Jööpwaipi held on and captured the spirit of old Rhabwê. Then the spirit said to him: 'You fought well with me, learn to recognise this pole on the altar, for this is the wood that covers me, so that I can act when there is illness. If a god strikes, if a spear pierces, in case of sudden death, you will take this wood, this plant and this herb to chew, and these are the corresponding prohibitions.' He spoke in this way. Jööpwaipi then took the ancestor's spirit and immersed it in the water so that it became a stone. The Ëribee mâ Boè keep that stone, and Bwêêyöuu Ërijiyi knows this medicine [*deewi*]. (English from author's French translation after Leenhardt 1932, pp. 334–36, and the text reconstituted by Aramiou and Euritéin 2003, pp. 22–23)

It is to be noted that here the process of acquiring the war stone occurs in the place of invocation of the ancestors (*ka-mwârö*), in the immediate crisis of a current war, and not when a mourner is watching over a dead

---

7   The translation of the term *vinyêê* poses a delicate problem of interpretation, to which I shall return. As an initial indication, it covers the semantic field of distraction, madness, ecstasy – in short an altered (second) state of consciousness, though the nature of this alteration is difficult to define precisely. It can be compared to the term *nyênyê*, meaning distraught, disoriented.

8   This band can also be used to roll up or carry objects, hence one of my interviewees' reference to a 'little pouch' in which a war stone can be carried (see above, note 1).

body – thus differing from the accounts I was able to record directly. There are nevertheless a number of by now familiar elements: the invocation of the ancestors in the steam from a pot, within a sacred place; the agonistic transformation of the spirit into a stone; and the revelation of plants, herbs or medicines (*deewi*) that reinforce the stone's efficacy.

The context in which this text was written up helps to grasp its meaning:[9] it forms part of the first notebook in the second series of Bwêêyöuu Ërijiyi's writings, in which he is responding, paragraph by paragraph, to the 'Questionnaire for information on clans' formulated by Maurice Leenhardt in the Houaïlou language in March 1918.[10] The questions, drawn up when Leenhardt thought he was about to leave New Caledonia for good and addressed to his pastoral pupils, relate to the internal organisation of the clans, the relations between the chief and the founding ancestor of the country, the offerings of yams made to the founding ancestor and accounts of the origins of the clans, war stones, ancestors and totems. More specifically, the text on Jööpwaipi forms part of one section, numbered '6', and is thus a direct response to the sixth question in Leenhardt's questionnaire: '6. All of these clans have gods … What is the power of each? What are the sicknesses each one can send? What is the (healing) herb for each one, and where does this herb come from? Who is its guardian?' (Leenhardt 1977, p. 91). Hence the text published under the title 'Jopaipi' in *Documents Néo-Calédoniens* constitutes part of Ërijiyi's response to a question on the origin of medicinal herbs (*deewi*),[11] specifically those he personally holds. In the original notebook, the text 'Jopaipi' immediately follows these statements by Ërijiyi:

> There are medicinal herbs for each ancestral power [*bâö*] … These herbs are found through dreams: the man who dreams receives them from the spirit of the dead person … Men in ecstasy [*vinyêê*] can also find these herbs, the name is revealed to them as they sleep, along with the way they are to be used and all the prohibitions on food, meat, sugar cane, everything they should not eat … Seers [*mèrhî*] also find them, those who dream awake or sitting: when the voice comes to them when they are awake, their vision is disturbed. (Aramiou and Euritéin 2002, pp. 21–22, English version after author's French translation)

---

9   I began analysing this context in Naepels 2007b, some elements of which are taken up here.
10 Leenhardt 1977; Naepels 2007b.
11 See Salomon 2000a.

Here, the acquisition of the herbs is linked to that of a war stone, allowing Ërijiyi to complete, through this text, 'Jopaipi', his response to Leenhardt's previous question that specifically related to war stones, *panyaö*: '5. Show the clans which have a panyao stone. What is this stone and where does it come from?' (Leenhardt 1977, p. 91).

Inner experience and technologies of the self

The two types of experience of meeting with the spirits of the dead, that of the mourner (*âvii*) and that of invocation at the 'altar' (*ka-mwârö*), constitute accounts of visionary experiences bound, within the accounts themselves, to a degree of disturbance of the senses, an alteration of consciousness (*vinyêê*). They are inscribed within a set of existing means for communicating with the spirits of the dead and acceding to a higher knowledge and power (*arinadö*), the other great domain of which is through dreams.[12]

Despite many attempts at clarification,[13] the descriptive vocabulary used in anthropology to describe such subjective experiences – possession, trance, ecstasy, shamanism, mediumship – is neither fully stabilised nor truly satisfactory. These terms are difficult to dissociate from their normative connotations of monotheist denigration and devaluation or New Age rehabilitation.[14] I propose nevertheless to outline a few elements of typology: according to Erika Bourguignon, in trance the subject's spirit is said to leave his body to travel in the realm of the spirits or the dead, the subject remaining in a state of deep sleep or profound calm; when he 'returns' he is able to recount his experience. In possession, by contrast, a spirit speaks to an audience via the body of a subject who shows violent motor behaviours and incarnates the spirit; when she comes out of it, she remembers nothing.[15] For the Oceanian examples, Edward Schieffelin proposes a congruent classification: the soul of the shaman travels out of his body to effect a cure, while the spirits speak to those present through the mouth of the medium they are visiting.[16] The most detailed and, probably, the clearest definition is that proposed by Gilbert Rouget in *Music and Trance*, where he contrasts ecstasy (characterised by

---

12   On dreams in the transmission of knowledge, see Naepels 1998, pp. 135–36; and Stephen 1979.
13   Bastide 1972; Geertz 1973; de Heusch 1971; Juillerat 1975; Lewis 1971 and others.
14   See Hamayon 1995.
15   Bourguignon 1972 and 1973.
16   Schieffelin 1977.

immobility, silence, solitude, the absence of crisis, sensory deprivation, memory, hallucination) with trance (marked by movement, noise, taking place in company, crisis, sensory overstimulation, amnesia and absence of hallucinations).[17]

Albeit with major variations in the vocabulary used, we thus have a general distinction between that which relates to ecstasy on the one hand (the spirit of the subject leaves her body to enter into contact with the world of the spirits – shamanism in Schieffelin, trance for Bourguignon, 'transport' for Leenhardt)[18] and that which relates to possession on the other (the spirit speaks through the man it visits: mediumship for Schieffelin, trance in Rouget).[19]

In what can be grasped of the Kanak case through the accounts available, the experience described does not relate to public 'possession', the incarnation of the spirit of a dead person in the agitated body of a living person, followed by amnesia and absence of control over one's actions. Most of my interviewees instead describe internal experiences, isolated in the singularity of the *ka-mwârö* or – for the mourner (*âvii*) – the solitude of the forest, which are subsequently reported, narrated, and thus relate to the category of ecstasy in Rouget's classification. In this sense, the fact that I did not directly observe the process of acquisition of stones, or the work of invocation conducted in the steam from the cooking pot, and more generally the absence of reports of direct observation of these situations in the ethnographic texts on the Houaïlou region, are perhaps not so far removed from the experience that many of the inhabitants of Houaïlou themselves might have had: the central element seems not so much the experience itself as the account of it and, still more, the power it engenders.

This broad-brush outline leaves many questions unanswered: what precisely were the techniques of ecstasy? Were they based on the hallucinogenic properties of certain plants? In particular, what was the significance of the anointing with the dye from the candlenut tree? In the texts quoted, modes of communication with the ancestors are connected with technologies of the self, among which prescriptions of abstinence

---

17   Rouget 1985.
18   Leenhardt 1937b.
19   It will be noted that the term 'trance' is the least precisely defined, and appears on both sides of the opposing pairs; it is for this reason that I avoid it in my translation of 'Jopaipi', whereas Leenhardt used this word to translate *vinyêê*.

are pre-eminent. We also need to examine the accounts of these practices, by comparing them to the healing practices described by Christine Salomon,[20] questioning to what extent they were made public, and what degrees of scepticism and pragmatism they arouse. Furthermore, we know nothing of the discursive content of the invocations.

This glimpse of the subjective experience associated with the invocation of ancestors and their power opens the possibility of considering another dimension of war: the emotions bound up with combat and preparation for it. This is a point emphasised by Maurice Leenhardt in his description of war in the Houaïlou region. In particular, he sees anger (*rhôê*) as a significant political sentiment (see Chapter 5).

> Preparation for war, among the Kanak, will consist … of creating the state of excitation necessary to accomplish it, of holding oneself in a state of warrior perfection, and also of maintaining one's equipment in the same state, and all the possible imponderables that might play a role at decisive moments. There is no training or organised exercise. 'War,' says the Kanak, 'is an individual matter, it is the effect of an anger that you stoke up inside yourself.' …
>
> Well before the fire in the hut is lit, a man tasked with preparing for war has made himself ready to fulfil this role. This is the youngest member of the clan, the priest who holds the stones containing the ancestral spirits, the *panyao* stones … The priest's task is to propitiate the warrior ancestors. For a long time he will make sacrifices, all alone, in a tiny pot that he must have made himself …
>
> The hour of combat has arrived. The priest touches his spear to a virility stone or a magic ring; on his left arm he wears a *moawe* band that is wrapped around a pebble selected from among the *panyao* (ancestor-spirit) stones,[21] and at the moment of setting out, he dances up and down on the spot, possessed by a sensation of burning in the soles of his feet that forces him to leap forth. (Leenhardt 1930, pp. 38–39, pp. 40 and 41)

These texts may be compared with Leenhardt's first article on the stones:

> As soon as his weapon touches this part of the stone [here Leenhardt is referring to a phallic stone], he is as if possessed. 'The soles of my feet are burning,' he says; he ties a long band around his left wrist, binding a small

---

20   Salomon 1993 and 2000a.
21   Here we encounter the dual sense of the word *mwaawé*, a band or pouch of beaten bark, which holds the stone chipped from a principal war stone (see above, notes 1 and 8).

> stone into it; this is as it were a representative of the sacred stone which is not taken, and he runs to the battle, shouting, gesticulating, bringing all the warriors with him. He will go on until he has killed an enemy. Stopping immediately, he cuts the finger that holds the spear-throwing cord off the dead man, and runs back with his trophy to lay it before the protective phallus, as a sign of gratitude. The warriors, intoxicated by his success, certain of the spirits' approval, display their greatest valiance. If, by chance, the priest should be killed at the start of the battle, their courage would fail all of them, crushed as they would be by the thought that the spirits were no longer with them, owing to the transgression of their priest, who must have broken his vow of chastity. (Leenhardt, 1909a, p. 295)

This spiritual and emotional aspect of war is also pointed out by some of my interlocutors, who thus likened the figure of the war chief to that which appears in the descriptions of the mourner (*âvii*) or the person who invokes the ancestors at the *ka-mwârö*. It will be noted, too, that dye from the candlenut tree (*tâi*) was used by both warriors and mourners.

> When it comes to war, there are all the prohibitions, so your wife shouldn't be pregnant, you had to bathe and prepare yourself several weeks before, you had to sleep on your own, cook your own food, there was the consultation of the seers [*mèrhî*]. There was all that, then, and then there were the ceremonies you did yourself, I mean your opponent … you were already putting him at a disadvantage, it was magic, you know. Then when you set off to war, like that … you're possessed by a spirit. The warrior, like the war chief for example … he is completely possessed by the spirit, he is no longer master of his actions. These are things you can trigger at any moment, for example us, when we make our war speeches. (Extract from interview, June 1995)

The story of a war

Who is Jööpwaipi?

Following this exposition of modes of propitiation for war, which are entirely absent from the colonists' and military officers' texts (see Chapter 1), I should like to complete my analysis of the 'Jopaipi' text by attempting to answer some sociological questions raised by this essay. First of all, who are the people mentioned, in terms of their social relations? Who is Jööpwaipi? Who is Rhabwê? Through these questions, a number of the wars described in the preceding chapter re-emerge, thus shifting the focus from the symbolism of war stones to their sociology, before refocusing on the colonial wars.

The first thing to be noted in terms of identifying the individuals named in this text is that in the language of Houaïlou, the name Jööpwaipi[22] literally means 'worn, spoiled, ancient pipe; old pipe'.[23] We are thus dealing with a name that postdates the sandalwood traders' introduction of clay pipes as objects of exchange. It therefore follows that the person whose experience is recorded in this text was born in the second half of the 1840s or after (or at least that this nickname was bestowed on him at that point).

The second thing to note is that the name of the ancestor whose spirit was captured by Jööpwaipi and transformed into a stone, Rhabwê, appears on several other occasions in the notebooks in which Ërijiyi wrote down the tale of 'Jopaipi'. The first mention comes in the second notebook of the first series, in two ceremonial speeches (*vivaa*) that present the ancestors of the Mèyikwëö tribe: section 8 refers to 'the descendants of Nörö and Gwâmee and Rhabwê and Wainô and Màjaa', and section 10 to 'the descendants of Nörö and Gwâmee and Rhabwê and Wainô and Varui and Kuayè' (Aramiou and Euritéin 2002, pp. 33 and 36). Moreover, the name Rhabwê occurs in a more detailed context in the same notebook in which the 'Jopaipi' text was written down, in section 4, in a paragraph headed 'The Mèyikwëö clan' (Aramiou and Euritéin 2003, pp. 14–15). This passage thus constitutes a response to the fourth question in Leenhardt's questionnaire: 'What is the origin of each clan? Describe the tales, *vinimo*, and the myths, *virhénô*, of each one' (Leenhardt 1977, p. 91). This section was translated by Raymond Leenhardt, the missionary's son, at an unspecified date, and revised by Jean Guiart and Gayô Karé before being published by Guiart in 1972, and again in 2003. In this text, Ërijiyi makes Gwâmee the founding ancestor of the maximal clan bearing the name Mèyikwëö. Gwâmee is said to have had five sons (Mâjaa, Bwa, Rhabwê, Jîîbwa and Mèvorhau) who founded a number of the clans in this tribe, and Rhabwê is identified as a member of the Kaviyöibanu clan: *Aè wi-a Rhabwê, wè néé mwâârö xie na Kaviyöibanu* – 'That man, Rhabwê, the name of his clan is Kaviyöibanu' (Aramiou and

---

22 I have followed the spelling proposed by Aramiou and Euritéin in their editions of Bwêêyöuu Ërijiyi's notebooks (2002, 2003), as it is phonetically more accurate than Leenhardt's version.
23 From *jöö* – old, worn-out, outdated – and *pwaipi*, derived from the English 'pipe'.

Euritéin 2003, p. 15, English version after author's translation). There are other versions of the history of this Mèyikwéö tribe. The important point here is that this is the version Bwêêyöuu Ërijiyi recorded in the same notebook as the 'Jopaipi' text.

These two pieces of information can be linked on the basis of the genealogical summary Narcisse Kaviyöibanu and I drew up during our first recorded interview, in June 1991. Starting from his grandfather Janô, who was born around 1900, two generations earlier there is an ancestor called Pwaipi, and four generations before that an ancestor named Rhabwê. Moreover, I conducted this interview in the village of Népèru, where Narcisse Kaviyöibanu was then living and which is very widely understood to be part of this clan's lands.[24] The fact that Ërijiyi locates the acquisition of this war stone in Népèru confirms this clan identification. Today, Rhabwê is a given name still used in the Kaviyöibanu family. Thus, both the text in Bwêêyöuu Ërijiyi's notebook and my genealogical research indicate the social location of the actors: the war stone was acquired by an individual in the Kaviyöibanu clan, which forms part of the Mèyikwéö maximal clan, and to which Jööpwaipi and his ancestor Rhabwê belonged.

1867: The Koro war

One further point requires clarification: while the identity of the protagonists seems established, what is the 'war between the Mèea and the Mèyikwéô' mentioned in Ërijiyi's text? Contemporary studies in the Houaïlou valley have much to say on this matter, for at least two reasons: firstly, this war and the movements of clans it gave rise to contributed to the current geographical distribution of families in the Houaïlou valley and the social structuring of this space between 'people of the valley' (*pâ néiriwâ*) and 'people of Mèaa' (*pâ Mèaa* or *pâ tëvo*).[25] Secondly, all of my interlocutors located this 'war between the Mèaa and the Mèyikwéö' at the confluence of the Koro valley and the main Houaïlou valley – it is also known as the Koro war. The fact that stories relating to this war can

---

24   At the time of writing, the area in question is occupied by another individual from this family; however, it forms part of the territory overseen by the organisation responsible for land reform, within the set of lands in the zone known as Dâô, the reassignment of which is a source of major conflict: see Naepels 1998 (see also Chapter 5).
25   Despite the fact it has been shown that some clans came down from Mèaa to various places in the Houaïlou valley and its tributary valleys prior to this war.

still be collected is no doubt due partly to the context of conflict over land in this Koro valley, in which I conducted my initial research during the 1990s (see Chapter 5).

This war arose between a group of clans then living in the Houaïlou valley (particularly, but not exclusively, the Mèyikwéö), gathered together in a small fort or protected by a barrier made from large wooden stakes (*mwâwêbé*), and families originating from the Mèaa plateau (particularly but not exclusively the Wéma family), who had come down to the outskirts of the Houaïlou valley via the Koro valley, for reasons that today are the subject of diverse and contradictory accounts. Given that these historical accounts form the basis for contemporary land or statutory claims, I have no intention here of putting forward a definitive version of the Koro war, nor obviously of imputing responsibility, since these reconstructions are also extremely hypothetical. It must be emphasised that a given protagonist can today set any localised account within a broader history, which links the episode to earlier accounts and justifies a given act by setting it in the context of a broader temporality. Despite the fact that much is uncertain about the causes and the precise sequence of events of this war, and notwithstanding the existence of differing versions, a certain number of protagonists and episodes are well known, as are the principal interpretations of the families concerned. I present here some excerpts from the accounts I collected:

> There, there is what was known as the *mwâwêbé*, it's like a fort, there are big stakes made of hard wood. And when the Wéma had trampled the fields, the Wéma, the Gowé, well all those who were called the Mèaa, you know, they also want to go and chase out the Mèyikwéö. But us, we had guns already. And they hid behind the stakes, you know. And then they waited for the chief to come and throw down insults, there opposite, on the other side of the river, he came to insult the Mèyikwéö, then it's from there they shot, then the chief fell … but only he wasn't killed. But it was above Koro up there that a warrior chief from X arrived ahead of the Mèyikwéö and killed the last one, it was the injured man, he killed the last one then he put his foot on him, then he waited for the Mèyikwéö to arrive, you know. He said: 'Oh! It's not worth running [chasing] them, here's your meat.' And that's where they stopped [chasing them], if not the Mèaa would have bene exterminated, that's the tale that all the elders told. (Guynemer Karé – whose clan forms part of the Mèyikwéö group, extract from interview, March 1999)

So I will just say that if we left Koro, it was because there were gunshots, but I don't think we were going to leave if there weren't guns, because X was a hell of a warrior, he had already won plenty of wars in the valley, but if they left, it's because of that. (Gilbert Wéma Gwâê, extract from interview, August 1995)

Maybe you've heard the story of Koro, if people tell it to you. I mean, we're in it too, we also chase away the people of Koro. And why do we chase the people of Koro away? It's to do with pride.

—Pride?

Yes. When they trampled the yam fields, they dug up and cut the yams [of the people of the valley]. The Wéma, they have to acknowledge their history, and even the Gowé, they have to tell the story of Koro to the end. Why did the people of Koro leave Koro? (Maurice Mèèvâ, extract from interview, December 1991)

They went to the others' fields, then they did bad things, they dug up the yams … Then they left Koro, that family, they did bad things in Nérhëxakwéaa, so in the end, I think they left one of their people there in Nérhëxakwéaa in the battle … So that's where all the family comes from, and then they ran away. (Joseph Wéma Nirikani, extract from interview, August 1995)

The Koro war has also been the subject of a literary account, 'The symbolic hole', courtesy of New Caledonian writer Georges Baudoux, in which the Coula tribe and its chief Sioupé come into conflict with the tribe of Nessakoaya, who are protected by 'a strong stockade made of stakes', also described as a 'fortress' (Baudoux 1949, pp. 50, 54). This version, which focuses on the use of rifles and the anecdote of the hole in a coconut palm created by one of the shots fired, has a number of traits in common but also some that diverge from the versions I collected.[26] For example, 'Sioupé' is indeed the name of a chief of the Wéma family, which was involved in this war. But locating this chief in 'Coula' and 'Boréaré' is a retrospective illusion, since it was precisely after they left Koro and following a complicated journey that the members of this family settled in Coula and Boréaré, where they were based when Baudoux lived in Houaïlou.

---

26 Baudoux 1949, p. 62. The same anecdote appears in an article published in 1956 by the Protestant missionary Raymond Charlemagne (see Chapter 4).

Contrary to Baudoux, who attributes the rifle concerned purely to the sandalwood trade and implicitly dates the conflict to this period,[27] some of my interlocutors insisted that the Koro war took place after Europeans were firmly established in New Caledonia – and even that they were directly involved in the conflict.

> The Koro war is from the time when the Europeans were already here. (Joseph Wéma Nirikani, extract from interview, February 1999)

> This war, for example, that took place in Koro, which started from the *mwâwêbé*, that's a different story, that's already in the colonial period ... That story, you shouldn't believe it, there are not only Kanak stories. (Narcisse Kaviyöibanu, extract from interview, June 1995)

One version I recorded offered detailed information on the relationship between the use of the rifle, the French military presence, and the auxiliary commitment of the Néjâ chiefdom (see Chapter 1):

> The version that is told at home, is that in the history of Koro, this story of the rifle, it's a rifle that came from Canala, it's through the relations of the Néjâ chiefdom, and that rifle they brought it from Canala to the *mwâwêbé* [fort] ... And there the elders, when they saw the rifle, they said: 'But that's a slingshot!' They saw it as a slingshot. They argued back and forth and then they said: 'It's a slingshot, but who holds the most powerful slingshot medicine here in the valley, well it's the X.' So then they went to look for the X family, they went to find the elder who was called Y, and the elder came, he took the rifle, and then he hid down there by the water's edge ... Then the chief of Wéma came with six warriors, they came to the other side of the river, they always came to taunt us from there ... So that means that is how the X there, old Y, he came, he hid on the other side of the river, and then in the war house, Z and T had already prepared the warriors, because they had to strike the people of Koro, they had to be driven out. And in the forest, there in Nérhëxakwéaa, Néjâ was hidden with the [French] soldiers. And when the Wéma came down ... Y there, X there, he shot, the bullet entered his leg, and then he fell, that's how the old people tell it ... That, that was in the story of that war, because us, we were supported by the big chief and the [French] soldiers, you see. (Extract from interview, January 1999)

Clearly, there is no way of establishing the truth of the details of any particular version. Nevertheless, the assertion of the presence not only of a rifle, but also of French soldiers alongside a 'Néjâ', chief of the coastal region of Houaïlou,

---

27 See the quotation from Nissol Euritéin (Chapter 1).

in a war that took place in the middle Houaïlou valley, suggests that this Koro war can be identified with the repressive operation conducted in that same zone in December 1867, by French troops supported by auxiliaries from the coast and the valley (see Chapter 1). This hypothesis is confirmed by the fact that accounts of the operation published in the *Moniteur* in August 1868 mention the people of Mèaa on two occasions. First they report the existence of a conflict between the people of the Houaïlou valley and inhabitants of Mèaa: 'Since February 1867, Chief Polinda of Bouéoua [in the Houaïlou valley] has been defending himself against Catamouino, chief of Méa' (*Moniteur*, 2 August 1868). Subsequently, they describe the destruction of villages associated with Mèaa during the repressive operation: 'The governor had the villages of Bouin-oué, Nindié, Houinbé, Méa etc. burned. The Houaïlou from the interior took refuge with the Honrôés' (*Moniteur*, 30 August and 6 September 1868).

Close reading of the *Moniteur* for the year 1868 reveals a further striking detail: in the description of the conflicts that took place in Bourail during that year, in which a number of individuals originating from Houaïlou seem to have been directly involved, the name 'Diopahipi', a Gallicisation of the appellation Jööpwaipi, which we have already encountered, appears: 'The two other murderers [of the freed prisoner Bridon], Diopahipi and Mindivi, are yet to be handed over' (*Moniteur*, 30 August and 6 September 1868).

Here we are clearly in the realm of conjecture, and much of the information about the sociological context is lacking: in particular, we know nothing about the source of the attribution of the murder of Bridon to 'Diopahipi'; conversely, there is no evidence to confirm the hypothesis that the individual named Jööpwaipi mentioned by Bwêêyöuu Ërijiyi could have gone to the upper Bourail valleys (specifically to Kikwé) in 1867–68. It will be recalled, however, that the name Jööpwaipi, the meaning and origin of which I discussed above, could not be a traditional (or a very common) given name in the language of Houaïlou in 1868, since forenames are generally specific to a particular clan. It is also worth noting the compatibility of a set of hypotheses, derived from various sources, that posit that Jööpwaipi was born in the second half of the 1840s, that he was directly involved in the 'war between the Mèaa and the Mèyikwéö' through his quest for a war stone in 1867, and that he played a part in the conflicts in Bourail the following year. Thus, according to the sources I have drawn on – and in line with my observations on the 1856 operation – the local issues of the 'Koro war' became bound up with the colonial concerns in the military operations conducted in 1867 in the valleys of Houaïlou and Koro. Just as we were able to shift the perspective on 1856 by focusing both on the gunboat and on the shark, we can understand the Koro war in terms of both the rifles of the colonial troops and the war stones of the Kanak inhabitants of Houaïlou.

The same kind of analysis would also be valid, to some extent, in relation to the involvement of people from Houaïlou in 1878: the best-known fact (see Chapter 1) is the way in which the Houaïlou auxiliaries protected the Ni tribe in Bourail by diverting the French reprisal toward the coast. We can now hypothesise that this protection was also a way for some of the Houaïlou auxiliaries to repay the inhabitants of the upper Bourail valleys, who had welcomed and protected them 10 years earlier.

War stones and conversion: The case of Bwêêyöuu Ërijiyi

> 'Twas in the age of darkness, before the gospel's light,
> The pagan lived a life of cruel and joyless blight …
> With crude tool he carved in wood, in strange misshapen style
> The features of the false gods worshipped on his isle.
> Philippe Rey-Lescure,[28] La sève monte … p. 82

A 'lesson in things'

I propose to continue the analysis of the spiritual and ideological stakes of the war by focusing on the interactions between Kanaks and Europeans around war stones. I begin by reading a text[29] by Étienne Bergeret, the Protestant missionary who replaced Maurice Leenhardt in Houaïlou when the latter was on leave in France throughout 1909. In an article published three years later in the *Journal des missions évangéliques* (*Journal of Evangelical Missions*), he describes how the father of Élia Mârârhëë (one of Leenhardt's first pupils) gave him a war stone:

> One day I met him [Élia's father] on his way in: but this time he had come to visit not only Élia, but me also, and it was no ordinary visit: Élia's old father had come to bring me his gods, two black stones, one of them

---

28 Rey-Lescure was a Protestant missionary in New Caledonia, specifically in Houaïlou, from 1922 to 1933.
29 I am grateful to Christine Salomon for alerting me to this text.

about fifteen, the other about thirty centimetres long, which he drew from the bottom of his basket … The first is a yam stone, *pè-mëu* [here called pémao]. The smaller pebble, which is shaped like the blade of a knife, is the pajao. This one is by far the more precious. You can find other pémao, but this pajao! This is the stone that rendered the Manarè [Mârârhëë] family invincible; it is owing to this stone that the warriors of Néaoua were feared as much by the coastal tribes as the tribe from the mountain! When it desired war, it turned blood-red, and the Manarè warriors, when they saw this sign, knew that they had merely to rush on their enemies, and were sure of cutting them to pieces. Élia's old father has seen it cover itself with blood, he assures me! And two young men who were present at the interview told me: 'But yes, it's true, Misher, we haven't seen it, because we're too little, but the old people have seen it!' So why does 'pajao' no longer become blood-stained as it did before? 'Oh, it's because of God's word. Since God's word arrived, it doesn't do it any more; it must be ashamed, and even it ran away, and for a long time we didn't know what had happened to it, it was hiding.' (I heard at least one other story like this, where the fetish fled and hid.) 'And then the other day, when we were rummaging in a corner, we heard something moving about inside a big shell. We looked! It was "pajao"! We put it in the fire to kill it, so as to be sure it wouldn't escape again. Otherwise, it surely wouldn't have stayed in your house, Misso!' But now that it has been burned, there is nothing to fear: since 'pajao' has been on my table, that is for over a year, it has not moved. Élia's old father has been a member of the Church for several years: he believes in the word of God … But Élia's old father persists in believing in the mysterious power of his pémao [*pè-mëu*, yam stone] and his pajao [*panyaö*, war stone], an active power, at least in past times. And that is why we must rejoice at seeing him give it up deliberately, so that he is not tempted to sew a new patch on the old garment. (Bergeret 1912)

This passage offers a further example of the image I considered above of a propitiatory stone that covers itself in blood and summons to war. This text seems to me particularly interesting in that it very clearly indicates a link between the missionaries' interest in stones, particularly war stones – which Bergeret categorises as a 'fetish' (see the title of his two articles, published in 1909 and 1912) – and a theory of the deep-seated conversion of subjectivities underlying Protestant missionary activity ('not being tempted to sew a new patch on the old garment'). Before they became a category for description or ethnographic interpretation, war stones were first the object of both practical and theoretical analysis by the missionaries – as embodiments of a pagan religion that needed to be simultaneously understood and eradicated. I have described elsewhere the missionaries' practice of collecting and destroying war stones, mainly by burning them, in the Houaïlou region during the first half of the twentieth century.[30] These acts of destruction began at the instigation of the first evangelists from the Loyalty Islands, even before the first European missionaries arrived:

> This is how Protestant worship began in the Houaïlou region. We had girded up our paréos, and the women had put on their dresses. One day Sawa Pierre said to us: 'We are going to burn all the altars, our war stones, our yam stones, all the things that were sacred to us and that we made sacrifices to, because from now on we will worship God who is our life in heaven.' In Néjéwa we did it for two days, but the people of Néaria did not move – I was there – for they were very afraid when we brought our thunder stone out of the sea at Katevui and put it on the fire. I was about ten years old and I was not afraid. (Nérhon 1969, pp. 41)

Notwithstanding the differences in their implementation of this policy (more spectacular among the Catholics, while the Protestants relied more on individual decision), these two Christian churches shared a focus on objects, of wood and stone, as metonyms of the old religion that had to be destroyed. To quote Victor Fraysse, the Catholic missionary in Bourail who was active at Karaxërë, in the upper Houaïlou valley, in the early 20th century, it can thus be said that the missionaries' practice was first and foremost a 'lesson in things' – as here in Fraysse's description of the sacking of a place of invocation of the ancestors (*ka-mwârö*):

> Then came a delegation of pagans from the neighbourhood, asking me to go and deliver them from their *lotous* [gods, fetishes, from the Wallisian *lotu* – religion, worship, prayer]. I willingly acceded to this request, accompanied by people from Karagreou [Karaxërë]. When we arrived at the designated place, at first I could not see much. Following closer examination, I entered a very dense thicket, and I saw a quantity of posts carved into strange shapes, long poles with bark pouches at the end, tightly tied on with lianas. They even showed me the place where victims were burned in honour of these singular deities. It was high time that these sacrilegious acts of worship were wrested from the devil. Although short, the ceremony was as solemn as possible. I put on my surplice and stole, and blessed the place according to the prescriptions of the ritual. Then I called the pagans, who until then had remained behind, in the grip of a vestige of superstitious fear. They leaped on their old wooden gods, and destroyed them with vigorous axe blows. Within a few minutes they were all in pieces, and were then consigned to the flames. It goes without saying

---

30 Naepels 1998, p. 62.

that they put up not the slightest resistance. This good lesson in things spared me the trouble of exposing the false nature and powerlessness of such deities through long disquisitions. (Fraysse 1905, p. 288–89)

Leenhardt and war stones

The missionaries' interest in objects was not only practical but also theoretical. Hence, Maurice Leenhardt concluded the 'Questionnaire' he addressed to his Kanak pupils in 1918, the most significant outcome of which are the notebooks of Bwêêyöuu Ërijiyi (in which the 'Jopaipi' text appears), with the following words: 'Thus it is important for us to understand the darkness and our work in this area, and that will give us wisdom in the way we speak the word of God' (Leenhardt 1977, p. 91). In other words, his interest in the internal organisation of the clans (question 1), the founding ancestors of the country (question 2), the qualities of yams (question 3), the history of the clans (question 4), war stones (question 5) and healing powers and communication with the ancestors (question 6) was also rooted in a theory of conversion: it was important to understand in order first to help people to change, then in order to better 'speak the word of God', and finally to ensure that the old man, the pagan, the one who invoked his ancestors and his gods in the steam from a cooking pot, through contact with a propitiatory stone, or using his medicinal herbs, had really died within the convert.

It seems to me that it is precisely this pragmatic agenda of conversion that forms the context for the answers Ërijiyi gave Leenhardt.[31] His answer to the fifth question, on war stones, thus ends with a long paragraph headed 'Here are the clans that have a war stone', and consisting of a list of the names of the clans and individuals concerned.[32] It is difficult to consider these pages as anything other than a denunciation – by the first Kanak pastor of Houaïlou, and addressed to the missionary who trained and converted him – of those who possessed war stones, who included the family of Ëribee[33] mâ Boè, precisely the family that is named at the end of the 'Jopaipi' text: 'There is also [a war stone] in another part of the Mèyikwéö clan, the grandfather is called Boé, and his son Bee.'

---

31 For further evidene in support of this argument, see Naepels 2007a, pp. 79–87.
32 Aramiou and Euritéin 2003, pp. 19–20.
33 This name does not appear in the civil register today, but a number of my interlocutors confirmed that this lineage still exists, under another family name.

Before appearing as objects of scientific study in the text and illustration plates of Leenhardt's *Notes d'ethnologie néo-calédonienne* (*Notes on New Caledonian Ethnography*),[34] war stones (and other propitiatory stones) first featured in the missionary pedagogic text *La Grande Terre. Mission de Nouvelle-Calédonie* (*Grande Terre. New Caledonia Mission*), from its very first edition in 1909.[35] And Leenhardt's first contacts with the school of anthropology in Paris, also in 1909, consisted of the presentation of various stones at the Anthropological Society.[36]

'Readily giving up his treasure'

Following Raymond Leenhardt, James Clifford and Jean Guiart,[37] I have emphasised the importance of Bwêêyöuu Ërijiyi in the construction of Maurice Leenhardt's knowledge,[38] particularly through his notebooks. Leenhardt indeed acknowledged the enormity of this debt: 'Everything I have been able to clarify in the obscurity of native questions, I owe to Boesoou', he wrote in the second edition of the pamphlet popularising the mission, entitled *La Grande Terre: Mission de Nouvelle-Calédonie* (Leenhardt 1922a, p. 111). Clifford rightly points out that 'such acknowledgements are all too rare in the annals of ethnography' (Clifford 1982, p. 142). I have quoted elsewhere the more ambivalent assessments of Ërijiyi that Leenhardt gives in his private correspondence.[39] And indeed, the enthusiasm of Leenhardt's published appraisals of Ërijiyi tends to decline over time. He still renders homage to Ërijiyi in the preface to *Notes d'ethnologie néo-calédonienne*: 'Old Boesou Ërijisi, formerly engaged in carving masks and organising pilou ritual dances ... rewarded us for teaching him to write by slowly setting down, lying on his mat, the best of the legends reproduced below, and the pilou speeches he used to teach to the Nindia chiefs (Neja clan)' (Leenhardt 1930, p. viii). This description, however, obscures the missionary context in which Ërijiyi learned to write and his status as convert (and further, as pastor), as he is here presented

---

34 Notably plates 8 (4. Fingerstall and pierced stone into which the spear is thrust before combat), 18 (1. Fossil crab propitious for crab fishing; 2. Fertility stone buried with the crops; 3. Taro stone; 4. Rain stone; 5. Yam stone) and 19 (1. Virility stone – phallus touched by spears before combat; 2. Virility stone; 3. Aphrodisiac stone).
35 Leenhardt 1909b.
36 Leenhardt 1909a.
37 R. Leenhardt 1976; Clifford 1982; Guiart 2003.
38 Naepels 2007a and 2007b. It is interesting to compare Leenhardt's interactions with Ërijiyi with those between Franz Boas and George Hunt, in terms of both the compilation of notebooks and the collection of objects. See Berman 1996; Jacknis 1991 and 1996.
39 Naepels 2007b, pp. 100–02.

as a traditional scholar.[40] In 1932, he still appears several times in the table of contents of the *Documents néo-calédoniens* (*New Caledonian Documents*), as the writer of legends and ceremonial speeches (though his rich sociological analysis, on which Leenhardt nevertheless draws extensively, does not appear in this volume), before practically disappearing from *Gens de la Grande Terre* (*The People of Grande Terre*) in 1937 and *Do kamo* in 1947. In a movement that Clifford (1983) has analysed in other contexts, the construction of Leenhardt's discursive authority as an ethnographer, aimed at winning him professional legitimacy, involves the inverse relegation of Kanak pupil pastor Ërijiyi to the role of informant, then to the anonymous embodiment of a generic category ('the Kanak', 'the Melanesian', or even 'the Austro-Melanesian').[41]

Ërijiyi's commitment to Leenhardt was not to the exclusion of other close relationships with Europeans; for example, when Leenhardt was on leave in 1909, Ërijiyi presented pastor Bergeret with the significant gift of his family's most precious shell currency, a gesture that points to a similar pattern of consolidating conversion through the abandonment of objects linked to ancestrality:

> The day before he left [for Kùa where he was going to take up his first post as pastor], he came to find me, and gave me a package wrapped in a very dirty rag, bound with a sort of netted strap. Bosoon [Bwêêyöuu] unwraps it, and very carefully spreads out the contents before my eyes. There are two flattened spindles, each with a very slender point, and a small piece of wood carved into the form of a pirogue, and stained with something that looks very like blood. 'Look,' Bosoon says to me, 'it's the god of my family, and also that of Mindia, the paramount chief, and also that of Sétei (one of our Do Néva boys). Now that we have "the Word" we no longer need this and I thought to give it to you, because you brought us a word of God.' … The spindles are made from coconut fibre and the hairs of the fruit bat, the enormous creature that roams the skies of Caledonia in the evening. The point is made up of tiny shells or carved fragments of mother of pearl, strung end to end. These are Kanak currency, the money with which the pagans, and even still some people who call themselves Christians, are paid for their daughters when they give them in marriage … But what I have before my eyes are not just money: Bosoon told me that this little package contained the most precious thing his family owns.

---

40 The missionary context does, however, feature marginally in the legend of illustration plate 36, where Ëriyji is singled out: 'First pupils and best instructors. Do Néva, Houaïlou, 1902. On the left, Boesou Erijisi.'
41 Leenhardt 1979.

> If they were forced to flee, this is what they would take before all the rest. As long as the family was able to keep it, it held a guarantee of prosperity and victory. (Bergeret 1909, p. 410)

More strikingly still, Ërijiyi was – without any missionary context – one of the principal guides in the Houaïlou region of Marius Archambault, the Houaïlou postmaster who became the first expert in New Caledonian petroglyphs – stones engraved with geometric motifs.[42] Thus, in an article also published in 1909, Archambault recounts how the 'devoted Boasaou' took him to Gondé, where there were several petroglyphs, naming some with reference to his guide – the '*dicona* [deacon]' group and the 'Boasaou stone' – and concludes, 'Boasaou is almost as passionate about archaeology as we are':

> This devoted guide, Boasaou, raised on old tales and readily giving up his treasure, hastened to tell me what he knew about the 'stone for measuring men'. He also guided me into the central mountains, to a stone with rectilinear incisions, half submerged in a great pool of water, 'where men in olden times hacked into the stone with axes because they had plotted to seize the moon that shone in the water, and wanted to open up a passage to the star through the very stone.' In the same region, he showed me a tall conical rock, with a cave at the base, and explained to me that: 'the men of old wanted to cut down this stone to make a big post for a hut.' Along the way he gave me many others, marked with the same touch of humour. (Archambault 1909, pp. 151, 152)

Comparison of these testimonies from Leenhardt, Bergeret and Archambault confirms the scale of Ërijiyi's involvement with Europeans, with whom he systematically appears 'readily giving up his treasure'.

An alliance (second half of the 19th century)

I should like to supplement what can be known about Bwêêyöuu Ërijiyi on the basis of interviews I conducted, with the combined intention of better understanding the 'Jopaipi' text and returning to the history of the Néjâ chiefdom (see Chapter 1). Both interviewees, who independently and two years apart drew up the genealogy of two members of the Kaviyöibanu family, assert that Bwêêyöuu Ërijiyi was indeed a member of the Kaviyöibanu family, adopted by the Ërijiyi family:

— Did your grandfather have brothers and sisters too?

---

42 Archambault 1901 and 1902; Luquet 1926.

He has another brother that I know of, he is adopted by Ërijiyi there …
— Who is that?
Bwêêyöuu, the one who used to be Mr Leenhardt's pastor. (Wainô Kaviyöibanu, extract from interview, September 1993)

I had already been given this information, with an explanation, by another member of the same family:

Bwêêyöuu, you know, he gave Leenhardt stories in the books … Paramount chief Mèèjâ [Néjâ], his mother was a woman of the great mountain Yöuma … so the Néwau went to settle in the Néjâ chiefdom … Thinking about power in war, they saw our house here, it was certainly a powerful clan at the time and to get my family involved, they sent back this woman, Bwèda … telling her: 'You can't come back to the chiefdom, you can only come back on one condition, if the Kaviyöibanu family send you, then you can settle in the paramount chiefdom.' So the woman came back, came here, to our house, here in Dâô, so she told people from here the answer they gave over there … So there were customary exchanges between my family and the people of Néjâ.[43] The exchange took place on the Kaviyöibanu path, but the person who made the woman leave, the one who holds the breath of the children this woman bears, is the Ërijiyi household … Once the child of this marriage – so he's the paramount chief Mèèjâ Néjâ – became chief … he asked that among the Kaviyöibanu, they talk and they send a Kaviyöibanu to the Ërijiyi clan, so that he has power to speak. And that's how Kaviyöibanu Bwêêyöuu became Kaviyöibanu Bwêêyöuu Ërijiyi. (Narcisse Kaviyöibanu, extract from interview, June 1991)

The process described thus refers to a threefold movement, intended to meet the demands of the various families involved in this alliance: the ceremonies enabling the marriage of the parents of paramount chief Mèèjâ Néjâ would take place not among the Néwau (the bride's clan), but among the Kaviyöibanu; in this place it would then be the Ërijiyi, not the Kaviyöibanu, who made the key exchanges; and, subsequently, a Kaviyöibanu – Bwêêyöuu to be precise – was adopted into the Ërijiyi family. This is the link that enables us to understand Leenhardt's report that Ërijiyi 'taught the chiefs' of the 'Néjâ clan' 'pilou dance speeches' (ceremonial speeches) (Leenhardt 1930, p. viii). Moreover, such exchanges are in no way exceptional, even now: marriage is first and foremost the occasion for creating, expressing or reinforcing political bonds among a number of families, and it is thus not unusual for the 'maternal uncles' of future children to be selected, at the time of the marriage ceremony,

---

43 To seal the marriage of Bwèda Néwau in the Néjâ chiefdom.

from within a clan that is not that of the bride, but which has a special relationship with this clan (see Chapter 6). This exchange is usually the means of repaying or creating a debt. Adoptions derive in part from the same practice.

It should be noted that in the interview I conducted in September 1995 with Paul Ërijiyi, who was then the oldest representative of this family, he did not mention this adoption. If we assume, however, that this information is correct, it throws new light on the 'Jopaipi' text: it allows us to understand not only how Bwêêyöuu Ërijiyi knows this story, which as we have seen concerns the ancestors of the Kaviyöibanu clan (Rhabwê and Jööpwaipi), but also how he knows precisely the healing plants (*deewi*) that are supposed to have been revealed when the stone appeared ('Bwêêyöuu Ërijiyi knows this medicine'). This revelation made to Leenhardt, who perhaps did not grasp its significance, once again shows Ërijiyi 'readily giving up his treasure'. His investment in a subjectivity profoundly marked by conversion, the abandonment of ancient practices and the revealing of private knowledge are confirmed by the following interview extract, which shows Ërijiyi playing an active role in the missionary destruction of propitiatory stones:

> Me, I know that grandfather said that I had a great-grandfather, a grandfather's father, old Bwêêyöuu Ërijiyi, who was adopted Ërijiyi, him with the Protestant religion, grandfather said he took the liberty of burning other people's stones, taking other people's medicines. (Narcisse Kaviyöibanu, extract from interview, February 1999)

The Néajië war (second half of the 18th century)

The alliance discussed above between the Néjâ family and the clans of the Houaïlou valley (Ërijiyi and Kaviyöibanu of the Mèyikwéö tribe in Dâô and Nérhëxakwéaa, and Néwau in Karaxërë) itself refers back to an earlier history:

> Paramount chief Mèejâ, his mother, she's an Ërijiyi woman, as I was saying, one of our women, of the Mèyikwéö[44] ... [The Néjâ] left Nindiah there, well, the stone up there[45] because there was an incident ... and in order to reconcile them, an Ërijiyi girl was given, and the Néjâ paramount chief, Néjâ Mèejâ, was born ... Piecing together the movements [of the Néjâ

---

44 The tribe that includes the Ërijiyi and the Kaviyöibanu.
45 *Néjâ*, a rocky limestone outcrop that overhangs the lower Houaïlou valley and gives its name to the Néjâ family (one branch of which is recorded today in the civil register under the name 'Nédia'), as well as to the village of 'Nindiah' and the district of 'Nindien'.

clan] … they left and then they stayed down there in Néwèö. Afterwards when the Whites came … he found us, his uncles, the Mèyikwéö, the Ërijiyi, he came to find the whole Mèyikwéö clan, to say that we should leave Dâô and go to Nérhëxakwéaa. (Wainô Kaviyöibanu, extract from interview, September 1993)

These highly euphemistic references to an 'incident' refer to an old war, the Néajië or Nindiah war. In the accounts I have been given, the protagonists in this war were, among others, the two Kakus (the ancestors of the Néjâ and the Népörö, see Figures 2 and 3) in conflict with Ayèrhari (ancestor of the Néwau) and Gwâmee (ancestor of the Mèyikwéö). This war (see Chapter 1) is widely held to be at the root of the displacement of these clans, who formerly lived in the lower Houaïlou valley, on the coast and in the middle and upper Houaïlou valley respectively.

On the basis of the figures in Chapter 1 and my genealogical research, I put forward below a synoptic, albeit hypothetical, table bringing together a set of data that are not all equally reliable, but that indicate the relative positioning of actors and sequences of events (see Table 1).

Table 1. Chronological and genealogical relationships between some of the individuals referred to in this text

Generation	Néjâ clan	Népörö clan	Ayèrhari and Néwau clan	Mèyikwéö and Kaviyöibanu clan	Date of birth	Event during adulthood
+5	Kaku	Kaku	Ayèrhari	Gwâmee	1760?	Late 18th century: Néajië war
+4	Nemwanô	Parö		Rhabwê	1785?	
+3	Wâga	Béra			1810?	1856: repression in coastal region
+2	Ai	Kavo	Bwêda	Jööpwaipi	1835?	1867: Koro war
+1	Mêêjâ	Jénô		Bwêêyöuu	1856 (Mêêjâ) 1866 (Bwêêyöuu)	1918: writing down of 'Jopaipi'
0	Apupia	Mwâdéwê			c. 1890–1900	

Source: Author's research.

WAR AND OTHER MEANS

1899–1900: The departure from Dâô

Under governor Paul Feillet, Mèèjâ Néjâ, paramount chief of Houaïlou, made a decisive contribution to the policy of disentitlement of reservations, in other words the Kanaks' forced departure from lands that had previously been recognised as belonging to them, a policy that Feillet instigated for the purpose of obtaining new land for colonisation. While Mèèjâ's attitude toward colonisation was complex and ambivalent (see Chapter 3), his involvement in the process of expropriation of land was a way of reinforcing his control over the valley chiefdoms, with whom his family had long been in conflict (at least since the Néajië war in the late 18th century). Thus the request he made, or order he gave, to the Dâô families to leave the place where they lived in order to make it available for colonial settlement has been remembered and passed down in the families concerned, in relation to the powers embodied by war stones:

> And once we'd accepted religion, paramount chief Mèèjâ … asked us, well, our ancestors, to give the war stone, to give him the war stone that was the source of our strength. The ancestors said no, it was not possible, because that was our strength, and then if he was paramount chief now, that was because his power was also based on that power [as nephew of the valley families, following the matrimonial alliance discussed above]. Him, this was his response: 'If you cannot give your war stone, I ask you to leave this place for 30 years because you have accepted religion, and religion asks that we burn these stones. But if you say that you cannot do that, now you do as I ask, you leave this place for 30 years, until the power of this medicine fades away, and after 30 years, you can come back to your land.' That's how our ancestors, they left Dâô and went to the Nérhëxakwéaa area. (Extract from interview, September 1993)

> I think I told you how the last grandfather left Dâô, with the X there, they didn't want to leave, paramount chief Mèèjâ came in person with his soldiers, he came to Dâô to ask one of grandfather's brothers if he could leave the place. Well, he came with his white horse, and then … he came with his soldiers, he was accompanied by [French] soldiers. He dismounted from his white horse, he crossed the river, and the grandfather climbed a banyan, because he had the war stone, he climbed the banyan, he took the war stone, he put it between his legs, and then from the top of the banyan … he wept as he spoke, you know. But the other [paramount chief Mèèjâ Néjâ] had money in his hand,[46] he came

---

46 Shell currency signifies the contractual relations of alliance formed through exchange ceremonies (see Chapter 6).

with Kanak money, to ask the old man to leave. That's when the old man, when he saw he had the money … chief Mèèjâ was his *nyaa*, like his nephew, and at that time, that was something big, it was something that was respected, there were alliances. So him, he was torn between all that and the desire to kill. He began to weep in the banyan, and then he reproached paramount chief Mèèjâ, he said: 'Today you're coming to force me off my land, but if you're here, all the same it's thanks to me.' He wept as he said that. Well, in the end he gave in, that means that chief Mèèjâ did after all succeed in telling him to give up the land, you know. (Extract from interview, September 1995)

Analysing the 'Jopaipi' text with a focus on the author of the account, Bwêêyöuu Ërijiyi, has enabled me to understand the reasons he had for writing it, within the framework of his privileged relationship with Leenhardt. Ërijiyi's position in his lineage also allows us a deeper understanding of the relations between certain families of the Houaïlou valley (within the Mèyikwéö group) and the Néjâ chiefdom on the coast, and to articulate the Koro war (which is also the repressive operation of 1867) with the pre-colonial Néajië (or Nindiah) war and the land seizures of the late 19th century.

The collectors

The Europeans were interested in Kanak warfare from more than just the missionary point of view, as demonstrated by the size of museum collections of objects related to war (weapons and war stones). This curiosity was very broadly based on ethnic stereotypes (in particular the reputed Melanesian ferocity).[47] But, a more detailed history of collecting in Houaïlou helps to understand the mechanisms that brought artefacts to European collections. In his article 'Objets kanak dans les collections européennes' (Kanak objects in European collections), Roger Boulay provides the essential historical background to the collection of Kanak objects.[48] I should like to focus more specifically on the Houaïlou region in an attempt to grasp how the actors involved experienced the donation of these objects.

---

47 Thomas 1989a; Boulay 2000; Douglas and Ballard 2008.
48 Boulay 1990.

First collections: The military, administrators and naturalists

The collections of Kanak objects that are held in a number of European museums were built up between 1875 and 1905, following the model of collections from other regions.[49] The military, administrators and naturalists thus contributed to the export of objects from Houaïlou.

If the sandalwood traders exchanged weapons in Houaïlou (see Chapter 1), there is no trace of this in the collections of Kanak art. During the first years of colonisation, however, the French military did take an interest in objects of war. For example, as early as 1860, army surgeon Bougarel wrote an article on 'New Caledonian weapons', most of which was devoted to a pragmatic evaluation of their efficacy: 'What is to be feared above all when one is at war with the New Caledonians is ambush, which is an especial danger to soldiers who have been imprudently left alone on watch' (Bougarel 1860, p. 286). Still, this analysis was accompanied by collecting. We may doubt Maximilien-Albert Legrand's claim in 1893, in *Au pays des Canaques* (*In the Land of the Kanaks*) that, because weapons had been forbidden since 1859, it was difficult to procure any. While bearing arms was heavily restricted in Nouméa, the very slow progress of military and administrative takeover of rural areas meant that the situation there was very different – particularly given that the French military came into contact with Kanak weapons during each repressive operation. This is retrospectively confirmed by the presence of pieces from Houaïlou derived from military collections, like the Venge collection donated to Grenoble Museum in that same year, 1893.[50]

The early naturalists, men such as Xavier Montrouzier, a Catholic missionary in the far north of Grande Terre, and Benjamin Balansa,[51] the French Natural History Museum's envoy in New Caledonia from 1868 to 1872,[52] compiled important plant collections at the same time as establishing the first foundations of naturalist knowledge of the territory. They seem to have been less interested in collecting artefacts. Nevertheless, some pieces brought back by Balansa were deposited in the

---

49 Boulay 1990; Cole 1995; Schildkrout and Kaim 1998; Thomas 1989b.
50 Lavondès 1990.
51 See Chevalier 1942; Astre 1947.
52 See Balansa 1869, 1872–73 and 1873.

Toulouse Museum.[53] We know that Balansa's explorations took him to the Houaïlou region,[54] but not whether the objects donated to Toulouse Museum come from there.

Finally, the first era of collecting, in the latter half of the 19th century, ends with the great universal expositions, which included sections devoted to the colonies;[55] hence objects from New Caledonia were among the displays at the Universal Exposition in Paris in 1878. The objects exhibited in Group IV, 'Fabrics, clothing and accessories', Class XI, 'Weapons' included 'Collections of spears, clubs, slingshots, slingshot stones and bags for carrying stones, stone-shields, wooden and shell knives, bows, arrows, angled stone axes, stone chief's axe' (*Exposition ...* 1878, p. 318): weapons were almost the only ethnographic objects exhibited. But there is nothing to indicate that any of these pieces came from Houaïlou. However, at the 1889 Universal Exposition in Paris, Jules Moriceau showed a large number of Kanak objects, without specifying their places of origin. Moriceau was practically the only provider of 'ethnographic' objects from New Caledonia at this exhibition. It is known that some of these pieces came from the Houaïlou region, of which Moriceau served as administrator before becoming head of the Native Affairs Department a few years later. Thus, 'Chief Cambo's staff' was exhibited (*Exposition ...* 1889, ref. 1772; this is Kavo Népörö, whose career as a colonial chief I outlined in Chapter 1). Moriceau's collection is known to be the source of most of the Kanak objects held in the Berlin Museum, to which he sold his pieces in 1895.

Leenhardt and Rey-Lescure: Missionary collectors

I discussed above the conditions under which missionaries came to make collections of objects. It should, however, be added that alongside the pieces that were destroyed, some were converted into ethnographic specimens. For example, Maurice Leenhardt sold 32 items to the Neuchâtel ethnographic museum during his home leave in 1909–10.[56] These included a Mèyikwéö traditional money piece that was shown as part of the 1990 international touring exhibition of Kanak art *Of Jade and*

---

53 Laroche 1953.
54 Moncelon 1887.
55 Jacquemin 1990.
56 Leenhardt 1910.

Mother-of-Pearl.[57] A number of other pieces collected by Leenhardt later entered the collection of the Musée de l'Homme (Museum of Mankind) in Paris. Leenhardt's position, as one of the pioneers of scientific collecting and mission work, is very similar to that of the Neuchâtel missionary Henri Junod, whose cross-disciplinary practices have been the subject of admirable analysis by Patrick Harries.[58] Similarly, Philippe Rey-Lescure used his time as a missionary in Houaïlou as an opportunity to take on the role of collector for the Trocadéro Museum. It is likely that this was at the behest of Leenhardt, who was then publishing his great monographs through the French Institute of Ethnography.

It is thus that the collections in the Quai Branly Museum in Paris come to include, among the Kanak objects identified as coming from the Houaïlou region, 12 'magic stones' donated by Rey-Lescure, and four by Leenhardt.

'A veritable open-air ethnographic museum'

As far as the Houaïlou region is concerned, the most significant period of collecting was certainly that ensuing from the succession of competing scientific expeditions undertaken just before the First World War. Once again, this period highlights the enmeshing of local stakes with global flows in a social landscape where the Kanaks' scope for action had altered substantially since the French takeover. In the expeditions led by the French explorer Maurice Piroutet, the Swiss researchers Fritz Sarasin and Jean Roux, and the British explorers Paul D. Montague and Robert Compton, the figure of the naturalist still predominated over that of the ethnographer, but with marked theoretical modulations. I shall attempt to trace these, focusing on what they tell us about Kanak people's relationship to their weapons and their propitiatory stones in the early 20th century.

Piroutet still belonged to the class of explorers who collected ethnographic objects as a supplement to his main collection. A geologist, he spent time in New Caledonia in 1901, 1905 and 1909–10, periods that formed the basis for the *Étude stratigraphique sur la Nouvelle-Calédonie* (*Stratigraphic Study of New Caledonia*), which constituted his thesis.[59] He also brought back a collection of objects that were deposited in the museum in Saint-Germain-en-Laye, and later entrusted to the Musée des Arts africains et

---

57 Boulay (ed.) 1990, pp. 66–67 and 83.
58 Harries 2000 and 2007.
59 Piroutet 1917; see also Piroutet 1903.

océaniens (Museum of African and Oceanian Arts) in Paris.[60] Many of the objects he brought back originate from the 'Nindiah' or Néajië tribe, in the middle Houaïlou valley.

Sarasin and Montague were the first professional ethnographers the Kanaks encountered. Both followed the models of exploration and cataloguing then dominant in the nascent discipline of European anthropology: Sarasin was well acquainted with Felix Speiser and his mission in Vanuatu, and followed the model of German geography;[61] Montague was a student of Alfred C. Haddon in Cambridge and, with Compton, undertook natural history research in New Caledonia along the lines of the Torres Straits expedition that Haddon coordinated during the last years of the 19th century. Both Sarasin and Montague stayed in the Houaïlou region, from where they brought back substantial collections of objects; Montague, moreover, wrote the first ethnographic monograph on the Houaïlou region, which was never published.[62] Sarasin spent some days in Houaïlou in early February 1912:

> Last Saturday had visit from two Swiss scientists who are travelling all over Caledonia and Loyalty, Dr Sarazin [sic] (conservator Basle museum) and Dr Roux (Geneva). They are part of the expedition led by Speiser who is in the Hebrides. They only spent one morning in Houaïlou, I cannot understand why, but I led them straight to the finest sculptures, and they took them away. (Leenhardt, Lettre à ses parents, 17 February 1912)

> The morning after our arrival, Mr Leenhardt kindly offered to accompany us in our search for ethnographic objects, particularly traditional sculptures … In one place on the left bank of the river, our arrival gave rise to a very curious scene: the natives, forewarned of our visit, had already gathered in the village square, where they had assembled a quantity of old objects they wished to sell. It was a veritable open-air ethnographic museum. Seven roof spires were planted in the ground one beside the other, we were spoiled for choice! Close by lay spears, bows, arrows, slingshots and wooden awls used to stitch together straw for the roofs; further on there were hammers used to make balassor [beaten bark cloth], belts of fibre, formerly worn by the women, combs, dishes made from plaited reeds (Fig. 118), earthenware cooking pots, sacred stones of all kinds and many other objects. There were so many objects it was difficult to examine them. (Sarasin 1913, pp. 200–01)

---

60 See Boulay 1986–87.
61 See Kaufmann 1990.
62 Montague n.d. [c. 1914–15].

Propitiatory stones were especially prized among the objects collected:

> These objects include one particularly rare piece: this is a magic stone, in the form of a double-headed dagger, very carefully polished (Fig. 106), which was used, according to the information we were given, to ensure progeny; with this intention, the man and the woman would each touch one end of the talisman, while invoking the spirits of the ancestors. We were also brought a number of other magic stones; they were perforated, either naturally (Fig. 107a) or artificially (Fig. 107b); the point of the spear was inserted into their hole before it was used in war or for fishing, in order to endow it with power; the hardness of the stone was no doubt thought to strengthen and toughen the wooden lance. (Sarasin 1913, pp. 194–95)

Sarasin puts forward an explanation for the changed status of the Kanak sculptures and stones: it was the fact that they had become socially disconnected that made it possible for them to enter the ethnographic museum.

> They were all the more keen to sell the old objects and tools because these vestiges of an era now past no longer held any value for the current generation. (Sarasin 1913, p. 194)

Before we accept this hypothesis, three important contextual observations need to be added: the public health policy implemented by the Native Affairs Department required that huts be abandoned and rectangular houses constructed, rendering the majority of wooden sculptures, which were also architectural elements (roof spires, doorframes, carved lintels and shelves for huts) useless; then, as we have seen, the Catholic and Protestant missionaries condemned the use of war stones and themselves collected them; finally, access to monetary income was a serious concern in light of the head tax.[63]

> I know that grandfather also told me about for example lintels, roof spires, things like that. They were very popular with the colonists … People sold them, there were even thieves in the tribe, you know. People would come then if the worst came to the worst they would demand your lintel to sell or your roof spire to sell, because it's more to make a bit of ready cash. (Narcisse Kaviyöibanu, extract from interview, February 1999)

---

63 A flat-rate tax payable annually by all Kanaks from 1894.

2. OBJECTS OF WAR

Sarasin used this expedition as the basis for a popular account of his travels,[64] and particularly for a monumental *Anthropologie*, most of which is devoted to physical anthropology, but two volumes of which are genuinely ethnographic: the analysis section draws on close reading of the entire bibliography then in existence to describe Kanak social practices.[65] The production of this scientific knowledge had no basis in Sarasin's field trip.[66] His *Atlas ethnographique* (*Ethographic Atlas*), by contrast, constitutes an extraordinary assemblage of 73 large plates illustrating ethnographic booty.[67] These include, for example, Table 51, which presents a collection of traditional money pieces from Houaïlou.

Montague and Compton conducted zoological and botanical research two years after Roux and Sarasin's visit: 'Mr P.D. Montague and I spent the whole of 1914 in making zoological and botanical collections and investigations in this most interesting French colony' (Compton 1917, p. 81). Both came from Cambridge and followed the model of the Torres Straits expedition, which represented a major innovation in ethnographic field studies, a precursor to those of Bronislaw Malinowski.[68] Montague devoted one part of his time to an ethnographic survey of the Houaïlou valley: 'Mr Montague spent some time in the tribe of Gondé at the head of the Wailu valley … His discoveries as to religion, magic, music, and ceremonial are of great interest, but I must not forestall his account of them' (Compton 1917, p. 97). We may assume that he followed the methodology set out by William H.R. Rivers, who had participated in the Torres Straits expedition and was tasked with writing a 'general account of method' for the fourth edition of *Notes and Queries on Anthropology*.[69] We do know that Montague made sound recordings on wax cylinders, as Haddon had in 1898:[70] the British Library holds the cylinders that Montague recorded on 30 November 1914 among the Gondé tribe (song, flute, genealogical recitation). Montague's presence certainly simultaneously, or by turns, irritated and stimulated Leenhardt, who saw

---

64   Sarasin 1913.
65   See, for example, the sections on war ('Krieg', p. 205–11) and cannibalism ('Kannibalismus', pp. 211–18) in Sarasin and Roux 1929.
66   Unlike his physical anthropology, which was largely based on measurements he himself made.
67   Sarasin 1929.
68   Herle and Rouse 1998; O'Hanlon and Welsch 2000.
69   Rivers 1912.
70   See Stocking 1995, p. 111.

in his work everything that an ethnographic investigation could produce. The evolution of his attitude can be detected in two letters, written at the beginning and end of Montague's stay:

> Mauss, one of Durkheim's followers, has just published a great article championing French ethnography, and he is right. But one of his great arguments is how little we know about Caledonia after sixty years of occupation. And this is perhaps, he says, the key to ... all that Durkheim and his school envisaged. He devotes two pages to criticism of Caledonia, and also concludes his essay by stating that it shall not be said that the French learned nothing from Caledonia, etc ... A newspaper announces that the British Association, a formidable research machine, is coming here. If they come, should I tell them what I know, and what I am now trying to record, when Laffay leaves me time? I am training Kanaks to conduct this kind of enquiry – little that is reliable will come from others. Should I give their names so that they can be called on? ...
>
> Montague, the young English naturalist who stayed here for a few days ... is going to put his papers in order and will then enlist for the war. He has made a detailed ethnographic study of Houaïlou, and that is why I should like to follow him. (Leenhardt, Lettre à ses parents, 7 and 20 December 1914).

In fact Montague's manuscript *Ethnological Notes from the Houaïlou Valley, New Caledonia* was never published, owing to the death of its author at the end of the First World War.[71] Montague devoted his sixth and final chapter to 'Religion and Magic of the Natives of the Houaïlou Valley', which deals principally with stones and includes a description of their origin in the period of mourning that matches the accounts cited at the beginning of this chapter:

> When a body, wrapped in white awa, was taken to the forest to be placed among the Banyan-trees, three or four men went out in the evening and watched by the corpse. No man would have dared to go by himself, so they always went in company. In the dead of the night the Bao [ancestral spirit] would appear, as lizards, birds, rats and strange forms which had no counterpart in nature. The object was to seize and capture some of these elusive spirits – a matter of some difficulty as they would change form suddenly, becoming like men of great strength. If, however, they could be once overpowered, they were carried to the river-margin and plunged into the water, whereupon they changed immediately to stones. Nobody could foresee to what kind of stone the spirit would turn, but its

---

71 A short passage on ceremonies was published in Leenhardt, Sarasin and Montague 1998.

virtue could be decided at once by its form. It might be good for yams, catching eels, making rain or have a phallic significance. (Montague n.d. [1914–15], p. 33)

The objects Montague donated to the Cambridge Museum in 1917 include two slingshots, a bag for slingshot stones, 11 slingshot stones, 18 spears, three spear-throwing cords, three clubs, and also an invisibility stone, a phallic stone, two seduction stones, two thunder stones, four rain stones, nine taro stones, eight yam stones, one swamphen stone, one mule stone and six eel stones. In his journal, Leenhardt notes the complex processes of alienation of objects (a process bound up with conversion) that led them to enter the museum's collection via Montague:

> M's child died here of indigestion after I cured him of dysentery and then enteritis, using hordenine. Two other children were cured at the same time, but M., a man of little faith, poured milk into his child as soon as he thought he was out of danger. He sent to consult the jaou [*jauu* – soothsayer, healer] in Nérin. He replied: 'These people (M.'s family) accept the word of God and follow another. They still have all their own gods and they are invoking a new one. Nothing can come of it. You have to do what you want to do.' So M. burned his abandoned kamoaro [*ka-mwârö*, place of invocation of the ancestors], where all the panyao (god stones) [*panyaö*, war stones] lay, still holding power. He brought me the principal one, without telling me what he had done, and two years later, sold some remaining fragments to Montaigu [Montague], an English scientist. (Leenhardt, Journal, 20 March 1915)

This can be recognised as the same process of social and ideological alienation that Sarasin hypothesised in relation to the objects he purchased. This thesis can, however, in no way be generalised across all of the inhabitants of Houaïlou: such subjective processes hold specifically for those who sold or gave away objects, but there is virtually no trace of those who did not do so, holding onto their propitiatory stones and keeping their distance from the collectors and missionaries, in the writings of these individuals.

Commenting on the conversion of 'M.' and the destruction of his *ka-mwârö* in an earlier entry in his journal, Leenhardt writes: 'But what a conversion, effected by a sorcerer (*jauu*)!' (Leenhardt, Journal 24 July 1912). The epigraph to this chapter, in which Leenhardt tells his parents that he, together with Paul Laffay, a young missionary recently arrived to reinforce the Protestant mission, and the 'young English scientist' Paul Montague, had 'cast a spell on the Kaiser' on 11 December 1914, 'on a rare magic stone', can be reconsidered in the light of this remark: what a strange invocation, made by two missionaries and a scientist! The conversion of 'M.' was entirely governed by the question of efficacy: what prohibitions should be respected in order to heal one's children? Where does power come from – the word of God, or the old gods? Which mediator should he prefer, the missionary or the soothsayer (*jauu*)? How was the death of a child to be prevented? With regard to this question of efficacy, Leenhardt's use of the 'magic stone' should be held up against its limited result: while the Kaiser eventually lost the war, Leenhardt's two companions, Laffay and Montague, lost their lives to it.

***

In focusing in this chapter on statements from my interlocutors as they relate to representations of ancestrality, I have sought to examine the forms of preparation and propitiation for war that the present-day inhabitants of Houaïlou recount, particularly in relation to war stones (*panyaö*) and their origins. This has given me the opportunity to analyse anew a classic text collected by Maurice Leenhardt, 'Jopaipi', which proves to present a traditional local version of the Koro war, and in which I have been able to identify the repressive operation conducted in 1867 in the Houaïlou valley (see Chapter 1). Through analysis of the proper names cited in this text and the social position of the author, in terms of both lineage and relationship to Europeans, I use the text as a basis for revisiting the local political stakes in auxiliary involvement and religious conversion. It has led me to understand the motives and forms of European interests in war stones (missionary, scientific, collecting), and particularly to refer back and forth between 1867 and 1918 (the probable date when the 'Jopaipi' text was written down), and set this war more broadly still in a history of conflict that runs from the middle of the 18th century (with the Néajië war) to the early 20th (with the collection of war stones by a chief on the coast, at the time of the land seizures organised by governor Feillet).

3

The Chiefdoms within the Colonial Order

Organising the chiefdoms

1897–1903: Mèèjâ Néjâ and governor Feillet's reforms

Over the second half of the 19th century, the undefined narrative use of the term 'chief', in both military accounts and administrative documents, became gradually more defined through the creation of a legislative framework that developed as colonisation progressed from simple military control to economic exploitation. As early as 1867, the tribe was constituted as a legal entity, with collective responsibility and collective ownership of the land, and represented by a chief. The latter, in exchange for a small stipend, served as an interface with the administrative authority (the gendarmes[1]) and its economic demands: provision of labour from 1863, compulsory work days (service) from 1871 and head tax from 1894. The chiefs were also responsible for applying the disciplinary regulations of the *indigénat* (introduced in 1887).

At this point, I should like to consider in more detail the forms of political activity at work in the Houaïlou region in the early 20th century, following the radical reform of the legislative framework and land ownership in the

---

1 The *gendarmerie* is a division of the French military, and one of the two branches of policing in France. Its duties include policing in small towns and rural areas, security, and maintaining public order [trans.].

colony instituted by the governor Paul Feillet. This reform ushered in a period of increased control of local social life under a colonial government that was manifested principally through the institution of the chiefdoms. At this point the segregated and policed order that had gradually been introduced over the second half of the 19th century and which, I would argue, constitutes the model that is implicitly, yet paradoxically, evoked when reference is made to 'custom' in New Caledonia today, can clearly be seen in operation. This new colonial governmentality was also manifested through the restriction on freedom of movement and the disconnection and marginalisation of rural spaces that was made possible and organised by placing the Kanaks in reservations. Rather than approaching this situation from a purely juridical point of view, I propose to examine political moments and singular events, through the various concrete forms of mobilisation of individuals and management of conflicts, in which rationales of both physical violence and sorcery, as well as a considerable number of actors, were brought into action and, on this basis, to try to grasp the modalities, the stakes and the possibilities involved.

In the preceding two chapters I sought to expose the rationales underlying the development of a privileged relationship between French military power and the coastal chiefdoms of Houaïlou. The career of chief 'Mindia', Mèèjâ Néjâ, is closely linked with the government of Feillet who, between 1897 and 1903, oversaw the great colonial enclosures in New Caledonia,[2] and the reorganisation of the government of indigenous people via the restructuring of the Native Affairs Department and the toughening of the *indigénat* system,[3] completion of the relocation of Kanaks onto reservations,[4] and an active policy of land expropriation supported by the administrative chiefs. The aim of all of this was to advance an aggressive policy of free settlement by colonists. It was, quite logically, as the direct descendant of the auxiliary chiefs with whom the French were now in the habit of cooperating in the Houaïlou region, and after personally participating in a military operation in early 1897 at Hienghène,[5] that Mèèjâ was named high chief of all Houaïlou when the office of high chief with authority over a number of tribes was introduced into the organisation of the colony (under the 'Decree on the subject of organisation of native tribes' of 27 October 1897). He also took part in

---

2   Merle 1995.
3   Merle 2002 and 2004; Muckle 2010.
4   Saussol 1979; Dauphiné 1989; Merle 1998.
5   Dauphiné 1989.

3. THE CHIEFDOMS WITHIN THE COLONIAL ORDER

the 'Peace of Pamalé' in 1901, during which Feillet ended protests against land seizures in the Poindimié region. Mèèjâ Néjâ became an efficient mediator of the demands of the Feillet administration with regard to land ownership in Houaïlou. It was at this point that the scene described in the previous chapter, outlining his role in the seizure of land in Dâô (applying the governor's decree of 9 January 1899, which appropriated part of the Nindien reservation) took place; as we have seen, this episode also achieved Mèèjâ Néjâ's personal objectives in his inter-clan relationships with his maternal uncles from the greater Houaïlou valley (see Chapter 2).

This privileged relationship, however, was not in any way a linear one. Structurally, it might be considered that this was due to the paradoxical position in which administrative chiefs were placed by the system of indirect government of the colony. The chief was responsible for both land expropriation and control of labour, but all variations were possible in the chiefs' involvement with the French: they could amplify the demands of the authorities, relay them neutrally, or offer passive or active resistance to them. They could also use their position to work towards objectives other than those laid down by French law: fines, days of banishment, designation of providers of forced labour and those who were to pay tax could be used to resolve problems of authority or internal conflicts. These contradictions were quickly manifested in the case of Mèèjâ Néjâ, who was subject to a punishment of administrative detention in 1899. Here are the deliberations on this punishment in the minutes of the Privy Council:

> Mindja – Chief of Houaïlou (7th district). Bad subject and drunkard; has several times disobeyed the administration and the gendarmerie. Abused his authority by preventing natives from buying goods from certain traders and working for certain settlers. Sentenced to exile in Maré under the decision of 21 July 1899. Although Mindja has behaved well in exile, the Native Affairs Department proposes that he continue to be held in Maré until 1st July 1900. This chief is an alcoholic who needs some time to acquire habits of intemperance [sic]. (Privy Council, 28 December 1899)[6]

This text seems to suggest that the chief's influence was only acceptable to the colonial administration and the gendarmerie in charge of Native Affairs on condition that it satisfied the private interests of 'certain traders' and 'certain settlers'. It may be surmised that it was a conflict with these interests – a reluctance to satisfy their demands – that was at the origin of the punishment to which Mèèjâ Néjâ was sentenced. Examination of

---

6   I am grateful to Adrian Muckle for alerting me to this reference.

the electoral registers for Houaïlou for the years 1903 and 1905, which list voters' occupation and are the closest in date to this administrative sanction of deportation, identifies two traders: Eugène Bozon-Verduraz and Alexandre Renevier. I shall have occasion to return to these individuals.

In the Protestant sources, Mèèjâ Néjâ's stay in Maré is initially presented as the result of his personal relationship with pastor Philadelphe Delord, and as a symbol of the vigour and even the resurgence of Protestantism, countering the deadly effects of colonial alcoholisation: it is represented as an episode that justifies the mission. It is within this discursive framework that Maurice Leenhardt recounts how he was received by Mèèjâ Néjâ when he arrived in Houaïlou, in one of the first letters he sent from his mission field:

> A number of small boats approach the ship. The finest contains Mindia, the high chief, formerly a drunkard so hardened that the authorities were on the point of withdrawing his title and bestowing it on another, when Mr Delord, who was in New Caledonia at that time, asked if he could take him to Maré. He returned completely transformed, and now polices his tribes to prevent them from drinking. (Leenhardt 1903, p. 132)

The account given by Delord two years earlier presents a more complex picture: it could be considered that Mèèjâ Néjâ's alliance with the Protestants came to substitute for, or at least augment, a failing alliance with the colony's administrative authorities:

> You know high chief Mindia of Houaïlou. Here is a letter from him that I received yesterday: 'You brought me to know my Saviour. I had become an inveterate drunkard, to the point where I was put in prison, in Houaïlou, on 23 June 1899, me the high chief of all the tribes of Houaïlou, and two days later sent to Nouméa, where I was in the orphanage (prison for natives)[7] for three months, mad and sick … You had pity on me, you obtained permission from the Governor to take me with you to Maré where, thanks to your good and constant care, I am returned to health in body and mind. In Maré I promised, for one year, to cease drinking completely. The year has passed, and thanks be to God, I have been able to keep this promise – a promise that I have just renewed for two years, on 1st January 1901, in my Church, in the presence of the nata [Protestant evangelist] Weimith and my Christian subjects. I pray God to give me the strength to fulfil this promise. Signed Mindia.' (Delord 1901a, pp. 329–30)[8]

---

7 The Native Detention Centre, Baie de l'orphelinat (Orphanage Bay), in Nouméa.
8 See also Delord 1901b.

Nevertheless, his conflict with 'certain traders' did not end there: on 5 July 1912 *La France australe*[9] noted that the lawyer representing 'Mindhia of Houaïlou', 'charged with assaulting two of his subjects', had condemned the machinations of the Houaïlou 'taverns', in other words the managers of bars, at a time when the 'the six-stripe high chief' wanted to avoid 'the degradation of his subjects through alcohol'. Mèèjâ Néjâ was eventually acquitted by the court.

The fact that the administration continued to recognise him also allowed him to assert himself within his clan:

> Néouéo. – Tribe of high chief of Houaïlou, Mindia. Poor order and discipline, because it is split between the authority of Mindia and that of his heathen brother. (Leenhardt 1907, p. 270)

This 'brother' appears in a number of other early 20th-century sources under the name 'Mindaïl' or 'Mandai' [Mâdai]. His position in the family of high chief Mèèjâ can be determined by reference to the genealogy presented in Chapter 1 (Figure 2); Mâdai Néjâ appears here as the grandson of 'chief' Wanga (mentioned in 1856), and Mèèjâ Néjâ as the son of 'chief' Ai (mentioned particularly in the repressive operations conducted between 1863 and 1868). Thus Mâdai is the son of the son of the brother of Mèèjâ's father's father: they are indeed, in the classificatory terminology of kinship in the Houaïlou region, 'brothers' and potential rivals for the position of chief. Some years later Mâdai in his turn was subject to a sanction of administrative detention and deportation: Lucas Mindaïl of Néouyo (Houaïlou), who called himself a 'war chief' 'under the sway of old customs' was sentenced to two years internment on the Île des Pins 'for indulging in all sorts of abuse of the natives in his district' (*Journal officiel de la Nouvelle-Calédonie*, 15 April 1912).[10]

1912: Establishing high chiefdoms in Houaïlou

The ambivalent figure of high chief Mèèjâ is all the more interesting because it offers us a valuable window into the changes in colonial governance in Houaïlou in the early 20th century. Let us start with the division of the territory of Houaïlou into administrative districts enacted by decree no. 353 of 3 April 1912:

---

9   *Southern Hemisphere France*, daily newspaper published in Nouméa from 1889 to 1979 [trans.].
10 I am grateful to Adrian Muckle for alerting me to this reference.

Article 1. The whole of the tribal lands known as Houaïlou shall be divided into four districts as follows:

1st District of Neouyo, high chief Mindia, comprising the coastal tribes located on the right bank of the Houaïlou or 'Boa-Ma' river, those located in the valleys of the Kamoui river and the Méré river.

2nd District of Waraï, high chief Mandaoue, comprising the coastal tribes located on the left bank of the Houaïlou or 'Boa-Ma' river, the tribes of Lebris Bay up to and including those of Moné, and the tribe living in the valley of the river La Thu.

3rd District of Nindien, high chief Notouo, comprising the tribes in the settlements of Mé, Nindieu, Nessakouya up to and including the tribe of Gondé.

4th District of Boréaré, high chief Paul, comprising the tribes of Boréaré, Koula, Karagreu and Nérin.

Article 2. Mandaoue of Waraï, Notouo of Nindien and Paul of Boréaré shall have the right to wear four gold stripes.

High chief Mindia of Neouyo will retain the six gold stripes he is already entitled to wear, with the understanding that he is chief only of his district and has no authority of any kind over the high chiefs and the natives of the other districts. (*Journal officiel de la Nouvelle Calédonie*, 15 April 1912)

This 'division of the tribal lands known as Houaïlou into four districts', to quote the exact title of the decree, is pre-eminently a limitation on the authority of high chief 'Mindia', the first 'high chief' of Houaïlou: this limitation is the actual subject of the second paragraph of Article 2 of the decree. The division should not be read only as a measure to frustrate Mèèjâ Néjâ; it was also a result of the administrative reform carried out in 1912 when, under the decree of 2 March 1912, the Native Affairs Department was separated from the Immigration Department and made directly accountable to the governor's office.

We have no information on the details of the process that led to the appointment of the three new high chiefs, 'Mandaoué' [Mwâdéwé], also known by the name of 'Métou' [Métu], of the Népörö clan; 'Notouo' [Nötuö], also known by the name of Casimir, of the Bwéwa clan; and 'Paul', of the Wéma Nirikani clan. Paul was certainly not unknown to the administration since, as tribal chief of Boréaré, he had been awarded one stripe on 31 July 1906.[11] A 'report No. 20 of 19 February 1912, by the Administrator of Houaïlou, communicating the results of agreements concluded between the councils of the tribes in the Houaïlou region', cited in the preamble to the decree of 3 April 1912, makes reference to prior discussions, but I was unable to find this document. Most visible among the reactions to this decree are inevitably the more negative or critical responses. The most vociferous on this matter is undoubtedly Leenhardt: in his letters to his parents, he regularly takes issue with Paul, 'the governor's great poodle' (Leenhardt, Lettre à ses parents, 20 November 1912) and with Nötuö: 'As he has installed the Catholic mission in his home, upon which he became, just like that, a four-stripe high chief' (Leenhardt, Lettre à ses parents, 26 May 1914). I shall come back to the persistent conflicts between Leenhardt and Mwâdéwé. This hostility stemmed from the fact that, from Leenhardt's mission-focused point of view, these appointments were primarily an attack by the colonial administration against the influence of Protestantism in Houaïlou, which had hitherto been protected by the goodwill of high chief Mèèjâ Néjâ.

> [The constable of Houaïlou] has completely won over the Houaïlou chiefs, that is, he has created new ones who owe him everything, while at the same time crushing Mindia. With these tame chiefs, and Mindia crushed, he turned generously to the latter, raising him up, guiding him, giving him authority, and by this wily strategy winning full authority over him. All the natives who do not understand are being sent to Nouméa, the Administration applauds the excellent reports it receives, and it's all wonderful. (Leenhardt, Lettre à ses parents, 13 October 1912)

It is possible that there were also local Kanak reactions. For example, in a notebook belonging to Mèèjâ Néjâ we find the following (anonymous) remark, which perhaps constitutes the draft of a letter of protest: 'We want high chief Mindia to resume his title of high chief of Houaïlou as before' (Papiers Mindia n.d., p. 187).[12]

This notebook also offers invaluable insight into the struggles of the new chiefs to assert their authority. For example, it contains two drafts of letters relating to a conflict between the new high chief of Nindiah, Nötuö Bwéwa, the tribal chief of Öröibâô, 'Beudimin' [Bëdimwâ Bwéwa], and their families, on the one hand, and the inhabitants of Nérhëxakwéa and Gôdè, on the other. The first, dated 13 January 1915, is signed by the

---

11 Archives of New Caledonia, 97W18.
12 The family of Maurice Leenhardt holds a microfiche copy of Mèèjâ Néjâ's notebook.

chiefs 'Goakê' [Gwâkê Ëribwa] and 'Arou Péruche' [Arhu Kaviyöibanu] of Nérhëxakwéaa, and 'Baptiste' [Cibëi] of Gôdè (Papiers Mindia n.d., p. 140); the second, dated 17 January, is signed by Mèèjâ Néjâ himself. We do not know if these letters were sent to the governor, to whom they are addressed; in any case the matter was adjudicated at a simple police court in April 1915. The most significant point, I would argue, is that the letters were drafted in a notebook belonging to Mèèjâ Néjâ, suggesting a coordinated opposition by the tribal chiefs of the middle Houaïlou valley and the high chief on the coast against the new high chief of the lower valley:

> Houaïlou, 17 January 1915
>
> To the Governor of New Caledonia and Dependencies
>
> Dear Sir
>
> I have long experience of your generosity and your goodness the services you have been so good as to render me are indelibly engraved in my memory I am turning to you once again to beg for your favour on the present occasion. I turn to you in trust to tell you Mr Governor that since 6 January chiefs Notouo and chief Beudimin gather their men and are summoning them to declare to fight against the natives of chiefs Goake and Arou Peruche tribe of Nésakoéa and Baptiste of Gondé. Everyones fight among themselves. The others hurt and injure the natives Setèi and Poïba of the tribe of Nésakoéa. The pore men suffering day and nights because of the injuries of Notouo and Beudimin and compatriots.
>
> I pray you Mr Governor to receive my protest and my complaint and the idea of having added one happy man more. Mr Governor I humbly beg you to believe me your abslutely devoted servant.
>
> High Chief of the district of Houaïlou.
>
> Mindia. (Papiers Mindia n.d., p. 153)

This affair brings into play Pöiba Kaviyöibanu and Yetèi Ërijiyi, one of Leenhardt's students at Dö Nèvâ who was at that time attempting to seduce the daughter of tribal chief Bëdimwâ Bwéwa of the Öröibâö tribe:

> Sétei to secure the beautiful and serious Kouento sought to seduce her. Battle between the Nindiah and the Nessakoéa reciprocal complaints to the gendarmes. (Leenhardt, Journal, 14 January 1915)

We have no detailed information on the issues at stake in this dispute between neighbouring villages over a young woman. But it is striking that tribal and high chiefs drew on their relationship with the gendarmerie in this conflict, using the administrative resources available to them to the best advantage.

The 1912 reform integrated the high chiefs deeply into the colonial order, turning them into officials of the administration. The role of the chief subsumed multiple functions: supervision (of all), internment (of lepers), and mobilisation of economic resources through tax and requisitioning.

> The high chiefs and the tribal chiefs both have a duty to inform the authorities of events that arise in the territory entrusted to their supervision. The former are also responsible for isolating lepers in the places reserved for them. Under Article 41, they are also responsible, on pain of disciplinary sanction, for the payment of fines imposed on natives living in the territory under their authority. As regards fiscal duties, they are responsible for collecting taxes, of which they may use up to one twentieth (5%). They also receive a deduction at the same rate from the wages allocated to those natives of their tribes who are requisitioned or placed under immigration regulations. The sums received under these two heads constitute the entirety of their official remuneration. (Pégourier 1919, p. 20)

1915–17: Mobilisation for war

The new system of administration through the medium of high chiefs, set up in 1912, was quickly put to use in mobilising the young men of Houaïlou for war; they were called on first to enlist as volunteers in the First World War (in 1915 and 1916), and then as auxiliaries in the north of Grande Terre (in 1917). The two recruitment campaigns for the First World War were conducted primarily through the newly appointed administrative high chiefs. A table of mobilisation by district, based on names recorded in the census of tribes carried out by Maurice Leenhardt in 1917–19, gives an indication of this:

Table 2. Mobilisation for the First World War, by district

	Troops	Male population	Mobilisation rate
Boréaré district (Paul Wéma)	8	105	7.6%
Nindien district (Nötuö Bwéwa)	29	303	9.6%
Néwèö district (Mèèjâ Néjâ)	18	318	5.7%
Waraï district (Mwâdéwé Népörö)	26	261	10%
Houaïlou	81	987	8.2%

Source: Leenhardt n.d. [c.1917–19].

Thus it was in the districts governed by Mwâdéwé Népörö and Nötuö Bwéwa, the two chiefs then least known to the administration, that mobilisation was highest, while it was moderate in that of Paul Wéma, a tribal chief who had been awarded stripes in 1906, and much lower in the district of Mèèjâ Néjâ. Clearly, any suggestion as to the motives for this participation would be purely speculative, particularly as regards how much derived from each individual's personal commitment and how much was owed to influence or obligations imposed by the chiefs – which itself only reflected pressure from above.

> Our Military Commander must certainly have recognised that he was wrong to … treat the chiefs of Houaïlou rather too harshly when he made his recruitment tour of the East coast. (*Bulletin du commerce*, 30 June 1917, p. 8)

Leenhardt, for his part, offered three explanations for enlistment in a letter to his parents: the promises of equal citizenship (to which I shall return), attachment to France as the source of the Gospel (Leenhardt is clearly projecting his own feelings here), and love of war. This exposition at least has the merit of pointing out to the diversity of possible motives:

> The decree opening up freedom to enlist for the war in Africa has been extended to all the colonies … They said to the Kanaks: you will be like the Whites. In my sermons I tell them: 'You will have participated in the victory and will thereby have gained a new degree of dignity that will enhance your standing in the eyes of France.' This is more vague than what the Whites are telling them; it is also more accurate. They understand it and they accept it. But they come to ask for specific detail about what the Whites are promising: 'Will we be like them? What do they mean? They are defending their territory, but what territory are we defending? Our lands are State property, will they give them to us?' I let them hope that this will be the case; but do not imagine that the majority of Kanaks talk in this way. Most of them are enlisting for two reasons: either out of love for France, the country the Mishers [missionaries] champion, which brought them the light (the Gospel), or in order to see war. (Leenhardt, Lettre à ses parents, 31 January 1916)

Following the two phases of recruitment for the First World War, the inhabitants of Houaïlou were called upon once again during the year 1917, through their high chiefs, to participate in a wide-ranging operation of colonial repression. More and more information is coming to light about the sequence of events in the north of Grande Terre in 1917 known as the Kanak 'rebellion', and the repressive operations it triggered in the

3. THE CHIEFDOMS WITHIN THE COLONIAL ORDER

regions of Koné and Hienghène, thanks to the work of Adrian Muckle.[13] Here I should like to focus on what can be understood of the participation of warriors from Houaïlou in the two phases of repression, in July–August 1917 (in the Koné region), and in December 1917 – January 1918 (in the Hienghène region). One of my present-day interlocutors emphasised the responsibility of the chiefs:

> He participated in a pretty much fascist war, the war over there all the brothers in Hienghène … We've been criticised for that, recently, the brothers [from Hienghène] when I was at school with them, things almost turned nasty, they asked me the question … Because at that time it was the high chiefdoms that decided everything, it wasn't us, you can't accuse us … They were led there, you know, when they got there they were astonished. At that time it was the high chief who made the decisions, it was colonisation that pushed from behind. (Charles Pûkiu, extract from interview, July 2006)

Coming nearly 40 years after they had played their part as auxiliaries in the repression of 1878, but in the immediate continuation of their military support for the French in the First World War, Kanaks were involved in the repression from the early stages, and on a large scale:[14] as early as 27 May, a few days after the first disturbances in the Koné region, the people of Houaïlou offered their support to the French army. The men responsible for coordinating the repression, the surveyors Bernier, Antoine Martin-Garnaud and Nicolas Ratzel, organised mass recruitment of men from Houaïlou in response to the following statement, relayed by Eugène Bozon-Verduraz, the chairman of the municipal committee. In my view, mayor Bozon-Verduraz' intervention was crucial in determining in the form taken by the operation. Here is the text of the telegram he sent to the governor on 20 June:

> Have the honour of reporting that high chiefs Mindia Mandaoué Casimir and Paul whose devotion to France assured came spontaneously to ask us to communicate to you following: they request the honour of participating expedition against rebels in north assuring will immediately put end to insurrection. (Bozon-Verduraz 1978a, p. 71).[15]

---

13   Muckle 2006, 2008 and 2012.
14   Guiart 1970.
15   This message is signed 'David Bozon-Verduraz'. In the four electoral lists for Houaïlou between 1903 and 1919, there is only one Bozon-Verduraz, with the forename Eugène. This must therefore necessarily be the chairman of the municipal committee; David was most probably the forename by which he was usually known.

This statement prompted an initial article in the *Bulletin du commerce*, on 23 June 1917:

> The tribes of Houaïlou, including that of Boréaré, are universally known for their loyalty and patriotism which they have always shown, on every occasion: these tribes supplied a large number of volunteers for the Pacific infantry battalion. In 1878, the same tribes showed themselves admirably well disposed towards us. It is therefore no surprise that high chief Mindia and chief Paul have recently offered the Governor the support of their warriors in the campaign against the natives of the Koné region: we estimate that they can probably supply between 100 and 150 guns. We offer our warm congratulations to chiefs Mindia and Paul for their affection for France and the devotion they show to the cause of civilisation. (*Bulletin du commerce*, 23 June 1917, pp. 8–9)

This article in its turn prompted a response from Bozon-Verduraz:

> As of now the chiefs of Houaïlou alone have 140 men ready, distributed as follows: François chief Monéo 15 Mandaoué chief Nékoué 40 Paul chief Boréaré 12 Casimir chief Nindhia 40 Mindia chief Néouyo 33 … We have to inform you that chiefs Mandaoué and Casimir were deeply wounded at not seeing their name appear relative congratulations in bulletin of 23 inst. beg you to rectify. (Bozon-Verduraz and Satorek 1978, p. 76)

Through this intervention, Bozon-Verduraz appears to constitute an interest group that binds him with Mwâdéwé Népörö and Casimir Nötuö Bwéwa; we do not know to what extent this alliance pre-existed the 1917 mobilisation, but we can perhaps take it as an indication of the role the chairman of the municipal committee may have played in the appointment of the high chiefs in 1912 (let us recall that Mèèjâ Néjâ had been interned in Nouméa, and then deported to Maré, in 1899, and in 1912 was once again charged in relation to a conflict of interest with a trader in Houaïlou, who might well have been Bozon-Verduraz himself). The following issue of the *Bulletin du commerce* confirms this 'influence':

> The traditional preparatory palavers are proliferating among the natives, suggesting that our brave natives will not be long in 'joining the campaign'. Alongside chiefs Mindia and Paul, we must mention, among the most ardent and most devoted to our cause, other chiefs from Houaïlou: Mandaoué, Casimir and François of Monéo. We should also mention that the influence of Mr Bozon-Verduraz, the Chairman of the Municipal Committee, was very happily exerted to encourage all of these valiant

chiefs in their manly resolution. A shrewd trader, he even went as far as offering a number of small gifts to the chiefs, encouraging them to fire the zeal of their warriors. (*Bulletin du commerce*, 30 June 1917, p. 8)

The telegram of 28 June is another source that helps us to estimate the capacities of the four high chiefs to mobilise men; it can be compared with other quantitative evidence – including the partial list below, provided in the account by surveyor Nicolas Ratzel:

> The number of men who came to place themselves under my authority totals 347, as follows:
>
> Néouïo, under the command of chief Mindia 34
> Nékoué Ouaraye, under the command of chief Mandaoué 43
> Mindieu, under the command of chief Notouo 63
> Boréaré, under the command of chief Paul 15
> Monéo, under the command of chief François 18.
>
> (Ratzel 2006 vol. 1, p. 353, 12 July 1917)

and that of Maurice Leenhardt:

> 2½ hours to embark 195 men, including 163 Houaïlou. Mindia, poor Mindia, in his desire to always be the one with the biggest number, gave 65 men. (Leenhardt, Lettre à son épouse Jeanne, 27 June 1917)

Taken together, these data form the basis for drawing up a new table of the mobilisation capacities (MC) of the high chiefs of Houaïlou.

Table 3. Mobilisation for the colonial war in Koné and Hienghène

	Boréaré district (Paul)	Nindien district (Nötuö Casimir)	Néwéo district (Mindia)	Warai district (Mandaoué)	Houaïlou
Bozon (28/06)	12	40	33	40	125
Ratzel (12/07)	15	63	34	43	155
Leenhardt (27/06)			65		163
Male population (c. 1917–19)	105	303	318	261	987
MC Bozon	11.4%	13.2%	10.4%	15.3%	12.7%
MC Ratzel	14.3%	20.8%	10.7%	16.5%	15.7%
MC Leenhardt			20.4%		16.5%
MC infantry	7.6%	9.6%	5.7%	10%	8.2%

Source: After Bozon-Verduraz and Satorek (1978), Ratzel (2006) and Leenhardt (Lettre à son épouse Jeanne, 27 June 1917).

Notable once again is the low mobilisation capacity of Mèèjâ Néjà (unless we accept Leenhardt's estimate). Be that as it may, Leenhardt's assessment is broadly confirmed: 'And no one is left … The young men are in France, the old men are in Koné, only the women are left' (Leenhardt, Lettre à son épouse Jeanne, 27 June 1917). In fact, nearly a quarter of the male population of Houaïlou (all ages combined) was involved in the successive mobilisations between 1915 and 1917.

Accounts of the methods of colonial war used by the Houaïlou auxiliaries in 1917 refer to tactics that are by now familiar, and which I described in Chapter 1: the use of mobile columns as tested in New Caledonia in 1878, and total war via the destruction of dwellings and means of production:

> I strongly insisted, to the loyal chiefs who rallied to our cause, on the absolute necessity of burning all the villages without exception and laying waste, of totally destroying crops and irrigation channels to the taro fields. I was convinced that the Kanak, thus deprived of his native foodstuff and of his shelter that protects him from cold and bad weather, would not long resist being harried every day, every moment. (Ratzel 2006 vol. 1, p. 362)

The descriptions of the 1917 operation stand out from those of the wars conducted between 1856 and 1878 (see Chapter 1) in their emphasis on the material interests of those participating, in terms of exemption from taxes, bounties, loot and capture of women. This may be due to the appearance of new sources, given that the missionaries certainly took a different view from the military in their evaluation of methods of war; but it may also be due to developments in the evolution of these methods. This is Leenhardt's account of the looting during the two phases of the repression (July–August 1917; December 1917 – January 1918):

> We left the Houaïlous, Bayes with words of encouragement aimed at arousing their atavistic instincts, they set on these savages, and massacre without mercy. Some have already returned here, bringing a huge booty of cooking pots and tools … Our Houaïlous are scouring the bush conscientiously, and paid as they are in booty, indiscriminately loot those loyal to us as well as the rebels. (Leenhardt, Lettre à ses parents, 3 August 1917 and 19 January 1918)

While far removed from this moral reading, the emphasis on the material aspect of the war is equally explicit in Ratzel's account of the rules of war he instituted at the start of the operation, which constituted a direct and powerful incitement to violence:

3. THE CHIEFDOMS WITHIN THE COLONIAL ORDER

You shall make war on the rebels in accordance with your ancient customs; we surveyors will decide the places and times when you should act. Each man who enlists under my leadership shall be exempted from the head tax for 15 years.[16] For each prisoner taken, the bounty shall be 25 francs. It will be double that sum for each rebel killed …

I had promised the chiefs that for each prisoner taken by the men, they would receive a bounty of 25 francs, and that any auxiliary who killed a rebel would receive an allowance of 50 francs. It was easy to count the men who surrendered and were made prisoners, likewise the women, but those who were killed were a different matter. He who had killed an enemy on a steep slope or in the depth of a forest could not bring the body with him: the Houaïlous and the men of Bourail quickly found a solution to the problem. When the enemy was down, they cut off his head; they tied the hair, which all wore very long, to a flexible liana stem one or two metres in length, and brought the head to the camp by pulling it behind them. It followed behind, now rolling, now bouncing over the rough ground, roots and stones, giving off hollow yet muffled sounds that aroused no emotion of any kind in the victor … I saw sixteen heads brought back this way on 16 December, despite the fact that I wished to avoid a sight that could not but disgust me. I had to harden myself to it, given the insistence of the chiefs and the remonstrances of Martin, who assured me that this visitation from the fallen was a privilege accorded only to the high chief among the Kanaks. (Ratzel 2006 vol. 1, p. 349, and vol. 2, pp. 16–17)

In the new institutional landscape, with its four high chiefdoms, there is little doubt that the administrative chiefs were encouraged to pass on the French incitement to violence, in what can be seen as a competition for prestige – as indicated by the statements of Mèèjâ Néjâ, reported to Leenhardt by Bwêêyööu Ërijiyi:

Boesou has picked up a rumour that Mindia turned on his people: 'Why didn't you kill rebels, cut off their heads like the others? Don't you know that you are paid per head?' And his brother, the heathen Madai, replied: 'You called us here to come and speak to the men of this place, not to kill them, why have they changed what they said?' And clever Boesou adds that Madai is the war chief of Néwéo (with higher authority than Mindia). (Leenhardt, Lettre à son épouse Jeanne, 5 August 1917)

---

16 I found no trace of such an exemption, which was also promised to those who volunteered for the First World War: if it had been applied, a majority of the heads of family in Houaïlou would have been exempt between the First and Second World Wars.

This text also points to the competitive relationship between Mèèjâ Néjâ and his cousin Mâdai, mentioned at the beginning of this chapter, and the heterogeneity of moral frames of reference, where personal interests (material or political), traditional systems of reference (the status given to a 'war chief'), the influence of the administration and the work of the missionaries constitute distinct bases for the most widely varying individual positions. I shall return to this point later, when I consider how the capture of women and children proved a crucial issue in the local colonial field of Houaïlou, and in the colony as a whole.

Once the repressive operation was over, governor Jules Repiquet made a trip to Houaïlou, from 15 to 20 April 1918, during which he visited the administrative centre, the main centres of European settlement, the tribes of the high chiefs and the two competing missions. This can be seen as the material manifestation of the colonial alliance between the high chiefdoms and the administration, the high point of which was the ceremony at which colonial decorations were awarded to the Houaïlou auxiliaries:

> It was on the 17th, at 3.00 pm, that rewards were conferred on the auxiliaries of Houaïlou and Monéo. An impressive ceremony.
>
> At the appointed hour, the Head of the Colony arrived at the great plain, where he was awaited by the Chairman of the Municipal Committee and the local dignitaries. All the natives of the high chiefs Mindia, Notouo, Paul, Mandaoué and François were gathered there. He was welcomed with a rendition of the 'Marseillaise', sung by choirs from the tribes. Mr Repiquet, who has a strong speaking voice, thanked the chiefs and the natives for responding to his appeals in 1915 and 1916, giving many Infantrymen to France without hesitation, he congratulated them warmly on the part they played in repressing the rebellion, and he praised them for their consistent demonstrations of loyalty to the Government. He reminded them of the benefits they could expect from civilisation; he counted on their loyalty and assured them of the Administration's full concern for them.
>
> The Governor then proceeded to the distribution of rewards:
>
> *High-chiefs*: Mindia, of Néouyo, Nichan Iftikar. Paul, of Boréaré, Nichan Iftikar. Mandaou [*sic*], of Waraï, Silver-Gilt Medal. Casimir Notouo, of Nindien, Silver Medal. François, of Monéo, Black Star of Benin. Douba, junior chief of Boréaré, Silver Medal.[17]

---

17 Nichan Iftikhar [Order of Glory]: originally a Tunisian decoration that could be awarded to French nationals, cities and foreigners with a connection to Tunisia. Bronze, Silver-Gilt and Silver Medals for various periods of service: decorations historically awarded to civilians working for the French military. Order of the Black Star: decoration historically awarded to individuals working for the development of French influence in West Africa [trans.].

3. THE CHIEFDOMS WITHIN THE COLONIAL ORDER

Natives: Paul, of Nindien, Silver-Gilt Medal. Lucien Mérindieu, of Boréaré, Silver Medal. Kaiba, of Kouaoua, Bronze Medal. Victor, of Waraï, Silver Medal.

This last native having passed away on his return from the expedition to Tipindjé-Hienghène, the Governor, to the applause of those present, pinned the Medal awarded to him to the breast of his mother, Savioba, of Thù. Various tribal chiefs and natives were awarded Declarations of Satisfaction.[18] (*La France australe*, 26 April 1918)

The decorations awarded – Nichan Iftikar and Black Star of Benin – are among the colonial orders that reward services rendered to colonisation by civilians or military personnel throughout the French empire. Ratzel's description of this event is very close to the article in *La France australe*. However, it allows us to add a few more details. Firstly, he sets the auxiliaries' career in the context of an additional history:

> The decorations awarded to the chiefs of the tribes, to Mindia, Mandaoué, Paul and a number of natives, were bestowed on them by Mr Repiquet in the afternoon of 17th April, on the plain, on the right bank of the Houaïlou river, opposite Ouani and close to the shark hole where the Houaïlous, who embraced our cause in 1878, threw the bodies of the rebels they had killed. (Ratzel 2006 vol. 2, p. 140)

Ratzel goes on to emphasise the large number of Kanaks who attended the awards ceremony as spectators:

> During the morning I had a proper stage erected in this place, by Mindia's and Mandaoué's men, where the entire population of Houaïlou, dressed in their Sunday best, had gathered round the Governor to watch the award ceremony. [There follows a list of those receiving awards, identical to that in *La France australe*.] The natives danced a frenzied *pilou*,[19] with each man awarded being celebrated by the applause of the crowd and an explosion of fearsome cries, as if sounded by one voice, let out by hundreds of Kanaks. (Ratzel 2006 vol. 2, pp. 140–41)

---

18   Témoignage de satisfaction: a certificate recognising contribution to military action [trans.].
19   Traditional dance telling clan stories [trans.].

Figure 4. Award of decorations in April 1918: 'The stage'
Source: Ratzel 2006 vol. 2, p. 245; © Archives of New Caledonia (Nouméa), fonds photographique Nicolas Ratzel, 2Ph15.

Figure 5. Award of decorations in April 1918: 'The frenzied *pilou*'
Source: Ratzel 2006 vol. 2, p. 244; © Archives of New Caledonia (Nouméa), fonds photographique Nicolas Ratzel, 2Ph15.

3. THE CHIEFDOMS WITHIN THE COLONIAL ORDER

The ceremony staged a privileged alliance between the Kanaks of Houaïlou and the colonial authorities, and its choreographed character was heightened by Eugène Bozon-Verduraz's translation of the governor's speech into the language of Houaïlou, 'so that all, young and old, may understand and appreciate our gratitude'. Other Europeans present would have been capable of making this translation, notably Antoine Martin-Garnaud, one of the surveyors who had directed the repressive operation, who was also a Houaïlou voter resident in Nékwé. Bozon-Verduraz thus appears here in the dual role of one of those responsible for the event and a recipient of one of the awards. Finally, I should like to cite one last passage in Ratzel's text, which can be related to my analysis of the collection of weapons of war by Europeans in Chapter 2:

> Following this ceremony, we went to pay a visit to Mindia at his house. He gave the Governor a club in the form of a bird's bill, magnificent and very old, which had been passed down from father to son in the High Chief's family. The wood was blood-red, and the part that was shaped into a bird's beak was very long, longer even than the handle. I noted the following day, when we set off on the path to Boréaré, that the point of the beak of this weapon, which was being carried by a native on horseback, over his shoulder, almost came down to his mount's saddle. It was a valuable gift, and I am sure that it will take pride of place among all the exotic souvenirs that Mr Repiquet, like all high officials, has collected during his time here and in other colonies. (Ratzel 2006 vol. 2, p. 141)

I have so far been unable to identify this bird's-beak club in the European collections.

I should like to add a few remarks on the Kanaks who were decorated on that day.[20] In addition to the high chiefs, they included Duba, the tribal chief of Karaxërë (district of Boréaré),[21] and three ordinary native subjects. Their awards demonstrate that they were picked out for their military skills from the start of the operations, as indicated by the various materials collected in the file Récompenses accordées aux Auxiliaires Indigènes. Troubles dans les Tribus (1917) (Rewards Granted to Native Auxiliaries: Trouble in the Tribes (1917)).[22] Thus, in the draft of decision No. 666 of 21 September 1917, the following are proposed: a silver medal for the 'Native Lucien

---

20 Cross-referencing the information that follows, in terms of tribal affiliation and age, with the census carried out by Leenhardt, identifies them as Duba Néwau of Karaxërë, Lucien Kaadè of Kula, Paul Tëvèyû of Nérhëxakwéaa, and Victor Baöci of Tù.
21 On Duba, see Ratzel 2006 vol. 2, pp. 23–24.
22 See Récompenses … 1917. I am grateful to Adrian Muckle for alerting me to this information.

Nimindieu', from the district of Boréaré ('Always in front, pursued rebels into the most difficult terrain'), a silver-gilt medal for 'Paul of Mindieu', i.e. the district of Nindien ('Volunteer veteran of 1878, more than 70 years of age – armed with a small axe and spears fought hand-to-hand; wounded …'), and for 'Victor', district of Waraï ('who pursued rebels even while himself seriously wounded').[23] The 'Report of bonuses awarded to native auxiliaries from 11/10/17 to 27/1/18' identifies Paul more precisely (tribe of Nérhëxakwéaa).[24] This report reveals that 'Lucien Minrindieu', 'Douba (junior chief)' and 'Paul Mégonda' were all among the (many) auxiliaries rewarded for the murder of an enemy during the second phase of the operation. The letter of 26 February 1918 from the 'high chiefs who led the auxiliaries of Houaïlou in the second expedition' allows us to identify 'Lucien Maradie'[25] (tribe of Kula). This letter also shows that it was the 'high chiefs' who proposed the bestowal of awards or Declarations of Satisfaction on the 'junior chiefs' who took part in the operation, and in the second part of the list, to those natives who had performed particularly well in the military operations. Thus we can read here the trace of the network that the Feillet administration had put in place, the high chiefs' internalisation of their role and of the colonial hierarchies.

The network of tribal chiefs

This network took the very concrete material form of an instrument of state administration, the *Registre des tribus et des chefs* (*Register of Tribes and Chiefs*) that was used by the Department of Native Affairs to organise its system of indirect government through chiefdoms.

This pamphlet can thus effectively be read as a colonial roll of honour, in which the Third Republic enrolled its good subjects onto a trajectory of excellence. For example, Casimir Nötuö Bwéwa, high chief of the district of Nindien, received a Declaration of Satisfaction in 1916, a silver-gilt medal in 1918, a fifth stripe in 1922, and a further Declaration of Satisfaction in 1925. Paul Wéma Nirikani, high chief of the district of Boréaré, was awarded a silver-gilt medal in 1913, a Declaration of Satisfaction in 1916, a fifth stripe in 1922; he was made a Knight of the Royal Order of Cambodia in 1926, received a further Declaration

---

23 On Victor, see Bernier 1917b; for the date of 31 July, Ratzel 2006 vol. 1, pp. 366–67 and vol. 2, p. 53.
24 On Paul, see Bernier 1917a; for the date of 23 July, Ratzel 2006 vol. 1, p. 361.
25 On Lucien, see Bernier 1917b; for the date of 4 August, Ratzel 2006 vol. 1, p. 367.

of Satisfaction in 1927, succeeded Nötuö as high chief of the district of Nindien in 1926, following the latter's death, and was made a Knight of the Order of the Black Star in 1932. Mwâdéwé Népörö received Declarations of Satisfaction in 1914 and 1916, a fifth stripe in 1922, the Cross of Nichan El Anouar in 1926, the silver-gilt medal with a further Declaration of Satisfaction in 1927, before succeeding Paul as the head of the district of Bas-Nindien in 1940. Mèèjâ Néjâ's career ended with the Nichan Iftikar awarded by governor Jules Repiquet; on his death, he was succeeded in 1921 by his elder son Apupia, who received a third stripe in 1923. A similarly precise list could be given for the tribal chiefs, although they were less copiously rewarded.[26]

The corollary of this roll of honour was the capacity to exercise violence, or indirectly to have the gendarmerie apply sanctions in the case of internal conflicts. This point is made in the recent work of Adrian Muckle and Isabelle Merle, and I have given a few examples elsewhere.[27] However, I should like to add a few testimonies relating to the local situation in Houaïlou. Firstly, Maurice Leenhardt's evaluation of this situation:

> The Administration requisitions services, but at the moment requisition has become a *lettre de cachet*.[28] Any Kanak who is out of favour receives one. (Leenhardt, Lettre à ses parents, 22 August 1913)

There is one example in Mèèjâ Néjâ's notebook, which I have already cited. The notebook contains a draft letter from the chief of Ba asking the administration to intervene with three members of his tribe:

Houaïlou 18 January 1913

Chief Piénéba Asawa of the tribe of Bah (Houaïlou)

To the Governor of New Caledonia and Dependencies in Nouméa

Mr Governor,

By this present I beg you to be good enough to ridd me of three natives here are the names. Mandine and Betouo and Edit of m'y tribe by diclaring prepetual exile in a place as far eway as possible. Three natives and of m'y family. That is why I did not ask for their exile earlier. I have try to bring them better sentiments I have not been able to (Papiers Mindia n.d., p. 104).

---
26 See *Registre ...*, n.d.
27 Muckle 2010; Merle 2002 and 2004; Naepels 1998, pp. 274–76.
28 Royal decree imposing varying decrees of restriction on liberty [trans.].

We do not know whether this letter was sent to the governor, nor whether it produced any result. But we do know that at the time when the letter was drafted Piénéba Ayawa was a young man in his 20s and, following the death of his father, the latter was replaced by a 'Diemba' until Piénéba came of age.[29] According to Leenhardt's 1919 census, the three individuals named in the letter were all heads of family more than 10 years older than the new chief, and also belonged to the families of founding ancestors who were involved in long-standing conflicts with the Ayawa chiefdom. We do know that the sanction of perpetual exile was not applied: chief Piénéba and his recalcitrant subject Bétuö left together for France during the First World War, where Piénéba died in battle on 29 October 1918.

The colonial field in Houaïlou: settlers, gendarmes, missionaries and chiefs

> How strange it is, lay heathens. They are only contained by chiefs sold to the gendarmes. Caledonia is not a uniform laboratory. (Leenhardt, Lettre à ses parents, 11 August 1916)

The modes of action and range of political freedom of the Houaïlou Kanaks in the second decade of the 20th century were radically different from what we know of the 1850s, for example (see Chapter 1). The landscape of local mobility and incorporation of some actors in social networks of importance (Caledonian, Oceanian, global) was profoundly altered by colonial action, particularly under governor Paul Feillet. This action then included the differential categorisation, identification and spatialisation that contributed to an intense localisation of the local, for Kanaks in particular, accompanied by multiple forms of segregation, through the differentiation of rights and spaces superimposed on this. This change did not, however, eliminate Kanak political actors' capacities for action, but did shift the places and forms of expression of conflicts. Military operations such as that of 1917, as well as the introduction of indirect powers of government granted to chiefs, or the spaces opened by the competition between Catholic and Protestant missionaries, constituted sites of initiative and confrontation between actors whose resources were in part determined by their place in European categorisations. Let us consider the example of the 1911 census.

---

29   Archives of New Caledonia, 97W18, 9 January 1906.

Census analysis has been a central tool in understanding the state's regulation of colonial spaces. Before examining the picture it gives of a population and its development, or reflecting on its limits, it is vital to emphasise the categorisation it operates.[30] Here, in order, are the categories (which offer a crucial key to the approach to the colony during the first half of the 20th century) and the descriptive variables of the 1911 census, for Houaïlou:

Table 4. Principal categories and results of 1911 census in Houaïlou

Free individuals (men, women, children M and children F)	384
French born in France	85
French born in the colony	187
Foreigners	112
Individuals under penal sentence (men, women)	215
Freed	108
Transported individuals	79
Transported groups	23
Sentenced	5
Regulated immigrants (men, women, children)	130
Tonkinese	27
Indians	7
Javanese	5
New Hebrideans	9
Loyalty Islanders	59
New Caledonians	23
Natives of the tribes (men, women, children)	2042
Natives of the tribes	2042
TOTAL	2771

Source: 'Recensement général de la population, 5 mars 1911', Archives de la Nouvelle-Calédonie, 441W3.

In her exposition of the interwoven construction of the categories of subject and citizen, Emmanuelle Saada writes: 'Gradually, in the space of Empire, the key distinction is no longer that between nationals and foreigners, as in metropolitan France, but the split between 'French and

---

30   See Mamdani 1996 and 2001; Appadurai 1996; Saada 2003 and 2012.

assimilated' and 'natives and assimilated' (Saada 2003, p. 17).[31] This remark illuminates the New Caledonian case, which incontestably confirms the pertinence of this division. It is worth adding that the quantitatively largest category, the 'natives of the tribes' is also the least differentiated. It is also worth noting that the sharpest division within the population of 'French and assimilated' is between 'free individuals' and 'individuals under penal sentence' (the latter could, in fact, sometimes have lost their status as citizens) – a more administrative distinction than that between 'French born in France', 'French born in the colony' and 'foreigners' (by implication, Europeans and Japanese). The 'natives and assimilated' also brings together nationals (both the 'natives of the tribes'; that is, those living in the reservation assigned to their tribe, and New Caledonians and Loyalty Islanders; that is Kanaks not originating from Houaïlou who were there under contract or requisition to perform some task, as well as Tonkinese and New Hebrideans from other French colonies) with foreign subjects (Indians and Javanese). Thus the organising principle of the state's perception – and no doubt of the subjective perception of those concerned – of the New Caledonian social space has nothing to do with nationality. We may note finally that this categorisation corresponds to a more or less pronounced spatialisation: regulated immigrants are required to live on the premises of their employer, natives of the tribes in their reservations; place of residence is restricted for those under penal sentence, and free for the free individuals. In Houaïlou in particular, regulated immigrants (primarily Loyalty Islanders and Tonkinese) and those under penal sentence seem to have been employed almost exclusively in the mines. Although contact with 'French and assimilated citizens' was not impossible, the restrictions on freedom of residence and movement for 'natives and assimilated' testify to a segregational system where place of residence determines socialisation, and hence legal status.

This differentiation reaches its apogee in the disparity between the results of this census of 1911 (2,771 inhabitants) and the electoral register drawn up for the elections to the municipal committee in 1911, on which only 90 men were listed: 34 miners, 25 settlers, 11 employees, four traders, four missionaries, two day labourers, one cowherd, one baker, one skilled tradesman, one road-mender, one carpenter, one blacksmith, one painter and decorator, one member of the post and telegraph company, one telegraph supervisor and one accountant. The exclusion of women, children, a proportion of those under penal sentence, foreigners, regulated

---

31   See also her analysis in Saada 2012, Chapter 4.

immigrants and natives combined to make citizenship a rare privilege, reserved for 3 per cent of the population of Houaïlou (this ratio decreased even further between the wars: there were 58 individuals listed on the electoral register of 1919, and 50 on that of 1932).

The second striking aspect of these census results is the gender imbalance that can be read in them: the proportion of male individuals was 99 per cent for those under penal sentence, 90 per cent among regulated immigrants, 80 per cent for free individuals, 59 per cent among the natives of the tribes (this percentage being calculated for the adult population, as the gender of children was not specified in this category – the censuses of the tribes carried out by Leenhardt between 1917 and 1919 indicate a comparable masculinity ratio of 56 per cent). One consequence of this was the reiterated assignation of women to the space of the tribes and to the authority 'of husband, parents or chief', since the colonial authorities judged that, in this matter, their role was to keep women in the domestic space:

> In the light of the results of the census of 1911, which show that in the tribes, the proportion of native women continues to fall and that numbers are already much lower than for men … decree:
>
> Article 1. Native women and girls of New Caledonia and Dependencies are forbidden to leave their tribe.
>
> Article 2. They may be employed by local settlers, but without specification as to the period of work, and must always, even in this case, return to their tribe if they are summoned by their husband, parents or chief.
>
> Article 3. The current employment of native women and girls shall be terminated but will not be renewed.
>
> Article 4. Free residence permits will no longer be issued to native women and girls. ('Decree forbidding native women and children of New Caledonia and Dependencies from leaving their tribe', 12 February 1912, *Journal officiel de la Nouvelle-Calédonie*)

The quality of the results of this census and, more generally, of the first censuses carried out in New Caledonia, has been the subject of much discussion.[32] In particular, the data concerning natives of the tribes (2,042 individuals counted in 1911) are debatable, according to inspector of colonies Paul Pégourier:

---

32   See Shineberg 1983.

A general census was conducted in 1911. The fundamental flaw in the organisation of this census was the disruption it occasioned for the natives, since some tribes lived 30 kilometres or more from the office of the Administrator. Under these conditions, it is no wonder that the results recorded in the Civil Register were uncertain, as the Administrator of Houaïlou rightly remarked in his report on the subject in 1918. (Pégourier 1919, p. 25)

Pégourier put forward an estimate of the 'population of the districts' of Houaïlou of 1,878 individuals (without any indication as to how he arrived at this number).[33] On his prophylactic tour in 1912, Dr Lebœuf counted 1,983 inhabitants.[34] The census of named individuals conducted by Leenhardt between 1917 and 1919 counted 1,762 Kanaks in the tribes of Houaïlou.

These general outlines can serve as a basis for understanding the shape of the colonial field in Houaïlou during the early 20th century. The first thing to note is the separation between the world of the mines and everything related to the administration of the tribes: while the Kanaks were not excluded from the economic activity of the colony (as providers of labour, particularly for the construction of public facilities, and as employees of the settlers in order to earn money to pay the head tax), their absence from employment in the mines is striking. Secondly, within the social space stratified by colonial categorisation, the intense competition between a number of European actors for influence and control over the Kanak population is clearly evident: the administration, in the person of Administrator, particularly when it was implementing a 'new native policy' during the 1930s; the mayor (who in the person of Eugène Bozon-Verduraz was both trader and landowner); and the missionaries (Catholics and Protestants had been in vehement competition with one another since they arrived).[35] In this local play of forces, the 'colonisers' were no more united than the 'colonised', and the group of chiefs (the tribal chiefs but, still more, the high chiefs) formed the locus of maximum tension in the interface between these divided worlds. The division of Houaïlou into four districts therefore not only represented a performative moment in the colonial evaluation of the relative prestige and power of the various chiefs involved, but also reflected the conflicts between Europeans embodying

---

33 Pégourier 1919, p. 24.
34 Lebœuf 1912b.
35 See Naepels 1998, Dauphiné 1990b.

the diverse poles of colonisation. I should like to offer a few examples of these struggles to establish zones of colonial influence through interaction with the high chiefs.

My first example is the conflict between Eugène Bozon-Verduraz, chairman of the municipal committee of Houaïlou, and the Protestant missionary Maurice Leenhardt:[36] as the corps of auxiliaries departed in 1917, Bozon-Verduraz relied on Mwâdéwé to limit Leenhardt's influence, through an exchange of telegrams with the governor:

> Chief Metou [Mwâdéwé Népörö] informs me that Leenhardt asked to appoint a teacher [a Kanak Protestant evangelist] and participate expedition. The warriors decided to refuse these two men who could only be encumbrance. Believe necessary inform you of this. (Bozon-Verduraz 1978b, p. 77)

The governor's response indicates that this initiative succeeded:

> I shall not of course permit the presence among the native volunteers of persons foreign to their tribes, particularly against the will of the natives themselves. (Repiquet 1978, p. 77)

The dispute between the two men was not new:

> Our mayor is Bozon, who comes from the aristocracy of penal servitude, the supreme example that world can provide of a cold-blooded, intelligent scoundrel. (Leenhardt, Lettre à ses parents, 6 April 1916)

But the sources suggest that the conflict between the two men around the departure of the auxiliaries was heightened by the fact that Mwâdéwé held Leenhardt responsible for the first article in the *Bulletin du commerce* on 23 June 1917, cited above, in which only chiefs Mèèjâ Néjâ and Paul Wéma Nirikani were named:

> Mandéwé is angry, he thinks I wrote to Nouméa that only Mindia is offering to assist the Government, etc. (Leenhardt, Lettre à ses parents, 27–29 June 1917)

Through the conflict between Leenhardt and Bozon-Verduraz, a rivalry between Mèèjâ Néjâ and Mwâdéwé Népörö was being carried on; this was open in 1912, but had much older roots (see chapters 1 and 2). For his part, Leenhardt did indeed lean heavily on Mèèjâ Néjâ, while at

---

36 See Vasseur 1985.

the same time condemning his ambivalence and his excessive respect for the colonial administration. The welcome Mèèjâ Néjâ organised when Leenhardt arrived in Houaïlou in 1902, in an extension of his relationship with Philadelphe Delord, was particularly spectacular:

> You would not believe the welcome we received from the natives when we arrived in Houaïlou. High chief Mindia had summoned all his chiefs; the natas [Protestant evangelists] of the east coast had gathered, members of several neighbouring tribes had come to welcome the 'misher' [missionary]. And they welcomed him with the traditional ceremony, which consists in offering gifts in kind (yams, taro, chickens, pokas [pigs]) and coming to shake the hand of the guest while at the same time dropping a silver coin on a cloth spread at his feet. In Neoueo, the tribe of Mindia in Houaïlou, this salutation lasted a whole morning, and the personal greetings generated 115 francs 60 centimes. (Leenhardt 1903, p. 278)

This charmed relationship subsequently proved a source of disappointment for Leenhardt, who refused to understand Mèèjâ Néjâ's political interests in offending neither his matrimonial allies nor the administration. The first sticking point was Mèèjâ's polygamy: he had four wives. This made it impossible for him to convert.

> On Tuesday I went to see Mindia to speak to him once more about his wives. Poor Mindia ... Always two faces, the one he approves of, which speaks to us, and the one he berates and that he shows to the Whites and the heathens. (Leenhardt, Lettre à ses parents, 11 August 1916)

The administrative recognition of the high chiefs did not in any way presume that they conformed to French civil law: this was indeed a system of indirect rule, where high chief Mwâdéwé Népörö could have three wives, and high chief Paul Wéma two (according to the information in Leenhardt's census).

> It would have been very sweet to see Mindia a Christian, but I believe that if he does not change he will become more and more savage, rooted into his double life of heathen-Protestant, closed to matters of the spirit ... These native chiefs live in such fear of the local gendarme that their wits, always restricted, eventually fall into atrophy. They only give themselves to God with one eye on the Administrator, to see whether they are noticed. (Leenhardt, Lettre à ses parents, 11 September 1916)

3. THE CHIEFDOMS WITHIN THE COLONIAL ORDER

Some details drawn from the gendarmerie archives for the late 1930s offer evidence that this opposition between the administration and the missions influenced the structure of the local field, independently of the individuals occupying the offices of missionary, chief or Administrator. For example, the gendarmerie's monthly reports include reference to a conflict between a high chief and (in this case) a Catholic missionary:

> No religious conflict among the tribes, with the exception of the dispute between High Chief Paul and Reverend Father Robert. (Houaïlou Regional Squad, 1 October 1939)

This conflict was merely the visible manifestation of a broader struggle, more significant perhaps even than the conflict between Catholics and Protestants, of which there is evidence in these police reports from the late 1930s:

> [The natives] maintain good relations with the Administration and its Agents, towards whom they behave respectfully. Always show themselves willing to perform their services and meet the various requirements for labour. High Chiefs Mandaoué, Paul and Apoupia are a great support in this respect. No conflict between tribes and families. The sectarian conflict although more or less maintained unspokenly does not succeed in alienating the natives from their High Chiefs or from the Administration. To be noted that when the occasion arises the missionaries of the various denominations demonstrate their discontent with Mandaoué and Paul, who have remained completely independent and entirely won over to the Administration. Nor do we underestimate the efforts of the Administrator, who does his best to maintain their prestige, guiding them to exert healthy authority over their subjects. (Houaïlou Regional Squad, 1 September 1939)

There was real competition for control of the natives, and establishment of some authority:

> However the pernicious activity of the catechists and natas [Protestant evangelists], attempting to usurp the authority of the tribal chiefs, must be noted. They often organise tribal gatherings, with the support of the Missionaries, without informing the High Chiefs and Administrators in advance. The natives for their part do not recognise the authority of the High Chief and sometimes leave the tribe for several days without informing him. (Houaïlou Regional Squad, 2 December 1939)

Thus from this perspective, conversion can be seen as the enlistment of the convert into a group that enjoys a privileged relationship with certain European interlocutors in the local colonial field (the missionaries), and by this token distinguishes itself from other networks (gendarmes, traders, settlers). Let us consider the way in which Leenhardt describes a conversion he was particularly pleased about around the turn of the year in 1910–11:

> Something had been brewing for a month. Mindia [Mèèjâ Néjâ] was aware of it ... Tomorrow, 1st of January, Louis [Népörö Yéé] and his family are to go to the church in Warai to declare their new-found faith. After Louis, there is still Mandéwé [Mwâdéwé Népörö], who allows us to hope that he will follow later, and paganism in Houaïlou will have run its course as a Society. Louis was the principal heathen chief, and a very skilled administrator, highly regarded by the Administration. He maintained his paganism, having sworn the great oath that four tribes swore in the past never to become Christian. The conversion of Louis, the leader of all these heathens, represents the breaking of this oath, and is one of the most significant events since I have been in Houaïlou ... Mandéwé came to see me under the mango tree, and gave me some hope for the future. In the meantime, he promised to send two children from his family to our school. (Leenhardt, Lettre à ses parents, 31 December 1910)

I have been unable to find direct evidence, or any other trace, of this alleged 'oath' to refuse conversion to Christianity referred to by Leenhardt. My interest here is rather in understanding the local political stakes involved in this process of conversion, leaving aside the question of faith. The actors mentioned in this letter are all clearly identifiable: high chief Mèèjâ Néjâ, here playing the role of intermediary, Louis Népörö Yéé and Mwâdéwé Népörö. Louis, 'held in high regard by the Administration', was a chief who had indeed been recognised by France since decree no. 725 of 1 February 1905, and was awarded further stripes in 1918 and 1932. From my perspective the most important point in this text is that the 'chiefs' referred to, of the tribes of Nékwé and Warai, belong to the same clan, Népörö, and were therefore rivals for a recognition that had already proved problematic during the course of the 19th century (see Chapter 1). Moreover, there was at that time a conflict between Louis and Mwâdéwé, as Louis' wife had become Mwâdéwé's partner. In this context, where Louis was gradually losing his recognition from the authorities to Mwâdéwé, his decision to make contact with Mèèjâ Néjâ in order to draw closer to Leenhardt can clearly be seen as an attempt to find new support among the Europeans who were at that time promoting his young rival. In this context the description of Mwâdéwé's visit to Leenhardt can thus be interpreted as a way of maintaining some hold over the missionary, or at least of pre-empting his hostility. This wait-and-see attitude would, however, largely break down over the succeeding years.

Leenhardt was perforce blind to the social issues bound up in conversion since he would, and could, see only the progress of the gospel message he was bringing and the decline of 'paganism', and his missionary politics drew him into the local social field, and probably through this, resulted in the entrenchment of the conflicts between rival families. It is therefore no surprise that the end of his mission posting was marked by an extremely tense stand-off with high chief Mwâdéwé Népörö, centred on two issues: a question of land (situated in Wânii) and the issue of women captured by the Houaïlou auxiliaries during the repressive operation in the north in 1917.

Concern with the material establishment of the Dö Nèvâ mission is a constant in the messages Leenhardt sent back to France, both to his parents and to the Mission Society in Paris. In addition to the physical extension of the dormitories and classrooms, he particularly needed land for cultivation in order to feed the students.

> The question of food is at the heart of any material extension … Large expenditure would now only be justified for an invaluable property like … the fertile half of Do Néva, Ouani, which I shall purchase at any price, up to 10 or 20,000, as soon as we can, I hope for less … I have been waiting ten years for Ouani, and I shall perhaps have to wait another ten. (Leenhardt, Lettre à ses parents, 28 August 1916)

> Misher Leenhardt asks me one day to give him land to cultivate to feed everybody who will build the new house. I accepted and we gave them Nesu, Moagu, Peu, Boede. The oxen ploughed there, we planted potatoes, cassava, maize, taros, yams, vegetables etc. I supervised the work until it was finished when Misher Laffay arrived [in December 1912]. (Nérhon 1969, p. 53)

Thus a customary and administrative conflict arose between Mwâdéwé Népörö, high chief of the district concerned, and some members of the Nérhô family who had offered their customary lands for the mission's use. On the whole, the identity of the owner of a given piece of land is often far from universally agreed, given that additional and competing claims, based on the various ways of recounting the history of a place, can be adduced in relation to the same piece of land;[37] the plots in question in this case were no exception. The situation was all the more complex for Leenhardt to manage because the man who had made the land over to him, Acöömwâ Nérhô was absent at the point when the conflict arose: he had enlisted in the infantry, and served as the nurse for the Kanak contingent during the First World War.

> In November, in Nouméa I received a letter from the Administration informing me that chief Mandéwé had lodged a complaint that in his absence pupils at Do Néva had enclosed a plot of land that belonged to him, without his knowledge, and that he wished to protest as he needed this land. I replied that we had enclosed this land over ten years ago and were growing crops there by agreement with the owners, the Nérhon family, and that the chief, who was fairly new, had in fact long known about this situation, since he had asked the Nérhons to give him this land, and they had wanted to keep it … Since this land belonged to the Nérhons, I told them to stand firm and continue cultivating this land. They feared reprisals, and it was Acoma's wife who led them there, standing up to the chief alone, chasing away the animals he had sent there to graze. For three months, members of the Church, various chiefs, etc. went to speak with Mandéwé to ask him to cease his attacks. But he had the authorities on his side and that was enough for him. Three weeks ago the administrator arrived … The administrator gathered everyone together and began by declaring: 'The chief alone is master of the land.' Then there was a discussion, and he threatened the landowners with punishment if they persisted in claiming their rights, and in the evening, in view of their insistence and the intervention of one of them, a nata in Voh who had returned for this meeting and had declared himself to the Administrator on this occasion, the land was left with its owner … And since then chief Mandéwé, in whose favour he could not rule in fact, though he did so in word, has been seeking revenge against the Nérhons … But this has been a little revolution in the Warai tribe, and it has raised the question: can the Christians help Do Néva with their farming, with land or not? And the whole issue was provoked by that man Bozon and the gendarmerie he runs, as another sottish official said: 'I've got them by the throat.' The principle was acknowledged. (Leenhardt, Lettre à ses parents, 23 March 1919)

---

37 Naepels 1998.

One of the sons of high chief Mwâdéwé summed up this conflict in conversation with me:

> I heard that they argued over Mèènèkö's land, because Leenhardt took Mèènèkö's land, but they did not give it to him, so he insisted a bit … and then my father [Mwâdéwé] talked about it with Leenhardt, and that's how it was, I don't know what happened between them, they quarrelled, and then it's since that time that Leenhardt doesn't want to see the old man any longer, and the old man doesn't want to see Leenhardt any longer, but I don't really know what's at the bottom of the story. (Pierre Mandaoué, extract from interview, July 2006)

At the same time, Leenhardt was engaged in a campaign for the release of women and children captured during the repressive operations of 1917, and held by the families of the high chiefs in Houaïlou. Following several exchanges of letters, the governor initiated an inquiry and drew up a 'List of wives of rebels provisionally entrusted to the Chiefs of Bourail and Houaïlou'.[38] This notes the presence of five women and nine children under the responsibility of high chief Paul Wéma Nirikani, five women and five children held by high chief Mwâdéwé Népörö, three women and one child held by high chief Casimir Nötuö Bwéwa, and two women and one child under the responsibility of high chief Mèèjâ Néjâ, and goes on to demand that the captives be released. The response was a request for compensation in return, from three of the four high chiefs concerned, in January 1920:

> Sir
>
> We high chiefs Paul of Boréaré, Mandaoué of Ouaraïl, Notouo of Nindia, wish respectfully to inform you that in confirmity of the orders we received from the Respected Administrator of Houaïlou we have sent back the rebel women and children who were entrusted to us. Here are the numbers we had respectively: chief Paul of Boréaré, 16 persons, chief Mandaoué of Ouaraïl, 8 persons, chief Notouo of Nindia, 4 persons. Our task being complete we beg you to reimburse us for what we have spent on these rebels in both food and cloth. These expenses can be evaluated at 30 francs per month per person for two years. Hoping that you will render us justice, Mr Governor, we remain devotedly yours
>
> Mandaoué, Paul, Notouo. (Mandaoué, Paul and Notouo 1978, p. 91)

---

38 Archives of New Caledonia, 1W1.

As far as I have been able to find out, this bold initiative was not crowned with success. There is little doubt, however, that in taking action against the surveyors' tolerance of the auxiliaries' booty of captives (women and children), Maurice Leenhardt earned himself a degree of resentment among the high chiefs concerned.

The increasing complexity of the play of colonial alliances, the ever more tangled interweaving of the stakes defined at various levels, and above all the hardening of the rules of native government at this time meant that the chiefs were losing some of the freedom they had previously enjoyed in the intermediary position they occupied. The inter-war years undoubtedly constituted a period of localisation, enclosure and disappointment for many of them. The policy of appointing chiefs thus aroused bitter reactions that Leenhardt observed. Here are two examples:

> Baptiste [Cibëi, tribal chief of Gôdè], the chief, sick, easily managed by the gendarmerie, and beloved by his men, is sending his brother to the war. He told me: 'The Whites do not recognise anything. They are trying to bring me down from my position as chief, and are asking for men for the war. This is the third time I have helped them. The first time, it was my father, in the rebellion in 1878, he helps them a lot on the other coast. The second time it was me, in the Poyes war. I went myself, ready to do anything to help them. The third time, we have to go to France [for the First World War], I cannot any longer and what's more I am old and sick, but see, I am sending my brother and others with him. But the Whites do not understand that I am helping them and are trying to bring me down.' (Leenhardt, Journal, 10 February 1916)

> Bitter farewell with Mindia [Mèèjâ Néjâ]: 'I've done what I could for France, if there's anything good in Houaïlou, it comes from us. And the result? The drinkers and the bastards have the government's trust. OK, but I don't want anything more to do with them.' (Leenhardt, Lettre à son épouse Jeanne, 19 July 1918)

At the same time, the demobilisation of the First World War troops was the occasion for severe disappointment, despite the law of 4 February 1919 that allowed some Kanaks to request French citizenship (for example, those who had been awarded the Légion d'Honneur or the Croix de Guerre, non-commissioned officers, or Kanaks who had married a French woman). In fact it appears that this law was applied only in rare cases.

> The preceding considerations of themselves preclude the extension of voting rights to natives, despite the fact that some of them enlisted in the service of France in hopes of this. The following extract from a report by

3. THE CHIEFDOMS WITHIN THE COLONIAL ORDER

Mr Martin-Garnaud, surveyor, dated 28 February 1916, may be cited in this respect: 'It seems that Djouma enlisted with the conviction that he and his comrades would have citizen's rights on their return and that they would rise above the chiefs who would then no longer have authority in the tribes because they had participated in the War and thus would have the same rights as Whites.' The current social condition of the Kanaks is barely compatible with the use of the vote, and moreover overall the native population is not so demanding. (Pégourier 1919, pp. 79–80)

Pégourier's remarks, which are nevertheless highly critical of the functioning of the Native Affairs Department, show the breadth of the gap between the colonial administration's perception of the situation and that of the Kanaks who sought to increase their spaces of freedom. Thus, on his return from France, Acöömwâ Nérhô wrote a letter to the governor on behalf of the troops from the Houaïlou districts, dated 28 December 1919:

We ask you, Mr Governor, to make us naturalised French citizens, or to tell us what law you give us so that we are not obliged to remain always under the same barbarian leadership as in some tribes. (Nérhon 1969, pp. 66–67)

It is clear here how the demand for civil rights, which for the soldiers was a reward for their service to France (which cost the lives of one third of the Houaïlou volunteers), was also linked to the desire to no longer be subject to the indirect rule represented by the high chiefdoms – 'the same barbarian leadership'. In the case of Acöömwâ Nérhô, this demand went alongside a conflict over land which brought Nérhô and the Protestant mission into contention with the high chief of his district.

The thinking that evaluated chiefdoms on the basis of their capacity for mobilising men, including for military purposes, was the dominant factor in the appointment of chiefs for over half a century. The approach to the Second World War was one of the last occasions on which the situation was assessed in these terms; the positioning of the high chiefs in the local colonial field was then the occasion for renewed affirmation of their alliance with the administration, in a historical continuity underlined by the indirect allusion to the old conflicts between Mwâdéwé and Leenhardt:

At the recent monthly meeting of the high chiefs of the districts, the chiefs asked if the Administration was planning to recruit volunteers for the War from among the natives. These worthies offered apologies for the difficulties encountered during the last war, which according to them were due to the pernicious influence of a missionary who had almost managed to prevent the departure of the volunteer troops, and declared in essence: 'Despite the baneful and occult part played by this adversary, we were still there, we the Chiefs.' High Chief Mandaoué made a point of adding: 'We shall still be here, if necessary, when I give my word has still more weight despite everything that of those who would like to see the high chiefs divested of their authority among the natives.' (Houaïlou Regional Squad, 31 October 1939)

Thus, in Houaïlou the interaction between the chiefdoms and the colonial power continued to centre on war for more than a century, as the needs of the administration interwove with the local social issues pursued by the chiefs. But their capacity to mobilise men was also increasingly deployed toward ever tighter and more consistent control of the segregated spaces of Kanak co-residence.

Public health and Kanak war

The network of tribal and high chiefs during the first half of the 20th century was a way of managing the colonial order that entrusted the chiefs with most of the work of supervision and maintaining order. This was, however, not only a policing system and was not limited to the capacity for mobilisation of warriors that that entailed. It was also a public health regime.[39] The policy of demolishing straw huts and replacing them with wattle and daub houses, first introduced in the late 19th century and imposed still more vigorously between the wars, is well known: 'There is a very pronounced trend to move from huts made of niaouli bark, which are dark, dirty and poorly ventilated, to large square huts with verandahs, with whitewashed earth walls, both light and well ventilated' (Lebœuf 1912a, p. 134). This policy was based on an entirely fallacious analysis of the fall in population. The terrible irony of the policy in the Houaïlou region is that it led to the whitewashing of the new wattle and daub houses with a locally available white clay, tremolite, a form of asbestos that leads to pleural cancer rates among the highest in the world.[40] The decree of 20 September 1911, on protection of public health, stated: 'Isolation is compulsory for all patients suffering from one of the following: Cholera. Plague. Yellow fever. Smallpox. Leprosy. Recurrent fever' (Article 6).

---

39 See Thomas 1990.
40 Luce et al. 1994 and 2000; Goldberg et al. 1995. On the effects of colonial policies on indigenous mortality, see Davis 2001.

The chiefs were also involved in managing major epidemics, particularly of leprosy. The arrival of these new diseases was interpreted locally in the terms of a Kanak war. This is particularly striking in relation to the epidemic of plague that hit Houaïlou in 1912.

1912–13: Plague

Analysis of the epidemic of plague that arrived in New Caledonia in the latter part of 1912 was extremely limited, and very few general data are available. It broke out in Nouméa in September–October 1912, prompting the issue of decree no. 991 of 22 October 1912, 'setting out the measures to be taken against individuals suspected of suffering from plague'. It arrived in the upper Houaïlou valley in December 1912, specifically affecting the Nérâ tribe:

> Alas, the plague is at our door. It has just broken out in Nérin, in the upper part of the valley, and in Gondé. An old couple were the first to die in Nérin, a remote village close by an abandoned pass, with no communication with Nouméa or with the outside … The doctor is up there and in Nouméa Dr Leboeuf has succeeded in making a good serum that gives protection for five months. (Leenhardt, Lettre à ses parents, 20 December 1912)

> [In December 1912, Paul Laffay arrived in Houaïlou.] Two days later, the Christians of the region came to welcome him. Those from outside, alas, had been prevented from coming by the prohibition on travel that struck the island's natives when plague was declared in Nouméa. This did not prevent the disease moving in one bound to break out in the upper Houaïlou valley, in a remote location, where its appearance remains a great mystery. The natas [Kanak Protestant evangelists] from the mountain, who were in Do-Néva at that moment, hastened back to their churches, in order to be with their flocks in these solemn times of abandonment to God. Dr Béros worked tirelessly to halt the evil, and signalled the end of the epidemic while being himself very seriously ill, in the tribe of Boréaré. (Leenhardt 1913)

The epidemic claimed seven victims in Nérâ and two in Gôdè;[41] it was halted by a vaccination campaign.[42] The experience of this epidemic is today interpreted locally as the manifestation of a Kanak war, within a discursive framework that analyses it in terms of sorcery, with the deaths from the plague representing the resolution of prior conflicts:

> It's not a war here, but it's, how can I put it? Plague … It's war, in a way, but it's medicine [the action of sorcery]. People died, it's incredible … But when the sickness, the plague came, it cleansed the tribe. (Lévi Cibëi, extract from interview, October 1991)

On 28 August 1913 Dùré Bwérhéxéu was appointed tribal chief of Nérin, even though he was living in Gôdé.[43] This appointment was interpreted by several of my interlocutors as a mark of the role he played in protecting the inhabitants of Nérâ from the threat of the plague.

Leprosy

While Houaïlou saw only one episode of plague, the role of the high chiefs was much more marked in the control of lepers, for this disease required permanent isolation of those affected. In 1889 four leper colonies were created in New Caledonia, in Nouméa, Maré, Canala and Cap Bocage; that is, in Houaïlou.[44] The three colonies outside of Nouméa were abandoned when it was decided, in 1892, to consign the lepers to Art Island, in the Bélep archipelago (the obligation to do so was enshrined in the decree of 22 September 1893). Criticism of the Bélep leper colony led to the reopening of the other places of confinement.[45] Article 27 of the decision of 9 August 1898, on the organisation of the Native Affairs Department and, more generally, on the modalities of government of natives, which conferred on the high chiefs the responsibility for isolating lepers in the sites reserved for them, directly concerned Houaïlou, which was a one of the main sites of isolation of lepers.

---

41 Doucet 1913, p. 894; Béros and Bocquillon 1913, p. 927.
42 Lebœuf 1913, p. 909.
43 Archives of New Caledonia, 97W18.
44 Baré 1939.
45 For example Pierre 1898.

The visit of the medical officer of the colonial troops, Dr Lebœuf,[46] reveals how the chiefs approached this task:

> Currently all of them together [here he is discussing Boréaré, Karaxërë and Kula] have eight official lepers, efficiently isolated 8 kilometres from Boréaré. My inspection revealed a total of 11 lepers (8 official and 3 new ones) and 3 suspected cases. This represents approximately 4%. As regards the three new lepers, chief Paul could in no way be accused of negligence: if he could have confirmed the diagnosis of these three patients, he would certainly have isolated them straight away. But it should be noted that the Kanak resolves to accept a firm diagnosis, for himself or one of his fellows, only when the disease is blatantly evident to all, even the least experienced. (Lebœuf 1912a, pp. 133–34)

Lebœuf's visit also revealed that the Cap Bocage leper colony had been almost completely abandoned: the number of inhabitants had fallen from 53 in late 1901 to two in late 1911. Lebœuf therefore proposed a reorganisation of the isolation facilities, and the establishment of four leper colonies in Houaïlou, one per district: in 'Kananon' [Kananu] for Néouyo district, in 'Kouareu' for Nindien district, in 'Néouin-Néoué' or 'Riga-Thû' in Warai district (and we may assume that the colony in Boréaré, referred to above, remained the fourth):

> The high chiefs and tribal chiefs discussed these various sites at a meeting I called prior to my departure from Houaïlou, which was held at the office of the Administrator of Native Affairs. He informed them of the terms of the most recent circular from the Native Affairs Department relative to measures to be taken against leprosy: the various points of this document were explained to them in detail. They grasped the spirit of it perfectly. (Lebœuf 1912b, p. 351)

In his 1919 report, Pégourier included a table showing the 'segregation of native lepers in 31 leper colonies', as of 30 September 1918. Out of the total of 322 people interned in Grande Terre (293 from the Dependencies, Loyalty Islands and Isle of Pines), the largest number were in Houaïlou (62, not including the 36 in Koné and the 35 in Canala).[47] It is difficult to determine whether this situation was due to a real increase in the number of sufferers in Houaïlou, or whether it is accounted for by the high chiefs' improved capacity for identifying sufferers and forcing them to reside in leper colonies. Nor is it known whether the four colonies suggested

---

46   Lebœuf 1912a, 1912b and 1914.
47   Pégourier 1919, p. 37.

by Lebœuf were actually established. Decree no. 610 of 12 July 1921[48] set out a new organisational structure for isolation, with the creation of 'segregation villages':[49] Kananu was the one so designated for Houaïlou. But, by 1938, apart from the Ducos Sanatorium in Nouméa, there were effectively only two special agricultural villages on the east coast, in Hienghène and Houaïlou, and four on the Loyalty Islands. The village of Kananu 'in principle receives all the lepers from the South part of the East Coast' (Baré 1939, p. 186).

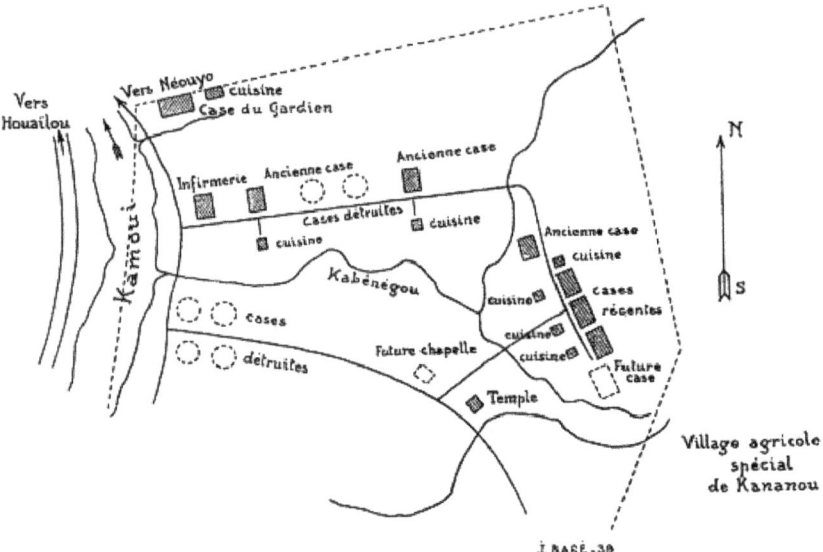

Figure 6. Plan of the partial leper colony of Kananu
Source: Baré 1939, p. 188; © Bibliothèque interuniversitaire de santé (Interuniversity Health Library) (Paris).

Christine Salomon has shown how the new diseases imported by the Europeans or through exchanges linked to colonisation became incorporated locally into Kanak medical knowledge, through a redefined aetiology.[50] Specialists in interpretation and healing were called upon, such as Kavimùrù Néröö, a seer (*mèrhî*) from Néawa:

---

48 Following on from decree no. 664 of 1 July 1913, which specified the conditions for internment of lepers.
49 See Genevray 1925, p. 173.
50 Salomon 2000a.

> Kavimuru (who is wrong, is mistaken) from Néawawa is a mèrsi (spirit chaser, exorcists, seer etc.). A remedy for leprosy was revealed to him. He announced it, treated patients, and even went to the Mévégon [Cap Bocage] leper colony to treat those interned there. He received dollars, Caledonian money, a horse from Mindia's stable etc., and died a rich man while his patients wasted away. (Leenhardt, Journal, 20 March 1915)

I shall consider other modes of intervention by such specialists into local social relationships, also in the Néawa tribe, in the next chapter (see Chapter 4). For all it was segregated, the space of the leper colonies was none the less integrated in a social space characteristic of local social life. There is evidence of this in the conflict that broke out in the Kananu leper colony in 1937, which involved, in addition to a group of residents, the Catholic missionary of Nindia [Néajië] and the gendarme, administrator of native affairs:

> 14 October 1937
>
> re: influence of Father Robert on the state of mind of the natives.
>
> I have the honour of reporting that on Monday 11th inst. the native Hmana, warden of the Kananu leper colony, presented himself at the office and made the following declaration:
>
> Last Thursday seventh October, in the morning, Father Robert from the Catholic Mission in Nindia came to say Mass as usual. When the service was over, he went to the house of Poukou Diopéri [Jöpéri Pûkiu], an interned patient, and accosted him, forbidding him from smoking, then called him a thief because he had married a Catholic woman in the leper colony. Poukou, vexed by the priest's offensive attitude, replied that he was not a thief, etc … The internees who were present at this scene egged Poukou on against the priest, but this patient, who was by nature calmer and older than the others, stopped short of assaulting Father Robert. Nevertheless, I have to inform you that the Catholic and Protestant patients are displeased.
>
> I feel it is my duty to make you aware of this state of affairs, which could have disagreeable consequences for this priest, who is excessively abusive towards Protestants. Proceeding to an inquiry into the facts reported by the warden, yesterday 13th October, as I was passing through the leper colony I interrogated the native Poukou, who declared:
>
> 'Thursday seventh October last Father Robert entered my dwelling. First he told me, in a cutting tone of voice, that if I smoked I would go to hell. Then, he said that I had stolen my wife Boisseba who belonged to

the Catholic faith before she married me. I pointed out to this priest that I was in no way a thief. He immediately objected that if I did not want to be called one, I should become a Catholic, or else I would go to hell like all Protestants. I admit that I was very angry at this attitude of Father Robert, as were my fellow-Protestants in the leper colony, who I did not want even to listen to, they wanted me to take revenge on the priest. When he left the leper colony Father Robert told me he was going to lodge a complaint with the gendarme and the doctor.'

… The patients in the leper colony wholeheartedly condemn Father Robert's behaviour toward the patient Poukou, who moreover is the son of the late Mindia, High Chief of Houaïlou, who was respected and idolised by all his subjects, and the brother of Apoupia, the current High Chief of the district of Néouyo. (Houaïlou Regional Squad, 14 October 1937)

We do not know all the intricacies of the dispute over this marriage. But we shall see in the following chapter that another brother-in-law of chief Apupia was at the centre of the conflict aroused by the visit of seers to the tribe of Néawa in 1955 (see Chapter 4). I believe we might reasonably imagine a link between these successive conflicts, and hypothesise a historical density of disputes that we perceive here only through a few snapshots in time and some imprecise documents. In this context, the understanding the Kanak inhabitants of Houaïlou had of the diseases themselves as continuations of war by other means makes complete sense. Similarly, the intervention of chiefs in the control of patients takes on a certain polemical dimension whose importance was undoubtedly not perceived by the gendarmes and French colonial doctors.

The invention of the 'council of elders'

As we saw, many auxiliary troops from Houaïlou participated in a major repressive operation in 1917, under the leadership of their chiefs. But the protest against the colonial presence in the north of Grande Terre in 1917, 40 years after the great colonial war of 1878, prompted a reflection focused on reform of this leadership throughout New Caledonia. While the network of indirect administration through high and tribal chiefdoms was established, the aim was to adapt colonial government more precisely to what was perceived of Kanak social realities, in order to refine it and render it more efficient.

The Pégourier report

In 1919 Pégourier, an inspector of colonies,[51] proposed a reform of the Native Affairs Department. This expert in colonial affairs, author of a thesis on *The Political and Administrative Régime of the French Colonies under the Restoration and the July Monarchy*,[52] 'a Polytechnique graduate[53] enamoured of social ideas, anti-democratic, pro-oligarchic' (Leenhardt, Lettre à ses parents, 3 December 1918), had been tasked with understanding the most recent crisis to shake the colony, the uprising in the north in 1917. His report ended with a draft decree on the status of natives; one of his most important proposals was that the structure of the high chiefdoms of districts and the tribal chiefdoms be reinforced through 'tribal councils'. In this draft decree, which was to remain at that stage, Pégourier proposed the following articles: 'The internal Administration of the tribe is entrusted, under the direction and supervision of the French authorities, to the chief, assisted by the Council of his tribe' (Article 41); 'The chief is appointed by the Governor on the basis of a recommendation from the Council of the tribe' (Article 42) (Pégourier 1919, p. 64); 'A Council, composed of tribal chiefs and members who may be appointed and dismissed by the Administration, and chaired by the high chief, shall be required to deliberate on the following matters' (there follows a list: punishment, internal police, services, contracts) (Pégourier 1919, p. 65).

He then suggested that a concept from the colonial lexicon that had been present in New Caledonia since the first days of colonisation be incorporated into the laws relating to natives. His report cites two documents: a report by Antoine Martin-Garnaud – the same Houaïlou surveyor who led the Houaïlou auxiliaries, with Nicolas Ratzel, in 1917 – and a text by a colonial lawyer:

> They [the tribal chiefs], together with a number of dignitaries, form the Council of the tribe, a very important body, which also serves as a court, and whose composition varies from one district to another (see note appended from Mr Martin Garnaud, Surveyor, dated 28 February 1916).
>
> According to Mr Girault (*Principes de colonisation et de législation coloniale* [*Principles of Colonisation and Colonial Legislation*], vol. II, p. 138), since the tribes live in a state of continual hostility, there is no security for the

---

51   Peripatetic official tasked with monitoring French colonies [trans.].
52   Pégourier 1913.
53   Graduate of the École Polytechnique, elite engineering school in Paris [trans.].

individual outside of his tribe. Even within the tribe disputes end with a battle, when the council of elders is unable to reconcile the interested parties. (Pégourier 1919, pp. 20 and 40)

The Algerian model

In a classic study on Algeria, Philippe Lucas and Jean-Claude Vatin sought to examine and understand the language of description used by the first 'ethnographers' of colonial Algeria: soldiers who sought to identify and know their adversaries better, and subsequently the administrators in charge of governing them, or rather of establishing a system of indirect government – the infamous 'Arab bureaux' – based on local nobility, traditional aristocracy, the high chiefs (*khalifa*, *agha*) and the tribes (with their tribal chiefs, the *qaid*). It was in part in opposition to this first model that what has been called the 'Kabyle myth',[54] which emphasised the local importance of village meetings and councils of dignitaries (*djemaa*), was constructed. According to Lucas and Vatin, the reason for this interest was the fact that, in the 1850s, Kabylia became the epicentre of Algerian conflicts; it ultimately resulted in one of the founding texts in the description of Kabyle social practices, Adolphe Hanoteau and Aristide Letourneux's *La Kabylie et les coutumes kabyles* (*Kabylia and Kabyle Customs*), which became the 'Berber Napoleonic Code'.[55] Thus, the perception of Algerian political organisation was structured by a two-sided model that contrasted Arab despotism with Kabyle democracy. Let us consider an example cited by Lucas and Vatin:

> Their political and social constitution is also very different from that of the Arab people ... Rather than the despotic patriarchy that crushes individual freedom, we find a democratic organisation that is its polar opposite. Each tribe constitutes a sort of large municipality, whose interests are managed by a council elected at meetings in which all adult men participate. A chief, a sort of mayor or president of the Djemmâ, also elected for a specified period of time, governs under the supervision of the council, polices the community, renders justice in accordance with customs, or with qanuns much more often than with the prescriptions of the Qur'an. (Pomel, *Des races indigènes de l'Algérie et du rôle que leur réservent leurs aptitudes* (*On the Native Races in Algeria and the Role Their Aptitudes Fit Them For*), Oran, 1871, cited in Lucas and Vatin 1975 pp. 132–33)

---

54 Ageron 1991; see Mahé 2001.
55 Hanoteau and Letourneux 1872–73.

Lucas and Vatin's analysis is remarkably striking when compared to the New Caledonian case, since the same conceptual vocabulary was used in New Caledonia, and the same implicit models were drawn upon first to describe Kanak society, and then in the organisation of native government – in particular the opposition between the model of the chiefdom (despotic) and the language of the council of elders (democratic), the two articulated in a feudal synthesis (with the chief as *primus inter pares*, and the council made up of an 'aristocracy' of 'elders' or 'dignitaries', or constituting a 'Senate'). The council combined with the chiefdom appears in all the major descriptions of New Caledonia from the second half of the 19th century. This is Victor Rochas, naval surgeon, in 1862:

> And as regards government, it should be known that in all important situations, the subaltern chiefs, who constitute the nation's aristocracy and enjoy privileges almost as extensive as those of the high chief himself over the little people, are called to council. The matter is discussed and decided collectively. In this barbarian senate, the sovereign certainly holds the greatest sway, but the principal lords, the war chief or chief general, and finally the old men, have great authority. Each tribe may be considered a little feudal state. (Rochas 1862, p. 244)

Here are Eugène Vieillard and Émile Deplanche, surgeons in the imperial navy, in 1863:

> Nevertheless, a declaration of war must be submitted to the high council, which has the final decision …
>
> In certain circumstances all the chiefs and some individuals belonging to the noble caste, particularly the old men known for their bravery and their wisdom, form a sort of council at which questions of general interest are discussed, such as a declaration of war, a peace treaty, the appointment of a regent etc. Opinions are freely expressed, the matter is argued, and then dealt with in accordance with the majority opinion …
>
> Among the various chiefs, if there is one who is senior in terms of the length of his noble line, the spread of his tribe, his wealth, his courage, he dominates over the others, he commands in war, in the council. (Vieillard and Deplanche 1863, pp. 68, 70 and 71)

And this is Ulysse de la Haütière in 1869:

> Each Caledonian tribe has a sort of meeting that we shall call the council, for if the chief is sometimes obliged to hear its opinion – for example, when there is a question of declaring war – he nevertheless commands as he sees fit. (de la Haütière 1869, pp. 76–78).

Writing in 1872, Jules Patouillet makes no reference to the 'council of elders', but does refer to the 'feudal period' (Patouillet 1872, p. 139) in which the Kanaks live. These descriptions are similar enough that, in 1894, the council appears in a compendium, *L'archipel de Nouvelle-Calédonie* (*The New Caledonia Archipelago*) written by Augustin Bernard, then a young teaching fellow at the École supérieure (college) in Algiers, who went on to become a renowned geographer and helped to circulate models of understanding of colonised people through the French Empire: 'He [the chief] is supported by a council of elders which assists him' (Bernard 1894, p. 291). Finally, this descriptive ambivalence is summed up perfectly by Jean-Baptiste-Maurice Vincent in his 1895 book *Les Canaques de la Nouvelle-Calédonie* (*The Kanaks of New Caledonia*), where he says: 'Their chief is an autocrat whose tyranny is tempered by the council of elders' (Vincent 1895, p. 26).

It is thus evident that the language of sociological description applied to local populations with which the French military and administrators arrived in the second half of the 19th century was – like the military techniques – the product of the circulation of colonial models largely forged in Algeria. It is of course impossible to judge the empirical pertinence of such a concept a century and a half later; all we can do is point out that it is a sign of the fact that the concept of despotism was inadequate, that the chiefs did discuss matters with other individuals, that they were not despots but political subjects who needed supporters and constructed relations of power. This does not, however, mean that a permanent institutional body, a 'council' or an 'assembly', sat alongside them. Moreover, one of the central elements of later anthropological descriptions of local political organisation, the balance between the chiefs and the 'founding ancestors' or 'masters of the land',[56] is entirely absent from these descriptions: the fact that these descriptions of a 'council of elders' date from long past is no guarantee that they are either apposite or accurate.

Evidence nowhere to be found

The most striking point is how little legal use was made of this concept in the organisation of native government, despite its omnipresence in the colonial lexicon. In the infamous decree of 24 December 1867, which

---

56   See Leenhardt 1937a, Guiart 1963, Bensa 1992, Naepels 1998.

3. THE CHIEFDOMS WITHIN THE COLONIAL ORDER

instituted the legal existence of the native tribe (in the sense of a collective political unit led by a chief),[57] the existence of a council of elders is barely implied in the preamble, through a reference to 'councillors': 'It is headed by a high chief, supported by village chiefs and councillors whom he chooses from among the most influential men.'

But, while lists of chiefs were progressively compiled over the next 50 years, to the point where they formed the comprehensive network of the Kanak population living on reservations that I described above, no further reference is made to any council of elders or old men in the legal texts. In the debates on the demarcation of Kanak lands in 1876 the wavering between chiefdom and council of elders re-emerges, and is resolved by the unanswerable affirmation of the colonial usefulness of the chiefdom:

> The influence of the chiefs is not absolute, being tempered by the councils of elders. These councils are, admittedly, not yet organised as a regular administrative form, but nevertheless represent an authority and are always consulted. It is by organising these sorts of councils that any arbitrary elements will be removed from the power of the chief, who must imperatively remain the representative of the tribe he leads vis-à-vis the administration, the work of the latter being thus simplified, and its intervention facilitated and delegated. (Privy Council, 6 January 1876)

Finally, in the two principal texts by governor Paul Feillet – that of 24 October 1897 which instituted the high chiefs, and that of 9 August 1898, under which the Native Affairs Department was organised around high chiefs of districts and junior tribal chiefs – no reference is made to the council of elders. It therefore has to be concluded that while both tribal and high chiefs were central elements in the functioning of colonial administration, aspects of which I have sketched in this chapter, no 'council' was deemed necessary to colonial governance: the interface between the chief, who bore the burden of obligation and enjoyed the concomitant privilege of arbitrary colonial power, was sufficient for the administration. And Pégourier's proposal for a more 'democratic' reform at local level bore no fruit.

---

57 Rather than in the sense of a Kanak village implanted in a reservation, which was a later local (and extra-legal) development of the term.

This tension between a 'council', which appears in many descriptions but yet is absent from the legal structure, is apparent in law scholar Éric Rau's very strange account of the council of elders, in a book where he attempts to codify Kanak customs. Firstly, he returns to Vieillard and Deplanche's analyses, cited above, and that of Victor de Rochas, while at the same time referring to a work of fiction by Georges Baudoux. The result is a massive confusion as to how the council might have operated, and Rau's consequent inability to codify the 'customs' he seeks to describe:

> From time immemorial, Kanak chiefs have had, for their government, Councillors and Councils. But the choice of the former and the composition of the latter essentially varies with each tribe and each chief. ...
>
> This High Council or Council of Elders comprised – both in former times [Rau refers to Vieillard and Deplanche 1869, p. 479, and Rochas 1862, p. 244] and today – all the chiefs of the vassal tribes, the ministers, old men belonging to the noble caste and reputed for their bravery and their wisdom. In a word, all the influential individuals of the tribe. But it also included – in former times especially – sorcerers [Rau refers to Baudoux 1928, p. 98] who were responsible for taking the auspices. In this sort of 'barbarian Senate' [the term is from Rochas], the matter was verbally introduced by the Chief, and was the subject of long debate; the decision, according to Vieillard and Deplanche, was taken by majority vote [note by Rau: Since the opinion of a great lord could equate to that of 4 or 5 lesser personages, this is a very particular kind of majority. Often, moreover, no decision is taken.] (Rau 1944, pp. 65 and 66)

Rau also states that the council was recognised by the colonial administration in a way that is doubly problematic. First, he describes the administrative organisation of the tribe: the chiefs, 'assisted by the council of elders ... maintain order in the tribe – decision of 9 August 1898, Articles 22 and 24' (Rau 1944, p. 71). In fact there is no mention of the council in this 1898 decree, either in the articles cited or elsewhere. Rau goes on to add: 'In the recruitment of chiefs too, the Administration to some extent follows the traditional rules we have considered. Is a high chief to be appointed? It leaves the task of nominating the candidate for the office of chief to the council of elders' (Rau 1944, p. 72). To back up this statement, for which there is no empirical evidence, he refers to another work of fiction, *À bord de l'Incertaine* (*Aboard the Incertaine*), by Jean Mariotti. Thus Rau offers a perfect illustration, in the New Caledonian context, of Lucas and Vatin's assessment of Algeria: 'The colonial head still weighs heavy on knowledge about Algeria' (Lucas and Vatin 1975, p. 7).

3. THE CHIEFDOMS WITHIN THE COLONIAL ORDER

***

Taking the division of the high chiefdom of Houaïlou into four in 1912 as my starting point, I have attempted to grasp the contrasting perspectives of the various actors in the colonial field in Houaïlou, by following the interactions between one section of the Houaïlou chiefs with the colonial administration during the period from 1897 (when Paul Feillet formalised the institution of high chiefdoms) to 1917 (when the four high chiefs of Houaïlou mobilised men for the repressive operation conducted in Koné and Hienghène), and then in the inter-war period, drawing on colonial sources but also on the remarkably rich Papiers Mindia. This has helped to reveal the development of the forms of colonial war, and also to understand how the management of both leprosy and plague could appear locally as the continuation of war by other means. Finally, this line of research serves as an entry point for perceiving the ways in which the colonial field was constituted in a small rural community, and the construction of a form of government that then dispensed with the legal framework of the 'council of elders' despite the fact that this was conceptually available in the Algerian lexicon.

4
Post-*indigénat* Mobilisations

I continue my exploration of the various forms of collective mobilisation by way of an analysis of the institution of the council of elders, and of witchcraft, as the pursuit of war by other means. These two strands of analysis, which have already been identified in the preceding chapters (see chapters 2 and 3), become entwined in a violent incident involving a number of Houaïlou tribes in late November and December 1955. This was the visit of diviners (*jauu*), invited to expose individuals believed to hold 'bad medicine' – in other words, powers of attack and sorcery.

In order to grasp all the intricacies of this affair, we first need to take into account the major political changes that accompanied the end of the *indigénat* system in 1946, and the gradual integration of Kanaks into the community of citizens in New Caledonia, which was completed with the 1956 enabling legislation and the parliamentary elections of 1957. In Houaïlou, this decade was a period of intense collective mobilisation in various forms, derived in particular from the presence of the Protestant mission in Dö Nèvâ, in the lower Houaïlou valley.

Interests and investments of various orders – political (in faith organisations and later in a party, the Union Calédonienne (Caledonian Union)), economic (through the establishment of cooperatives), customary (with the institution of councils of elders), and symbolic (in the search for, and putting out of action, those presumed to hold powers of attack) – were thus brought together, often through the local mobilisation of the same individuals.

1945–54: Administrative reform and Protestant mobilisation

The end of the *indigénat* and local autonomy

Following on from limited earlier studies on the subject,[1] three recent works offer a fuller understanding of the stakes involved in the transformation of New Caledonian political life just after the Second World War.[2] The right to vote, granted under the order of 22 August 1945 to certain categories of Kanaks (war veterans, chiefs, pastors and religious instructors – in total, 1,144 individuals), the creation of the New Caledonian Communist Party on 15 January 1946, the abolition of the *indigénat* system and the head tax in February 1946, the ending of requisitioned forced labour in April 1946 and, finally, the abolition of designated residence in May 1946, radically altered the jurisdictional landscape as a whole and, hence, also the roles of chiefs in village life (see Chapter 3). In the Houaïlou region, Denis Rousseau won a majority in the municipal elections of May 1947; the first Kanak was also elected to the municipal council, in the person of high chief Mandaoué (see Chapter 3). Moreover, Houaïlou was one of the places in Grande Terre with the highest levels of Communist Party activism, largely through veterans of the two world wars. Wakubwa Mârârhëë was one such, among many others:

> There up there, that's my grandfather, he was the communist activist in Néawa, my grandfather who was in 14–18, Wakubwa [Mârârhëë] there. (Ivô Mârârhëë, extract from interview, July 1995)

While it has often been noted that the Kanaks' demands for citizenship were voiced by war veterans, both between the wars and after 1945, in my view the importance of ideological motives for joining the Communist Party has sometimes been overestimated: in the accounts I have collected the greatest weight is given to the condemnation of forced labour:

> — Can you tell me how things were with the New Caledonian Communist Party in Houaïlou?
>
> It started in 1945, around then, it was the volunteers, those who did their service in Caledonia ... And in the army, they made the most of it to get all the soldiers on side, and when the soldiers were demobilised, they

---

1 Guiart 1966; Saussol 1979; Dornoy 1984.
2 Soriano 2001, see also Soriano 2000; Kurtovitch 2002, see also Kurtovitch 1997; Trépied 2010, see also Trépied 2007.

4. POST-*INDIGÉNAT* MOBILISATIONS

came here to the bush ... That party did some good things at that time, because it was that party that got rid of compulsory service and taxes ... whereas before we paid tax, and we had to do two weeks' service on the roads. (Guynemer Karé, extract from interview, August 1993)

They decided to come to Nouméa to get a Communist Party card ... When they arrived in Nouméa, they went to see a lady called Mrs Tunica ... and they were received by her secretary, they explained their problem, they said they had come from Houaïlou to get a Communist Party membership card, and then they complained that in Houaïlou there they were doing forced labour, all of that, they complained ... The secretary fixed them a meeting for the next morning, so the next morning, they were received by the lady, and that was it, they went off with their cards. Maybe they stayed two days, then afterwards they came back to Houaïlou, they had their Communists' cards. The instructions they had been given, they had to go straight to the gendarmerie and show the card, there was a letter, plus their Communist Party membership cards, they had to go to the gendarmerie, then show that to the gendarmes, and then say to the gendarmes that there was no question of them working any more because they were communists, they had their cards. And then in Houaïlou, that really put the cat among the pigeons, in Gwarawi for example the chief, he got angry, he said, talking about grandfather: 'But that one, I'm not going to let him walk all over me, he'll see what'll happen.' But everyone was waiting because they didn't really know how things would turn out, so then the three elders came ... they went home in the evening, they had a bit of a rest, then in the night, they walked, they arranged to meet at two o'clock in the morning, there at the edge of the village ... They went back to the gendarmerie, and then Tèn's dad [Bwéwé] gives the letter to the gendarme, and then the gendarme takes the letter, then he reads it, then when he's finished reading he looks at Tèn's dad, and he says to him: 'So you're a communist?' then the other old man says like grandfather: 'Yes me communist'. The gendarme, he looks at the letter, he says: 'OK, off you go home, you don't have to work.' So that meant they left there, then they went home, grandfather still tells me: 'There I arrived in Pwèi, there [a hamlet in the Gwarawi tribe], everyone was there with their pickaxes'; when the people saw him coming they said to him: 'So what did the gendarme say?' So he took out his card: 'Well, you see my card, me I'm a communist, I went to the gendarme, then the gendarme asked me if I'm a communist, but I told him: "Yes, me communist", he said to me: "Off you go home, you don't have to do any more forced labour".' So everybody dropped their pickaxes on the worksite, and then everyone went to get the car to go to Nouméa to get a membership card. That's how the system collapsed, you know, everyone ran away from forced labour. Well, it was a minor incident, if you like, but a fine story, because the chief was furious, he didn't know what to do, but everyone abandoned him, all at once, nobody worked any more. That's pretty much how forced labour sort of broke down, because everybody joined the Communist Party, and you can understand it's in that spirit that UICALO and the Union Calédonienne were formed afterwards, you know. (Narcisse Kaviyöibanu, extract from interview, February 1999)

These interviews reveal firstly that the system of compulsory service, under the coordinated management of the gendarmes and the chiefs, continued to operate after it was officially abolished, and that it was only through the mediation of Communist Party membership that it was ended in practice. The last extract also offers evidence that the ending of this system represented a direct challenge to the authority of the chief, implying a re-evaluation of the status and rights of each individual in village life. It is estimated that in 1947 there were more than 150 Kanak members of the Caledonian Communist Party in Houaïlou. This striking success in freeing themselves locally from the oppressive disciplinary structures of colonial governmentality prompted a sharp reaction from both the Catholic and the Protestant missions, which had until then adapted to the colonial order. This story is well known, from the creation of the Union des indigènes calédoniens amis de la liberté dans l'ordre (the Catholic UICALO) in 1946 to the establishment of the Association des indigènes calédoniens et loyaltiens français (the Protestant AICLF)[3] in January 1947. The UICALO was set up at the initiative of Father François Luneau, who had been a missionary in Houaïlou (in Néajië) before settling in Canala. He thus succeeded in recruiting large numbers of the Catholics in Houaïlou: at the UICALO delegates' meeting in May 1948 there were 150 members from Houaïlou. In September 1948 Roch Pidjot and Luc Wadé, respectively the chairman and secretary of the organisation, visited Houaïlou on behalf of UICALO. On the Protestant side, Houaïlou, as the headquarters of the mission on Grande Terre since the time of Maurice Leenhardt, was naturally directly involved in the establishment of the AICLF; the arrival of a very active young missionary, Raymond Charlemagne, at the Dö Nèvâ mission in May 1947, helped to strengthen the Association. There is evidence of this in the numerous association meetings that took place there (for example the general meeting of 27–30 July 1951 in Mèènèkö, that of 13–15 May 1952 in Nédivâ, that of 10–13 September in Lèwèö, and that of 10–12 September 1960 in

---

3   UICALO: Union of Native Caledonian Friends of Freedom with Order; AICLF: Association of French Caledonian and Loyalty Natives [trans.].

Ba). One of Pastor Charlemagne's first articles in the AICLF newspaper, *Le Messager* (*The Messenger*), concludes with this peroration, remarkable for its condescension, explicitly addressed to the communist lost sheep:

> The Association offers you another way: its aim is to preserve the life of the great native family, to preserve its houses and its lands, in order to remain free. Pride makes a person blind: you have to be able to see your weaknesses and shortcomings too. You want to walk alone, but there are many obstacles on the road ahead; you are the child who has let go of his father's hand and is going to fall. (Charlemagne 1948b)

The great fear of native communism led the two missions to take on some of the Kanaks' demands, and thus become involved in the process of renewal of political life that followed the collapse of colonial governmentality. For example, as has been noted, they contributed directly to the birth of the Union Calédonienne. From the Kanak point of view, in the late 1940s and early 1950s the AICLF and UICALO became sites of mobilisation, debate and political development within which the Kanaks sought to strengthen the autonomy they were gradually acquiring, and to construct it in positive forms. Éric Soriano, Ismet Kurtovitch and Benoît Trépied, in the recent studies cited above, have identified the stages and stakes involved in the Kanaks' entry into political life, and examined the contradictions that dominated the development of the Union Calédonienne's programs and the individual careers of some elected deputies. Here I return to the subject only in an attempt to understand the implications and issues of these developments for the inhabitants of Houaïlou.

By April 1951, on the occasion of New Caledonia's first parliamentary elections, the indigenous electorate had increased substantially, rising from 1,100 to around 8,700 (but still not amounting to universal suffrage). This led to the active involvement of the two missions (and specifically of pastors Marc Lacheret and Raymond Charlemagne for the Protestants, and Father Guillaume for the Catholics, Father François Luneau having died in 1950) in supporting of the candidature of Maurice Lenormand. Pastor Lacheret wrote to Maurice Leenhardt shortly after the election:

> You will have been rather surprised to learn that Maurice Lenormand is our deputy – and you will be still more surprised when you hear that the Protestant Mission was primarily responsible for this event, I myself first of all! With this new electoral law, we were faced with a native electorate that we estimated would amount to about 10,000 natives – and we

realised that it was at risk of succumbing to all kinds of propaganda.[4] ...
When Charlemagne visited me in Nouméa, we spoke much about this
matter. Lenormand seemed the kapani [fitting][5] man because: – good
knowledge of the native question – capable of bridging the gap, keen to
help the natives develop within their own sphere without raising them too
high prematurely – intelligent and open-minded enough to understand
and defend Caledonian interests – free from all political ties. In the eyes
of the Whites, he had against him his marriage 'to a popinée'[6] and the
fact that he is still seen as being from France. But in any case, whether or
not he was elected, he turned native votes away from communism ... You
will see Lenormand in a few days. His general manifesto, and his native
programme in particular, was wise and lucid. Now he needs help, because
he is not a seasoned politician. (Lacheret 1951)

Jean Guiart, a Protestant student of Leenhardt as well as being Lenormand's brother-in-law, was at the Institut français d'Océanie (French Oceanian Institute) in Nouméa at the time, and hence became heavily involved in the electoral campaign:

It was not easy to demonstrate how useful ethnology could be. In 1951
I had to overstep the limits of standard practice and cobble together
a campaign in the bush and in the islands for the election of Maurice
Lenormand as deputy, in close collaboration with both the Catholic
and the Protestant missions, who held the same opinions as I did on
the situation: to wit the necessity of capturing the rising tide of Kanak
awakening. (Guiart 1993, p. 54)

Lacheret's and Guiart's attribution of Lenormand's anti-communist success to their own efforts is brought into question in Houaïlou, given the local influence of Charlemagne:

To begin with when we started getting involved in politics, it was still
thanks to Charlemagne, I can tell you that for sure because it was me
who took them to Nouméa to look for a deputy who would represent
the Kanaks. So after the two Catholic and Protestant organisations, the
AICLF and the UICALO, formed a single political party, the Union

---

4   It is primarily Fernand Colardeau, the former Communist deputy for Réunion and left-wing candidate, who is in Lacheret's sights here. Madame Tunica, the founder of the New Caledonian Communist Party, had been attacked and did not stand in these elections.
5   A term from the Houaïlou language, from *ka*, relative, 'he who', and *pâri*, 'fitting, appropriate', here spelled *kapani* by Lacheret.
6   A pejorative term in the New Caledonian lexicon, denoting a Kanak woman. Maurice Lenormand's wife was the sister of ethnologist Jean Guiart's wife.

Calédonienne,[7] they looked for a deputy at that time. And it was in the Protestant church in Nouméa, they stayed there, and then there were the other pastors and all that, and then they prayed to find a name, and that was when Charlemagne spoke first and said he had thought of Maurice Lenormand, who was in the Hebrides. And they sent a cable to Maurice Lenormand ... to tell him they had decided to choose him as the representative of the Kanak people, or rather of the Union Calédonienne. And Lenormand didn't reply, but the registration closed at midnight, you know, and they waited for him, and at 10 minutes to midnight, the head of the Haussaire's[8] office telephoned the church to tell them that that was it, Lenormand had registered his candidature.[9] And that was how politics started. And then at that time, how did Lenormand get in? It was purely through the pastors, the *ékalésia* [the members of the Protestant church], the delegates of the AICLF and the delegates of the UICALO. (Guynemer Karé, extract from interview, August 1993)

Nevertheless the Catholic mission, which was heavily invested in this electoral campaign through the person of Father Guillaume, also had grounds for claiming credit for Lenormand's candidature, since the latter was himself Catholic. The Catholic mission's analysis of these elections was no different from that of the Protestants: 'The Mission therefore gave the Natives the only counsel it could give with any likelihood of being heard' (Correspondance et pièces diverses, 1951). Lenormand's election evidently rested on the mobilisation of a wide range of support from within Kanak society. For example, the seventh issue of the AICLF's newspaper, *Le Messager*, offered explanations on the vote and the various candidates in Drehu (the language of Lifou), in Ajië (the language of Houaïlou) and in French; it pointed out that the association's committee, at its meeting in Poyes on 1 June 1951, had urged electors to vote for Lenormand, the candidate who followed the association's own program, which it summed up thus: '1. Preserving the status of native reserves. 2. Recognition of the Council of Elders. 3. Establishment of native customary law. 4. Development of technical and vocational education. 5. Retaining anti-alcohol legislation' (*Moniteur (Le)* 1951).

In the special issue of the *Journal de la Société des océanistes* (*Journal of the Oceanian Studies Society*) that appeared at the end of 1953 to mark the centenary of the French taking possession of New Caledonia, under

---

7 Lenormand's standing for election to the assembly was effectively the point at which the Union Calédonienne came into being, though it was not yet formally constituted in 1951.
8 New Caledonian term for the French High Commissioner.
9 On this point, see Guiart 1966.

the title *Un siècle d'acculturation en Nouvelle-Calédonie (1853–1953)* (*A Century of Acculturation in New Caledonia (1853–1953)*), the task of presenting 'the political evolution of the indigenous people of New Caledonia' was entrusted to the new deputy. His long article also gave him the opportunity to expound the principles underlying his campaign, and thus constituted a historical justification of his own position as well as an account of his program:

> Of the candidates, the one elected was the only one to include in his manifesto, which some deemed too wide-ranging to be sincere, a chapter devoted to the problems of indigenous people. This section of the manifesto read as follows: *It is vital, without harm to any legitimate interests, to provide the conditions and means for continuing development of the governing framework of traditional life, through the following measures: Preserving the status of native reserves; Official recognition of the Council of Elders as the council of the Chiefdom; Surveying and registration of the names of families and clans and also of the lands belonging to each family; Establishment of customary native law; Development of technical and vocational education; Retaining the measures supporting the fight against alcoholism and for the protection of health and of the race; Organisation of production and institution of social welfare cooperatives; Regulations regarding accidents at work and support for dependents; Freedom for the more advanced to renounce native status and submit individual applications for ordinary-law status.* This programme was to rally the vast majority of indigenous Melanesian voters. It also received the support of two indigenous groupings, the 'Association' and the 'Union'. (Lenormand 1953, p. 281)

In placing indigenous issues at the heart of the new political order in New Caledonia, Lenormand's text echoes the chapter Leenhardt added in the second edition of *Gens de la grande Terre* (*People of Grande Terre*), which appeared in that same year. We may recall that Leenhardt was the founder and first president of the Société des Océanistes (in Paris), as well as of the Institut français d'Océanie (in Nouméa). Lenormand and Guiart had been his students at the Institut de langues orientales (Institute of Oriental Languages). Benoît de L'Estoile has shown how this chapter, entitled '1952', redefines the articulation between ethnographic knowledge and colonisation, putting forward a new, postcolonial, social contract:[10]

---

10   L'Estoile 2007.

The country thus no longer has a colonial class that asserts itself and natives who are in decline, an archaic group that is withering and a modern group that is flourishing. But there are two groups that have formed or re-formed in unequal conditions. They are growing alongside one another. They each maintain their own lives. But they can no longer ignore one another. Natives or Whites, they are all Caledonians …

It is possible that in a few months, the Centenary of the French arrival in New Caledonia may also mark the moment when the old misunderstandings die, and a new era begins. Ethnology will have an audience there, and will inspire a sociology in which each component of the population will work in accordance with the particular talents of his ethnicity, to further the development of the rich resources of Caledonia. (Leenhardt 1953, pp. 214 and 223)

Thus a conjunction of forces that were at once political (around Lenormand), religious (around Charlemagne, Lacheret, Leenhardt, Guillaume and Guiart) and academic (around Leenhardt and Guiart) contributed to the multifaceted promotion of a program of New Caledonian unity, on a level of expectation that the missions could control. Under this program, the Kanaks would be integrated into New Caledonian political life alongside Europeans: 'Therefore neither group is without its entitlements. Modern or traditional, they are all Caledonian, and all will participate in a future that they will build together' (Leenhardt 1953, p. 215). As we have seen, Pastor Lacheret informed Leenhardt about the election of Lenormand, although this might seem an unusual subject for mission correspondence. The celebration of the centenary of the French takeover was the high point of this Caledonian 'New Deal' project, but lost some of its lustre owing to the failing health of Leenhardt, who had to abandon his planned visit to New Caledonia for the 50th anniversary of the Dö Nèvâ mission and the centenary of the French takeover – he died in January 1954. Houaïlou was one of the key centres of the planned reform: it is noteworthy that the only contemporary chief mentioned in *Le livre du centenaire* (*Centenary Book*), the prestigious book of photographs by New Caledonian writer Jean Mariotti, is high chief Mandaoué, thus testifying to the significant place Houaïlou occupied in the system of indirect rule that had hitherto operated in New Caledonia.

Figure 7. The Mandaoué chiefdom in the *Livre du centenaire*, 1953
Source: Mariotti 2001, p. 162; © Association pour l'édition et la promotion de l'oeuvre de Jean Mariotti (Society for Publication and Promotion of the Work of Jean Mariotti) (Nouméa).

Of the various elements of Maurice Lenormand's program for the Kanaks, the identification of family names and official registration of the patronymic were the first to be implemented, in late 1952. Jean Guiart contributed directly to this process,[11] which had been rendered necessary by the extension of the vote. The decree of 4 October 1956, under which the identity card was introduced, was the logical consequence: 'Article 1. An identity card shall be issued, without restriction of age, to any individual of French Nationality, or holding either ordinary or customary civil status, who requests it.'[12] Considered in relation to my analysis of the 1911 census categories (see Chapter 3), the identity card can be seen as an indication of a profound reconfiguration of colonial relationships, where the crucial division is no longer only between Europeans and assimilated and natives and assimilated (a division that nevertheless persisted in the two forms of civil status) but between national citizens on the one hand and foreigners on the other. I have discussed elsewhere some of the difficulties engendered by the declaration and official recognition of family names;[13] I have pointed out (see Chapter 1) how both the Népörö and Néjâ clans were at that time identified in the civil register under two distinct names (Néporo and Mandaoué, and Nédia and Mindia, respectively).

May 1952: The creation of the Nédivâ cooperative

I shall now turn to a second aspect of Maurice Lenormand's program as it was implemented in Houaïlou, as described in the *Journal de la Société des océanistes*: on 14 and 15 May 1952, the new deputy visited Houaïlou to officially open the Nédivâ cooperative. Primarily a Protestant initiative, the cooperative nevertheless received the support of the Catholic tribal chief of the neighbouring Néajië tribe, where the Catholic mission was based.

> This week was an important one for Houaïlou and all its people finally fully rallied to the mission, secure in their trust. A huge amount of work has been accomplished since you left by Potin [the native director of the girls' school] and the Catholic chief. The cooperative is working at full capacity, a magnificent building was opened on 15th last by Mr Lenormand; our

---

11   Guiart 1997, p. 181.
12   Under French law, indigenous inhabitants of New Caledonia have 'customary' or 'personal' civil status, allowing their transactions (e.g., marriage, inheritance) to be governed by customary law, except in relation to persons with 'ordinary civil status' (as held by French citizens), in which case ordinary law applies.
13   Naepels 1998, pp. 208–10.

two tractors (there is a new one) are working in the tribes; a 2,000-hectare domain is being created to supply meat and milk to the natives, who for the first time in their history, without consideration as to religion, political party or clan, have come to agreement under the flag of Dö Névâ. (Charlemagne 1952)

This cooperative comprised a warehouse for storing goods, two tractors to help in agricultural production, a small truck for collecting and distributing agricultural produce, and a network of small shops in each tribe. The aim was clearly to support the 'organisation of production' and the 'institution of cooperatives', to cite the terms used in Lenormand's manifesto. It was also a direct attack on the colonial relationships that pertained in a small rural municipality, where the trading post economy was based on a monopoly of trading in products centred on the shop operated by the Ballande trading company; it was thus intended to contribute to the development of new social relationships in the relational space between Kanaks, settlers and representatives of the administration.

> Me I was the delegate for the AICLF, we set up the AICLF and it worked very well. But already in the AICLF, we were talking about independence, we were already talking about a lot of stuff, we created cooperatives, but the White man is still there suffocating us, you know. We bought tractors, and then we made fields, you know, everywhere in the tribes. (Guynemer Karé, former member of the cooperative, extract from interview, July 1993)

Lenormand's visit aroused the anger of one section of the settlers in Houaïlou; as can be surmised, this was due not only to the fact that he had chosen to visit a Kanak tribe rather than the European administrative centre, but also to the support the new deputy was thus bringing to the cooperative, in opposition to the clientelist networks that had been a major bone of contention in the conflict between high chief Mèèjâ Néjâ and Eugène Bozon-Verduraz, the trader and chairman of the municipal committee (see Chapter 3). Leenhardt, in the political testament he offers in the second edition of *Gens de la Grande Terre*, imagines an expostulation by the 'positive spirit' (in other words Europeans closed to Kanaks), defending colonial imperialism and dimissing the cooperative initiative: 'What do we care about their cooperatives, we earn more by making them drink' (Leenhardt 1953, p. 222).

4. POST-*INDIGÉNAT* MOBILISATIONS

We have no information as to how the concept of cooperative organisation was introduced into New Caledonia, nor why the Protestants of Houaïlou took it up in 1952. It may be noted, however, that Jean Guiart concerned himself with the development of the cooperative movement throughout the 1950s, in the New Hebrides, and in the Pacific more broadly.[14] In this final text from that decade, he mentions the Houaïlou cooperative:

> The cooperative based in Nedivin, in the lower valley of the Houaïlou river, owes its origins in part to the concern of the Protestant mission to restore equilibrium in a district split between fluid and indeterminate local political factions, where a heavy atmosphere was becoming established as a permanent feature of life in the region. Following years of fruitless efforts on the spiritual level, a well thought-out strategy for economic development was to see many return to the mission's fold ... Ultimately, it has held together perhaps less from economic than from political reasons, but this has been enough for the project to continue, and gradually become better organised: a central cooperative store receives merchandise from Nouméa and distributes it to the local shops which are initially looked after by individuals, but which tend to become collectively run. With a lorry and a truck, the central store also takes on collecting the coffee, which it trades with the capital. The cooperative currently handles about one fifth of the coffee grown in the valley. Its main handicap is primarily financial, since it does not have enough ready cash to pay the producer for the coffee, and the latter must wait for the final sale in Nouméa in order to enjoy the added value they gain from choosing the cooperative to sell their product. However, most Melanesians have no other means of existence than selling their produce, and in their pressing need for money, all too often opt for a less advantageous but immediate sale, selling the coffee to travelling pedlers. (Guiart 1959a, p. 22)

As part of the program of cooperative development in Houaïlou, a trainee was later sent on placement to a kibbutz in Israel, to find out about collective forms of rural development:

> All of Houaïlou lived through the cooperative, and they went so far those old guys, me I remember old Tèn [Bwéwé] coming back from Israel, he was the first person we saw driving a Renault lorry, a Renault Saviem. They organised a harvest in all the tribes, coffee was still the main product economically, and the Nédivâ cooperative handled the transactions, and collected the coffee in all the tribes in the region. And processing was done in the tribes, before it was brought in sacks, and then the transaction was done with Ballande, the big stores in Nouméa, you know. It worked

---

14   Guiart 1951, 1956a and 1959a.

so well that they built the big cooperative that is still there, you can still see the structure, they bought vehicles, they were able to fund some of the schools, construction. (Jean-Jacques Ayawa, extract from interview, July 2006)

While the Catholic tribal chief of Néajië, Louis Unu, initially participated in the Nédivâ cooperative, this initiative was countered when a Catholic cooperative was set up by Father Plasman, a missionary in Néajië, who was associated with the American veteran Lee. But this lasted only a short time, owing to a conflict between its founders that arose as early as 1956.

The high level of Protestant involvement in the reorganisation of colonial relationships in Houaïlou, under the aegis of the mission, through the defence of their lands, the cooperative's criticism of colonial relations, the openness to village reorganisation and training (evident in Lenormand's program), was matched in the political realm. Thus, in the municipal elections of October 1954, the winning list comprised five settlers (Leroi, Rousseau, Malignon, Magnier and Maradhour) and five Kanaks, all Protestants, who were heavily involved in the AICLF and the running of the cooperative. These were Auguste Parawi-Reybas, cooperative delegate and AICLF delegate for Warai; Kétiwan Ayawa, cooperative delegate and AICLF delegate for Ba; Georges Jöpöyöi, chairman of the cooperative and cooperative delegate for Nédivâ; Denis Yupé Wéma, cooperative delegate for Boréaré; and finally Uruva Néjâ, son of high chief Mèèjâ Néjâ (who died in 1921), former student at Dö Nèvâ and brother of high chief Apupia. We shall return to the role played by the two brothers Uruva and Apupia Néjâ in the life of Houaïlou during the 1950s.

> The list that won the majority of votes was that formed, with the support of Europeans which they themselves solicited, by the directors of the local Cooperative. This cooperative had been set up with the open sponsorship, and financial assistance, of the Protestant Mission; but its day-to-day operation was subject only to increasingly lighter monitoring, which has now all but disappeared. (Guiart 1955, p. 26)

Plans for councils of elders

It was in the context of the reorganisation of Kanak village life, necessitated both by the ending of the repressive colonial rules and by the fear of communism, that the two faith associations chose to take up the concept of the council of elders. Thus, the pamphlet marking the founding of the Catholic UICALO, dated 25 May 1946 and entitled 'Demands of the Union of Caledonian Natives Friends of Freedom With Order', includes the following: 'We call for the Chief to have a council elected by his subjects' (Correspondance et pièces diverses, 1946). This notion was developed in the UICALO manifesto of March 1947, which called for councils of elected elders with powers of coercion:

> To maintain inviolate the tribe under the direct authority of the Chief, assisted by a Council freely elected by secret ballot, by all adult subjects of both sexes. The purpose of the council is not to diminish the authority of the Chief, but on the contrary to assist and support him by providing the help of its wisdom and the support of its own authority. The delegates call on the French administration to derogate to the chief and his council those necessary judicial and coercive powers that are conferred on them by the ancient customs of the ancestors, for the purpose of settling conflicts arising between subjects within the tribe. ('Vœux émis par l'assemblée des délégués de l'UICALO à Paita', 1947)

The centrality of this institution in postwar Kanak campaigning was emphasised by the priest of Lifou in March 1947: 'They insist on only one point: the creation or rather the reinstatement of a chief's council, for the Council still exists but is no longer either summoned or consulted' (cited in Kurtovitch 1997, p. 64). The same emphasis on the need to recognise or establish councils of elders appears in the early AICLF texts, in 1946: 'The council of elders (or of atési[15] in the islands) must be reinstated, so that they, with the chief, can examine all questions concerning the tribe's wellbeing ('Pensées de base …', 1946). Shortly after his arrival in New Caledonia, in a 'chat' broadcast on the radio in April 1948, Charlemagne put forward the same idea:

> Of the planned roles devised between 1912–1918 by a committee chaired by Mr Cané, one custom remains: the council of Elders. Its creation emerged from the observation that the Caledonian chief, although all-powerful, never goes against the law of his men … This chief does not decide alone … Recognition of this state of affairs led to the creation of the council of Elders, the practice of which corresponded so well with the mentality of the people that it is now becoming established in every village, and 'the Elders', regardless of age, are recruited from among the local people of note. This custom ought to be enshrined in law. (Charlemagne 1948a, p. 6).

---

15 Spiritual advisers to the chief on the Loyalty Islands [trans.].

In fact the councils of elders had not been legally instituted after the First World War; those that were set up in the years after the Second World War were local Kanak initiatives, without any legal framework, sometimes based (in varying regional contexts) on locally recognised social functions (as in the Loyalty Islands, particularly Lifou), and sometimes not (specifically in Houaïlou). The councils of elders set up in the late 1940s had varying, generally fairly close, relationships with the two organisations that promoted the principle, and equally variable, generally somewhat conflictual, relationships with the chiefdoms:

> In some districts the reinstated councils were composed of elected members of the 'Union' or the 'Association', while in others, which remained attached to the traditional membership, the restored councils were formed by the heads of specific families. The tribal chiefs, dispensing with the support of the now eliminated administrative discipline, returned to their traditional role, and their authority, tempered by the presence of councils, returned to its original principles. (Lenormand 1953, p. 292)

As noted above, official recognition of the council of elders formed part of Lenormand's manifesto when he was elected deputy in 1951. During this campaign, and still more through the year 1953, it was promoted throughout New Caledonia, in a debate around reform of the status of municipalities. In a territory that was not yet living under the democratic rule of universal suffrage, and where the question of the dual electorate was a subject of debate, the issue was reproduced at the level of local communities. Was it better to create indigenous municipalities, alongside municipalities that preserved the European settlers' autonomy, 'in order to provide each of these communities with a framework appropriate to its conditions of development and its specific ideas', or 'mixed municipalities' (Lenormand 1953, p. 290)? At that time Lenormand supported dual municipalities, in order to avoid what he believed to be the risk of premature assimilation:

> The powers and responsibilities accorded to European rural municipalities and indigenous communities need to be defined respectively by a distinct status. In this way the particular character of these communities and the desire of their inhabitants to live according to their habits and their usage and customs will be respected. (Lenormand 1953, p. 291)

The idea, then, was to establish dual political representation at municipal level, one structure for Kanaks living in reserves, and the other for other residents. Within this framework, councils of elders would have served as the first step in the construction of indigenous municipalities. Thus the Kanaks' campaign for greater democracy within the tribal space via the election of a council of elders, and the small rural settlers' defence of colonial segregation, became strange bedfellows in the new deputy's plans. In fact in the municipal elections of 1954, the allocation of municipal elected officials for each ethnicity and each municipality was fixed in law, without any relation to the respective weight of the communities in question. For a decade, the terms of the debate on the status of municipalities was to be determined by the relationship between universal suffrage and colonial heritage: at the level of local politics, how was the difference between customary and ordinary civil status, resulting from the colonial distinction between subjects and citizens, to be resolved? What weight should be given to the division of non-state-owned space into reserve lands and private land? Would assimilation of the electoral colleges not lead to the disappearance of unique features of Kanak social and cultural life? Conversely, would plans to grant the councils of elders' autonomy in managing village affairs not simply reproduce colonial segregation, at the very moment when Kanaks were gaining greater mobility and increased opportunities for living on privately owned land? And finally, was universal suffrage to be applied within the space of customary life, or not? A difficulty of interpretation in relation to the recognition of 'customary authorities' began to develop, and to this day this recognition can be seen in two contradictory ways in the New Caledonian context, either as a means of achieving full Kanak autonomy or as a brake on it, blocking the path to genuine democratic representation.

To return to the councils of elders and their powers, the administration's response was that, now that the *indigénat* system had ended, the chief no longer held any powers of administrative sanction; nor was there any question of according such power to any councils that might be formed: 'The natives are currently governed by ordinary law, and it could not be otherwise' ('Étude des voeux de l'UICALO', 1947). Therefore, as Kurtovitch notes, 'neither native justice, nor the powers of chiefs, nor the change in status of tribal and district councils, nor tribal police, actually came into being' (Kurtovitch 1997, p. 140). Thus councils of elders, conceived as a counterweight to the figure of an all-powerful chief – a role that had been built up by the colonial administration during the first half of the 20th century – were never officially recognised. The relics of indirect administration, in the management of public order, did indeed remain in the hands of high chiefs and tribal chiefs, as indicated in decree no. 895 of 6 July 1954, which specifies the powers accorded to the Indigenous Affairs Department:

> Article 10. Indigenous high chiefs are responsible for maintaining order in their district. They shall take all measures necessary to ensure that public safety and peace are not disturbed by indigenous people.
>
> Article 11. Under the authority and supervision of high chiefs, tribal chiefs shall maintain order and calm within their tribe.
>
> Article 12. The indigenous high chiefs and tribal chiefs are required to inform the sergeant of the gendarmerie squad in their district about everything that happens in the territory under their authority.

1955–56: A witch-hunt

December 1955: The visit of the seers

It was in this context of high levels of political activism among many Kanak Protestants in Houaïlou, in the Nédivâ cooperative, in municipal administration, in a number of councils of elders and in the work of the AICLF, that a violent witch-hunt was organised in a number of tribes. A group of a dozen or so men from the neighbouring municipality of Ponérihouen, made up of *jauu* (seers) from the Goa tribe supported by AICLF representatives from the same area (Goa and Mou), had organised public meetings in a number of tribes in Ponérihouen, in order to seek out individuals suspected of possessing malign powers, and neutralise their activity. They were invited to Houaïlou to carry out the same task, at the instigation of AICLF delegates.

> It was all the people who represented the AICLF association there, I think it was them that invited the *jauu*, but to get them into the tribe, they had to go and see the chiefs or the councils of elders. (Ivô Mârârhëë, extract from interview, June 2006)

The dozen or so individuals involved, who formed themselves into an inquisitorial tribunal, stayed more than a week in Lèwëö, a tribe adjacent to the administrative centre of the municipality and the headquarters of the Néjâ chiefdom. They were lodged with the local AICLF delegate and cooperative representative, before leaving to spend a few days in Néawa, where they stayed with the chief, one of Leenhardt's Protestant students who was a former communist and also an AICLF delegate. Guiart published two accounts of this episode, in which he himself was indirectly implicated, through his faith (as a Protestant close to the AICLF and the Nédivâ cooperative), his academic interests (as a researcher at the Institut français d'Océanie, doing fieldwork in Ponérihouen and Houaïlou during this period) and his political associations (as Lenormand's brother-in-law).[16] These two texts confirm the Protestant involvement in this campaign: 'Themselves Protestants, the seers cracked down mainly in Protestant villages' (Guiart 1967, p. 135). They also give an idea of the methods used:

> The sorcerers' 'spontaneous' confessions were obtained by third-degree procedures that these days are standard procedure:[17] beating, placing red-hot embers delicately on the skin. It should be added that the *jau* were supported both by a number of dignitaries, who gave a veneer of respectability, and by a few strapping fellows … Yet this modern-day inquisition was not to everyone's liking, least of all the accused. The Protestant mission saw its best students involved in the affair, as accusers, alleged perpetrators, or simply believers in the virtue of the *jau*. (Guiart 1959b, pp. 42–43)

All of the testimonies I have gathered emphasise the extensive publicity given to these events, and the crowds that gathered around them. The accusation was public. In front of the gathering of seers, their supporters from Ponérihouen, representatives of the AICLF and the councils of elders from the Houaïlou tribes concerned, the accused were adjured to renounce the alleged powers of protection or attack they were supposed to possess (plants, leaves, bark, stones) on pain of violent punishment, including being made to stand all day in full sun, kneeling while holding heavy stones in their outstretched hands or being repeatedly slapped.

> I know that before there were two old grandfathers who came from there [Ponérihouen], they were *mèrhî* [seers] … So, and before, well in the years 54–55, all the people of Houaïlou, they went to look for them there to come and dig out the bad stuff here in Houaïlou, you see? Then they did it in Lèwëö, they went back and did it in Néawa, you see? Then there was a big outcry, because there were people who didn't want to give up their medicines or their stones, so the council of elders sort of kept an eye on them and then shoved them around a bit, you see? So it ended in court … There weren't too many fights or anything like that, it was just

---

16 Guiart 1959b and 1967.
17 Guiart is implicitly referring to the war in Algeria.

the councillors who sort of ... the police, the tribal police who roughed people up a bit, sort of ... And then they took away leaves, pebbles, bits of wood, bark. (Ivô Mârârhëë, extract from interview, February 1999)

The reference to 'councillors' in this interview indicates that the initiative ran alongside the reorganisation of village administration around councils of elders and faith organisations. The material adds to the ancestors' efficacy – 'medicines' or 'stones'[18] – obtained through a markedly unequal power relationship, and were taken as confirmation of the malign intent of the accused who was thus unmasked, and held responsible for deaths or misfortunes that had occurred in the recent history of the tribes concerned.

> It was decided by the whole tribe, I mean the *kâmöyaari* [subjects] together with the chief, in discussion, and they said that since there was quite a lot of stuff, deaths that couldn't be explained: 'It seems there are *jauu*, you know, we'll try to get them to come, then we'll see.' ... They held the court down there, you know. So the *jauu* brought everybody down, it was as if they were seers, you know, they were seers. They called, and their chief said: 'Look, I see Such-and-Such, make Such-and-Such come.' He is called; 'Come here!' Them, they question him, still got their medicine. The other he says: 'No, I haven't got anything', they argue, it's like a prisoner, you know, he tries to defend himself, until the moment when, well, he ends up saying: 'Yes it's true.' At that time it was a good thing. There are a lot of old people who everybody knew that him, he's got a bad medicine, him he's got a devil; well after the *jauu* came, they're nothing, they become powerless those guys, they haven't got anything any more, they're just ordinary guys like us, they can't do their little magic any more. (Marcel Mèèjâ, extract from group interview with the council of elders of Lèwèö, June 2006)

The aim was thus to 'clean up' the villages, to expose those responsible for disorder and to settle accounts – in short to start again from clean and transparent foundations for community life in shared spaces, countering all the alleged powers to attack 'in darkness', in the domestic space behind closed doors. It should be added that the accused came primarily from the tribes of Lèwèö district, but that some originating from other districts were brought in front of the tribunal, sometimes using the cooperative's truck.

---

18 See Chapter 2.

4. POST-*INDIGÉNAT* MOBILISATIONS

A fairly precise idea of the breadth of the accusations can be gleaned from a quite extraordinary document published by Jean Guiart, the 'List of witchcraft in the district of Neouyo', which was entrusted to him by some of the organisers of the campaign:

> [The team] had the local dignitaries issue victory announcements, to support an official request to intervene. Curiously, here the team targeted members of the chief's family most of all, particularly those who supported the political minority in the country, which included high chief Apupia, though they did not dare to accuse him. It was not that the *jau* were asked to participate in a political operation; their tendency was more simply to shape the forms of their campaign in line with majority opinion ... [This list] contains a request for intervention, formulated, according to the investigator, in ungrammatical French. (Giuart 1967, pp. 135–37)

The document is signed by the president of the Croix-Bleue (Blue Cross, the Protestant anti-alcohol temperance society), the chairman of the council of elders in Lèwèö, and the cooperative and AICLF delegate for Lèwèö. Fourteen individuals from the 'district of Neouyo' are identified by name, together with the various kinds of powers of attack they are accused of possessing: 'doki (bad spirit)' (*doki*), 'Jee (a kind of spear)' (*je*), 'Rhë gassu (medicine that makes women infertile)' (*rhëë gayu*), 'Gasu (medicine that poisons the blood and leads to leprosy, madness. etc ...)' (*gayu*), 'Gasu Koé (a sort of liana that prevents a person from growing)' (*gayu kwèè*), 'Arù (medicine that makes a person weak)' (*aru*), 'Kosèri (power of curse)' (*ko yèri*), 'Rhaï (a lizard)' (*rhai*), 'club', 'Bée (a sort of barrier that hides everything)' (*bé*), 'Jarua (a medicine for robbery that makes the thief's victim blind)' (*jarua*). The list is followed by a 'List of the Sick' that mentions (without naming) 132 individuals – a very substantial number in relation to the population concerned – who were in need of treatment: 42 from Lèwèö, 40 from Néawa, but also 13 from Warai, 12 from Kwawa, 10 from Kùa, eight from Nédivâ, six from Ba and one from Nérhëxakwéaa. By comparing the 14 names on the 'List of Sorcerers' with the genealogies I have constructed for the families concerned, we can sketch the genealogical diagram below (which completes Chapter 2, Figure 2):

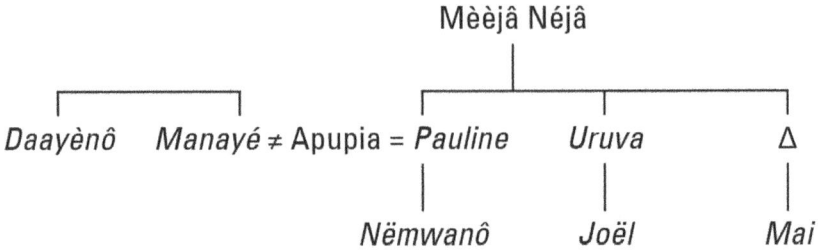

Figure 8. Genealogical identification of some of the accused related to high chief Apupia in 1955
Names in italics are those accused.
Source: Author's research.

It was in the context of this activity that the list of the accused was given to Jean Guiart, who was then in Houaïlou doing ethnographic fieldwork and was close to the campaigning Protestants: the document's signatories hoped thus to obtain authorisation for their intervention, 'I pray you to do what is required for authorisation of medicines to drink'. In the two articles he wrote on the subject, Guiart claimed that it was he who had persuaded the seers to return to Ponérihouen, after two weeks spent in Houaïlou, on grounds of potential interference in the forthcoming election campaign, new parliamentary elections having been scheduled for 8 January 1956: 'The ethnologist … however obtained better results than the administration in this matter, using the imminence of the elections to persuade the seers to go home in order to prevent their political adversaries from exploiting this upheaval' (Guiart 1967, p. 137). Thus he intervened here on behalf of his brother-in-law Lenormand's political interests; the need was all the more pressing given that the committee for revision of the electoral register in Houaïlou, on which some of the 'accused' were due to sit, had not been able to begin its work because of the activity around the Ponérihouen *jauu*:

> The administration watched this commotion anxiously and believed that at times they detected the result of political manoeuvring by the Deputy. The latter's party wondered whether the affair would excite resentment and fears that would be harmful in the forthcoming elections … The author of these lines had to resort to subterfuge and ask the seers, given the imminence of the parliamentary elections, to return home, making clear to them how inopportune this disturbance was. A few months later they reappeared in the criminal court, with some of their acolytes; but only the assaults were punished. (Guiart 1959b, p. 43)

There is little doubt that this campaign, conducted by the most ardent Protestants in Houaïlou with the aim of reconfiguring the local social order, was initiated without consulting pastor Raymond Charlemagne, who had returned from a visit to France in November 1955, just before the *jauu* arrived at the end of the month. When, two years later, Leenhardt's son Raymond, himself also a pastor, returned to Houaïlou (where he had been born when his father was a missionary there) in the company of his wife Geneviève, Charlemagne offered them his interpretation of a witch-hunt that he had not initiated, though his condemnation of it was on the mild side:

> According to Charlemagne, there are even more 'seers' here than in Paris! And the witchcraft crises that break out from time to time are aimed at purging the country of foreign devilry introduced by the Chinese, the Javanese, etc. In short it is salutary and well-intentioned witchcraft! … In 56 there was once again a lot of sorcerer activity,[19] and Charlemagne returning from vacation sent his instructors on a big Bible study tour of the tribes affected, on Moses and Pharaoh's sorcerers: 'These stories of magic, the Bible knows them and shows us that this is not good.' (Leenhardt and Leenhardt 1958, p. 78)

The question of witchcraft

In the discussion that follows, in order to avoid exoticising witchcraft, I propose to follow Marc Augé's definition:

> When using the term witchcraft, we simply indicate a set of beliefs structured and shared by a given population that relates to the origin of misfortune, sickness or death, and the set of practices of detection, healing and sanctions that correspond to those beliefs. (Augé 1974, p. 53)

Augé goes on: 'Beliefs in witchcraft are only manifested and acted upon during procedures of divination, interrogation or accusation' (1974, p. 62).

In New Caledonia, when the person responsible for misfortune (sickness, accident, death) is not identified, the wrong suffered may be analysed in terms of witchcraft.[20] This distinction from other modes of evaluating behaviour and responsibilities can be discerned in the expression used by some Kanaks who describe witchcraft as 'Kanak justice'. The relations

---

19 In reality, at the end of 1955.
20 For this exposition, see Salomon 2000a.

between natural phenomena and moral phenomena, between social affiliations and the individual body, that emerge here are very different from those constructed by the values of either the Christian missions or the French legal system. In order to understand the social logic at work in witchcraft affairs in New Caledonia, I follow Christine Salomon in distinguishing two principal categories: illness, accident, failure and death can be perceived either as punishment for deviance inflicted by the ancestors, or as the consequence of a malicious attack by a third party.

In the first case, 'witchcraft' denotes:

> illnesses sent by ancestral powers, who ensure respect of social rules. These illnesses represent a response to transgression of norms, a punishment or simply a warning intended to induce the individual to reflect and encourage him to make amends for his error ... By means of sickness, the omnipresent and omnipotent ancestors punish deviance both within the lineage they founded and outside of it. (Salomon 2000a, pp. 72–73)

The transgressions thus sanctioned may be of the order of negligence toward the ancestors (poor upkeep of cemeteries) or toward the contractual obligations linking different clans (for example, matrimonial alliance and the ceremonial exchanges it calls for at various stages of the life cycle), or of failure to fulfil one's obligations to maternal uncles (refusal to obey, speaking ill). 'Kanak justice' thus has a strong ethical dimension and a powerful element of social control. Sickness and its variants prompt a work of enquiry, interrogations in the family about any social conflicts in the recent or more distant past. This investigation sometimes includes consultation with a seer who can identify the origin of the harm.[21] Given the social aetiology of the misfortune, the victim is not necessarily the person directly to blame for the transgression thus identified, but may be one of his relatives. The sickness in effect punishes the behaviour of an individual insofar as he belongs to a family group (lineage or clan, patrilineal kinship group), which is also a political unit in local social life. Thus the individual implicates his group through his actions. This social belonging is complex because, in a segmentary system, an individual can claim to be a member of more or less encompassing groups depending on the circumstances. Thus we cannot talk of a principle of 'collective responsibility' as such in 'Kanak justice', but rather of a political and military system of inter-individual relationships, mediated by family

---

21   There are several different types of healer in the Houaïlou region, notably seers (*mèrhî*, literally those who search by vision) and diviners (*jauu*); see Salomon 1993, p. 255; Leenhardt 1935, p. 181.

affiliations. In this first case, the process of assigning responsibility may lead to reparation, according to a specific logic: it is the person guilty of the transgression who makes amends, because he is the target of a potentially lethal sanction sent by the ancestors, to which he wishes to put an end.

In other situations, other illnesses, other diagnoses, a second type of witchcraft is identified, in which the evil spell may be more individualised. An individual may come to believe himself the victim of an aggressive attack through witchcraft. Every individual is believed to have the power to bring about the illness and death of another, including one of his relatives, either directly by means of the powers he holds, or by commissioning it from another. In such cases there is a variety of possible responses: one of them consists of accusing, in private but also sometimes in public, the individual one believes to be responsible for the wrong one has suffered. This leads to the circulation of large numbers of witchcraft accusations, which sometimes give rise to customary trials and violent settling of scores. The witch-hunt conducted in Houaïlou in late 1955 is an example of this second category, a sort of continuation of war by other means.[22] The vision of the diviners, who are able to identify illness and its cause by various means, such as dreams, defines a way of seeing distinct from eyewitness testimony and carrying the same evidential value as catching someone in the act: 'I saw an innocent man, accused by the diviner, dragged before the court and accepting being sentenced to several months in prison. How was he to know what his spirit might have done? But the jau [diviner] could know, and all he could do was passively lament the revelation that this divination had brought forth' (Leenhardt 1930, p. 248). Confession at the customary trial or, more precisely, the gesture that amounted to confession, which consisted in surrendering plants, pieces of wood, bark or pebbles that might constitute the material aids for practices of witchcraft, is then often followed by private retractions. As Salomon writes: 'In most cases, the sorcerer identified confesses, pleading guilty, for fear of incurring the censure of the group (and physical mistreatment), in the expectation of subsequently retracting in better times, when the current balance of forces has altered and his accusers have been discredited in their turn' (Salomon 1993, p. 142). Thus, 50 years later, one of my interviewees returned to the accusation made by the *jauu*

---

22   See Salomon 2000a, pp. 110 and 114–15.

against his grandmother in 1955, explaining that, under physical duress, she had been forced to reveal the protective powers of her clan ('to preserve the house'), but these were in no way powers of attack ('Satanic objects'):

> The medicines at that time, there weren't really what I would call Satanic objects. They kept all of that, to preserve the house [to protect their own clan] … I remember grandmother's story, X's grandmother, she held the medicine from the great mountain of X up there, but it didn't come like that the medicine, it was her fathers, her grandfathers who put it [who had given it to her] … And then how many times they [the *jauu*] sent uncle: 'Hey, go and get your mother', the old man kept going and coming back. 'No but that, that's mine, it belongs to X, what do you want with it?' Grandmother, she was beaten. (Extract from interview, July 2006)

The accused person's gesture appears to have stood principally as a guarantee of good behaviour or, sometimes, the promise to give something up, rather than an act indicating admission of a 'transgression'. The public meetings organised by the *jauu* thus fall into the context of public handling of a social problem. It is worth remembering also that it was the missionaries who inaugurated the collection of stones and 'medicines' during their campaigns of evangelisation and eradication of 'paganism' (see Chapter 2): for those who gave up these objects at this time, the point was to turn a page, rather than to feel guilty. I have already cited the example of the father of Élia Mârârhëë (one of Maurice Leenhardt's students who was involved in the witch-hunt operation in 1955) handing over a war stone to pastor Étienne Bergeret. Bowing the head, keeping silent, bringing the plants specified by a seer are thus ways of acknowledging the power of the accuser or the powerful person in an interaction, if need be under physical duress. But after the crisis, perhaps following a minimal confession and a sanction in the public spaces of judgment, retraction is always possible in private or after the local balance of power has shifted and the context of the past confession has been recast. The confession then appears as a temporary capitulation, in a context that may vary and where the stronger individual may lose his power. Nevertheless, in Houaïlou in late 1955, the dominant collective dynamic, reinforced by the *jauu*, was certainly on the side of the Protestant mobilisation around the AICLF and the cooperative.

Political and judicial consequences

Following the witch-hunt conducted by the *jauu* in Ponérihouen, a man lodged a complaint about the violence that had been inflicted on him when he refused to hand over the powers he was accused of holding: 'He didn't want to confess to his thing, so they did things to him to make him confess, you know' (extract from interview, June 2006). Coming on top of similar complaints filed in relation to previous *jauu* activities in the Ponérihouen region, this case became the subject of an investigation by the gendarmerie, a judicial inquiry and then a court judgment in Ponérihouen in January 1957. Several members of the Ponérihouen group, in particular the two *jauu*, were given prison sentences, while two individuals from Houaïlou were fined.

> At that time old Daayènô, he was like the brother-in-law of high chief Mèèjâ Apupia [see Figure 8]. Well, it was really Apupia who was pointed [targeted, hit] through his brother-in-law, so he pushed the man to lodge a complaint against the council of elders, the *jauu* [diviners]. (Ivô Mârârhëë, extract from interview, July 2008)

This interpretation is both interesting and convincing, because it clearly situates both the witch-hunt and the formal complaint, with the concomitant displacement of the conflict into the judicial arena, within the context of a more general struggle between the authority of the high chief of Lèwèö district on one hand and the councils of elders, associated with the AICLF Protestant activism, on the other – even though Apupia was not the direct object of the *jauus*' accusations, as Guiart notes.

The political commitment to the reorganisation of communal tribal space, and the feeling that it was necessary to eliminate alleged causes of misfortune, in order to achieve greater local unity around the councils of elders and full mobilisation of the Protestant villages, were powerful forces. Even after the conviction of the diviners in early 1957, those who had initiated the visit of the Ponérihouen *jauu* to Lèwèö district, that is, the AICLF and cooperative delegates, planned for them to return to 'clean up' the other districts of Houaïlou, starting with the tribes in the main valley; this aroused the concern of the administrator for native affairs. This, along with other cases in other parts of Grande Terre, was one of the main reasons for the circulation of a memorandum from the New Caledonia Ministry of the Interior, addressed to the gendarmes who served as native affairs administrators, on the subject of witchcraft cases. This document offers a prime example of administrative ethnology:

It has come to my notice that there has been a sharp increase in witchcraft cases recently. Some of you seem somewhat uncertain as to the attitude to take and the precise role of the Administrator in this kind of incident, I believe that a clarification will not go amiss in informing you as to the feelings of the government concerned on this question. First of all it should not be forgotten that these cases are closely bound up with the affective bedrock of native mentality, and will only die out through a gradual evolution of minds. Repressive action in this arena would risk running counter to our goal, causing ceremonies to be hidden; they would thus escape your oversight and might take aggravated form. In my opinion, it would be equally inappropriate for you to officially acquiesce, as this would give the 'sorcerers'' activity a sort of administrative endorsement that must be avoided at all costs. Your role in this domain therefore appears to me essentially one purely of informing people and warning those involved about certain limits they cannot go beyond without incurring penal sanction (serious mistreatment, ordeals by poison, etc.). It goes without saying that in cases of manifest breaches of the law you must draw up a report and submit the matter to the judicial authorities, the only authority competent to initiate an inquiry and punish the guilty. I hope that this clarification will facilitate your work by indicating the path to follow. I count on you to conform to it, and to keep me fully apprised as before about any incident of this nature that comes to your attention. I would add that when you draw up such reports I would see no harm – quite the contrary – in your giving your opinions on the underlying reasons for this resurgence in witchcraft cases. It is almost certainly due to quite serious social discontent. Your knowledge of the local situation and of the native mentality will be invaluable to me in this matter of drawing out the exact and real causes of it, and if necessary putting forward structural reforms that might bring lasting improvement in the current situation. (Memorandum No. 287, from the General Affairs Department of the Ministry of the Interior, on cases of witchcraft, 28 January 1960)

This text reasserts the gendarmerie's detachment (which was also the position taken by the surveyors responsible for the 1917 repression) in its activity of indirect rule (while, of course, maintaining its role of ensuring that penal law was respected). In short, the stated desire of the government council was that the Kanaks reorganise their village life as they saw fit. We have, indeed, a quite remarkable cinematographic record of a witch-hunt in the neighbouring region of Canala[23] – one of its most striking features being that it was filmed by a gendarme during the 1960s. In my analysis, the issue in these witchcraft trials was at least as much the

---

23   Some extracts are included in Dagneau 2008.

4. POST-*INDIGÉNAT* MOBILISATIONS

local definition of a new village governmentality following the end of the indigénat as it was the 'affective bedrock of native mentality' – since forms of subjectivation are clearly linked to forms of government. Of relevance here is the intuition of Peter Geschiere, who examines the question of the 'modernity' of witchcraft in a Cameroonian case (Geschiere 1995, p. 9), showing how it operates as a 'political language' (p. 7), contributing to 'the emergence of new forms of domination or resistance' (p. 16).[24]

In addition to its judicial consequences, the visit of the *jauu* contributed significantly to the political rallying of the Protestant tribes (a movement that could of course include widely varying forms of adherence): thus in the parliamentary elections of 8 January 1956, the sitting deputy, Lenormand, who was supported by the Protestant mission of Pastor Charlemagne, won 645 votes in Houaïlou, while his main opponent from the social republicans, Georges Chatenay, who was supported by the Catholic mission of Father Plasman, obtained only 190.[25] The two other candidates, Bastien and Raighasse, obtained nine votes and one vote respectively. In a text dated August 1956, Guiart notes that the two high chiefs of the coastal area, Apupia Mindia (the son of Mèèjâ Néjâ) and Félix Mandaoué (the son of Mwâdéwé Népörö) supported not Lenormand, but Chatenay.[26] This confirms once again how the issue of local governmentality was bound up with the political mobilisation of the AICLF, the economic investment of the cooperative and the institution of the council of elders.

Following this renewed victory, the Union Calédonienne was officially inaugurated in Nouméa on 13 May 1956. Both the AICLF delegates from Houaïlou and Pastor Charlemagne participated in the founding congress. The Defferre enabling legislation of 19 June 1956[27] was implemented in New Caledonia under a decree of 22 July 1957, finally introducing full universal suffrage around a single electoral college. An AICLF congress, chaired by Dui Matayo Wetta, was held on 10–13 September 1957 in the Lèwèö tribe, which was deemed cleansed of its 'bad medicine', in order

---

24 See also Taussig 1987.
25 My point is not to deduce ideological adherence from the vote, but simply to note the efficient mobilisation of voters, whatever the individual motives behind their behaviour.
26 Guiart 1956b.
27 Law passed by the French parliament enabling the French government to introduce reforms in overseas territories, particularly electoral reforms [trans.].

to complete preparations for the campaign for the territorial elections of 6 October 1957, in which the Union Calédonienne won a large majority on the government council.

1957–60: Dynamics of division

A return to the council of elders and political suspension

Owing to the preponderance of the UICALO and the AICLF, and their importance in Lenormand's program, legal recognition of the council of elders and the definition of its areas of authority were debated throughout the second half of the 1950s. In 1956 Guiart wrote 'Notes à propos de l'organisation intérieure des tribus autochtones en Nouvelle-Calédonie et aux îles Loyalty' ('Notes on the Internal Organisation of Native Tribes in New Caledonia and the Loyalty Islands'), in which he proposed assigning to the council of elders the procedures for choosing the chief, discussion of problems of land ownership, questions of succession, the establishment of a native police force and the allocation of shared labour, thus making the council both a 'customary court' and a 'low-level municipal council' (Guiart 1956b, pp. 12–13). This document seems to have formed one of the bases for reflection in the New Caledonian territorial assembly when it debated a plan for recognition of the councils in March 1958:

> Article 2. Customary Councils called 'Councils of Elders' shall be recognised or established in the tribes, the members representing the various clans constituting the tribe being appointed according to customary rules; these appointments shall be submitted to the Ministry of the Interior for validation.
>
> Article 3. The powers of the Council of Elders include ruling on problems of land ownership within the reserve or the part of the reserve assigned to the tribe.
>
> Article 4. The Council of Elders shall appoint its Chairman and Vice-Chairman, with renewable mandates of two years' duration. A secretary responsible for keeping the record of decisions shall be appointed by the Council of Elders from among its number or outside.
>
> Article 5. The Council of Elders shall be convened by its Chairman or in his absence by the Vice-Chairman. It may also be convened at the request of half of the constituent members, or at the request of the Ministry of

the Interior. Any council may at any moment, and by invitation of its Chairman, coopt any person whose presence it judges necessary; this person shall not have voting rights.

Article 6. Decisions of the Council of Elders may only be made by a majority of two thirds of the constituent members. Within two months of notification of the decision taken, parties may appeal to the Ministry of the Interior, or if necessary to the Courts. The final decision of the Ministry must be notified within three months of receipt of the appeal. (Régime … 1958)

The members of the council, representing the different clans of the tribe, are here 'appointed according to customary rules', rather than elected as had been envisaged in the UICALO's initial demands. Nevertheless, in terms of the power relations within the Houaïlou tribes, this text still represents a partial divestment of the authority of chiefs. This is clear from a letter written by high chief Apupia Mindia (Apupia Néjâ) to the high commissioner, effectively a cautionary reminder of the state's neutrality of the state in customary affairs, established through the system of indirect rule in return for the loyalty of the chiefs.

> I have just learned that the government council has decided that the composition of the council of elders should be submitted to the ministry of the interior, for validation, and that this council shall elect a chairman who is not the chief. I protest in the name of customary rights, recognised by the 1946 constitution, against these violations of the prerogatives of tribes and traditional chiefs. It is to them and them alone that the choice of the council belongs, and the territorial administration can only approve the choice made according to customary rules, chairmanship of the council of elders rests with the chief. On the occasion of the forthcoming replacement of a tribal chief who died, I have just sent to the gendarme administrator of native affairs a list of the members of the council of elders for my district. I protest in advance against any manoeuvre that would challenge this list, the only one valid in the eyes of custom, and against any political and partisan intervention in the operation of the rules handed down to us by our ancestors. I count on your authority to ensure that the rights and freedoms recognised by the Constitution are upheld, in the name of France. (Apupia Mindia, Letter to the High Commissioner of the Republic, May 1958, private archive)

Such a protest recalls the bitter animadversions of Apupia's father Mèèjâ Néjâ on the state's failure to reward loyal chiefs (see Chapter 3). This draft legislation was aborted owing to the events of 1958 in Nouméa, when a large demonstration in opposition to Lenormand developed into an attempted coup and resulted in the suspension of the government council.[28] In the subsequent elections, on 7 December 1958, the Union Calédonienne remained in the large majority in Houaïlou, with 840 votes; the social republicans won only 272. The local balance of political forces remained stable.

Split in the Protestant church

However, the structure underlying the mobilisation of a large number of the Houaïlou Protestants on a variety of levels (economic, customary, political, organisational), which culminated in the gatherings around the diviners (*jauu*) in late 1955, broke apart not long afterwards. From at least 1954, a serious conflict arose between Marc Lacheret and Raymond Charlemagne, two of the Protestant missionaries sent to New Caledonia by the Mission Society in Paris.[29] It resulted both in visits from various leading figures in the Mission Society to New Caledonia and to the missionaries concerned being summoned to Paris. Over the years, a great mass of disagreements had accumulated between Pastor Raymond Charlemagne, the missionary established in Dö Nèvâ, on one side, and pastors Marc Lacheret of Nouméa (and later Lifou) and René Dolfuss of Lifou (later Nouméa), on the other. Marked differences of character were exacerbated by financial disagreements (Charlemagne criticising Lacheret's financial management and his ability to protect educational investment projects linked to the development of Dô Nèvâ), by political differences (Charlemagne being accused of being close to Lenormand, while Lacheret was more closely linked to the wealthier classes in Nouméa;[30] added to this were their conflicting evaluations of the political situation in Maré) and by accusations that Charlemagne was excessively strict with the Kanak pastors (owing particularly to his conflict with pastor Élia Tidjine). Despite four years of mediation, the Paris Mission Society failed to arrive at a solution. Rather the reverse: throughout the year 1957 the conflict became more entrenched. During his visit to France in July 1957, Charlemagne's position appeared indefensible to the Mission Society:

---

28 Following the events of 13 May 1958 in metropolitan France and the involvement of the Gaullist party in the management of Algerian affairs.
29 For the remainder of this chapter, I shall refer to the interpretation proposed by Trépied in relation to the case of Koné, in Chapter 8.1 of his 2007 book ('The 'Charlemagne-ist' Protestants: from the UC to the RPCR (1957–1977)'); see also Trépied 2010, Chapter 6. I am grateful to Benoît Trépied for the various archival documents he has alerted me to.
30 His daughter Évelyne married Jean Lèques, the future conservative mayor of Nouméa, in 1954.

'Whether wittingly or not, he had become a symbol of political order, which the Executive Committee could not accept, in New Caledonia any more than in any other field' ('Bref rapport sur les origines …' 1959, p. 7). Lenormand then intervened to protest against the possibility of Pastor Charlemagne being recalled to France, given the imminence of the elections in October 1957, and received assurance that he would not be recalled before the elections. In August Charles Westphal, a delegate granted high-level powers, was sent to New Caledonia. Charlemagne, against the wishes of the Mission Society, returned to New Caledonia in early September and refused to go back to France as Westphal requested. Westphal finally published an article in the *Bulletin du commerce* in Nouméa announcing that Charlemagne had been relieved of his duties:

> Pastor R. Charlemagne, recalled to France by the Committee, is relieved of his office with effect from 30 November 1957 and no longer belongs to the Territory's Mission Staff. The Protestant Mission henceforth denies any responsibility for his actions. (Westphal 1957)

This interpretation, according to which the conflict that resulted in the founding of the Free Church of New Caledonia (Église libre, Nédivâ) arose from arguments between missionaries, is today supported by those in Houaïlou who remained loyal to the Paris Mission Society (the Autonomous Church, Église autonome, Dö Nèvâ):

> It's very harsh, they even came to force my mother to sign a paper, at that time they worked a lot with paper and signatures. Ultimately it's a problem between missionaries, normally we shouldn't be involved, but we couldn't help it, the other one [Charlemagne] tried to hole up in Caledonia so he didn't have to go back to France, and then look what happened, people split, right up to now even. (Abisai Bwawé, instructor at Dö Nèvâ following the split, extract from interview, July 1993)

Seen from Houaïlou, home of the Dö Nèvâ mission where Pastor Charlemagne was established, it is difficult to abstract this conflict from the context of politico-religious mobilisation I have described in this chapter, and understand the local interpretation of these disagreements. Charlemagne's supporters emphasise first and foremost the issue of education.

> Charlemagne, he didn't think so much about prayer, but about education, for the education of the Kanaks in New Caledonia. Well the problem started because Mr Charlemagne set up a high school in Dö Nèvâ. But he set up the high school with money from state subsidies from the New

Caledonia Mission Society. But since all of that is in the name of the Paris mission, you know, the pastors got up a petition to get Charlemagne out of Dö Nèvâ … He built it, and then the Mission Society asked him to go back to Paris. With Pierrot Ayawa, and then Olèn Jöpöyöi, and then Porâ Pidra, they started to gather all the deacons, all the representatives in the tribes, the tribal chiefs. We stayed nearly a week over there in Dö Nèvâ, trying to ask all the pastors to keep Charlemagne, we're going to tell the Mission Society not to leave, we will keep Charlemagne, it's for teaching. It's no good, the Mission Society says he's got to leave. That's why Charlemagne chose to come to Nédivâ. Me I'm here because I lived through the whole thing. There are three delegations that went off, there's one that went from the east coast, over there up to Hienghène, there's one that went from the north, north-west coast, it went from Pöya to Koumac Poum, and there are others that went from here to go to Nouméa to get all the people to sign so that Charlemagne stays in New Caledonia … Because when Charlemagne left Dö Nèvâ, he came to Nédivâ, and then the school began to develop. (Honoré Jöpöyöi, extract from interview, July 1993)

You want to know exactly how the Church got cut in half. It was in the time of pastor Charlemagne, and I was right there at the start of the split in the Church, because at that time, I'm in Dö Nèvâ learning to drive, because the old people, they were preparing to set up a big cooperative. The other pastors when they taught at Dö Nèvâ, there was a barrier in education, they shouldn't cross that barrier, it's a contract between the Paris Mission Society and then the government, they mustn't raise the native, the Kanak, a bit higher. Well, when pastor Charlemagne arrived, he threw all that out, he smashed that barrier, and then he started to send students to France, like Naisseline and then all his first students, he sent them to France, Pierrot Ayawa and all them, it's not by chance that he sent them to France. And that was the start of the story. There are some who've tried to talk about it, and to ascribe other motives, but all that is false, absolutely untrue. The start of this business was purely education. Why? Because the French government wasn't pleased with the Paris Mission Society … That's the split in the Church, it's about education, it's not about anything else. (Guynemer Karé, extract from interview, August 1993)

When Pastor Charlemagne arrived in 1947 I think, him, he wanted to start to really teach the young Melanesians there in Dö Nèvâ. Him, he saw what a handicap French was. So he really opted for dropping the *Ajië* language at school, and teaching French so that the school would start to be effective, you know. Because before up there in Dö Nèvâ, the school was more oriented towards training pastors, deacons, it was a bit for teaching young people to do manual work. But the people did not really get very far in education. It was more geared to manual stuff, practical work and all that. Then there, when there were splits, it was there that most of the old people in Houaïlou, they really saw the work. Since they were closer, then they were for father Charlemagne when there was the split with the pastors all of that, father Lacheret all of that.

— So that means that in Néawa people moved over to the Free Church too?

We stayed with father Charlemagne, you know, pastor Charlemagne. Yes almost all of Houaïlou. (Ivô Mârârhëë, extract from interview, July 1995)

The first consequence of Charlemagne's dismissal was his departure from Dö Nèvâ, the missionary post belonging to the Paris Mission Society, when an interim order from the civil court in Nouméa of 27 January 1958, upheld on appeal on 17 February 1958, required that he leave the premises. A few days before the start of the new school term pastor Charlemagne, accompanied by the majority of the staff at Dö Nèvâ, set up a few kilometres up river, in the Nédivâ tribe, where the Kanaks who supported him – in particular the local leaders of the cooperative – gave him land for the construction of a new education centre. The Fédération de l'enseignement libre protestant (Protestant Free Education Federation, FELP), chaired by Dui Marayo Wetta, was founded there on 23 February 1958.

> The primary reason for setting up this Federation is the perennial failure of the Evangelical Protestant Mission in Paris until now to improve the level of its schools and its instructors. Thirty years ago the Steering Committee of the Paris Mission adopted the point of view of pastor Bergeret, that is that it was enough to have religious classes led by pastors to teach students to read the Bible in their indigenous language and some basic arithmetic. On the basis of this decision one teacher, Miss Peter, did not train any instructors during a 25-year period, and one missionary, Schoolmaster Rey-Lescure who stood up for the opposite view, was sent to Tahiti. We trained the first instructors to teach the Certificate in Primary Education in Do Néva in 1949, and in 1956 I obtained funds from Fides[31] for construction of the Elementary School in Do Néva, despite the Paris Mission Directorate intervening with the Fides Steering Committee. Today, through their autonomous Federation, the indigenous people are completely free to provide for improving their level of education and to attempt to remedy their general educational disadvantage. (Charlemagne 1961)[32]

---

31   Fonds d'investissement pour le développement économique et social de la France d'outre-mer (Investment Fund for Economic and Social Development of non-Metropolitan France) [trans.].
32   I am grateful to Benoît Trépied for sending me a copy of this document.

In retaliation for the expulsion of Raymond Charlemagne from Dö Nèvâ, the pastors and evangelists who had remained loyal to the Paris Mission Society were forcibly expelled from the Protestant tribes where the majority had rallied to Charlemagne (particularly in Kula, Gôdè and Nérhëxakwéaa). For their part, the opponents of the FELP took back the infrastructure belonging to the Paris Mission. The conflict thus spread to all the Protestant tribes in Houaïlou; the most serious incidents occurred in Warai in spring 1958, with the result that the FELP's primary school had to move premises. Taï Wahéo, a pupil at the Warai school who originated from Ouvéa, recently told this story in his memoirs:

> One Saturday morning, a non-working day, angry men entered the Protestant church in Warai. They were shouting and yelling, taking out the tables and benches used by the students. It was barely a week after school had started. They even went to Eika [a site the tribe had granted to the Protestant mission] to chase away the students who were there.
>
> — *Névâi, ge ve tu bèri xè-réé. Koa wi gèvè yömi ve* (Hey you! Get out of here now! Or else we'll kill you) …
>
> One young man kept his cool. Having witnessed the whole scene, he recognised the culprits in the disturbance … Michel, that was his name, ran to warn his father, Waxuié, and a few others …
>
> When they arrived at Eika, Auguste [Parawi-Reybas] asked:
>
> — Who brought all the benches and tables out of the church?
>
> — We did. Why, don't you like it?
>
> Immediately, it was a general punch-up. Blows rained down, mingled with shouts and curses …
>
> — That's enough, said Pierrot [Ayawa], the courts will rule on this disagreement.
>
> So people stopped fighting. Everyone went home. The gendarme, in his role as administrator of indigenous affairs, was informed by chief Nérhon Acomâ … When the class from the Warai church was transferred to the tribe of Thü, the children assumed that it was as a result of a court judgment, to allow them to study in peace … Those two years 1958 and 1959 were very hard for the pastor's family. With the split in the Protestant church, the pastor had lost all his fields. The parishioners who remained loyal to the Paris Mission left the parish and took over the fields that had been granted to the pastor. (Wahéo 2008, pp. 86–87)

This account introduces a number of important players in the Protestant mobilisation of the 1950s and 1960s, whom we shall meet again later in this chapter, in particular Pierrot Ayawa and Auguste Parawi-Reybas. Noteworthy also is the physical violence aroused by this educational and religious conflict, emerging in these moments of political mobilisation well beyond the bounds of the witch-hunt described above. Geneviève and Raymond Leenhardt, who were travelling in New Caledonia at the time, offered a political reading of these religious and educational events, associating the (armed) opponents of Pastor Charlemagne (and hence of the Free Church and the FELP) with the conservative activists supporting the social republicans – and thus implicitly aligning Charlemagne with Lenormand's party. As we shall see below, this association was also to break down.

> On our return tonight, we find Charlemagne on the road; he tells us that when he returned last night he found his school in Warai empty. He is told that they are in Tu because there are problems. He learns from the women that one of them has heard via her son that 41 social republicans gathered at Afchain's house with 14 rifles, and that they wanted to empty the Warai school. Charlemagne runs to Tu and sees that for their part his people have decided to enter Do Néva … He tells them that this would be a serious mistake and dispatches messengers to all parts. He manages to get them to turn back. (Leenhardt and Leenhardt 1958, pp. 26–27)

Ultimately, detailed examination of the protagonists in the Warai conflict presents a more complex picture of the local stakes in the brawls of spring 1958. The two opposing sides were led by two brothers who were thus rivals into a violent segmentary conflict:

> There are stories, me I lived through that time, Michel, where we were at Warai – the first FELP school was Warai on the east coast, Tiéta on the west coast – and at the time in Warai, we lived through the time when the old people were still there around the fire with spears, and it was war, you know. What I don't accept is that there was war between siblings, between members of the same family, some supporting the causes of the Evangelical Church, and the others the Free Church. In fact it was the Church that appeared on the surface, but when you took a good look beneath, there was politics, but the base of it all was culture, it was the customary relations we had, you know. (Jean-Jacques Ayawa, extract from interview, July 2006)

Aside from the isolated case of Warai, the two classes of reasons given retrospectively for the split (conflict between missionaries or investment in education) are not sufficient to account for the division of the faithful between the two churches and the two schools. Reluctance to fall in with the new leaders who had emerged during the recent Protestant mobilisations, based on an assessment of personal character or social status, could on the other hand be a much more decisive factor:

> [In our tribe] Everyone went to the Free Church, everyone. The only one who stayed attached to the Autonomous Church was grandfather X, but even there you understand the cultural split, the split at the level of custom. (Extract from interview, July 2006)

In the Lèwëö tribe for example, we may thus note that Uruva Néjâ, one of Leenhardt's former students at Dö Nèvâ, brother of high chief Apupia and victim of the *jauu* in late 1955, remained loyal to the Autonomous Church (associated with the Paris Mission Society). During the same period, he was forging links with the social republicans (even though he had been elected municipal councillor in 1954 on the list supported by the Nédivâ cooperative) – thus refusing to follow those who defended Charlemagne, who had prompted his accusation by the *jauu* and were campaigning for the reduction of his brother's powers, in favour of the council of elders.

Jean Guiart published two texts in 1959, 'Naissance et avortement d'un messianisme. Colonisation et décolonisation en Nouvelle-Calédonie (Birth and Death of a Messiah Cult: Colonisation and Decolonisation in New Caledonia)' and *Destin d'une Église et d'un peuple (1900–1959). Étude monographique d'une oeuvre missionaire protestante* (*The Fate of a Church and a People (1900–1959): A Study of a Protestant Mission*). These, like the travel journal of Geneviève and Raymond Leenhardt, take a clear stance toward the split in the Protestant church in New Caledonia, justifying the position of Charlemagne, who they thus present as the faithful follower continuing Leenhardt's missionary and educational work. What is interesting is that, in taking this position, they also found themselves taking sides in local discussions on the reform of village life:

> The high chiefdoms are losing their power to the tribal chiefs. I think this is no bad thing. An elder explained to me that in order to choose a new chief, following the death of the previous incumbent, there are now three points that must be considered by the council of elders who will elect him: his knowledge of traditional customs, his religion, which

must correspond with that of the tribe, his relations with the Whites. The high chiefs have in effect allowed themselves to be too easily bought and their subjects have not followed them in elections. All of this reveals a consideration that the mission needs to take into account. (Leenhardt and Leenhardt 1958, p. 24)

Split in the Union Calédonienne

Finally, the interlinked mobilisations instigated in Houaïlou in the early 1950s also broke down as a result of political developments in France and in New Caledonia as a whole. Following the events of 18 June 1958,[33] the substantial autonomy that the Defferre enabling legislation had allowed the New Caledonia government council, on which the Union Calédonienne held the majority, was gradually reduced, in a Gaullist process of recentralisation that lasted almost 10 years. This was initiated by governor Laurent Péchoux, who thus stood in direct opposition to Maurice Lenormand. Once again, I am interested in these political events only in terms of their effects on the social and political life of the Kanaks of Houaïlou, how they mobilised and around what issues. In fact, the result was a rapid breakdown of the alliance between Lenormand, Charlemagne, Guiart (supported at a distance by Geneviève and Raymond Leenhardt), and a certain number of rural European settlers in the Union Calédonienne on one side, and the AICLF activists, the founders of the Nédivâ cooperative, the defenders of the councils of elders, and those who had promoted the visit of the *jauu* to Houaïlou, on the other. While their interests and programs had converged during the early 1950s, the alliance had already been damaged by the split in the Protestant church.

Thus in March 1959 the Kanak municipal councillors who belonged to the AICLF resigned from the Houaïlou municipal council in support of Lenormand; the European municipal councillors from the Union Calédonienne (headed by the mayor, Denis Rousseau) refused to do so. Lenormand's local support then gradually disintegrated: firstly he came into conflict with Dui Matayo Wetta, the AICLF chairman from Ponérihouen who had been a member of the New Caledonia government council since 1957, and with Michel Kauma, the vice-chairman of the government council; secondly, a personal and political disagreement[34]

---

33 When de Gaulle became president of France and was granted emergency powers by the French parliament in order to resolve the constitutional crisis [trans.].
34 See the analysis put forward by Guiart (1966).

pitted him against Jean Guiart following the death of their father-in-law, Jules Calimbre, leading Guiart to disseminate notes that were highly critical of Lenormand, to which responses appeared in the Union Calédonienne's newspaper *L'avenir calédonien* (*Caledonian Future*);[35] finally, Pastor Charlemagne drew increasingly closer to Péchoux, principally in order to obtain the money needed to finance the new FELP facilities.

> It was Charlemagne who founded the UC [Union Calédonienne], because the UC, it's UICALO and then the Association that formed the UC. Me, I know because I lived through it, because before, when old Roch [Pidjot] and Lenormand are still there, the big meetings they hold in Houaïlou, they hold at the [Nédivâ] cooperative down there. Me I'm down there with the cooperative's big truck, I do all the tribes in Houaïlou to bring people when Roch Pidjot is coming, and then Mr Lenormand. It's a long story, because Charlemagne is for the side where there's money, it's so he can build his school quickly … He's maybe really on the side of important people who've got a lot of cash as well, yes because it's to get loans to build his school, the Federation's school, because the Federation is Charlemagne's school … Charlemagne and the others left the Union, Charlemagne he goes over to the bigwigs, it's money … I know because me, I'm there, I saw what happened, it's me that goes everywhere cutting timber, trees to build the school … It's me who does the other side up to Hienghène, with my baby-car [minibus], the cooperative's baby-car, to get the people to sign, tribe by tribe. And then there is [Auguste Parawi] Reybas who goes over to that side with Pierrot [Ayawa], they go to Canala, yes. (Honoré Jöpöyöi, extract from interview, July 1993)

> At that time, he [Pierrot Ayawa] got closer to the political circles, it was more from the need to make the FELP work. He had an ideology that he didn't articulate openly, that he didn't expound openly, for him it was a form of independence that he wanted already. He split off from the Paris Mission, because politically, his mission, as he saw it, was to train people, so that there were people capable of leading the country. I believe all the elders shared this philosophy. Then after there were splits with Charlemagne, there were splits, and then in politics it was Lenormand, it was Pentecost, at the time they were the people who held the power, who had the money, who could help. (Jean-Jacques Ayawa, extract from interview, July 2006)

> Before at the beginning, I remember when I was still a kid, everyone was in the Union Calédonienne, AICLF and UICALO. People started to vote, I can't remember if it was 51 or 52 for the first time in Caledonia

---

35   Nos 251, 252 and 254, April 1960.

there, the Melanesians. And then that worked for maybe about six years, you know. And the big split happened at the same time as the Protestant church split, it was in 58. That was when the Protestant church began to break apart, and the UC, the Union Calédonienne starts to split. The AICLF they went over to the other side, and then UICALO was still with the UC, you know. (Ivô Mârârhëë, extract from interview, July 1995)

These converging developments, moving towards the break-up of the Union Calédonienne, were particularly strong in Houaïlou (as in Ponérihouen) where, as we have seen, mobilisation around the AICLF had been high among the Protestant Kanaks. It is therefore no surprise that it was in Houaïlou, in the Ba tribe, that a crucial general meeting of the AICLF was held, at which the association expressed its support for Dui Matayo Wetta and Michel Kauma in their opposition to Lenormand, and strident criticism of the latter's proposals for reform of the status of municipalities ('The second day was devoted to studying the various plans for reorganisation of Municipal Committees. The Union Calédonienne's two versions were examined in detail and rejected by all the Delegates present, who are categorically opposed to the introduction of an electoral majority system at tribal level' ('Assemblée générale de l'AICLF' 1960)). The text drawn up at the general meeting merits detailed examination. First, because in opposition to Lenormand's position, the AICLF insists on maintaining the division between municipal matters and customary aspects of village or tribal organisation:

> The AICLF opposes any introduction of municipal sections, because it is in practice impossible to operate in local circumstances, because they are discriminatory in principle and because, owing to the automatic confusion of municipal matters and customary issues, they risk causing serious difficulties within the tribes, both in Grande Terre and in the Loyalty Islands.
>
> Our customary affairs should not be mixed up with those of the municipalities. The proposal before us is for the establishment of sections with councils elected within the Municipalities, these local councils being responsible for managing the municipal interests of districts. The municipal Budgets are not large enough to be cut into small portions. We are opposed to our life being transformed by mixing politics and elections in places where our understanding and our solidarity depend on the balance established through custom. ('Assemblée générale de l'AICLF' 1960)

Second, because in this way the plans for recognition of the council of elders regained an element of local, 'customary' self-organisation independent of the general political issues in New Caledonia. The AICLF's reflections reached a level of detailed elaboration sensitive to the diversity of local configurations of social relations:

> The problem of official recognition is therefore that of the Council of Elders which has been reinvigorated in the last few years, renewing an ancient custom, but too often in a disorganised fashion. In order to prevent any challenges, and any intervention by Politics where it does not belong, a number of conditions need to be met, in particular no election should intervene on the customary level:
>
> 1. The Council of Elders of the Tribe should be composed of one representative of each clan resident in the tribe. This representative is normally the oldest man in the senior branch of the clan, unless all the members of the clan agree on another person, for example if the normal incumbent has moved elsewhere. No clan must be excluded from the Council, once it has been settled there for at least one generation.
> 2. The decisions of the Council of Elders must be unanimous, in which case they can be considered final. If there is prolonged disagreement, the decision can be taken by a two-thirds majority; this opens the possibility of a challenge in law, which is in any case already possible in the Courts. In no case may a decision be made by simple majority, for fear of leading quickly to violent opposition in the reserves resulting in the collapse of indigenous society, especially through the politicisation of the problem.
> 3. The role of the Council of Elders is to serve as an organ of conciliation for settling problems of land ownership within reserves, conflicts around the attribution of family names, any difficulties resulting from marriages, and everything that, according to local custom, concerns the internal life of the tribe.
> 4. The Council of Elders must not be attributed any responsibility on the municipal level. This does not preclude it from formulating opinions on points of interest to the tribe and tasking the Chief with taking any steps in the general interest.
> 5. It is for the Council of Elders to appoint, according to local custom, the successor to a Chief who has died or stepped down. The Council of Elders is chaired by the Chief as part of his duties; he has the responsibility of holding, or having another hold, the notebook in which at each meeting the date, names of those present, subjects discussed, decisions taken or wishes expressed, are recorded. Where any firm decision is made, the members present must initial the notebook under the record of the decision.

6. As regards the appointment of High Chiefs in Grande Terre, the diversity of individual practices is such that it is better to pass the task of recording the appointment of post-holders to the Administration, following upon general agreement in the district. Subsequently, a consultation among the various officially recognised Councils of Elders will determine whether it is necessary to make legal provision for them to meet in Assemblies or Districts, under the chairmanship of the High Chief, whom these Assemblies shall have, among other things, the duty of appointing. ('Assemblée générale de l'AICLF' 1960)

In light of the articulation of these positions, the congress of the Union Calédonienne that was held in November 1960 resolved to expel Kauma and Wetta, thus triggering the departure of the AICLF from the Union Calédonienne, which then drew closer to the conservative parties. Thus, in the municipal elections of May 1961 in Houaïlou, Paul Malignon, who had succeeded Rousseau as mayor on the latter's death in 1959, was re-elected, with the support of the Kanak municipal councillors who were the mainstays of the AICLF, Auguste Parawi-Reybas, Pierre Ayawa and Kaléba Boai. And, in the parliamentary elections of November 1962, Lenormand lost the election in Houaïlou for the first time since 1951, with only 350 votes against 733 for Édouard Pentecost. Thus Houaïlou became a regular provider of Kanak elected officials opposed to the Union Calédonienne's proposals for autonomy and, later, of anti-independence representatives, some of whom, like Auguste Parawi-Reybas, Victorin Boéwa and Delin Wéma, were well known throughout New Caledonia.

The splits in the Union Calédonienne, Lenormand's political trajectory, the state's resumption of control in New Caledonia (Jacquinot law 1963, Billotte law 1969)[36] and the AICLF's demands effectively helped to separate the municipal issue from that of the councils of elders. And, when the reform of municipal administration was finally passed in 1969, there was no mention of councils of elders. It was merely established that, in accordance with a 'consideration relative to the clan council and the council of clan chiefs', on 10 December 1981:

> Article 1. The clan council settles all matters involving the clan's property. It is composed of representatives of each family group included in the clan.
>
> Article 2. At the level of the tribe, a council of clan chiefs may be set up, comprising each of the customary representatives of the clans making up the tribe.

---

36 French government legislation reducing the autonomy of New Caledonia [trans.].

Article 3. Once it is fully constituted, the council of clan chiefs replaces the council of elders as regards the powers exercised by this latter. The council of clan chiefs manages the general customary Administration of the tribe.
(*Journal officiel de la Nouvelle-Calédonie* 1981)

Houaïlou was a crucial location in New Caledonian political life in the 1950s, particularly because of the presence of the Protestant mission and its role in the political reorganisation that followed the dismantling of the *indigénat* system. This decade was marked by the transition from chiefs with a monopoly on representation of the Kanaks in the public arena (like high chief Mandaoué, the first elected Kanak municipal official in 1947) to a new generation of local actors (such as Pierre Ayawa, Georges Jöpöyöi, Jona Pwâdi and others). The successive conflicts that were played out in the late 1950s led the majority of them to espouse conservative policies, some developing political careers at territory level. One of their aims was to challenge colonial chiefdoms by promoting the postcolonial councils of elders. This challenge ran alongside the attempt to build economic autonomy through the cooperative, the quest for political harmony through witch-hunts, and the pursuit of educational success in their support for pastor Charlemagne's breakaway venture. This mobilisation was in fact based on a coalition of new actors in the intellectual, religious and political spheres: Charlemagne, Leenhardt, Guiart and, to a lesser extent, Lenormand thus saw their fates closely entwined with that of Houaïlou. In addition, the 1950s were by far the most productive for Guiart; as far as the Houaïlou region is concerned, he relied massively (but not exclusively) on Protestant interlocutors from the AICLF. Thus, in the pages 'honouring those who have been of greatest assistance in the writing of this study' that open the first edition of *Structure de la chefferie* (*The Structure of the Chiefdom*), 10 men from Houaïlou are mentioned in the acknowledgements;[37] eight of these were mainstays or supporters of the AICLF, and some also of the cooperative (Kétiwan Ayawa, Pierre Ayawa, Yené Bwérhéxéu, Philippo Cibëi, Georges Jöpöyöi,[38] Élia Mârârhëë, Acöömwâ Nérhô, Auguste Parawi), the ninth being the Catholic chief of Kamwi (Adrien Lecê Bwêé), and the 10th, pastor Charlemagne himself (who disappears from the acknowledgements in the second edition).

---

37 Guiart 1963, pp. 9–11.
38 Under the name 'Bwéowé'.

4. POST-*INDIGÉNAT* MOBILISATIONS

While the level of military activity in Houaïlou was low in the 1950s, physical violence nevertheless remained a significant component of the register of possible actions drawn upon by those involved in the reorganisation that political, economic and customary mobilisations aimed towards. Thus, the blows and mistreatment that accompanied the visit of the diviners (*jauu*) from Ponérihouen in late 1955 and the split in the Protestant church are not an incidental element in the formation of apparently relatively consensual social spaces: intimidation and harassment here represent the margin of the spaces of autonomy that the Kanak inhabitants of Houaïlou were in the process of constructing.

***

In this chapter I have chosen the organisation of a witch-hunt conducted by seers (*jauu*) in Houaïlou in late 1955 as a point from which to observe the huge transformations that took place in colonial governmentality after the end of the Second World War. By following the mobilisation of one group of actors, I have sought to reveal the broader connections between political stakes (access to universal suffrage), economic questions (the cooperative organisation of production and consumption), religious divisions (within the Protestant church in particular), educational issues and village concerns (through the councils of elders and preoccupation with questions of witchcraft), over an extended period that runs from the granting of voting rights to a few Kanaks in 1945 to the AICLF congress in Ba in 1960, where the conjunction of interests that had made Houaïlou one of the centres of political life in the 1950s finally broke down.

5
The Subjectivity of Violent Action

In her analysis of the municipal elections of 13 March 1977, Myriam Dornoy writes: 'Due to the combination of the mining centre at Poro[1] and the influence over Melanesians of the conservative Protestant mission of Pastor Charlemagne, Houaïlou was the sole example of a region with a majority of Melanesians and a minority of autonomist votes' (Dornoy 1984, p. 247). And indeed, in 1977 (as in 1971), Auguste Parawi-Reybas, a leading figure in the Association des indigènes calédoniens et loyaltiens français (AICLF) and in Kanak 'loyalism', whose activity during the 1950s has already been noted (see Chapter 4), was elected mayor. The 'autonomist' list, the umbrella for candidates from the Union Calédonienne, the Union multiraciale de Nouvelle-Calédonie (New Caledonia Multiracial Union) and the Union progressiste mélanésienne (Melanesian Progressive Union), garnered only 38 per cent of the vote. The key elements contributing to the emergence of the independence movement in New Caledonia[2] included the activism of the Foulards Rouges and 1878 Group[3] from 1969 onwards, the emergence of a land rights movement, the founding of the Parti de libération kanake (Kanak Liberation Party, Palika) in 1976 and, finally, the Union Calédonienne's congress in Bourail in December 1977, at which the organisation resolved to rally to the independence

---

1   Many mine employees – Europeans, Wallis and Futuna Islanders and Tahitians – were living in Poro in the 1970s; they tended to vote for conservative parties.
2   Barbançon 2008; Bensa 1995; Chappell 2003; Colombani 1985; Coulon 1985; Dommel 1993; Gabriel and Kermel 1985 and 1988; Leblic 1993; Mokaddem 2005.
3   The Foulards Rouges (Red Scarves), a student-led campaign group, and the 1878 Group, a more radical independence movement focused particularly on land reform, came together with other groups to form Palika in 1976 [trans.].

campaign. From this date on, the land rights movement took off in Houaïlou, with a succession of settlers' properties being claimed from December 1977 – starting with those that had been assigned in the second process of land demarcation conducted by governor Paul Feillet at the turn of the 20th century. In August 1979, it was in Gwârü, in Houaïlou, that the Autonomous Evangelical Church announced that its delegates were unanimously in favour of independence. On 24 September 1979 the commemoration of the French takeover of New Caledonia in Houaïlou village was disrupted by Palika demonstrators, in a scene far from the consensual atmosphere of the centenary celebrations in 1953 (see Chapter 4):

> I remember in 79, when we had a demonstration in the village, on 24 September, to protest against the raising of the flag over the town hall, we don't want it there any longer. It was organised by the regional Palika branch at the time, people jeered at us, they insulted us in the village; it's because back then, people were still too far to the right, dug in on the right. (Raphaël Wéma Néèè, extract from interview, May 1991)

At this point I turn my focus to the forms of violent conflict that accompanied land rights claims and the Kanak independence movement in the Houaïlou region, ending more than a century of special relationship with French colonial power. The period known as the 'events', which began with the 'active boycott' of the territorial assembly elections stipulated by the 'Lemoine statute'[4] (a campaign famously incarnated by the image of Éloi Machoro destroying a ballot box in Canala with an axe) on 18 November 1984, ended with the successive events, in spring 1988, of the Fayawé gendarmerie's murderous attack in Ouvéa, the massacre of hostage-takers in Gossanah, the signature of the Matignon-Oudinot agreements,[5] and finally the murder of Jean-Marie Tjibaou and Yéwéné Yéwéné in May 1989. The land reform begun in 1978, on the other hand, is still under way today. My ethnographic research in Houaïlou began, in 1991, under the shadow of those years of tension, and the ongoing discussions about land rights. I had the opportunity to meet a number of those active during this time and I, therefore, focus here especially on their account of these 'events'. As far as the means at my disposal allow, I shall

---

4   Introduced on 4 September 1984, the statute strongly reinforced New Caledonian autonomy and provided for a referendum on independence within five years [trans.].

5   Agreement between New Caledonian separatists and loyalists in 1988, providing for a 10-year period of development and a new referendum on self-determination, while the Kanaks were a minority in the electorate [trans.].

try to understand the subjective implications of what was experienced, at least in part, as a war of independence. My microsociological and pragmatic description focuses on three moments of conflict: the events of 18 November 1984, the death of a man during a land rights meeting in 1987, and a family crisis around a padlock in 1991.

The 'events': Collective campaigns and individual initiatives

1984–88: Return to war in Houaïlou

18th November

The day of 18 November 1984 saw a large number of roadblocks erected in Houaïlou, and opened a period of struggle for the control of space (land) and movement (primarily on the roads). Roadblocks were set up on roads along the Houaïlou valley and the coast and, for four years, any passing vehicles were liable to be targeted by stone-throwers. The retrospective account of the 'events' often paints these as heroic actions. The interview extract below gives an idea both of the epic tone of such accounts – despite the fact that, in this case, the planned action did not take place – and the way the 'events' are inscribed in a history of war, rooted in the use of ancestral family powers of protection or propitiation (see chapters 2 and 4).

> When I left for France [to do military service], grandfather showed me family things. When I left, he gave me them, I took them with me: 'If war comes, well you do this, you do that.' What I'm telling you is, there were family secrets, you know. He showed me that, but it was funny ... On 18 November in Houaïlou we nearly got killed, but I used that medicine. I'll never forget it, I believe that's what saved us, because we were in Néajië, and then here comes X ... he egged all the young people in the valley into going to attack the town hall, and they came with two trucks ... I said to the others: 'No, in the strategy we've planned, our role is to block the valley, here the mood isn't so much in favour of the independence movement, so we need to take that into account.' ... We talked for a bit, it was hard, and then X was still pushing, so in the end all the young people decided: 'OK, we're going!' and they came with balaclavas, a whole pile of things, and everyone was there, everyone was silent. And then I said to X: 'Listen, you're pushing the young people, but look, among all these young people, there are some who won't come

back, they'll all get themselves shot down there, there are people in the town hall, there are sure to be RCPR[6] people down there, and they're armed, and they're people whose backs will be covered. But look, if the young people get killed, who's going to take responsibility? Will you? Will it be you that takes responsibility for that?' And he wasn't planning to go, he was pushing the young guys, but he wasn't going ... so I called the people, I explained to them, I said: 'Things like that, they're things we shouldn't do', I explained why, and then I said to them: 'Well, since the others insist on going at all costs, I'll go with them, but I want you to be clear that we're going, but we might not come back.' I said it straight to everyone – grandfather Y was there, he wasn't saying anything, it looked like he had tears in his eyes – I said to them: 'OK, but I'm going to tell the others that you're not going on your own, I'm going with you. Wait here for me, I'm going down, then I'll come back up.' I went down [to the river], I bathed with the medicines, then I got my gun, I went back up. You should have seen the looks they were giving me. I got into the first truck. When I arrived, I told the young people what they had to do ... I said: 'Inside we're going to have to shoot. You fire into the crowd, the one who's going to pick up the ballot box, he takes the ballot box, but you mustn't aim, there's no question of aiming, you have to shoot, anyone who has a gun you have to kill him, because it's him or us.' So off we went, we'd already planned where to take up position, there were several positions, and then off we went, but you know, we were saved by Z, it was as if he did it on purpose. He stopped us, he said: 'Listen, turn around, it's not worth it, we can't get to the bridge, and down there, the reinforcements from Ponérihouen, it's packed with armoured cars, and then the people are in the town hall, they're drunk, but they're armed.' So that's what happened, that's why we turned back. But the reason I'm telling you is because I used the medicine that day. I've always wondered whether it wasn't just a coincidence, I think it was the medicine that saved us. Because it's a medicine that's like that, it's a medicine that helps you to pass through dangers ... So talking of the medicine, that's the time when I used it. (Extract from interview, February 1999)

Christine Demmer uses the example of Canala to demonstrate the importance of the period of the 'events' in the development of a new generation of political actors at local tribal level.[7] The epic and dramatised recounting of the various episodes of the 'events', the narrative elaboration of memories, the staging of the self, and the exclusion of subsequent generations too young to have been involved in these heroic feats,

---

6   Rassemblement pour la Calédonie dans la République (Rally for Caledonia in the Republic), the local branch of the RPR (Gaullist political party in France), led by Jacques Lafleur.
7   Demmer 2002 and 2008.

undeniably colour the historical awareness of this period. This awareness initially developed through the shared experience not only of collective mobilisation on the day of 18 November but, also, in the following months, of arrest, prison, and the violence of mobile police and military units.[8]

> We carried on with our disruption and all that, and then there were clashes here, I got caught up in quite a few raids, around the reserves here, the mobiles [gendarmes] arrived, they smash everything, they mix everything up, washing powder, sugar, rice, salt. (Raphaël Wéma Nééè, extract from interview, May 1991)

As well as being a serious challenge to the inequality of colonial relations, the 'events' were also a time when people took action in a multitude of microlocal situations, harking back to political conflicts around the establishment of administrative chiefdoms, the arrival of the missions and the split in the Protestant church (some of which I have examined in previous chapters). For example, the mention of the local 'right wing' forces or the RCPR of course refers to the presence of European settlers in Houaïlou, and their extensive hold over land, but also includes a considerable number of Kanak 'loyalists', among them a number of elected representatives.

> We were putting up barricades in the tribe, we put up a sign saying 'No RCPR members permitted to enter the tribe', and so we put a chain across the two parts of the road. He came, he saw that, he came right after the death of Éloi [Machoro], he came back, he saw the barricade, he said: 'What's all this?' We answered: 'You saw the sign.' He said: 'Even me?' and I called him over because he's a nephew of mine, in the family. He came down to see me, we talked a bit, I told him: 'It's better not to insist, because you've seen all the young guys there, you should understand.' He said: 'Yes, but I'm from the tribe.' I said: 'Me, I understand, but will the others? Because yesterday and the day before, we saw you on the TV, alongside the old guy who's categorically against what we're doing. We're demanding our dignity as Kanaks, but if you want to deny your identity, that's your problem.' That's how it was, that's it, when I said that, he tried to sweet-talk me, so then the young people started to come over. And then it was the mobiles [gendarmes] who escorted him through the tribe. (Extract from interview, May 1991)

---

8   See Feldman 1991.

A warrior

Going beyond the chronology of the 'events' in Houaïlou, the following four extracts from one interview offer an outline of the forms of military actions mounted, and the subjective involvement they reveal. Alongside the roadblock campaign, which is better known from the widely disseminated media images (both press photographs and television), and was more structured, being coordinated by leading political elements (in New Caledonian parlance, the 'pressure groups' making up the FLNKS[9] and the local 'committees of struggle'), the war in the 1980s in Houaïlou was also a time of marked autonomy and great freedom of individual initiative. Here I consider two scenes of fires (in a house and a shop), and two examples of attacks on drivers (of a lorry and a car):

1. The business at the As' place, I was involved. There was one of B's uncles there, who the A family had left there to guard it, then at that time there was also a company working on the road there. In the evening, they would park their machines at A's place … And then one night, I said to a nephew and a cousin, I said: 'Hey, guys, we're going down and we're going to set fire to A's house, and then burn a few of the machines that are up there as well.' … I got there, and then I chucked a Molotov cocktail at the little house, and it flared up brilliantly, but it only burned the wall. It didn't do a lot of damage, you know. Then him, he was inside, well, he wasn't asleep yet, he was inside, and when he saw the light, the fire, he came out. We were in the dark, we saw him come out, and then he came out with a gun, he looked around and then when he saw the light he went back in, he grabbed a bag, he shut the door, he took off, and he ran all night, he said he ran until he got to B, that evening … That's it, we made sure he'd definitely left. So then we set fire to the house, we set fire to the machines, then we scarpered. Afterwards, a long time after, when we told the story, it was one of our uncles, he was a runner, then we told him one day when we saw him again, we cracked up laughing after. Oh, there are some actions I still laugh about, because there are some that are funny, there really are …

2. The C family, they had a shop there, before the events … There were two people there, two Kanaks to guard the building. And in the evening, I saw that they had both gone into the house below with two guns. I said: 'Well then, let's see.' And then I waited until it was late. And then around midnight, that's it, I got my things ready, I

---

9   Front de libération nationale kanak et socialiste (Kanak Socialist National Liberation Front), formed in September 1984.

> made two Molotov cocktails … I threw one at the window, it broke the window, then exploded inside. And then … it caught fire straight away, then on the ceiling as well, there were boxes, all of that. I heard the two shouting inside, then all of a sudden I saw the fat one, the one called D, breaking down the front door, then the other one behind him. Me I was killing myself laughing up there, I was hiding behind. But hey, they weren't burned, you know, but they were scared by how big the fire was. Afterwards they looked, I saw them standing there, they looked around, they couldn't do a thing, you know. After when the fire had gone out, I saw the two of them go down towards where grandfather E lives, because they live there. Then after, I saw the two had left, after I went up. There's a house behind, well, I set fire to all of that, and then I went off to the mound to watch it all burn. Then I went calmly back home. Afterwards, in the morning, I heard on the news, and they said it was FLNKS activists. But down there even now, people don't know who it was. At A's place they know, but at C's they don't know who did it. (Extracts from interview, August 2004)

Another of my interviewees put a political slant on this second fire, setting it in the historical context of commercial and affective relationships between Kanaks and settlers, which I have referred to at various points throughout this analysis (see chapters 3 and 4):

> The houses that were burned, they belonged to the settlers, C. We took advantage of the political events to chase them out, because we'd asked the council of elders to get up a petition to ban the sale of alcohol, he was selling alcohol there. So for us it was too close to the tribe, we saw how that caused problems in a lot of families. A father who sells a bunch of bananas, as soon as he's got three or four hundred francs,[10] he can walk to go and get a bottle of beer. So as the council of elders, the customary authorities, weren't really doing anything, we took advantage of the political events to get rid of it. (Extract from interview, May 1991)

Thus, as in the 1950s, political activism had as much to do with the singular local relationships of proximity and exploitation as with the national slogans of the political parties. I continue with two further extracts from the first interview:

> 3. There's the story of F. When everything starts to blow up down below, he started to evacuate his stock to Bourail. And then one day, I go to the Col des Roussettes, I had my gun, loaded, and I had the bullets I needed and everything, and then I just happened to go up there.

---

10 CFP francs (currency used in Francophone ex-colonies), a sum equivalent to 2.5–3.3 euros.

Because in my head, I was saying: 'Oh, I'm going up to the Col des Roussettes, if there are mobiles [gendarmes] passing through there I have to get one of them in the head.' And I was going to do it, you know, I was! And as the Col des Roussettes was a good place for that sort of thing, forest everywhere around, well I went off, I set up camp in a little spot up there ... And then here comes F with his big truck full of cattle, I said: 'Oh, look at you there, you who used to shoot at G's brothers sometimes when they go to fish down there, there you are.' ... Then when he got there, I'm there, I've already got the gun trained on him, I said I'm going to plug him. Then I said: 'No, let it go', into the truck tyre, on the driver's side, his side, he passed right in front of me, and the lorry tipped over on his side, and I saw him panic, he starts to look all around, he must have heard the noise of the gun too, he knew as well, but since the front wheel on his side is completely blown out, and the truck is starting to slow down ... So after I reloaded, the two back wheels on the left, the driver's side, I plugged two bullets in there. The truck accelerated like crazy, it was smoking and everything ... And then people don't know who did that either. There are quite a few tricks like that that I pulled by myself. Without anyone knowing. But I don't know, I like pulling those tricks alone like that. Without anyone noticing ...

4. With H it was the same as well, he said he's had enough because every day there's a roadblock at I, every day, and him, he's fed up with it. And then one day, he said to all his work colleagues down there: 'All the little rabbits in I, one day I'm going to slaughter them up there.' And that didn't fall on deaf ears among his workmates. And then J told us what he said. I said straightaway: 'Oh, that's how it is, just wait, let's wait for him down there.' I went down, I always had a little knife like that, nicely sharpened, he comes with his car, he comes down from the pass, he saw us there, I came out, I said: 'Stop', and he stopped, and then before I started talking with him, I cut the wheel, I cut two tyres, after the third wheel, I came up to his side. Then I said to him: 'Oh, it's you, do you remember, you said to J that we were rabbits and you were going to slaughter us like in Hienghène[11] – he said that, the little rabbits of I – you were going to slaughter them, it was you said that, wasn't it?' And then J was with us that day too, because we brought him along so he told the truth in front of him. Because he was a witness, he heard what he said. And then he started to panic, because some of the guys had sticks, others had tamiocs [hatchets], and I had my knife ... Then I said: 'But why

---

11 An allusion to the murder of 10 independence campaigners near the tribe of Tiendanite, in Hienghène, on 5 December 1984.

are you lying? You should tell the truth.' And then I started to yell too, and I started to roll up my sleeves, all of that, getting ready to hit him. Then I said: 'If you don't tell the truth, you see this knife? I'll stick it in here and it'll come out here, if you don't tell the truth.' And then his son beside him, his name is K, he starts to talk over there, I turned to him over there, and I made him get out of the car, I opened the door, and I made him get out of the car, and when his father saw it was going to turn out badly, he started the engine, first gear, but he was driving with three flat tyres. The others saw that he'd started off, first gear, that's it, stones were raining down, break the windows, he must have got hit a few times as well but they got away. (Extracts from interview, August 2004)

The first point of note is the similarity between this last scene and the accounts of confessions elicited during the visit of the seers to expose alleged witches (see Chapter 4): here again, the use of violence is deemed legitimate as a means of producing truth. Equally striking is the resemblance between this account and the hunting scene – a genre narrative of a type frequently encountered in New Caledonia, and not only among my Kanak interviewees. Characteristic features include the staging of the self in the account and the extremely precisely remembered details (which may have been reworked over time: this interview took place more than 15 years after the events recounted). In the four extracts cited, the interviewee highlights the techniques of ambush, keeping watch and waiting, which are not unrelated to those of pre-colonial wars, as far as can be known.[12] My interviewee's actions are also set in the context of his family's history in war, one of his grandfathers having enlisted in the French army during the First World War, and other members of his family during the Second World War (see Chapter 3). Finally, these incidents of violence take place in a more general social context in which opposition to the 'structural violence' of colonisation meant that, for those involved, the use of war and physical violence was on some level justified.

Acts of violence during the 'events', as presented in this interview, are not of the order of direct confrontation or pitched battle. Rather, these are guerrilla techniques aimed at control of space: fires to intimidate or chase out settlers, especially those deemed most implicated in relations of inequality; roadblocks built with stones, felled trees or trenches dug across the carriageway; and stone-throwing (or occasionally shooting) at cars

---

12 Leenhardt 1930, pp. 34–46.

driving the roads – regardless of the political opinions of those driving them. In response, the state sought to maintain its control of the roads by operating convoys under military or police protection. Many Houaïlou men involved in the 'events' also participated in expeditions into the region's mountains and forests, returning to the footpaths linking villages that were remote from one another by road, and thereby coming into contact once more with the old cemeteries. In this struggle for control of the roads, Simone Heurteaux, a teacher, was killed in April 1985 by stones thrown with great force as she drove past; this was the only death attributed to the 'events' in Houaïlou.

In returning to this focus on gestures, words and their contexts, we need to take a moment to interrogate the notion of 'violence', in terms of both the precise definition of the actions it covers and its moral connotations. In the sociological analysis of violence, the researcher faces questions of ethics and sentiment that cannot always be resolved in practice by the anti-ethnocentric anthropological principle of suspension of judgment. Some anthropologists use the concept of the 'grey zone' – a decontextualised concept borrowed from Primo Levi, which alludes to the way frames of moral reference are overturned in violent situations – to address this difficulty but, in my view, this simply reifies the paradox.[13] The conflicts under consideration here have led me to meet murderers in New Caledonia who in other situations prevented violence; victims beaten to death who were known locally for their domestic abuse; politically and economically dominated individuals, victims of serious structural violence, who also perpetrate violence in unequal social relations within their own group (particularly in relations of gender, generation or status). 'Physical violence' is not a unitary reality, and portraying it as a political evil obscures rather than illuminates the specific features of each case.[14]

A judgment in Néawa

Alongside the actions against settlers, against anti-independence Kanaks and against Europeans using the municipality's roads, the 'events' were also a period marked by tension among the local leaders of the independence movement, particularly in relation to actions undertaken. This is evident from the first interview extract cited in this chapter, in the conflict between my interviewee and X around the potential attack on Houaïlou

---

13   Scheper-Hughes and Bourgois 2004.
14   Naepels 2006a.

town hall on 18 November 1984. Another FLNKS activist told of other internal disagreements: 'I called out to Y, during the events: "If we were at war, I'd kill you, and the people defending you as well." There are too many wimps. There are things you don't need to argue about. A bullet in the head' (extract from interview, February 1999). These tensions continued throughout this period, and culminated in a 'judgment' in the Néawa tribe, where there were disagreements among a number of local political leaders who were also organising military operations linked to the campaign. Although the issue in question was different, this form of collective judgment, within the setting of the village, echoes the tribunals organised by the *jauu* (diviners) in 1955 (see Chapter 4), including in this same Néawa tribe.

Insults and blows: Engagement of the self in land reform

The land reform on which the state embarked in 1978, as a way of countering the emerging demands for independence, gathered pace after the 'events'. This was due both to the departure of a number of settlers (following threats of physical violence or the burning of their houses) and to the conclusion of the Matignon-Oudinot agreements. From the start, by questioning the legitimacy of the families making land claims, it also resulted in a plethora of internal conflicts within the Kanak population.[15] Under the procedures for redistribution of state land operated by the body charged with land reform, the Agence pour le développement rural et l'aménagement foncier (Agency for Rural Development and Land Use, ADRAF), land was only assigned once a local consensus had emerged – in other words on condition that no claim was lodged by a third party contesting the presumed ownership. The conflicts that arose at this time were manifested in the long-term deadlock on reassignment of a number of sites. They also led to a general rise in social activity, particularly in the form of meetings and discussions, sometimes organised by the ADRAF. I shall examine two examples of violent actions linked to land conflicts, in Dâô and Koro, considering the forms of engagement brought into play.

---

15   Naepels 1998 and 2006b.

1991: A visit to Dâô and some meetings about land reform

During the first week I spent in Houaïlou in 1991, I was invited by the person I was lodging with to accompany him on a visit to a site in Dâô. We went with a dozen or so other men, members of the three main lineages of one clan, a week in advance of a meeting called by the ADRAF to discuss the potential assignment of this land.[16] There was a palpable tension during the visit and all the men present, apart from myself, were armed with machetes and guns – for clearing the paths and hunting, but also to put up a front and be ready for all eventualities. The journey was remarkable for the fact that very few of the participants spoke during the two hours it took us to walk the site: one of the men present, however, identified the places where these three lineages had been living around a century earlier, before the colonial expropriation of the land. Some men, older than the speaker and members of other lineages than his, seemed rather surprised by what they heard him say. This visit allowed the three lineages to formulate a common position at the meeting organised by the ADRAF the following week; it also fed into the stand-off between these individuals and their adversaries at this meeting, in an exchange of insults:

> Yes when [the ADRAF land agent] starts his report, talking about boundaries, all that, and then how the land is to be shared, and then he finished his report and invited everyone to speak. And then as the B family has a little plot in that bit of Dâô, me personally I didn't know, I found out the day we visited that site ... So it's in relation to that that grandfather A starts to say what he thought, you know. So he started his speech, he was really saying what he thought, what he wanted to do, all that. And then after, he starts to attack the B family about the site in Dâô, and how there was a plan for a GIE there,[17] well he didn't agree, and you know he thought of himself as the one in command of all the families in that sector. So he doesn't recognise the B family there, and then he said that if the B family did anything in that part, they risked coming up against him, him and then his family, you know. And then that was it, so he insulted us, because he was talking to dad B ... So he let loose the first insult, then the old man didn't say anything, second time he didn't say anything, third time he didn't say anything, so then I replied. I told him what I thought. Yes, and then it didn't come to any conclusion that meeting, then everyone went home.

---

16 I described the conditions of colonial expropriation of this site in chapters 2 and 3.
17 GIE: groupement d'intérêt économique (economic interest grouping), a legal vehicle for development projects at that time.

— And father B, you think he didn't answer, why was that?

I don't know, I can't tell you why he didn't answer. Anyway, he just answered: '*Ah! Tëvë e ma kwa tëvë yaané!* (Speak then speak well!)', you know.[18] There's no point insulting people. That's what he said. That's what he said, and then no, he didn't react. (Extract from interview, August 2004)

The same disagreement over the attribution of the site in Dâô was expressed at the following meeting, a few months later, which ended with a renewed exchange of insults and then a brawl:

So the chairman of the council of elders opens the meeting. And then he invites everyone to speak so everyone can state their position and say what they think and all that. And then C starts to speak, and then he was stating his position, you know. Then he came back to what happened down below. And then uncle D replied to him, uncle D stood up, and he was talking loudly, and then he showed C that he didn't agree with what he said about what happened down below, you know. So they were speaking, we were on the road, and them they were on the verandah, sitting on a bench, all the elders there, him, he was talking and going towards C, and C stands up, and then he raises his voice on the other side as well. And then uncle D threw the little tamioc [hatchet] he had. He threw the tamioc, well it was just to make the point, you know, that he was there too. Well he didn't want to hurt him, the tamioc fell just next to him, you know. And then when C saw that, he calmed down straightaway. And then after, there are voices that start to speak, he's calmed down, in the end he's sat down, he still carries on talking, uncle D, after he's thrown the tamioc. Me I got in ahead of uncle D, I went after C, and that's when the fight started, that's it, that's how the meeting ended, you know. (Extract from interview, August 2004)

In dialogues, a collective is formed around oneself both through traditional historical appeals to a pre-colonial legitimacy, like those produced during the visit to the site, and through the delegitimisation of the speaker by means of mockery, insult or provocation. There is thus a continuum from speech to violent gesture.

1987: The death of K

The second case I should like to analyse had more serious consequences. It throws a very clear light on the way physical violence is articulated with the account of history and with local ways of interpreting misfortune,

---

18 Literally, 'Oh! Speak well but don't speak ill!'

in relation to the alleged powers of the ancestors. In October 1987, an open-air meeting was held to address conflicts over the reassignment of the Devillers property, involving the village of Koro.[19] This meeting was remarkable, and its consequences particularly significant, in that one of the people present, whom I shall call K, died as he was speaking, while criticising the actions of the Z family. This situation helps to deepen understanding of the forms of subjective engagement in conflict, in its articulation not only of words and gestures, insults and blows, but also of the physical and the symbolic.

> The way uncle was speaking, he was yelling at them, you know, and then he told the story, how they were thrown out of Koro, how they were chased away, how they came back from Bourail, all those stories, the name they bore as well, and then he came to that, why that name as well. And then all of a sudden, three times, we heard a tree falling, because there's a little forest just behind there … then all of a sudden we heard 'crack', a big tree falling, and we turned round, and apparently nobody saw anything, you know … we heard, everyone heard, everyone stopped, the old man stopped talking, then he started up again. Second time, same sound, a tree falling, everyone stopped, we looked, and third time, it starts again the tree about to fall, we're still hearing little creaks, all that, and then after, uncle crashed too, he was talking, talking, then he was biting his tongue. When we saw him, he starts to turn like that, and then crash, laid out, fell down dead. And then I don't know who jumped up, when he fell, the first to react was A, he got up from where he was sitting, and he went straight for B, then he said: 'That's your fault, and if he's dead, that's your fault', and then he hit B, crash bang wallop, then it all broke down, then it was a free-for-all, in the end a free-for-all, we beat up the whole family there, and then there were some who went to hospital, and uncle K they tried to take him to hospital, no luck, he arrived there, and the doctor said he was dead you know. And that was it, that's how it ended, everyone went home, and it ended with uncle's death. (Extract from interview, August 2004)

My interviewee's insistence on the simultaneity of the cracking of the trees and K's death indicates that he attributes this death to a non-accidental cause, referring implicitly to the part played by the powers attributed to ancestral forces.

---

19 I have considered the Koro war, which preceded the colonial expropriation of the land, from two different angles (see chapters 1 and 2).

5. THE SUBJECTIVITY OF VIOLENT ACTION

So when we were discussing, well that's when he fell. We started to talk, only I told them first: 'We're going to meet, I'm going to see fair play. When the Z arrive, let me talk, I'll talk first.' No but him, by custom he talks, he's so annoyed when the others arrived, straightaway, I didn't even see him, he went off. He didn't talk for long, not even five minutes, he fell flat. So it was after that there was the punch-up, then I felt bad, oh, it was terrible. If I hadn't been there, some of the Z would have been killed. They brought out tamiocs, machetes ... Then I made them get out of there, I told them: 'Come away, now, if you stay here you'll die, it's better to come away', so I made them come away, they came away. But there had already been kicks, so the tamiocs, the machetes, I said: 'Hey, calm down, calm down', I had trouble stopping them. When they left all the cars were vandalised, they went off with the cars, there were no windows left and all that ... I got them to calm down, I said: 'Take the guy to hospital.' So they take the guy to hospital ... When we heard he'd died, I told them we'd take him up there ... I go up there, in the afternoon, I try to calm them down, the day of the burial, I try to calm them ... Then I said to them: 'The business with this site, there's already one person dead, if there are more who die tomorrow or the day after, you have to try and think about that.' (Extract from interview, August 1995)

All of my interviewees without exception made a link between this sudden death and the conflict over land that was under discussion at the meeting. As the two interview extracts describing the scene demonstrate, some of those present immediately attributed this death to the Z, who were in dispute with K's family – hence their violent reaction to members of this family who were at the meeting. Other interviewees emphasise the responsibility of K, who must, in either form or substance, have said things that should not be said:

Them, before they're defending the Z, and now they've quarrelled with the Z. When he's speaking, well you shouldn't insult others, you have to settle problems the right way, what's the point in insulting people? Shouting and insulting other people, it's not good ... K, then his brother, they were standing up both of them, they hadn't come to listen, that's it, that's how it starts, when you do things in anger, it's not good ... But that's not how it should be done, when the others are sitting all around, and then you talk. (Extract from interview, June 2006)

K told us once that it was thanks to them that the Z exist, because all of that, it's buried by our ancestors, you shouldn't say that now, because it brings bad luck. And him when he said that, what happens? Well he fell down dead. (Extract from interview, September 2002)

Whichever interpretation of this death is put forward, it refers to one of the two types of causality described in Chapter 4, as defined by Christine Salomon: either the dead man is the victim of powers of attack brought into play by his enemies, or he incurs the wrath of ancestors (his own or those of other clans) irritated by his transgressive behaviour. As one of my interviewees said to me in relation to this death: 'There's the other world, behind, that settles disputes' (extract from interview, August 1991). The process of reassigning lands in Koro was subsequently resumed and the various families concerned are now settled there (with some tension between them at times). However, the varying interpretations of the death remain. The conflict was resolved on the practical level through the intervention of the ADRAF and the mediation of a number of senior local figures:

> After the claim, there were difficulties between the clans, all the clans. Then in relation to Karhövâ and then Koro down there, the Z and us, there, that's created the difficulty … When Devillers [the former European proprietor] gave it up, they were the first to go in … That's where the problem is a bit hard. Then it's there that my big brother was lost [died] … We wanted to have a meeting to tell them to leave Koro. It's there my big brother died … Then after a while the ADRAF worked on that to organise meetings … I can tell you it's thanks to the ADRAF, they worked hard so that they came to an agreement with us. That's that, and now they've already built in Koro, but we're still not reconciled … What's serious is that my big brother died, because he fell down dead, it's like when a guy's shot with a bullet. (Extract from interview, August 1995)

> It was me who worked on that, after K died, because they went back there, and they said the Koro valley was theirs, there are no other clans there. So the others responded, so we organised the meeting, that's where the brother fell down in front of us, among us. Then after he fell among us, then the people from Koro left, they left Koro … So I tried to organise a meeting there in Koro … Only I said to them: 'I'm settling the land issue, but the issue of reconciliation, that's between you.' … Only I told them they had to respect the limits: 'If you overstep the limits tomorrow or the day after, once you've overstepped, it's for ever, there's no one else who'll settle the dispute, I'm the last.' So that was it, they've respected that up to now … I did the work for the site, but reconciliation, that's up to them … So when their old man died, he was buried over there. As for reconciliation, that's how it is, but there's still one more thing, according to custom, because when they came from Mèaa, they settled there, there's someone there in Koro, there's the owner of the site. So the owner of the site gave his land over to them, then he left … They have to try to see those people to try and reconcile with them. (Extract from interview, February 1999)

This last extract introduces an additional element into the historical issues bound up in the reassignment of this site, by connecting the conflict between K's family and the Z family to their common origin in the Mèaa plateau, from where they came down to the Koro valley: hence their (more or less conflictual) relationship with the people of the Houaïlou valley. Two other interviews also point to this historical aspect:

> It's like in Koro, when the Z came, even the Mèaa if they want to come, according to custom, they have to look behind a bit why did they leave by violence? But who began the violence? Then you see clearly that it's the Mèaa. So I'm telling you, this is just my opinion, according to custom, first of all you have to make a customary gesture as a reconciliation with the people of the valley. (Extract from interview, August 1995)

> The problem for them is the problem of rights, because on lands like that, there is a history that speaks after all. For them, as long as things haven't been recognised on the customary level, it will always create problems … Me what I can say is that the history of Koro, you never see the end of it … People talk a lot about Koro, the Mèaa clans, but the problem is that Koro is secondary. The actual base of the Mèaa clans is up there in Mèaa … That's why I'm saying, there they talk a lot about being from the Koro area, but Koro is the second zone. If they follow their origin to Mèaa, there they'll become really small. And they don't want to start that discussion up there, precisely because that's where the truth will be found … The people of Mèaa, the thing that characterises them, we say *pâi pa néjâö ma kwé* [literally, 'the people of straw and liana']. *Néjâö ma kwé* are old lianas. What does all that mean? It means they're people who are always in conflict, who are always tearing each other apart and always fighting each other, who are envious of each other. But you must never get involved in their game, because once you get embroiled, you'll suffocate … So that's a kind of clan character, and would you believe they're proud of it, the people of Mèaa, that they're like that. (Extract from interview, July 1993)

Readers will have noted that the villages in question in this chapter (Dâô, Koro, Mèaa) are places that have been mentioned in the first two chapters: the intensity of the conflicts described here is directly related to the complexity of the pre-colonial and colonial issues embedded there. And it is precisely the aliveness of the issues linked to these places, and the consequent local mobilisation of historical knowledge, that allows access to their history[20] – and at the same time makes it so difficult to write about without intervening in the conflict.

---

20 See Naepels 2008.

Political emotions

Experiencing affect (some political sentiments)

As these selected examples from the period of land rights claims and the 'events' show, the social relations described here are manifestly not regulated by any convention or a contract. As a general rule, each individual has first to take his/her position in a relation of power. It is therefore war, and its many avatars following the colonial 'pacification' (including witchcraft conflicts, conflicts over land and brawls), that are used to resolve conflicts originating in relations between individuals and between groups of belonging, relations that, if necessary, are formalised through contractual forms after the event (see Chapter 6).

> Him, the day I go and talk to him, he's going to have a heap of problems ... I don't mean to boast, but they owe me respect. X, I'm waiting for him. One day I'm going to get him, and he's as good as dead. It's people like that you have to shut up. There's no point talking any more, today you have to kill people to express yourself. (Extract from interview, February 1991)

In the interviews I gathered, anger (*rhôê*) emerges as a systematically aggravating factor in violent confrontations, an intensifying element in the continuum of violent acts and a justification for action.[21]

> So in the end, he hits him ... he's so mad and he has to do something with it, he goes to hit him. (Extract from interview, August 1995)

> When I went to see him, the guy, instead of speaking well, straight away [he gets] angry. I said to him: 'Hey! One day I'll get fed up of telling you to go, one day I'll smoke [set fire to] your house.' (Extract from interview, September 2002)

Although my interviewees use anger as a descriptive concept to account for certain behaviours, they do not themselves necessarily subscribe to them:

> But them, they're always fighting, arguing and angry. No, that's not how [things should be done]. What use is it to show your strength to say what? You have to show your strength in another way. (Extract from interview, September 2002)

---

21 See Harrison 1993, and my analysis of the role of emotions and anger in war, following Leenhardt (see Chapter 2).

5. THE SUBJECTIVITY OF VIOLENT ACTION

Anger is also sometimes ascribed to specific family traits (linked to the agnatic group of the person concerned, or that of his maternal uncles), thus identifying characteristics, or habitus, that are embodied and, occasionally, supported by a discourse about the self as warrior.

> When someone shows that he is angry, or when he behaves in a certain way, people say: 'Oh, it's not surprising, it's in that family's blood', because in that house they have that very specific character. (Extract from interview, June 1995)

In the same explanatory register, accounting for the resort to violence, alcohol is put forward as a disinhibiting factor (particularly in the context of anger). In his famous article on the grief and rage of an Ilongot headhunter, Renato Rosaldo emphasised the need for the social sciences (and anthropology in particular) to give proper place to emotion in understanding the actions these disciplines seek to account for.[22] This project presents us with an analytical difficulty, however: in the retrospective narrative (the account I am able to gather from my interviewees), there is a constant oscillation between calculated rational decision-making and loss of control, between spontaneity and premeditation, between rage and calm.[23] But we will never know what goes on within an individual consciousness or the depths of subconscious decisions; we shall never enter the 'unbreakable kernel of darkness that their action is to themselves' (Veyne 1984, p. 191). This is evident if we compare two explanations of the same action, given by the same interviewee (a few years apart): one emphasises premeditation and calculation, the other immediacy and rage:

> You saw my business with the old man, I almost put a bullet in his head, but it was a conscious act, I mean from the moment I decided to do it, I thought about it a lot, it's not the first time he's done the dirty on me … I couldn't carry on closing my eyes to it, I had to stand up for myself at least a bit … Now if the Whites' court convicts me because I've killed someone, that's up to them, for me it's nothing to do with me. But me in my reasoning, it's based on my values. I reckoned there was a boundary he shouldn't overstep, and then I reckoned he'd gone too far, it was the accumulation of everything he did, I reckoned I was within my rights, that I had to do it … When people overstep a certain limit, you in relation to who you are, your past, what you should be, in relation to the society

---

22   Rosaldo 1989.
23   See Feldman 1991 on the narrativisation of violence.

you live in, you're a man after all, and you have rights to defend after all, and you can't carry on letting yourself be walked over all the time like that. (Extract from interview, January 1999)

A moment after, it was evening. It really came home to me in the evening, but me when I'm angry, when I fly into a rage like that, it's very hard to control. (Extract from interview, July 1995)

After he was beaten up by a group of several men, another of my interviewees told me in July 2008 that in hindsight he was glad his wife had reacted as she did: if she had not hidden his gun, he would have gone after his attackers in a rage, and killed them all. In speaking of violence and the move to action, we must avoid over-functionalising violent practice, identifying its relation to the uncontainable, the overwhelming, at the same time as to calculation. Hence analysis cannot be set within this psychological register, and we can only come back to the gestures, the words and the contexts as a way of producing the most specific description possible. In fact this is what my interviewees often do: thus the account I cited at the beginning of this chapter, of four actions during the 'events', distinguishes between military-style operations (the aborted action against the mobile gendarmes, then that carried out against F – see extract 3) from angry reaction and exhilaration (against H, who had denigrated the independence movement – see extract 4).

The laughter in these accounts (explicitly evoked in extracts 1 and 2, above, and sometimes interrupting the narrative itself, though I have not noted this in the transcriptions) clearly indicates the legitimacy of the use of violence. Most tellingly, physical violence or taking action are very often interpreted as 'legitimate self-defence' against attacks by witchcraft. The powers of healing ('medicines') are also held to be powers of potential attack, and local conflicts are systematically shadowed by the fear that oneself or one's family might fall victim to persecution from adversaries who are all the more redoubtable because their actions are neither visible nor foreseeable. In this context, words are at least as important as gestures, and words of curse may serve as explanation and justification of the resort to violence.[24] The accounts of crisis situations that I gathered consistently show a movement from actions deemed unacceptable to words (insults, warnings or curses) and from words (insults or curses) to actions (processes of asking forgiveness or taking violent action). This continuity, which is

---

24   See Salomon 2000a.

5. THE SUBJECTIVITY OF VIOLENT ACTION

demonstrated by the examples below, makes it difficult to fully separate physical violence from psychic forms of internalisation of conflict. The following account, given immediately after a tense meeting, points to the potential for shifting from insult and provocation to fighting, as well as to the long history of witchcraft attacks between the families concerned:

> Oh yes, X, he was lucky because I don't want to respond to him, because if I respond maybe there would be a fight just now, because the other there, Y, he's already angry … because X insulted him up there, Y is annoyed, he said: 'Stop, stop speaking ill.' Oh yes, I think the others are going to leave by the window. Luckily there aren't very many of us, because if all the kids were there, my Lord I think there would be a fight up there. Him, he's already annoyed because when we speak, you have to speak well, you have to know how to discuss, we have to develop nowadays. That's why me when they started to speak ill, and the bastard calls on anyone who has the balls … [understood: comes to fight him], but I didn't answer, you shouldn't speak ill. We speak well nowadays. They want to claim to speak today, but it's because before they eliminated all our elders, because they've always got bad medicine, me I accuse them of having killed my elders. (Extract from interview, September 2002)

Another account makes reference to a curse causing tension between families:

> So there, the old man said: '*Gwè yè öi wênénââ-î*' [literally: 'I'm going to eat your heart'],[25] those are serious words, with serious consequences. Me, I always remember grandfather, my mother's dad, he always says, the old people when they talk like that, it's not good, it's not good, then if you manage to sort it out straight away, it's good. If you don't manage to sort it out, then it has endless consequences, if nobody takes steps to resolve it, and to say: 'Well, maybe I was out of order', that he recognises he did wrong and that's that. It's quite simple … Saying well, I did wrong, I'm sorry, for the Kanaks it's difficult to take that first step, nobody wants to make the first move, and look where we end up, you know. (Extract from interview, August 2004)

One of my interviewees referred to the protective practices that were required, owing to the risk of being subject to a curse:

---

25   These words can be understood in several, more or less metaphorical, ways, but the anthropophagic connotation is certainly present.

So there are always thoughts, because among us, we say that there is a back side to the word, *ko mêrêa, ko mêrêa*, that's bad. When you have bad thoughts about somebody, well that has an effect on the person. When you are anger, you curse him, you send him words of cursing, that has an effect. So why do I give the kids [protective medication] to drink? It's because of that, I'm still protecting myself, otherwise the children suffer in school, they can't work properly, they are sick, loads of things happen to them, you know. (Extract from interview, April 1999)

Thus, with social relationships rooted in relations of force, a paradigm of tension arises. This tension is grounded in ways of interpreting misfortune that establish word, insult, curse as significant moments in violent conflicts. Land claims mobilised a historical knowledge that had been relegated to the background during the years of most intense colonial oppression (from the government of Paul Feillet to the end of the *indigénat*), and hence aroused or exposed inter- and intrafamilial conflicts that were powerfully experienced, sometimes with extreme levels of tension, owing to the awareness of the risks (for oneself and one's family) that went alongside the assertion of the self in these conflicts. The local landscape of Houaïlou was transformed by the departure of one section of European settlers during the 'events' of the 1980s; this together with the collective but disputatious reflection on the forms of social life to be constructed meant that the issues entailed in establishing a new governmentality became embedded in bodies and psyches – as one of my interviewees made very clear:

And there are also all the histories related to the political situation. For example, we claimed rights, and that aroused conflicts, whether it relates to problems over land, whether it relates to problems of clans and all that, it gets tangled up, so it makes a big deal after all. The consequence of the policy we implemented is that we didn't have control over all of that, and that meant there were a lot of conflicts at the level of all the tribes, and that results precisely in misfortunes like that, where ultimately it leads to curses, conflicts, situations, things like that happening. Me, what I can tell you, is that when A died, when B died … each time I had a lot of visitations.[26] What I'm saying is that for us, in our culture, there are realities on the other side. Creating conflict, that unleashes things. Well, they are things we don't necessarily have any control over, but anyway there we noticed it happening. (Extract from interview, June 1995)

---

26 My interviewee refers to manifestations of his ancestors in his dreams.

Both within and outside the family, including in relations between neighbours and in political relationships, physical violence and intimidation form part of a repertoire of actions in which many Kanaks are socialised, accustomed from childhood. Conflict and violence are significant aspects of social relations, an everyday presence in moral landscapes through accounts of attack, in both public and private and domestic spaces (which form a continuum, in the segmentary understanding of the inclusion of the self in groups of varying size).[27] Insults and blows feature, as does the interpretation of misfortune in terms of aggression. Information drawn from legal and public health statistics, especially from the Christine Hamelin and Christine Salomon's study for Inserm[28] on the health of New Caledonian women, indicates high or even very high levels of violence in New Caledonia today. This is true of physical violence (assaults, homicides, suicide and road violence), sexual violence (rape, incest) and moral violence (insults, bullying, sexual harassment).[29] Where figures are available, they show that these levels are higher than in metropolitan France (twice to nine times as high, depending on the indicator selected), comparable to those in some Pacific states, and lower than in other countries such as South Africa. Nevertheless, this does not imply that physical violence is uncontained or that it constitutes the only register of political action (see Chapter 6). On the contrary, incidences of violence have a converse in moments of contractualisation and pacification of social relations:

> Well, at the level of custom as well, these are things that get sorted out among us. You let a little time go by, so the grudges dissipate, anger fades. Then after you take steps to get them to come and ask forgiveness. (Extract from interview, December 1991)

1991: An action halted

To conclude this chapter, I should like to offer a relatively detailed ethnographic description of a scene of 'ordinary' violence, by way of returning to some key points of my analysis.[30] I was not present at this scene, which took place before my first field visit to Houaïlou. As Jean Jamin writes, 'the ethnographer can generally proceed only by means

---

27 See Naepels 1998, Demmer 2009.
28 Institut national de la santé et la recherche médicale (French National Institute for Health and Medical Research) [trans.].
29 Salomon 1999; Hamelin and Salomon 2004; Hamelin et al. 2007; Salomon and Hamelin 2007.
30 See also Naepels 2004 and 2006a.

of reconstructing and investigating alleged incidences of violence, like a police detective, rather than observing them directly' (Claverie, Jamin and Lenclud 1984, p. 20). This assertion needs to be qualified, however, bearing in mind that some ethnographers have witnessed scenes of violence of which they have subsequently given an account.[31] In general, much of what is learned through ethnographic enquiry refers to moments or episodes that are not witnessed by the ethnographer, rendering the formula 'participant observation' doubly problematic.

By 'ordinary' violence I mean firstly that this is not a scene of 'extreme' violence. In the 'continuum of violence' described by Nancy Scheper-Hughes and Philippe Bourgois, in which the scale runs from 'symbolic violence' to 'extreme violence', via 'everyday violence', 'structural violence' and 'terror', this is an incident of low intensity.[32] What is more, we are dealing here with an action that was interrupted, halted. In this sense, it is as much a moment of nonviolence as of violence: aiming at the enemy – and ultimately deciding not to shoot. The term 'ordinary' here also indicates that such incidents are not entirely uncommon; at the same time, it is still an action of the order of an event, therefore unexpected, exceptional, even if it can be understood, and to a certain extent explained, with hindsight. This event or episode relates to crisis, but also reflects certain aspects of Kanak social relations in Houaïlou.

Here is how the main protagonist in the scene recounted to me how he almost killed a member of his family who had put a padlock on a gate, thus blocking the path the narrator habitually took to reach the river:

> When I saw the padlock, I was annoyed, and I hit [it] with my tamioc ... On the customary level, that was going too far, they had done things, they overstepped the mark. At a push, making things difficult for me at the back, I can live with it, but that was just tying my hands, well, so for me it was a challenge, you know. So at that point I said: 'Oh no, I think he's gone too far, I've got to put a stop to it.' At that point it was maybe 10 o'clock, I took my tamioc, I took my gun, I went down, I smashed the padlock with my tamioc, I chucked it in the water, then I grabbed the gate, I chucked the gate, and I said: 'I'm going to wait, because the person will come.' Then there were A and B there. I said to them: 'Don't get involved, this is my problem.' And that's when one of the little cousins passed by, and he saw the gate was open. So when I saw him pass, I said

---

31 See Bourgois 2002, in Harlem; and Bourgois 2001, in El Salvador.
32 Scheper-Hughes and Bourgois 2004.

5. THE SUBJECTIVITY OF VIOLENT ACTION

to B: 'There's the guy.' He passed by and then he went back maybe to see his father, then when he came back he slowed down, and I looked at him, at that moment he slowed down, then he backed off, he asked me: 'Who opened the gate?' I said: 'I did', I said: 'Why are you asking?' He said: 'No because it was locked, the gate.' I said: 'Yes, but who closed the gate?' He said: 'It was dad.' I said: 'But what right does your father have to put padlocks on my property?' The little guy didn't say anything, I said to him: 'Go and tell your father that if he doesn't like it he should come, but he should bring his coffin at the same time, I've had enough.' At that point he left, and then he went to tell his father, and then they came back. The old man when he came down, he came with the idea of punching me. I was waiting for him, he came down, I let him come, when he got to about that far away, my gun was just behind the pile of sand, he hadn't seen it, I went and got the gun, I got out a bullet, I bit it, I loaded a cartridge in the gun. When he saw that he stopped dead, he was dumbstruck, and I pointed it between his two eyes, I said: 'If you come one step further, they'll be picking your brains up with a spoon.' I told him: 'Stay where you are, now we're going to lay it on the line face to face.' The first thing I was angry about, I told him: 'I've been waiting two years for you, your brother and your children, because I called you to a meeting, because we have family things to talk about, because we have the same name, but you do a lot of things behind my back, and you tell your children a lot of things that aren't true. And two years ago, I went to see you so we could talk and deal with the things between us. You always ran away, you and your children, I've been waiting two years for you. And these are your manners, you do this, you do that.' At one point he perked up a bit, then he was trying to smooth things over … he said: 'Yes, you're like your big brother', speaking of C, 'You're like your big brother over there, you're both little jerks.' Then I couldn't hold back any longer … I don't know what I said, there was a cartridge on the ground, I ran and grabbed it … that was it, I was ready to kill him. And when his son saw that, he started [ran off]. Then I loaded the cartridge, yes I cocked the trigger, when he felt that he turned round, he started as well, so when they ran, I aimed for the old man, but because they were pellets I wanted to shoot him dead … I was still pointing the gun, and when he arrived at the metalled road, he tripped on the edge of the road, he fell behind the barrier, but the bit behind the barrier was covered with lianas, so you couldn't see behind the barrier. I ran up, then I aimed at the back of his neck, I thought: 'When he gets up, I'll shoot him in the neck, he'll die straight away', I wanted to kill him quickly, you know. But I'm going to kill him, that's what I'm thinking, then I'm going to kill his son, then I'll have taken the car, I'll have killed his wife, then the kids right up to the youngest, I'll have killed everybody. For me killing one or killing 10 or 20, it's all the same, the result will be the same, it was in a rage … And at that moment B shouted, but it was a shout from the guts, and that's how I came to my senses, in my rage I got hold of myself again, then I stayed like that with the gun, you know. At that moment he put his head out the other side, when he saw me with the gun, he hid behind the gate again. Afterwards I went back down, I didn't say anything more. Then he yelled, and I was so angry I wanted to hit him, but I pulled myself together a bit, and it was then I spoke, and for a long time he was shocked, traumatised by what had happened. He told a lot of people that I almost killed him, that he almost died. He was shaken, you know. (Extract from interview, July 1995)

A number of the subjective aspects of the use of violence that I have described in this chapter can be recognised in this account. First there is the oscillation between rational premeditation and uncontrollable affect. Secondly, the mingling of words (reproaches, insults, provocations, shouts and curses) and gesture (fight, pursuit, aim and holding back from firing) is also key to both the move to action and its interruption. A witness to the scene (B in the above account) also points this out:

I panicked, I don't know what else to say, I don't know what else to do either, and I just said: 'Uncle, think of your daughter.' And when I said that, he stopped talking, and I saw him lower the barrel of the gun, and then after I came up and I picked up the gun, and I discharged it, and I took the gun down to the banana field, and I left it there. And then after, they yelled at each other, argued without any other consequences, you know. (Extract from interview, January 2004)

This moment of crisis can be accounted for on the basis of a set of elements, cross-contextualising it at increasing levels of generality. The gesture of placing a padlock is thus seen as an extremely serious 'physical attack':

When the old man came to put the padlock on, they showed their cards there, they had to attack me physically, why? Because at the level of using medicines, it wasn't working any more. (Extract from interview, March 1999)

This is effectively an act of appropriation or privatisation of a space that was contested, ambiguous, a space where superimposed layers of rights and concurrent usages existed (one of the protagonists cultivating crops and the other raising cattle behind the gate in question). Given the context of land rights issues in 1991, this conflict between two members of the same family over an unattributed piece of land is an expression of a more general conflict between two groups of actors. These two groups clashed in the land attribution meetings then being organised by the ADRAF, drawing on different versions of history (pre-colonial and colonial) to justify their claims. But this land ownership conflict also reflects a more fundamental segmentary conflict, with the two protagonists each claiming to have greater legitimacy in the clan than their adversary, basing their arguments on their own appraisal of the value of the other's adoption into their common clan. The personal dimension of the conflict, the reciprocal reference to a multitude of wrongs, the disagreements in the approach taken to the ADRAF or to the organisation of customary ceremonies (of mourning in particular) are thus set in sites of habitual tension in New Caledonia. These contextual factors do not, however, constitute explanations, as Wolfgang Sofsky points out:

> The context is not a causal factor and is neither a sufficient nor an essential condition of violent behaviour. At most it encourages or hampers violence. Determining the circumstances, whether they are biographical, social, political or historical, pinpoints significance and sometimes opportunity, but not causes. It may offer plausible stories, but not explanations. The context does not explain a single act of violence. (Sofsky 2003, p. 20)

Contextualisation always runs the risk of portraying an action as functional (or even inevitable, in the most rigid forms of causalist sociology) and, at the very least, of offering a retrospective justification of it. Perhaps it is sufficient to describe.

***

I have sought in this chapter to focus on the engagement of the subject in relation to violent action, without seeking either to explain it causally, or to justify it. This engagement arose in a context of high levels of mobilisation around political and land rights issues: individual or collective actions during the 'events' (in 1984), a collective trial process, brawls and a death (in 1987) in the course of land rights meetings, an action interrupted before it became murderous (in 1991). Long-lasting tension and fear, as well as explosions of anger, emerge as recurrent modalities of affect brought into play by the engagement of the self in local political life. These affects are overdetermined by accounts of attacks by witchcraft, and fanned by the exchange of verbal challenges and insults. Along the way, my analysis of these selected episodes has connected them to some important political developments in Houaïlou in the period from 1977 (with the municipal elections and the Union Calédonienne's Bourail congress) to 1991, the date of my first period of fieldwork in New Caledonia, when I began this research, in the shadow of the Matignon-Oudinot agreements. In Houaïlou this phase of emergence of the demand for 'Kanak socialist independence' – that is for the development of a postcolonial social organisation – was lived as intensely as the transformations of the 1950s (see Chapter 4), following the end of the *indigénat*. In both the 'events' and the land rights campaign, political engagement came through the constitution of collectives mobilised in relations of power. This engagement occasionally involved the use of physical violence, in the form of roadblocks, brawls or gunfire, individually or collectively, spontaneously or with premeditation, and sometimes supported by 'medicines' employed in the hope of obtaining the greatest possible assistance from the ancestors. In this chapter I have sought to grasp the forms of subjectivity, of emotions, of affects and of calculations brought into play by this use of violence. Finally, I would add that the conflicts I have referred to in this chapter are recent, not always resolved and still sensitive – and, for this reason, the interview extracts I have cited are often anonymous and relatively uncontextualised.

6

The Construction and Fiction of Consensus

In Houaïlou today, since the 'events', social relations appear more peaceful, especially in communal spaces: ceremonies, villages, tribes and places where Kanaks live together operate as public space. Having observed how these spaces were imbricated with a colonial order, my ethnographic research reveals how they are being reconfigured at the current time. Through the production of collectives and forms of public consensus, these realities are emerging in relationship with violence and conflict. The point here is thus to grasp not the opposite of violence, or its end, but rather the internal articulation between social relations, contractual relations and relations of power, at the heart of the ambiguity from which this book takes it title: what do the people of Houaïlou today do to ward off war?

Ceremonial politics

During the time I was conducting research in Houaïlou, from the early 1990s on, the most frequent occasions for large gatherings (from several dozen to many hundreds of people) were the few marriage celebrations and the more numerous ceremonies marking the beginning and end of mourning that took place there; these formed key moments in local political life. Ceremonies of exchange between groups probably represent the most significant site of public affirmation in local social life: before a gathering of members of various clans, without equivalent in everyday life, numerous speeches are made in which the historical and social links between the groups present are extolled, justified, remembered, euphemised or quietly ignored. These events are moments of both collective joy and high tension, in which the issues emerge very clearly through a series of actions peculiar to the ceremonial context, enacted by its participants. They are the occasion for affirming, reconfiguring or contesting a public order, with speeches or challenging claims sometimes giving rise to protests or fights. They may also be considered as one of the sites of naturalisation of a social order that is nevertheless riven with tensions and even violent conflict, an order essential to the consolidation of relations of power and influence, through the construction of ordered collectives. They are, therefore, doubly interesting for my purposes: first, because the contractual relations formed there may help to resolve or settle a past disagreement or contribute to the present-day mobilisation of those assembled; second because, conversely, they can on occasion reveal the failure of such projects, manifested in the aggressive language, exchanges of insults or scuffles that can break out there.

In the case of customary ceremonies, however, the reference to 'public' space or 'public' gatherings cannot go unquestioned. In a segmentary system, the duality of public and private has to be understood as a continuum rather than a binary opposition. In the physical terms of use of space, ceremonies always take place on someone's land, in an appropriate place into which one should not enter without invitation (although there are sometimes exceptions). Nevertheless, given the size of the gathering, what goes on there and what is said there may be considered more public than anything that happens at other times in local life.

A sort of theoretical dualism prevails in the anthropological analysis of ceremonial exchanges. Ritual procedures and actions are often considered as one aspect, strategic actions and political contextualisation of ritual as another. Thus Stanley Tambiah notes:

> On the one hand, it can be said in general that a public ritual reproduces in its repeated enactments certain seemingly invariant and stereotyped sequences, such as formulas chanted, rules of etiquette followed, and so on. On the other hand, every field anthropologist knows that no one performance of a rite, however rigidly prescribed, is exactly the same as another performance because it is affected by processes peculiar to the oral specialist's mode of recitation, and by certain variable features such as the social characteristics and circumstances of the actors which (aside from purely contingent and unpredicted events) affect such matters as scale of attendance, audience interest, economic outlay, and so on. It is therefore

necessary to bear in mind that festivals, cosmic rituals, and rites of passage, however prescribed they may be, are always linked to status claims and interests of the participants, and therefore are always open to contextual meanings. Variable components make flexible the basic core of most rituals. (Tambiah 1985, pp. 124–25)

This dualism partially overlaps with the opposition between structure and event, rules and strategies, grammar and style. Thus, using the term 'ritual' to describe these ceremonies would already be to adopt the dualistic approach, privileging form and repetition over the political context of exchanges and speeches that occur within them. Following Tambiah's suggestion, then, I believe it is essential to attempt to describe ritual procedures and strategic actions together.

Some ceremonial forms

The ceremonies under discussion here are complex events. Leaving aside the annual ceremonies celebrating the first yams (or first fruits), which today in Houaïlou are confined – when they do take place – to the family space, the main ceremonies held there are linked to the 'life cycle', on the occasion of birth, marriage, mourning and the end of mourning. Older descriptions can be found in some of Maurice Leenhardt's writings: his article 'La fête du pilou en Nouvelle-Calédonie (The Pilou Festival in New Caledonia)'[1] (reprinted almost word for word in the eighth chapter of *Notes d'ethnologie néo-calédonienne* (1930), before being substantially reworked in the chapter 'Le pilou, moment culminant de la société (The Pilou, the High Point of Social Life)' in *Gens de la Grande Terre* (1937a)), is a linear paraphrase of Bwêêyöuu Ërijiyi's series of notebooks on this subject;[2] there is also an account in the fifth chapter of Paul Montague's manuscript, on 'Social Organisation and Customs'.[3] My own research indicates that all these ceremonies follow a general model of reciprocal exchange between families gathered into two groups sitting opposite one another: the people of the house (*ka-wêmwâ*) and the guests (*tewö*). This division is made in accordance with a central alliance: for a birth, exchanges are made between the clan of the father of the child (and of the child) and that of the mother (and the maternal uncle);

---
1 Leenhardt 1922b.
2 Aramiou and Euritéin 2002, pp. 15–102.
3 Translated into French in Leenhardt, Sarasin and Montague 1998, pp. 32–39. I referred to this manuscript in Chapter 2.

at a marriage, the organisers (the bridegroom's clan) and their relatives sit opposite the family of the bride and her relatives; at the formal start and end of mourning, the masters of ceremony (the clan of the deceased for a man, that of the deceased's husband for a woman, and those allied to them) face the family of the maternal uncle of the deceased and his relatives.

When a child is born, a gift known as *mèèpèmaa*[4] (which may consist of shell money laid out on a square of cloth) is made to the baby's maternal uncle by the father, or by his close family. The uncle must then visit his nephew or niece to speak a blessing. This exchange, though fairly informal, seems particularly important for the eldest child, especially if it is a boy, the birth of whom testifies to the success of the alliance between the two clans.

The celebration of marriage was a site in which the missionaries invested heavily: the first focus of mission policy was matrimonial alliances. Both Catholic and Protestant missionaries issued a series of prohibitions on 'mixed' marriages (between members of the two faiths), polygamy, forced marriage, and marriage promises contracted at birth. The effect was such that it is worth considering to what extent present-day marriage between young adults is a missionary creation. Leenhardt wrote: '[The elders] give [the young initiates] and the woman they will marry holy water to drink, removing the final dangers to their union. They then send the two to a hut (Gomen). They are given a mat to sit on (Houaïlou), the woman is given a yam to cook afterwards and eat with the young man (Voh, Garope) – parallel details which all represent the *unique ceremony of marriage*' (Leenhardt 1930, pp. 140–41, my emphasis). Two of my interviewees offered similar accounts:

> When she is about 3–4, the girl is given to the grandmother, and the boy is given to the grandfather, and each one will do his/her duty of education. The grandmother teaches everything that is the woman's work, even bearing children, or weaving mats, or cooking, all of that, the things that are women's concern. And the grandfather does the same for the boy. That boy doesn't see the woman, he is only [told] 'You are going to marry such-and-such a girl', but it's the grandfather who makes the decision for him. He is obliged to say yes, you know, but he doesn't see the girl. He only sees the girl on the day of the marriage. (Guynemer Karé, extract from interview, July 1995)

---

4   Literally, end (*mèè*) of coleus (*pèmaa*).

In the time of the ancestors, for example, there was no big wedding like you see there, because marriage ties were already established, you're somebody's wife as soon as you're born, you're destined, you know. All the big show you see today, it came with colonisation because there was a big reorganisation, the rules are no longer the same, today you choose your wife, you choose your husband, and you make do. You make do and not only do you make do, but the social structures are disorganised. Whereas before, you didn't touch a woman like that ... And when a woman left, you go and sit over there and that's the end of it. She came, when you saw her come with the subjects, well she was your wife, you know, you knew she was your wife. It was a different life, different rules. (Narcisse Kaviyöibanu, extract from interview, January 1999)

In earlier times a similar system of bride price seems to have given rise to exchanges at the time when the marriage was arranged, like those that take place today at the marriage ceremony.[5] Three significant moments can be distinguished in the proceedings of present-day marriage ceremonies in Houaïlou, each of which may be accompanied by a specific speech:

- the request or reservation (*pè ërë bwè*: ask for the woman; *pè tuwiri bwè*: reserve the woman)
- the sending of the woman by her clan to the clan of the bridegroom (*vinôâ*: send the woman, say goodbye, marriage custom)
- the payment of the bride price to the bride's clan, an amount greater than that paid previously by the maternal relatives (*urhii bwè*: pay for the woman, provide bride price). This act may be supplemented by specific gifts related to any children born before the marriage (*yawîî mèômwâ*: close the door, or apologise for already having taken the woman; *pubwaara* or *kî mârâ*: doff one's hat or tug one's forelock, that is legitimise children already born, or thank their uncles for their birth). Elsa Faugère on Maré, Christine Salomon in the Poya region, Dorothea Deterts in Koné, and Hélène Nicolas on Lifou have identified the different elements of matrimonial exchanges in these regions, and how they may be interpreted, particularly in terms of gender relations and the domination of women by men.[6]

My experience in Houaïlou suggests that mourning and the end of mourning are the most complex ceremonies today, engendering the greatest investment of time, work and money; their form is more difficult

---

5   For informative definitions, see Testart 1996–97; and Testart, Govoroff and Lécrivain 2002.
6   Faugère 1998; Salomon 2000b; Deterts 2000; Nicolas 2012.

to describe. It is at the formal end of mourning that the largest gatherings of men and women occur, the most substantial gifts are given, and the rights of the maternal relatives are most significant.

There seems always to have been a distinction between two stages: death and burial (*pè yöwîî*: to close the coffin, *pè pètùrù*: to carry the coffin out of the house and take it to the cemetery, *bûrû ma mâ kwa*: meal to bid the deceased farewell) and then the end of mourning a year later (*néjaumé*: one year of mourning). Each of these stages is accompanied by small gifts and specific speeches. But the heart of the ceremony of exchange, the gift of shell money (*kurumé*: custom of mourning) and the exchange of more substantial goods (*lèèwi*: wealth, that is to say yams, taros, sacks of rice, cloth, clothing; *mie* shell money and European money),[7] may take place either five days after the burial (*mèè bwênii*: fifth day), during the first ceremonial phase, or at the end of mourning. Both the availability of foodstuffs and the importance that the organiser wishes to ascribe to the ceremony, or the complexity of the gathering he hopes to bring together on this occasion, seem to be important criteria in this choice. It is also at the *kurumé* that some of the most poetic and beautiful Kanak ceremonial speeches are made (*pèvipö*: speeches of condolence). Finally, a meal is offered to all those present, in the form of piles of foodstuffs (*bwêê*) shared between the different families in attendance. A further speech is made at the distribution of these piles of foodstuffs (*pè pawirè bwêê*: speech for the presentation of piles of foodstuffs). These exchanges are weighted slightly in favour of the maternal relatives (*tëvö*) in terms of the circulation of money, and more so in relation to the other goods. The dominant ideological model of restricted exchange (exchange of sisters or bilateral cross-cousin marriage) suggests that obligations are matched and, in the medium term, exchanges between clans balance out. A simple genealogical review of alliances refutes this assertion and, in fact, imbalances give rise to recriminations among the groups who feel they have been wronged.[8]

Even where the exchange is formally reciprocal, and the organisers' 'gift' is met with a 'counter-gift' from the maternal relatives, there is a certain asymmetry in shell money (the first black – most prestigious – shell money is not returned) and in other goods (a certain proportion, which I did not quantify, is not returned) as well as in time and labour, weighted in favour of the *tëvö*. On the death of the last surviving sibling

---

7   See Faugère 2000.
8   See Leblic 2000.

6. THE CONSTRUCTION AND FICTION OF CONSENSUS

in a family, the maternal relatives have a substantial right of appropriation or even destruction (*jèdo*) of the goods owned by members of the 'house' side, since the ceremony then closes the debt occasioned by the alliance between the parents of the deceased:

> What does *jèdo* mean? It means that people come and then they take everything they want in your house. They do it because they can no longer eat at your house, since relations are no longer renewed. So there is that *bwêê*, and that *bwêê* [pile of foodstuffs] so that's the last meal you owe them, after that there's no more. (Narcisse Kaviyöibanu, extract from interview, April 1999)

Inclusion/exclusion

Beyond the simple formal description of the ceremony, and the modalities of reciprocity it brings into play and thus its role as a process of contract agreement between those assembled, some aspects of the ceremonies make them more than just a formal mechanism for exchange repeated identically from ceremony to ceremony. They become a singular political event, in which aspects of the relations of influence and power between the groups involved are at play on each occasion. I should like to outline some elements of this political play, on the basis of a number of examples. It appears that, to begin with, a ceremony is the site of an organisational dualism: two groups face one another to exchange goods, words and sometimes people. This dualism results from the production of the groups involved, a social labour that unfolds in various ways.

Structural exclusions

The central actors in the various stages of the ceremony demonstrate by default that the many individuals present at the public display of exchanges in an open ceremonial space are highly differentiated as actors. The young women are almost always kept at a distance (usually cooking); the young men take on the tasks of handling goods (putting the piles of foodstuffs in place, transporting yams); and, while older married women are sometimes present in the ceremonial arena (at a number of stages in marriage and at mourning), most of those present are men, and they alone have charge of the most prestigious acts of unrolling shell money and making speeches. It is worth remembering, in this context, what Pierre Bourdieu wrote: 'the *social* function of ritual ... [is to institute] a lasting difference between those to whom the rite pertains and those to whom it does not pertain ... Thus sexually differentiated rites consecrate the differences between the sexes: they constitute a simple difference of fact as a legitimate distinction, as an institution.' (Bourdieu 1991 (1982), pp. 117–18, emphasis in original). In the New Caledonian context, Christine Salomon has shown that the exclusion of women often leads to them being present at ceremonies at a distance:

> Their attitude in the ceremony ranges from active though silent participation to more or less resigned passivity (waiting in their place until the ceremony ends, or chatting until the men tell them to be quiet), right up to discreet disparagement and acrimonious remarks on the content and above all the length of the speeches (when the meal they have prepared is long since ready). (Salomon 2000b, p. 331)

Invitations and the destination of custom

Ceremonial action produces collectives, through a series of operations the most basic of which is the distribution of the invitations that, on the occasion of a death or a marriage, will form the two groups who face one another to circulate goods, words and sometimes persons from one side to the other during the ceremony. If this is a public event, how is that public constituted? It is the organiser of the ceremony, in other words the head of the family of the agnatic group of the bridegroom or of the deceased, or of the husband of a deceased woman, who takes responsibility for communicating the news or appointing messengers to inform those concerned by the ceremony. The choice of which heads of family he will notify and which words he will use offers the possibility of bypassing some, of drawing support from marginalised groups – in short of reinforcing or overlooking the social role of any given person – and is thus politically tactical. The construction of a collective uses the grammar of social relations: one invites the members of the houses of one's lineage, one's clan, of allied clans, sometimes one's political or religious associates, thus accentuating the value of these relations. In 1999, I asked Narcisse Kaviyöibanu what he was planning to say at the forthcoming marriage of a young man from a family with whom his clan then had close relations:

> The day I arrive with my ceremonial gifts ... I shall have to recall the deep ties that bind us. And when I recall those ties, that's the opportunity for me to say things that are not said every day. First I will thank them for inviting me to come to be at their side, that's the first thing. The second important thing I will say is why their father [the organiser of the ceremony] has asked me to come. And that's when I'll tell them: 'The words I'm going to say to you are words that belong to you and to me, words that must stay in our houses, none must leak away because that is what binds us.

> In your clan there are lineages bearing the names Kamwinô, Nébürüwaa, Wéavèra. Those names are not just names in the air, they are words that mean we are bound today. What does Kamwinô mean? In the time of the elders I called on you, you the warrior clan, because I was in difficulty and to translate that difficulty, you bear the name Kamwinô that means where the word of the Mèyikwéö [the maximal clan to which Kaviyöibanu, the speaker's clan, belongs] finds relief [literally, 'where the word breathes']. The house of Nébürüwaa [literally, 'messages of war'], why? Because all the warriors come with their war medicines in relation to the house of Nébürüwaa, which is your house. The house of Wéavèra [literally, 'one word'], what does that mean? One single word, that's your house, when you say "It's OK", it's OK. If you say "no", it's no. That is how we are bound together by words. The elders have passed on, but the word they left, it's that in difficult situations, in difficult moments, I will never be against you. I shall always be by your side.' (Narcisse Kaviyöibanu, extract from interview, April 1999)

This speech mobilises historical knowledge both to extol the warrior role of the clan being honoured (citing the name Nébürüwaa, 'messages of war') and still more to emphasise the importance of the relationship that binds it to the clan of the speaker, both in protection in war (glossing the name Kamwinô, 'where the word breathes') and in political decision-making (on the basis of the name Wéavèra, 'one word').

As well as changing over time (now incorporating political or religious associates), this grammar is not unambiguous: it always permits more or less significant exclusions. The choice of people to be invited and of words to be uttered allows the organiser to bypass some potential guests or to draw support from marginalised groups. In consequence, invitations may arouse resentment and lead to frequent refusals to come, or even public protests on the day of the ceremony.

> I yelled at him here, every time when something happens at his house, well, he doesn't let us know. He doesn't let us know, he goes off with his wife and they go into the customs, and then we're not there. Or else they go off before with the family down there, and then we go, and then that creates [a] bad [impression], you know. (Extract from interview, March 1999)

One of the key points of the invitation is the decision as to the destination of the principal money, with a number of possibilities deemed legitimate: maternal relatives (the mother's clan), *pûûpèmöö* (clans of the grandparents, particularly the maternal grandmother), *bééniaa* (clan of the son of the mother's sister) or even the clan of the brother in the case of a ceremony for a woman who has died. Similarly at marriages, it is not always the man's clan that provides the principal money of the bride price,[9] nor the woman's clan that receives it, depending on the prior relations between the clans involved. Thus in one mourning ceremony I attended, one of the maternal relatives protested vehemently against the way the invitations had been made and the attribution of the custom to a clan other than his, shouting out his grievances in front of everyone present. In another case, in front of the shell money laid out in the ceremonial space, two members of two different lineages in the same clan came to blows to establish who should receive the first money offered.

In his turn, the person selected chooses whether or not to disseminate the information to the *tëvö*. I witnessed conflicts that manifested these difficulties around invitations, in other words the inclusion or exclusion of a given person in a particular group. For example, on the day of preparation for the mourning of the grandmother of one of my interviewees, his uncle (with whom he was in conflict) tried to join the organiser's group of agnates (*ka-wêmwâ*: the people of the house). The agnates already present refused this uncle's help, however, seeing him as a maternal relative. Embarrassed by this refusal, the uncle did not return on the day of the ceremony. As one of my interviewees put it:

> Often there are protests like that because you've forgotten such-and-such a person. After the event, I don't know, a drunk or something like that, that's when you get criticised, and sometimes they shout at you in public, when you come to talk, they reproach you: 'Oh yes, you come today, but yesterday the day before? Did you think of me when that happened?' (Extract from interview, January 1999)

Finally, it is quite common for individuals to be invited to the ceremony by the two groups who sit on either side, and are thus free to emphasise one or other of the bonds concerned. The way in which members of a given family may be split between the two groups varies, and is primarily determined by the local social and political context. For example, at the marriage of the son of the chief of a village in the Houaïlou valley, the bride's maternal uncle, who was a member of the same village, invited all

---

9   As I showed in the case of Bwèda Néwau (see Chapter 2).

the village's inhabitants, as had the chief. With one exception, they chose to sit on the maternal relatives' side as a way of contesting the legitimacy of the chief, thus arousing his anger.

Rather than asking what is the collective subject of the collective action constituted by the ceremony (which is thus reified by being described as a 'society' or 'the whole'), the question can be turned round to ask how ceremonial action produces collectives. As can be seen here, it is through a series of operations, the most basic of which is the choice of participants, the choice to include or exclude. But while this group is constructed from highly valued categories (one invites the members of one's lineage, one's clan, of allied clans, sometimes political or religious associates), this does not mean it is perceived in terms of collective identity. The staging of 'the whole' and the production of 'consensus' in ceremonies thus always rests on more or less important conscious exclusions or avoidances, and therefore on the prior construction of a collective (actor).

The choice of money

At the ceremony, the internal work in each group to decide who is going to offer his shell money to the exchange partners who are to be honoured is another site of potential political affirmation for social actors: 'Your aim has to be true, you can't be off target, if you're off target the people on the other side aren't happy' (Guynemer Karé, extract from interview, August 1993). The organisers have to agree among themselves how many pieces of money they will offer to their guests (one piece which is not reciprocated, plus one piece per clan or group of clans present on the opposite side), and decide who will offer them. This offering is the focus of intense preparatory political work. For example sometimes, contrary to prevailing practice, a piece of money is attributed to an absent clan so that someone who claims to be of that clan can take it. On the day, some hours are devoted before the guests arrive to a discussion among mature male representatives of their clan or lineage, to choose together which families will have the dignity of publicly demonstrating their wealth and importance by offering a piece of money to those invited groups they wish to honour. At this point all of the families, gathered around the master of ceremonies, try to persuade him to accept theirs because of this or that relationship that binds them with the guests. This discussion is an opportunity to demonstrate one's rhetorical prowess and the breadth of one's historical and social knowledge, in what one of my interviewees called a 'diplomatic brawl':

Everyone tries to get a position, there's a whole art to it, it's at that point that, in the house, you learn things, or you reassert things you all know, you know, your rank, or your rights, or stuff like that. What's dangerous is that when you reassert that, now there are people who make use of it to settle scores. (Narcisse Kaviyöibanu, extract from interview, September 1995)

I was not able to record these discussions when I witnessed them, and I do not know enough about the nature of the arguments, but be that as it may, 'the clans are not happy when you take out their money [when it is excluded from the exchange], because they came to support us' (Guynemer Karé, extract from interview, August 1993).

Equality/hierarchy: An order and its production

The order of money and foodstuffs

While reciprocity (between the two assembled groups) and proportionality (between goods brought and goods received) are essential components in the exchange,[10] thus demonstrating that material wealth is not the principal factor in prestige, some moments of the ceremony also contribute to the definition, or the production, of an order.

Firstly, the offering of money generates a classification, an ordering of the clans in attendance: the first piece of money, generally presented to the bride's clan at a marriage, and at mourning to the clan of the deceased's mother, is followed by a series of other money offerings to the other clans present on the side of the maternal relatives, the equivalent being strictly returned in a counter-gift. The way these pieces of money are laid out, which is based on the proximity of the clans present to the maternal clan, can be seen as an action defining a hierarchical order: 'There's a whole customary hierarchy that's referred to every time there's a death or a customary act: when you place the money you can't put the one who's lower before the other, you have to place people *in order*' (Narcisse Kaviyöibanu, extract from interview, January 1999, my emphasis). Guynemer Karé gives an example of this practice:

> When the dead person's mother is from one of these clans, if you do it *in order*, here they are from Wéma Gwâê, and their money is classed as first. And then, among the Wéma, it's like you recite *in order*, the Wéma Gwâê, the Wéma Nirikani, the Wéma Néèè. They're *greater* than the other two,

---

10 See Bensa 2006.

but *in order*, you put them there. So the second money is Wéma Nirikani, and the third is Wéma Nééè. The fourth money is Mèèvâ, because Mèèvâ is *greater* than Bwawé and Gowé. And then fifth money [Bwawé], sixth money [Gowé], and that's it. (Guynemer Karé, extract from interview, February 1999, my emphasis)

Similarly, the arrangement of the piles of foodstuffs that are distributed at the end of a mourning or marriage ceremony testifies to an order: 'Everyone comes, but *in order*, you see?' (Guynemer Karé, extract from interview, February 1999, my emphasis).

While my interviewees refer to a hierarchical order that seems true or self-evident to them, the perspective can again be reversed by stating that it is precisely this work of placing in order that contributes, on the ceremonial stage, to influencing established hierarchies, for example by altering the relative classification of a series of lineages. Finally, one variant of these classifying and ordering operations consists of deploying, more or less extensively, the layered segmentary levels of social organisation, bringing together or splitting the agnatic groups present. Thus a piece of money or a pile of foodstuffs may be offered to one lineage, to all the lineages of a clan, but also to more complex subgroups ('In the division, I separate [lineages] L1 and L2 [on one side] from them [L3], to one side'), or to a clan or even a group of clans. Uniting and dividing are thus potential new actions available to the master of ceremonies, allowing him to bring out (or not) the specificity of any given group.

Names in speeches

During the course of the ceremony itself, exchanges of goods are accompanied by speeches. Some of these, which only a few specialists know by heart, correspond to a very specific stage of the given ceremony, and can therefore be reproduced almost identically at different ceremonies. Two other types of speeches may be given, more specifically adapted to the particular local and social context of the ceremonial event. Firstly, relatively free speeches of thanks and criticism are delivered; almost all heads of family can improvise these. In these free, contingent speeches, the rhetorical subtlety of the best orators allows them to demonstrate great skill in insinuation, implying or making listeners believe that they know more than they are saying, and thus suggesting that their private social knowledge is greater than it might seem and that they are not fooled by public politeness, nor satisfied with the existing political situation. These speeches may be more or less public (in the house or in the open, unenclosed exterior space of the ceremonial arena).

There is also another form of speech, the highly formalised genealogical declamation (*mêrê vivaa*), which cites, in the form of a list of proper names, the clans gathered for the ceremony. In my view this form is important as a manifestation of an authorised version of history and the current relations between clans that should derive from it. *Mêrê vivaa* are lists of proper names of two types, either of ancestors or of residential alleys that are precisely and specifically attached to certain clans, or even to certain lineages. Formally, these lists are presented as discursive blocks corresponding to local social groupings (*mwâciri*: hamlets or sections of larger villages), broken up into large agnatic units, where appropriate accompanied by their servants, within which the different lineages proceed in order. Depending on the situation, an indication of the connection between names of ancestors and alleys, and names of clans, may or may not be given, sometimes in rather vague form. Here is an example:

> I shall honour and call attention to the descendants of Miimö and Pawirigu and Kakè and Yakörui and Gùyi and Kaa'bwèèwè [six names of ancestors] in Nékoè [name of residential alley]
>
> and Udo and Mèèvara [two names of ancestors] in Néwari [name of residential alley]
>
> and Béyixémi and Javèru [two names of ancestors] in Wâkiâ [name of residential alley]
>
> and Leregu and Apwarö and Akuii [three names of ancestors] in Wèèbénéxö [name of residential alley]
>
> and Payù [name of ancestor] in Némi [name of residential alley]
>
> Lee and Bèidowa and Jiirua and Kayarhëë [four names of ancestors] in Néii [name of residential alley]
>
> who make up the Bwêêua Gwâê downstream, and here the Bwêêwua Mii and the Bwêrê and upstream the Néii [four names of clans]. (Bwêêyöuu Ërijiyi in Aramiou and Euritéin 2002, p. 33, English from author's translation into French)

If speeches can be said to manifest a social order, in my view it is in the *vivaa* that this function is most clearly seen: these lists of names declaimed are far from transparent to their audience, requiring a knowledge that is unequally distributed in order to interpret them. The location of the residential alleys cited is not always known, nor the history of some of the ancestors named. Even today, however, heads of family know all or some of the names corresponding to their own lineage, and sometimes also to other families, which is enough to identify their own place in the speech. Two things are then particularly important: who is cited (or not) in relation to a given space of residence, and in what order. Names of ancestors or of prestigious or sordid alleys may be forgotten or taken over (by one agnatic group rather than another), and with them the part of local history pertaining to them (and the local status implied therein).[11] And the order of naming of clans in a given space of residence refers to their local status, in a complex way: thus the first clan cited may, depending on the situation, be the founding ancestor of the country or the chief. Given that the declamation is public, and that there are several versions of *mêrê vivaa* relating to the same spaces of co-residence, it acquires a degree of official stature, which changes it into a potential site of humiliation or homage. These lists would be recomposed by communal decision during agnatic integration processes (or at the welcome or adoption of clans from outside) if the adoption gave rise to a local reorganisation or the change in social relations led to modification of the speeches.[12] Delivery of them is, therefore, problematic, as indicated by the fact that their recitation can arouse great discontent among some listeners about the way their clan is cited. Neither a simple manifestation of a pre-existing relation of power nor the pure construction of a new order on the blank slate of free speech, speaking in a ceremonial context emerges as a risky act, in which each person has little room to manoeuvre.

> That's why now there is difficulty, fights and all that, because the guys who *vaa* [who deliver the *vivaa*] take the one who is at the top and put him at the bottom, and they take the one who is on the bottom. '*Wi-rè*! [Hey you!] Did you just say my name above the other?' Then the other one is anger. (Gilbert Kaparâ, extract from group interview with the Lèwèö council of elders, June 2006)

It is in the ceremonial space that the dominant version of history, and the relations between the groups making up the local group, are constructed or ratified today. Every ceremony thus has a retrospective gaze on social

---

11   See Harrison 1990.
12   There seem to have been major revisions of speeches of genealogical declamation in the early 20th century, at the time of the displacements following the demarcation of reserves described in chapters 2 and 3.

relations, which is necessary both to bring together enough participants around oneself and thus put on a good appearance, and to give meaning to the ritual event itself. Public utterance testifies to a moment, by its very nature unstable, in a local organisation that is legitimised by a historical discourse, but which can be altered by a range of political events: changes in place of residence, fights, deaths or speeches made in public. The violent forms of public confession at the time of the visit of the seers to Houaïlou represented an alternative way of visibly inscribing a relation of political power (described in Chapter 4). The recitation of *vivaa* can, therefore, be an opportunity for lateral historical reminders, or for introducing new interpretations of particular historical events. The proper names of residential alleys and of ancestors cited in these speeches all refer to episodes in history or events that are considered important in the history of the clans, and therefore have a political significance:

> A name is not innocent, it always contains a history … so the composition of *mêrê vivaa* is a whole pile of concepts, well of words that contain histories. Well, people tend to say: 'Yes, that name, it's that ancestor.' But that's too easy, they don't know the content. Yes it is a name, but it's a name that corresponds to a history, it's the name of an ancestor, the name was given to an ancestor so that he can carry the history, but you have to know, you have to peel back, what does that name mean? That's where you find the history of the marches [the displacements of clans] … The genealogical speeches, like the name of houses, the name of alleys, all that, it's history. It's written, the history. And when you analyse it there, when for example I take the history of Gwâmee [from *gwâ*, head and *mee*, split, cracked, the name of an ancestor of the Mèyikwéö clan mentioned in Chapter 2], eh, it's a history. When I tell the history of Gwâmee, there you go, Gwâmee was this this this this and this. You say the name Gwâmee, it's an envelope, I would say it's a concept, but what's behind it is a whole history, it's a whole page, two pages of history. That was the old people's thing, the genealogical speech, it's simply that. People today give speeches, speeches are a hierarchy, a treasure. It's a treasure that we've lost. That's why the people who gave the genealogical speeches, they were protected by medicines, because you can wound people too. When the person concerned, for example, whose pride is wounded, they know it's their history. Maybe he was defeated in a war, well, the word then there, when you analyse the word, you'll say it's him, but him when they make the speech, him in his heart, even if there were agreements between the old people, he's still wounded, because when the history is recounted, his history will be told, eh, that his ancestor was defeated. That's an example. (Narcisse Kaviyöibanu, extract from interview, February 1999)

6. THE CONSTRUCTION AND FICTION OF CONSENSUS

The risk that speakers take is not so much that they will be attacked verbally or physically during the ceremony – although that possibility exists – as that they expose themselves and their family to accidents or illnesses that could be caused by errors on their part or by witchcraft attacks from third parties.[13] In the view of local commentators, sickness or death are then seen as retrospective proof that a given speech was inopportune or incomplete. Participants in the public acts of communal life are aware of this death risk; silence (or non-participation in ceremonies) thus comes to seem the simplest way of avoiding it.

> For example if there is a custom that comes back to you and then him [the giver] he gets on well with me, then he'll say something like: 'No, we're not going to give him the custom, we're going to give it to this other one', you see, they're not going to give to you, they're going to give to me because you've fallen out … But that can cause problems for them, he can fall ill with that, but nobody will look after him. You'll take him to the doctor, he won't get better; you'll take him to another healer, he won't treat him. He has to come back here, and then ask forgiveness, he has to recognise he did wrong like this: 'I am sick because I did that, I turned away something that belongs to you, I gave to another.' (Philippe Kaviêrênèvâ, extract from interview, March 1999)

However, there are encompassing rhetorical forms allowing the speaker to avoid such faux pas; these can be thought of as the reverse side of the political game played by those who deliver speeches at ceremonies:

> So that's a way of saying that if anybody is forgotten, there are taros and yams there, that you will eat, you know. There are also the *lèèwi awa ma kwèèbe* [literally, the ceremonial goods made of beaten bark and banyan root] that are there … So that's the way of saying in case you have to correct yourself, you know. You always say it in case you haven't named someone, because if you don't say it, well you might get swallowed by the custom, I mean the person over there, who hasn't been mentioned, but they'll have a heavy heart, and when they go home it's heavy, so automatically in return, you'll catch a misfortune; but if you say that, you close the door [to misfortune]. (Narcisse Kaviyöibanu, extract from interview, April 1999)

The tendency of some of my Kanak interviewees to gloss names openly (particularly the proper names contained in the *vivaa*) should not obscure the silent corollary: a no less significant number of the individuals I met

---

13   See Chapter 4, and Salomon 2000a.

asserted their lack of understanding of these speeches, and of their poetic, metaphorical and social impact. It is empirically impossible to confirm such 'ignorance', and we have to settle for noting the repeated assertion by a number of people that the understanding and functionality of these speeches are diminishing, without drawing conclusions one way or the other.

> When you work on that … that's when you'll realise people's limits. That many of the elders, for example, actually they don't know a lot … Today, in the Kanak population, I'm talking about Houaïlou, there are maybe, I don't know if there are even 5 per cent who understand Kanak society that way, the way the old people understood it, saw it, you know, eh. And the proof is that today they're incapable of making a speech. We're incapable today of making those speeches, the young people … who haven't been brought up with that, that vision of Kanak society … Before, everybody could speak, and that's where you'll see the weak point in the Kanak people. We hide behind custom, we hide behind a lot of things, but actually inside, it's empty. It's a great void. (Extract from interview, February 1999)

Conversely, confidence in intrafamilial transmission of knowledge gives some courage in their truth:

> My strength is my faith in what the old man told me. When you have truth with you, you have nothing to fear, even if you're all alone. With time, you'll get them … The true version is gaining the upper hand. (Extract from interview, March 1999)

Notwithstanding these reservations, one sign of the continuing political importance of ceremonies is the fact that some older men decide themselves to organise, in their lifetime, exchanges that should take place after their death, in order to honour their maternal uncles and ensure as far as possible that the ceremony and its effects run smoothly. This ceremony of anticipated mourning, known as *pèuwè*, demonstrates that, for the actors themselves, the stakes in ceremonies are first and foremost political.

In the Houaïlou region, Kanak ceremonial speeches consist of a set of specific genres of formalised speeches, and free speeches that correspond to the various moments of rituals performed on the occasion of birth, marriage, death and the end of mourning. While their poetic dimension makes reference to a metaphorical field peculiar to this region (which it would be useful to compare with other parts of New Caledonia and even of Oceania), their inclusion in the proceedings of the ceremonial event and their articulation with other ritual practices make them one tool among others in the local political play (through operations of equalisation and hierarchisation, inclusion and exclusion, uniting and dividing). The ceremonial gathering thus represents a particularly important space of political manoeuvring, given its relatively public nature. The temporal structure of the ceremony means that these political choices mobilise a social knowledge referring to a more or less distant past. The mobilisation of afferent history thus allows those involved to recall the origin of the relations between the clans principally concerned in the ceremony. The wealth of history that can be drawn on depends on the knowledge of the organiser and his relatives, but also on the current situation and the present state of relations between the clans involved.

Hence a ceremony is made up not only of the exchanges and discourses that take place onstage (in the open-air space where goods and words are exchanged) but also of the less formal moments, at times accompanied by consumption of large amounts of alcohol, that are the occasion of jokes, ironic comments, provocations, and sometimes fights. These moments arise as people become more drunk, and represent the chaotic counterpoint of the tightly controlled speeches that precede them. In some cases, fights resolve tensions that date from before the ceremony, or arise within it. For example, in early 2008, in a tribe in the Houaïlou valley, a hundred or so participants in a mourning ceremony decided to go and have it out with one of their neighbours with whom the organisers of the ceremony had, for various reasons, been in conflict for several years. They ended up destroying windows, doors and household equipment in his house, as well as his car, before beating up both him and the two people who had come from neighbouring houses to intervene. Thus the production of ceremonial agreement between groups results from multiple operations that bring into play political subjects bearing their own plans and emotions. The reverse side of this celebratory moment of consensus and apparent agreement of contract is the maintenance of tensions due to ongoing conflicts, which sometimes lead to physical violence, and frequently to a shared anxiety about the risk of witchcraft attacks at public gatherings.

Four spaces of mobilisation following the Nouméa Accord

I turn now to consider contemporary forms of political mobilisation in the Houaïlou region, keeping in mind the connection between the production of consensus and the persistence of violence in the ceremonial arena. I base my consideration on case studies of a party political campaign in 1999, a village conflict that has continued since 2002, the public management of this conflict and, finally, the work of collectors of oral heritage that has also been under way in Houaïlou since 2002.

Departure from reserves and abandonment of farming

> [Modern] processes of denucleation in Ilahita are operating through a diversity of practical situations which are, in aggregate, pulling the village apart. Internal land disputes, political defections, business rivalries and even sectarian discords are undermining ward solidarity, but only in the absence of positive reasons for this solidarity and of traditional means for ensuring it. The modern dismantling of Ilahita village is both cause and effect of, both indicates and accelerates, the decay of Ilahita's ideological nuclei. (Tuzin 1988, p. 95)

Since it was launched in 1978, and particularly since it was sped up following the Matignon-Oudinot agreements in 1988, land reform has contributed significantly to the transformation of rural worlds in New Caledonia. In particular, the reserves are no longer the sole frame of reference for Kanak rural life on the east cost of Grande Terre. Between 1978 and 2005, 6,582 hectares were assigned to Houaïlou. Of this, 699 hectares was allocated to enlarge the reserve, 1,493 hectares as clan properties, and 4,390 hectares in the form of 'local specific rights groupings'.[14] Hence over 30 per cent of the municipality's customary lands are now located outside of the reserve (without taking individual private properties into account). The effects of Kanak recuperation of the lands expropriated in the 19th century are materially evident here, in a lower density of houses and gardens, and a tendency for people to move away from the reserve lands. This geographical evolution, combined with (and sometimes intensifying) internal frictions in the spaces of collective habitation of the tribes, means that the forms of social organisation centred on the reserve that were established in the

---

14 According to Sourisseau 2006, p. 24.

late 19th century (the small tribal chiefdom and the district-wide high chiefdom) are no longer fit for purpose. It cannot, therefore, be assumed that the chiefdom continues to structure all the various aspects of village social life. In fact, successions to the status of tribal chief have become highly problematic in Houaïlou, and there has been no high chief in any of the municipality's six districts for several years. Moreover, this same period has seen a huge shift in tribal village economies, as Marcel Djama has shown for Grande Terre as a whole:

> There seems thus a clear trend towards reduction of the area under food cultivation … But this decrease has not been made up for by any marked increase in agricultural productivity …
>
> The main constraint on all farmers in New Caledonia is that of access to a limited and highly concentrated internal market …
>
> Although still focused largely on subsistence of individual domestic units, [agricultural production] does not supply the majority of their food, as it did in the pre-European period. Nor does it constitute a major source of income as it did during the era of colonial development of the tribes. (Djama 1999, pp. 9, 15 and 23)

The general drop in agricultural activity, the fall in the number of farms and the increasing age of farmers noted in the most recent agricultural censuses (1991 and 2002) are also evident in the Houaïlou region. The first analysis produced by the ADRAF (Agence pour le développement rural et l'aménagement foncier (Agency for Rural Development and Land Use)) in 2006, for the purposes of creating a Grouped Land Planning Operation (OGAF)[15] in Houaïlou, reveals the same tendencies, with a very sharp fall in horticultural food production and in small commercial production (coffee cultivation has collapsed, and cattle farming is declining markedly, in Houaïlou). Fruit orchards live on year in year out, and 'there is in the municipality a growing interest among producers in production of lychees, which is less labour-intensive than coffee farming, offers greater added value in sale price terms, and has technical facilities available nearby' (ADRAF 2006, p. 17). This production is supported by an annual lychee festival held in Houaïlou since 1997. These developments are partly linked to the more numerous opportunities for paid employment amid the economic growth that followed the political settlements of the

---

15   Opération groupée d'aménagement foncier, a local planning structure set up under the state-run territorial development program [trans.].

Matignon-Oudinot and Nouméa accords. Within Houaïlou, however, income from paid employment is limited to statutory public employment (for the municipality, the province, schools), subsidised contracts (for example, young development interns), and a few dozen jobs directly or indirectly related to the mines that are worked nearby. The alternative is temporary or long-term migration to Nouméa or to the (few) other employment hubs in the North Province (Houaïlou residents being fairly sceptical about their chances of getting jobs in the mining development region of Voh-Koné-Pouembout).[16] Overall this picture testifies to the rapid transformation of a context that is no longer that of an economy of colonisation, which more or less persisted until the events of the 1980s. Djama has shown that these developments should be seen as the result of local adaptation to the very marked structural imbalances in the agricultural market in New Caledonia as a whole, which are such that for Kanak producers:

> the economic reproduction of average domestic units is based neither on paid employment nor on agriculture, but on a *combination* of paid employment and production and harvesting activity. At the level of the individual this combination needs to be understood in the context of a professional life cycle: this is not really an organised portfolio career, but rather an alternation between cycles of activity on a pattern that follows the fluctuations of the job market. At household level, the mobilisation of resources needs to be understood in terms of both economic diversification and division of labour. (Djama 1999, p. 22)

The preparatory study for the Houaïlou OGAF confirms this analysis: 'In general, while agriculture predominates in the economic life of the population, it is no longer experienced as real work capable of generating regular income. It competes with mining work and paid employment' (ADRAF 2006, p. 16).

In both their conversation and their practices, residents of Houaïlou seek to imagine new ways of living together, in the face of a shift in the political and economic framework of their lives at least as significant as that experienced at the end of the *indigénat*. They are grappling with the need to develop the forms and terms of this reorganisation of a local social life where village solidarity seems to be in decline, sometimes with other solidarities (of clan, for example, or political affiliation) taking over. In my view, all the recent forms of mobilisation express, either explicitly or

---

16   Sourisseau et al. 2006, p. 167.

pragmatically, a point of view as to the need for local reorganisation, and often, though not always, stress the importance of customary rules and values, while still reflecting on the forms and uses of legitimate violence. The following examples of these mobilisations, emerging from widely varying registers of action and discourse, highlight 'politics', 'clan', 'custom' or 'culture'. While far from exhaustive, I present four ways of emerging from village life as it was articulated in the colonial and neocolonial forms of the chiefdom, the council of elders and the missionary associations (see chapters 3 and 4). Thus, in some of these registers, the levels of municipality, province and *ajië-arhö* customary area prove more relevant than the 'tribe' to the understanding of contemporary forms of collective living. All of these levels contribute to shaping and organising the new situation of residential dispersal noted above, and thus compete with one another to determine a new postcolonial governmentality. I shall seek in particular to grasp the contemporary shifts in the modalities of individuals' engagement and the use of physical violence in the conflicts they encounter, in order thus to understand the way my interlocutors devise ways of increasing their autonomy or their emancipation.

1998–2002: A new political party

At the time of my field research in Houaïlou in 1999, discussions were marked by the recent signing of the Nouméa Accord, in May 1998. Under this agreement, New Caledonia entered a new dynamic, for a transitional period of 15 to 20 years, extending the Matignon-Oudinot agreements of 1988. These had brought Kanaks into the process of determining the institutional future of the territory, following the violent 'events' of 1984–88. Thanks to a wide-ranging transfer of responsibilities and the establishment of new institutions (local government, the New Caledonia Assembly, the Customary Senate, provinces with increased powers), New Caledonia currently has a status without equivalent in France. The preamble to the Nouméa Accord, a remarkable text in the context of French colonial history, is effectively a call for decolonisation:

> The time has come to recognise the dark side of the colonial period, even if it was not devoid of light. The impact of colonisation had a lasting traumatic effect on the first people. Clans lost their names when they lost their land. Extensive colonisation of land led to considerable displacement of the population, in which Kanak clans saw their means of subsistence reduced and their places of memory lost. This process of dispossession led to a loss of reference points for identity. Kanak social organisation,

even if its principles were recognised, was brought into disarray by this process. Population movements broke down its structure, ignorance or power plays too often led to the denial of legitimate authorities and the installation of authorities with no customary legitimacy, reinforcing the traumatic loss of identity. At the same time, the Kanak artistic heritage was ignored or looted. To this denial of the fundamental elements of Kanak identity were added restrictions on public freedoms and a lack of political rights, despite the fact that the Kanaks had paid a heavy toll in the defence of France, particularly during the First World War. Kanaks were relegated to the geographical, economic and political margins of their own country, a process which, among a proud people not without warrior traditions, could only provoke rebellions that were met with violent repression, aggravating resentment and misunderstanding. Colonisation damaged the dignity of the Kanak people and deprived them of their identity. Men and women lost their lives or their reason for living in this confrontation. The result was enormous suffering. These difficult times need to be remembered, the mistakes acknowledged, and their confiscated identity restored to the Kanak people. For them this equates to a recognition of their sovereignty, prior to the foundation of a new sovereignty shared in a common destiny. Decolonisation is the way to rebuild a lasting social bond between the communities living in New Caledonia today. ('Accord sur la Nouvelle-Calédonie signé à Nouméa le 5 mai 1998', p. 8039)

This agreement led to a reconfiguration of the political space in New Caledonia. One noticeable effect in the Houaïlou region was a split in one of the independence parties, the Parti de libération kanake (Palika), some of whose members came together with activists from other movements to set up a new party, the Fédération des comités de coordination indépendantistes (FCCI, Federation of Pro-Independence Co-operating Committees). This party, which formed a territory-wide alliance with the anti-independence Rassemblement pour la Calédonie dans la République (RPCR), demonstrated that the issue of independence was being put on the back burner following the signature of the Nouméa Accord.

> So, what is the FCCI right now? It's the third way, the way of people who reflect and think about this country, you know, we're obliged to live together. It's not possible for us Blacks to be all alone on one side, and the others on the other side; for development, for all the rest, it's not possible … There with the FCCI, we're bringing together people on our side who want to take initiative, who want to take responsibility for the future, you know, so that tomorrow we build a future of peace, of happiness and above all of peace together for all the young people of this country, whether they're Black, White, Yellow, Green or Red, there you are, that's how we see it. (Extract from interview, March 1999)

6. THE CONSTRUCTION AND FICTION OF CONSENSUS

In the Houaïlou region, some individuals' decision to join the FCCI was accompanied by a customary procedure in which a number of pieces of ceremonial money were offered to one of the chiefdoms in Yaté, the municipality of origin of one of the leaders of the party:

> We'd like the FCCI to be set up on a solid foundation, in relation with Yaté … That's why us here in Houaïlou, we took a custom, presented it to the Yaté chiefdom with that idea, that today the FCCI is going to become a political party, and in order for that political party to be strong and when people hear the word FCCI, it sounds better to them, well we need to make its base in Yaté. There you have it. And that's why, when we went to Yaté, we took that custom, to bind ourselves whether to the people of Yaté, or the people of Bourail, the people of the north, the people of the south, the people of the islands, and it's that custom that bound us all. (Extract from interview, March 1999)

> So, why did we take the Kanak money? … We thought that in order for the FCCI to last as long as the Union Calédonienne, we needed to put in something strong as well, and what's the strong bond that unites two families or two clans among us Kanaks? It's Kanak money; Kanak money acts as glue, for something, a construction … And that's how, talking in that way, but instinctively, we went there, each of us took a piece of money … And the word that went with the Kanak money from the Houaïlou people that was laid there, in front of everybody, it was the protection of leaders. That Kanak money will correct their words if they are not straight, that Kanak money will be a bodyguard in their work. And at the same time that Kanak money will be Kanak justice, Kanak law, if they ever deceive their people. (Extract from interview, March 1999)

This decision to circulate a piece of Kanak money thus acts as a public formalisation of a political commitment, as in the ceremonies examined at the start of this chapter (hence the reference to the 'word that went with the Kanak money from the Houaïlou people that was laid there, in front of everybody'). This formalisation mobilises the presumed powers of the ancestors (alluded to in the mention of 'Kanak justice' in the second interview extract, an expression I commented on in Chapter 4). This close articulation of 'politics' and 'custom' can be understood particularly in the light of the fact that this party political split led locally to major commitments to reconfiguring village life: while the national goal of constructing a 'common destiny' played its part, in Houaïlou the high level of local activism was rooted, for those leading it, in a desire to restore what they considered authentic customary hierarchies at village level.

Thus the first decision of the activists in Nérhëxakwéaa was to become involved in the local council of elders (in an extension of the political movement of the 1950s examined in Chapter 4). Christine Demmer has also shown, in relation to a different activist context in Canala, how Palika activists chose to become involved in the council of elders and ceremonial activities during the period of the 'regions' (1985–88), as a way of supporting the economic autonomy project of 'constructing Kanaky' from the bottom up, instituting a *de facto* independence.[17] While in Houaïlou the issue of economic development and initiative was probably less significant, the mechanism of local mobilisation of the FCCI through the councils of elders was the same:

> That's really the work that we're doing there, when we take on the restructuring of the council of elders, the political work we've been trying to do up to now. If we want to bring people back to the right balance, people need to recover cultural values, really. And those cultural values, in a way, today they don't exist any longer in houses, the word no longer exists in each house, so we have to teach people to respect one another again. We have to teach them how society was organised, teach them again how you should speak … So that we can resolve problems of lands, so we can resolve problems of conflicts. The conflicts are just a reflection of that reality, people don't know their custom any more, there's no respect for the uncles … Because there are always conflicts, in every society there are conflicts, but a conflict can be managed, there are rules, but here that isn't the case. (Extract from interview, February 1999)

This was a pragmatic and proactive extension of the diagnosis made by the same individual a few years earlier, in a different political context:

> People speak any old how nowadays. That explains the mess we're in. Because if people referred to the respect to each house, well, a lot of problems would be resolved. But the problem is that a lot of houses no longer have any structure, there's no respect any more for the clan elders, the clan house … Well, maybe that's a bit of a retrograde position, but it's the best position to ensure security in the tribe, a more pleasant environment to live in, you know. (Extract from interview, June 1995)

Thus, campaigning activity was based on the mobilisation, redefinition and even the invention of 'customary' social relations, in a process that has a long history in Oceania.[18]

---

17   Demmer 2002.
18   See Jolly 1982; Keesing 1982.

The FCCI is where families come together in custom, not just in politics. It's the opposite of selfish demands. (Extract from interview, February 1999)

Conversely, all the weight of 'customary' relations between families was harnessed to ensure maximum possible support for this project, with strategies including transmission of historical knowledge:

That's what I explained to X yesterday, I told him: 'You see, there are things you don't know.' And I said to him: 'The FCCI in Houaïlou, I based it on the foundation of our strength, the strength of your house and my house, and you are missing from that, because me I wanted to give it deep roots. You haven't understood that because there are a lot of things you don't know', so that's what I said to him, I told him: 'You see, there are things I'm going to tell you now, things I don't [usually] say but now I'm going to tell you, your father is there, he knows, and you'll hear it from my mouth.' So then I explained all that to him. (Extract from interview, April 1999)

In this example, the relations between two clans were directly articulated in order to facilitate a shared political mobilisation, brushing aside (or bracketing) the political reservations of a man who was not persuaded by the FCCI's general political arguments. Education in certain elements of the history of the clans involved and their relations served as the ultimate justification for a commitment from which no individual should be missing. The effort to clarify local history and modes of social life in the Houaïlou region that some of these campaigners agreed to make, in the interviews I conducted with them during my fieldwork in 1999, resulted from their desire to reform village life, which then made sense of their activism in the FCCI. In short, what some of my interviewees told me during this field research could perhaps be considered the consequence of their investment in these 'customary' structures.[19] This combination of political engagement with a view towards electoral timeframes (provincial and municipal elections) and the desire to reorganise village life on the basis of a model of imagined social and customary order, which arose in 1999 out of a party political split, is again apparent in the following interview extracts:

That's when we felt the need to reclaim our values, our way of speaking, be closer to people … That's why for example we need to sort out our situations in the tribe, we have to make our customary marriages, we have to baptise our children, we have to get married, because you can say what

---

19   See Naepels 2008.

> you want, but those are the values people pay attention to … People live their ordinary life, judge according to their way. And what's their way? It's: who goes to mass? You're in order, before you speak you start first by having a house, being married by the book, not stealing girls, you have to pay for girls, and then you have to get married and then you have to baptise your children. Those are after all the reference criteria that can't be bypassed, if we want people to be with us. That's it, that's what's lived in the tribes. (Extract from interview, February 1999)

> On the political, FCCI level, we have to refer back to the history of colonisation, how did colonisation become established? How did religion become established? It was on the basis of family units, chiefdoms, things like that. So the FCCI, if we want it to be something strong, we have to take that into account … And when [a party member] gets married, or at the end of mourning, all of that is what we've taken into account. (Extract from interview, January 1999)

Ceremonial formalism emerges here as a legitimate aid to political mobilisation. The activist team, therefore, decided to implement a strategy of irreproachable adherence to custom, through assiduous attendance at ceremonies of mourning and marriage, sometimes speaking at them, and by organising a number of marriage ceremonies in their own families, so as to resolve their overall position in this new tribal balance of forces. Thus, the takeover of the council of elders and investment in custom represent the spearhead of a political campaign of local development, through the revaluation of customary functions: as one of my interviewees said later, 'politics succeeds when the link with custom has been made' (extract from interview, September 2002).

> Me, how I see the FCCI today, well, what we're trying to do, is to base ourselves on cultural values, in the way we do things. For example not keeping to ourselves, for example if tomorrow the FCCI is well established, well we'll still carry on seeing people from the RPCR or the Union Calédonienne or other parties, whatever, it's not a problem, if there's work to be done, let's do it together. That's the customary spirit, the spirit of the people of one country … all of that is really what we need, well, to learn to live together again, you know, to ensure that everyone has freedom of opinion, but without wanting to crush the other at all costs because he doesn't think the same way as you. (Extract from interview, February 1999)

Although more limited in scope, a certain similarity emerges between the political project developed by the FCCI in Houaïlou in the late 1990s and the Protestant mobilisations of the 1950s, where the council of elders also served as the principal vector of a reorganisation of local social relationships following the abolition of the *indigénat* system (see Chapter 4). Indeed, according to those involved the claimed success of the campaign in support of the FCCI was also due to the implementation of nutritional restrictions and rules of abstinence, following the visit of a healer who had come to the most active tribes at their invitation. Their aim was both to ensure the purity of the members of this new party and to protect them from witchcraft attacks. While this visit did not result in a witch-hunt like that which accompanied the visit of the Ponérihouen diviners (*jauu*) in 1955 (perhaps because the FCCI activists were not powerful enough to instigate it), the aims were certainly comparable, and justified the use of protection against potential witchcraft attacks. For some of my interviewees, then, political activism ran in parallel with a war between shadowy powers, justifying the use of a whole arsenal of 'medicines':

> We're in the period of politics … So there you have to be vigilant, you know. So, among the medicines I've prepared there are several compounds … there's the medicine for when people activate things to hurt you, so I've got the medicine to block that; I've got the medicine of words of curse; I've got the medicine of the clan's spirits, the devils … and then in there I've put a slingshot medicine … and there's one last medicine I've put in, it's to remove, because when people do something bad, they'll take their medicine and they'll attach it, when somebody makes bad medicine, they'll cast a spell on you, they'll talk to you, and they'll attach … But the medicine I put in there, it's a medicine that'll jump over all those medicines, but not only will it jump over the medicines, it will remove what he's done. And not only will it remove, I've loaded a slingshot, that'll blow up in his face. So that's how there are screw-ups that happen, you know, accidents, or this or that. If the person who's making the stuff protects himself, it's his family that gets hit, you know, that's their problem. Well, I've got other medicines I can load up, I've got very powerful things but I don't use them, I often keep to just that. But the ones I'm already using are strong. But I've got other, more powerful medicines, so if I want to send them to the graveyard, I send them, but that you only do in extreme cases, you know. (Extract from interview, April 1999)

This political mobilisation also meant continual calls on the wives and children of the main activists involved: the large number of meetings organised to establish the new party, of village fêtes to finance it, and of marriage ceremonies planned relied on a substantial labour of production, practical organisation and availability of domestic labour, principally that of women. This process was made particularly visible in Houaïlou by the women FCCI activists who organised the region's first International Women's Day demonstration, in the municipality's main town in March 1999; it was also highlighted because the prohibitions recommended by the healer included one on women preparing food while menstruating, which several times obliged older men to take on this work during campaign meetings, whether they liked it or not.

2002–08: A clan war in Wakaya

I turn now to the second space of collective mobilisation I saw in operation during my research, around a serious village conflict between two agnatic groups.[20] In 1996 (the date of the most recent census providing such data), the village of Wakaya comprised 15 households, with a total population of 75; 45 other people stated that they belonged to this village, but did not live there. These families form part of two agnatic groupings that I shall here call the 'L' and the 'R'. The tribe lies about 10 kilometres from the main town of Houaïlou municipality (administrative, medical and commercial centre), at the end of a dirt road some way away from the major communication routes, which serves a total of five villages. Wakaya is the name of one of the tributaries of this small valley, lying along a dead-end branch of the road that passes by the houses of the L, then those of the R, making up Wakaya village.

Here I offer an ethnographic description of a social situation of conflict that has been going on for several years, marked by the most serious confrontations that Houaïlou, and probably the whole of Grande Terre, has seen since the political 'events' of the 1980s. These have involved gunfights between several dozen men, as well as many brawls. This 'low-level war' is not dissimilar to the classic ethnographic descriptions of pre-colonial wars in Oceania.[21] It also shows some continuity with processes of militarisation of village conflicts, including even the formation of militias, as far as they are known in the Solomon Islands and Papua New Guinea.[22]

Since 2002 a conflict between these two clans has taken a somewhat violent turn, resulting in an escalation or intensification of the forms of physical violence used. This is a conflict of low or very low intensity. Nevertheless,

---

20   An initial analysis of this conflict appeared in Naepels 2012.
21   See for example Knauft 1990.
22   See for example Dinnen and Thompson 2004.

incidents are frequent enough and violent enough to be at the forefront of concern for the individuals involved, other members of the two agnatic groups, and the population of Houaïlou well beyond them. I sought to understand this situation through interviews with members on both sides, drawing on relationships I had that predate the conflict, and on third parties who have good enough relations with the two sides, and often (but not always) conducting interviews outside of the village (in other Kanak villages in Houaïlou or in other municipalities, mainly Nouméa and its suburbs). This does not answer all of the methodological and ethical questions relating to securing sources, verifying their reliability, the extent to which they can be deemed relatively comprehensive, and the forms of account it is possible to construct. I certainly cannot claim exhaustive knowledge of all of the events linked to this conflict (in particular the detail of exchange of insults and gunfire).

In June 2002 an argument in the municipality's main town degenerated into a fistfight between two of the R and one of the L. The latter, on his return to Wakaya, went to get his gun and fired buckshot at the son of one of his opponents that day. In January 2003, when he was released from prison, there were several exchanges of gunfire between the two families. A dozen of the houses and huts belonging to the L family were burned. In retaliation, one of the L shot one of the R, seriously injuring his leg. The ambulance taking him to the health centre was attacked. In October 2003 another shootout resulted in two people being wounded, and then the burning of a number of houses. In September 2005 there were further exchanges of gunfire. In July 2007, following a reconciliation meeting that the R family failed to attend, a more substantial gun battle resulted in six wounded, including four members of the R family who drove past their adversaries' houses, gun barrels at the windows of their car, in a gesture of defiance and who were then caught in an exchange of gunfire and had to be evacuated to hospital in Nouméa owing to the seriousness of their injuries. Following this gun battle, roadblocks were set up on the road (which here serves only the two families involved). In November 2007 there was another shootout between the two families in the main town of the municipality, during a fête, and four people were wounded. The gun battles continued in the tribe, with more casualties, four houses were burned, the gendarmerie vehicle that came to put a stop to the incident was shot at. In January 2008 a 17-year-old man accompanying his L cousins was killed. The alleged gunman gave himself up at the gendarmerie a few days later. In the following months, during the first half of 2008, a number of representatives of institutions called on the R family to leave the place temporarily. They did so, moving mainly to a site in a disused mining settlement in the municipality. All of their houses and huts were burned. Shortly afterwards, a member of the L family who had come to get drunk in the mining settlement was beaten up in his car. Hospitalised in Nouméa, he was attacked again by members of the opposing family living in the capital.

In order to understand this conflict, I begin with a few remarks on the forms of social organisation it brings into play. Firstly, it arises between patrilineal groups that are extremely close, and are listed together in the *vivaa* (the ceremonial speeches whose sociological significance was discussed in the early part of this chapter). Nevertheless, the conflict is not confined to a simple agnatic definition of the actors involved, primarily because there are internal divisions in each of the two groups around their varying levels of engagement in the conflict. For example, following the burning of a number of houses, one member of the L family was reproached by members of his own family, was beaten and suffered lasting neurological damage. Segmentary principles of fission and fusion characteristic of family commitments in the Houaïlou region are thus being brought into play. Secondly, the conflict continually spreads beyond the principal families involved, following the individual lines of alliance or affinity of the people in question: the maternal nephews, brothers-in-law and maternal uncles of a given individual sometimes participate directly in a given incident. For example, V, a young man, was hit by buckshot in 2006 as he was walking with his L brothers-in-law; after the fête in November 2007, some of the maternal uncles of the wounded joined in the burning of the shooters' houses. More crucially in terms of physical violence, the young man killed in 2008 was not himself a member of either the R or the L family; and today, with hindsight, some of my interviewees link the current conflict between the two families with the death of a young R man killed in a knife fight by a member of the other clan in 1999.

'Youth', moreover, is a distinct characteristic of those involved in the violence; as far as I was able to tell, the vast majority are men, although women are often present at scenes of violence, and women originating from or married into both clans consider themselves deeply involved in what is happening, and contribute to the circulation of accounts of it.

The deviant behaviour of those involved is very widely stigmatised, both by local Kanak commentators and by the media, who relate it to their youth, and to the consumption of alcohol and cannabis.

> It seemed obvious to us that people were taking too much liberty in the tribes, and since at the same time they can't solve the problem of youth among their own children, the young people have become the mainstay of the disorder in the tribe – cannabis, alcohol and then theft and all that. And at the same time, you've got the conflicts between adults over land rights and the legitimacy of social hierarchies, whether it's at the level of customary authorities or of older/younger brother, and so on. So the two came together somewhere: the adults sort of used the young people, well, they didn't use them on purpose, I mean the young people, there is delinquency, but when it's connected to clans to families who themselves have conflicts over legitimacy, that creates bombs, you know, that's the whole of the big problem. (Extract from interview, July 2008)

In the New Caledonian context these variables are not unique to this case, but incidents of physical violence do not necessarily result in tension and escalation like those discussed here. This could be a case of social patterns that are well known elsewhere: the instrumentalisation of 'youth' in local conflicts, but also the autonomisation of violence (though here it does not result in the creation of specialist institutions, militias or armies, but rather refers back to a specific practice of physical violence and weaponry), over and above the reasons given for it. These acts of physical violence emerge as moments of greater autonomy for young people, who do not always have much say in decisions that involve their family; it also seems to be the continuation, in another form, of a period of warrior initiation prior to marriage that may have existed during the pre-colonial period, if we are to believe Maurice Lenormand in one of his articles on Lifou:

> In olden days the young man was first a front-line warrior who had to remain physically fit and observe a number of rules of abstinence. Therefore he could only marry after several years of service among the warriors of his tribe … In order to marry, he had to prove himself as a man, that is to say, as a warrior. (Lenormand 1970, p. 52)[23]

---

23   I am grateful to Hélène Nicolas for alerting me to this passage. Accounts along the same lines can be found in the second series of Bwêêyöuu Ërijiyi's notebooks, in Aramiou and Euritéin 2003, pp. 95–102.

Pragmatically speaking, older men certainly have more to lose when violence is resorted to:

> X wanted to help defend us, he wanted to give us a hand; result of the chases, his house was burned, but him, he's got his kids, he loses out in the story. His wife and children, they went to the grandmother's house ... He would have done better to stay calm. He should have left it to the ones who were still unmarried. (Extract from interview, July 2008)

As far as cannabis use is concerned in relation to this conflict, Houaïlou is the municipality with the largest number of arrests for breaches of the drugs law, and the largest seizures of cannabis, in Grande Terre in recent years.[24] Wakaya is one of the three Houaïlou tribes most often mentioned in the local daily newspaper in relation to cannabis seizures and convictions for drug dealing. The profitability of cannabis is very probably far higher than that of the rural development projects that compete with it. Christophe Pommé writes that 'household income [from cannabis] in tribes amounts to 36,390 CFP francs[25] in Houaïlou' (Pommé 2006, p. 22) – a figure that can be put in perspective by comparing it with the ISEE (Institut de la Statistique et des Etudes Economiques, Institute for Statistics and Economic Studies) data: in the North Province, one quarter of households receive less than 80,000 CFP per month, and half less than 176,000 CFP francs per month.[26]

In Houaïlou itself, Wakaya and its groups of 'young people' have a rather bad reputation, mainly owing to the disturbances they cause in the municipality's main town. Similarly, the village is mentioned in relation to car thefts (some vehicles stolen in Nouméa having been found burnt out there). Some members of one of the families involved in the conflict deliberately play on this, choosing to adopt the alias 'Al-Qaida'. Finally, certain young men from the two families are regularly (rightly or wrongly) accused of exporting both the problems dividing them and the methods that unite them (in thefts and assaults in the neighbouring mining settlement of Poro, but also in relation to burglaries in a low-income Kanak neighbourhood in Nouméa, or in a neighbouring tribe where a senior member of the community was threatened at gunpoint in June 2008). The point that interests me here is not the question of

---

24 See Pommé 2006, p. 17.
25 Currency used in French overseas collectivities of French Polynesia, New Caledonia, and Wallis and Futuna [trans.].
26 ISEE 2009.

6. THE CONSTRUCTION AND FICTION OF CONSENSUS

'delinquency', but rather understanding that this is a case where physical violence has become autonomised, going beyond the manifestations linked to the conflict between the two families. The involvement of those concerned in the destruction of public facilities, and some of the assaults at the municipal health centre, also testify to this development.

As we have seen throughout this book, conflict (including the resort to physical violence) is not an unusual way of performing social relations in the Houaïlou region. But this conflict is striking in both its duration and the escalation it demonstrates. We therefore need to examine its origins, which invites broader reflection on the historicity of the conflict and the way history is or is not mobilised within it. My interviewees pointed to a period in the 1970s when relations between the neighbouring families deteriorated sharply. Evidence of this is the claim for a private settler property situated in the Néawa valley, initiated in December 1977. This claim, accompanied by the threat to occupy the land to force the settler to leave, was one of the first public claims brought in Grande Terre (see Chapter 5). It was mentioned in the territorial assembly as early as 1977, resulting in a visit by the high commissioner and the head of the civil service, sent by the French Ministry of Overseas Domains and Territories to launch the land reform in 1979. The important point here is that, from 1978 onwards, despite the fact that the land rights movement also involved other clans, the two families came into conflict, by launching competing claims to one part of the land; on this issue, there has been barely any movement in the conflict over the last 30 years. This situation indicates a pre-existing opposition between families and recalls earlier episodes from a few years before the land claim was lodged, at the very beginning of the 1970s, when there was a serious disagreement between some members of the two family groups over the ownership of coffee trees planted on reserve lands and a harvest. While a knife fight involving a woman from the R clan and a woman married into the L clan took place, insults deemed extremely serious that were exchanged between the husband of the R woman and men of the L seem to have been the immediate source of a breach in the moral relations implied by residence in the same village.

It seems that, from this breach onward, all of the past disagreements that might have divided the two groups at one point or another were communicated en masse within the opposing families. Thus the background to the violent incidents today is based on a conflict of legitimacy, and competition between divergent historical knowledges relating to older disagreements, which have become current again since the fights in the 1970s. The conditions of introduction of the Catholic and Protestant religions in the late 19th century, the installation of administrative chiefdoms in the early 20th century, and also the reasons for the two groups' arrival in this valley prior to colonisation and the social position occupied by each of the families, are the subject of accounts that agree on certain points, and diverge on many others.[27] At the times when the state has intervened in this conflict (in particular during the land reform operations and in the courts), these differences have been widely disseminated (in the form of letters sent to state institutions, statements made to the police or in the courts, and public declarations at meetings organised by the municipality or at customary councils), beyond the habitual confines of the transmission of history within the family. The accounts I was sometimes given of elements of the history of the families involved obviously fall into this register of justification.[28] There is thus a powerful capacity for escalation in the naturalisation through knowledge of the enmity between the adversaries, which is exploited in different ways depending on the individual: it could be said that more of the individuals concerned now know more things about the history of their family, but also that, even when they do not possess this legitimising knowledge, the perpetrators of the violence fall back on the certainty of being supported by their relatives in this context of enmity. The question that arises then is under what social conditions this construction – and also the success or failure of any potential mediation – comes into being.

2008–10: Warrior ethics and public management of the conflict

One of the striking aspects of this conflict is the willingness of the families involved to pursue it despite the public disapproval it arouses – or alternatively, their strong resistance to media and political pressure to reconcile with one another. Contrary to the usual procedure for resolving conflicts by broadening the issue out to other actors (allies or co-residents), mediation by third parties and an attempt to reach a historical synthesis by emphasising agreements and passing over discord, here an apparently self-sustaining dissenting logic prevails. The choice of the alias 'Al-Qaida' falls into this logic. When one of my friends asked him how

---

27 See Naepels 2000a.
28 See Naepels 2008.

he saw the attempts at reconciliation then under way, accompanied by ceremonial exchanges and pleas for forgiveness, one victim of a gunshot wound replied: 'The war continues.' It is worth considering how collective factors and individual determinants are interwoven in this attitude. The fact that many members of one of the families have regularly appeared at the police court since the 1950s, and the way my interviewees frequently linked this fact to their pre-colonial status as 'warriors', certainly makes it possible to distinguish between an affirmative modality of the relation to physical violence, and a reactive modality that refuses to accept the unacceptable, experienced as a denial of rights – in short, not letting oneself be walked over.

> I've heard that the elders always told it like that, in the Kanak clans, there are some who find it easier to screw up that way. When you hear the elders say it, it doesn't surprise us because it's been going for generations like that. Yes, they don't know how to behave well, they'll always do bad. And the proof can still be seen today, you know. If they don't do it in their tribe or here they go to the city, Nouméa, to mess up. The elders, when they talk like that, they say it comes from the blood. (Extract from interview, July 2008)

It may be added that the weight of unequal gender and age relations in these forms of violent mobilisation makes the 'family' a key site for understanding the conflict and the violence, both as regards the acquisition of repertoires of action, socialisation, the construction of habitus (in which physical violence, sexual violence and intimidation are not necessarily seen as illegitimate) and as regards the segmentary erasure of the distinction between public and private. Christine Hamelin and Christine Salomon's work has moreover shown that, in New Caledonia, levels of domestic violence correlate with alcohol and cannabis consumption.[29]

One further analytical dimension that can be added to this description relates to the mode of regulation of social relations it reveals. The procedures for managing conflict in spaces of collective habitation that were current in the colonial period (that is, confinement to the reserves under the authority of an administrative chief, sometimes supported by a council of elders, collaborating with the colonial administrative authorities, primarily the gendarmes) are clearly failing here. As in the majority of tribes in Houaïlou, there is currently no administrative chief in Wakaya, since succession to the chiefdom is increasingly disputed.

---

29 See Hamelin, Salomon et al. 2005.

And the intervention of clans in a position to act as mediators (principally those who are matrimonial allies of both clans in the conflict, which is not unusual), or senior members of neighbouring Kanak villages, which has been attempted here through very many meetings of the council of elders and the district council, has enabled periods of calm, but not the suspension of the conflict. It therefore seems that this conflict is proof that colonial village governmentality has indeed fallen away. Faced with this shift, three types of actors are seeking to assert their central position in the local construction of a postcolonial governmentality and in the management of violence: individuals and families (in other words, 'clans'; that is, collectives constructed on a segmentary model), the state through its political and administrative bodies, and the state through its neocustomary structures. I should like now to address this point.

The actors in the conflict appear to assimilate a large number of public institutions with white colonial power: the shooting of a police car, the publicly declared indifference to court convictions, the vandalising of schools and the assaults at the health centre and the hospital are evidence of this. At the same time, state institutions can also be seen as resources: the successive bodies overseeing land reform regularly received letters from the two clans, or visits to offer justification, make claims or, occasionally, to contest their opponents' claims, and one of the first involved in the 1977 claim was himself a gendarme. Finally, the political authorities at the various levels of local administration, the municipality of Houaïlou and the North Province, were born out of the Kanak nationalist and independence movement and, therefore, take on the mantle of some local civil society initiatives (such as the march against violence that took place in the main town of Houaïlou municipality in November 2007). This is clearly a way of asserting their own legitimacy, refusing to be identified with white colonial power by asserting, on the contrary, their takeover of institutions. It is, then, significant that the new municipal team in Houaïlou, elected in 2008, insisted during the election campaign that it was essential that the courts and the gendarmerie be involved in resolving the Wakaya conflict.

Finally, following the murder in January 2008, some representatives of the customary council of the *ajië-arhö* area went to Nouméa to meet with members of New Caledonia's Customary Senate (both institutions created under the Nouméa Accord). The senators proposed to organise a conciliation committee (comprising members of these customary bodies, the councils of elders concerned, and churches). The presence of church representatives revives an experiment first conducted in the 'mission of dialogue' that followed the Ouvéa massacre in 1988, and sought to achieve the conclusion of the Matignon-Oudinot agreements; it also returns to work carried out in recent years to reconcile the families involved in the deaths of Jean-Marie-Tjibaou, Yéwéné Yéwéné and Djubéli Wéa in Ouvéa in 1989. This is how Georges Mandaoué, a senator from Houaïlou, explained the Senate's intervention in the attempt to resolve the Wakaya conflict:

> Because ultimately, from a conflict over legitimacy, we've ended up with an excess of violence, and today they're managing a violent situation, but they're no longer trying to resolve the problem of legitimacy; so I burn your house, tomorrow I burn yours, we meet in the village I shoot at you, and tomorrow I shoot at you ... So we tried to start all over again. (Georges Mandaoué, extract from interview, July 2008)

In July 2008 a meeting of around 80 people (including 10 from each of the L and R groups, representatives of the Néawa district council, of the *ajië-arhö* customary area, the New Caledonia Customary Senate, Houaïlou municipal council, the North Province, the gendarmerie and the land reform organisation) was held in Houaïlou. The aim of this was to set up working groups to look at the regrouping of Wakaya lands, the possible installation of mediating clans who could serve as a buffer between the two clans, the conditions for social and economic development that could benefit the Kanak villagers, and at the role, authority and powers of constraint of chiefdoms and councils of elders in this tribe. The process is currently under way, and it is too early to know whether it will achieve its aims: 'The first thing is to give back meaning to their communal life up there ... so people start to live again and their minds are more occupied with projects than with conflicts' (Georges Mandaoué, extract from interview, July 2008). This resulted, in March 2010, in the parties involved signing a 'charter of commitment to improving the security and development of the Ouakaya valley' at Houaïlou town hall.

Over and above the hoped-for reconciliation, the issue is clear: at this local level, in the management of a conflict and appraisal of the right to exercise physical violence, what is at stake is the construction of a postcolonial state, and of the spaces of autonomy it will allow to different categories of actors, in the context of the decolonisation initiated by the Nouméa Accord.

We can't live like that, each clan individually, and not be attached to an authority, we call that anarchy. That's not what we want ... That's why it's important to restore the customary authorities and if we had put the customary authorities in place, we could have made up for the lack of parental authority over these more and more chaotic young people ... Chiefdoms, councils of elders with a solid structure of constraints, we wouldn't be where we are now. (Georges Mandaoué, extract from interview, July 2008)

2002–12: The customary land register and collection of cultural heritage

Over and above the Wakaya conflict, the customary council of the *ajië-arhö* area is doing much work to re-establish a greater role for 'custom' in the organisation of municipal affairs. As has been noted, and in line with what is observed in other regions of Oceania, this is a highly ambiguous term.[30] By 'custom', my interlocutors understand the full range of norms and practices that governed local social life before the arrival of the Europeans – or rather, what they believe today to have played this role in earlier times. Doubly metonymic, as we saw at the beginning of this chapter, the word 'custom' also designates ceremonies of exchange (on the occasion of marriage or mourning, for example), which constitute one of the key moments in customary life, and the treasures exchanged during these ceremonies. Since 2002, the *ajië-arhö* customary council has been undertaking a toponymic and genealogical collection, sometimes under the encompassing term of 'land register', in view of the links between toponymy, family history and land rights.[31] This activity is rooted in the belief of a number of actors that restoring greater power to the 'customaries' would bring an end to most conflict situations, thereby justifying the work. There is, however, no consensus around either the assumptions behind this position or the demands that are being made:

– Hermesse Pwâdi: The customary council, they want us to put everything back again, bring back the chiefs, the high chiefs, the tribal chiefs. We went on a tour with a committee to inform people, they're not interested any more. We dropped it.

---

30 See Keesing 1982.
31 See Naepels 1998.

6. THE CONSTRUCTION AND FICTION OF CONSENSUS

– Marcel Mèèjâ: Yes it does, it interests a few people but there are gaps … It's all very well all that, but setting up this and that, you have to put it into practice, they have to be pretty solid rules. Well, I think that in these customary things, it just pisses everybody off, they're consultative. They ask your opinion, OK, well, we don't like your opinion, we're rejecting it, we're not taking your opinion into account, so what's the point? You're consultative, you're an observer, what you want isn't taken into account. (Extract from a group interview with the Lèwèö council of elders, June 2006)

The term 'land register', used particularly during the years immediately following the signature of the Nouméa Accord,[32] is admittedly still used. Nevertheless, the idea that creating a cartography of land rights could be a simple and rapid solution to the various existing conflicts on the one hand, and that the area customary council could constitute a suitable site for building a consensual customary truth on the other, no longer seems to carry much weight today:

In any case, there will always be conflicts, maybe not us, but I think the generations that come after, because each person will think: 'I've heard stories, I know my pine stump isn't here, my coconut palm isn't there.' And then that'll make even more trouble for the customary register. In one way it's good, but it makes you grind your teeth, because I don't know, Kanak mentality, at the time of the ancestors, the ancestors buried all that so that it didn't go any further, so there was harmony, social cohesion, so there wasn't any more dispute or war.

– Are the difficulties coming up again?

Yes, that's it, they're digging up the war axe, that's what's happening. Well, so much the better as long as each person takes responsibility. (Charles Pûkiu, extract from interview, July 2006)

Since 2004 the customary council of the *ajië-arhö* area, in partnership with the Cultural, Heritage and Research Development department (DCPR) of the ADCK (Agence pour le développement de la culture kanak, Kanak Cultural Development Agency), has been collecting oral heritage in an operation that has largely replaced the initial project of creating a customary land register. This program of collection of Kanak oral heritage was launched by the ADCK in 2002,[33] starting in the Canala region. Since 2004, a network of freelance collectors – trained, contracted

---
32 See ADRAF 2002, Le Meur 2003.
33 Following other similar projects carried out by the Cultural Office during the 1980s.

and paid jointly by the ADCK and the customary councils – has been built up. The collectors meet together once or twice a year to share their experiences and discuss problems raised by collection (as relates to both archiving and protection or transmission of the data gathered). The meeting of the collectors itself forms part of the process initiated by the ADCK, and aims to increase the interactions between those who collect, to reinforce their faith in the importance of what they are doing, and to contribute to motivating everybody when the collectors return to their regions of origin. The most important aspect is thus perhaps not so much the resulting collection as the process of bringing collectors and the institution into a relationship with local scholars and knowledge valued in and of themselves. I was present at the collectors' meetings that took place over four days in Houaïlou, in the Gôdè tribe, in July 2008. The director of the ADCK, Emmanuel Kasarhéou, himself from Houaïlou, invited me to participate, following our earlier conversations about the collection process at the launch of the program in 2002,[34] and in 2006 (with the entire DCPR team). My role was specifically to contribute to clarifying what is at stake in the collection, and to improving the means used in relation to the stated aims. I could not fail to be impressed by the number of people and the energy I witnessed at this meeting, which took place in the presence of collectors from the five customary areas of Grande Terre and Ouvéa, the DCPR's permanent team, members of the tribe (notably the Gôdè council of elders), and several members of the customary council of the *ajië-arhö* area originating from other tribes.

Thanks to the collection of Kanak oral heritage, the data collected has been archived in the mediathèque at the Tjibaou Cultural Centre (on minidisk), and transcriptions are made in vernacular languages and published in an annual report on activities sent to each customary council that has signed agreements with the ADCK. Two types of document are contained in these reports: texts describing practical skills related to weaving, horticulture, medicine, dance, fishing and hunting, the organisation of ceremonies and the vocabulary of kinship; and texts made up of knowledge about society and history: clan histories, genealogical speeches and explanations of place names.

---

34 See Naepels 2003.

What are the effects of this process of 'collection'? Firstly, it changes the status of 'intangible heritage': however rigorous the collectors and however faithful the transcriptions, to collect is to alter. The oral tradition is adapted to context: narratives are drawn on in certain circumstances (in ceremonies, local conflicts, land claims for example). Historical and social knowledge is still transmitted in this way in Houaïlou, as a living knowledge to the extent that it is linked to current practices and issues, such as land rights or the place of each family in local social relations. The first effect of collecting is materialisation, the transformation of what is held in one or more individual memories into a material object – cassettes, minidisks, digital files and video recordings – and then, via a process of transcription, the writing down of these oral accounts. Collection thus establishes a mode of existence for the narrative that is disconnected from the speaker and from the context, in other words first and foremost without the rhetoric linked to the people present and the social situation. This is the process of all museography.[35]

Secondly, the notion of 'heritage' poses the question of the owner: through collection, individual, lineage or clan knowledge becomes a knowledge deposited with the ADCK and the area customary councils, where it is archived. This is the second transformation, from a knowledge located in a clan to a knowledge located in the institutions of culture or Kanak custom.

Finally, for the collectors themselves, the very process of collecting reveals the diversity within each area as a treasure, not just a web of contradictions: each one can observe that there are different versions of the histories of clans and lands, different versions of speeches, different ways of organising ceremonies, different explanations of proper names. The very process of collecting involves bracketing, at least temporarily, the (scientific and practical) question of truth. Otherwise collection could be accused of becoming a weapon in the fight to promote this or that version. This was precisely why a collector from Wakaya eventually had to stop working, for fear that the historical and clan accounts he was attempting to collect might aggravate the conflict situation within his tribe.[36]

---

35 I described the first steps in this process in Houaïlou in Chapter 2.
36 Described earlier in this chapter.

There is without doubt a tension between the pragmatic and immediate aims of the Customary Senate and some area councils, and the ADCK's heritage agenda. One of the points of friction is the level of confidentiality instituted, with varying periods of consultation negotiated with speakers, described here by one of my 'customary' interviewees:

> For us, collecting the information is so it can be used now, it's not to make a thing you'll consult in 20 years, that's not much use to us. For us society is being constructed now, so we need the data now, you see. People didn't understand the point of collecting data that can be used to identify people and legitimacies through creation of the customary land register, so [the ADCK collectors] do their work which is linked to their own concerns, but it's not linked to our concerns. Well, in short, the kid who in 20 years or 30 years is going to reread the thing, won't that revive conflicts? … Inevitably in the history of oral societies, the more you have information that goes back in time, the more you say it's the truth. But which truth? Is it really the truth? (Extract from interview, July 2008)

This comment raises the question of the goals of the customary councils and the ADCK, as actors involved in the process of collection. Beyond a discourse that highlights safeguarding, restitution, promotion and dissemination in a general way, there is the reality of conservation activities (and hence of material safeguarding) at the Tjibaou Cultural Centre. Nevertheless, the local political stakes need to be clarified. What is the status of the collection's annual reports? How can their dissemination be ensured? And what practical implications are there for local social relations on the ground? It sometimes appears that there is an abstract confidence in the practical efficacy of safeguarding the 'heritage' of the 'elders' that partakes of the scholastic illusion. It should be pointed out, however, that those involved in the collection are themselves often aware of this problem:

> The collection of Kanak oral heritage and traditional knowledge is first and foremost a collective matter. Its preservation depends in large part on this. It concerns both the ancestors' generations and the generations to come. It concerns both this multifaceted past and this future to be constructed … Writing the history of the Kanak land is no simple matter. It is a perilous and extremely complex exercise. To work on one's own history is to work in a minefield, it is to work at one's own risk and peril, it is to dig up things that have been buried, it is to bring up a painful past, it is to bring up things that are not pretty to see. (Justin Monawa, vice-chairman of the *ajië-arhö* customary council (*Collecte du patrimoine immatériel de l'aire ajië-arhö* 2005, p. 3))

Thus the general views held in New Caledonia about the articulation of politics and custom cover a wide variety of forms of mobilisation that seek, in singular social contexts, to imagine new relations that take into account the departure from reserves that, for many, accompanies land reform and the relative decline in agriculture. I have tried to show how, in Houaïlou, a great variety of collectives has formed for this purpose, drawing on diverse references: party political structures, the neocustomary institutions created under the Nouméa Accord, cultural institutions and agnatic groups. Such mobilisations sometimes fail (the FCCI is virtually non-existent in Houaïlou today); they are always subject to criticism focused on the individual interests of the people active in them, and they are often met by the scepticism of observers who note the persistence of some local conflicts. Nevertheless, they testify to the stubborn desire to create spaces of autonomy in place of an oppressive colonial governmentality – a desire that is also paradoxically revealed by those who seek the paths of emancipation elsewhere, in the new churches or in migration to Nouméa.[37]

* * *

In this chapter, I have focused primarily on the various ways of constructing collectives, and forms of political mobilisation, in the context of decolonisation initiated by the Nouméa Accord. The ceremonial, political, clan, institutional and cultural engagement of the different inhabitants of Houaïlou here emerge as actors' strategies for reorganising the place of each individual in the village space, following the breakdown of the colonial order (whose forms of exploitation rested essentially on the combination of land reserves, subsistence economy, the administrative chiefdom, and the management of native affairs by the gendarmerie). While in the 1950s and the period of the 'events' of the 1980s (see chapters 4 and 5) these different sites of mobilisation sometimes, at least to begin with, converged fairly broadly, in Houaïlou today they appear much more disconnected, and even competing, in the plans for collective life put forward by one and the other. This competition is manifested particularly in the high level of conflict that accompanies the invention of postcolonial social relations in the village. The awareness of the risk of witchcraft, in both ceremonial action and political action; the direct violence in the conflict between

---

37   See Dussy 2012; Hamelin 2000; Naepels 1999 and 2000b.

agnatic groups in Wakaya; and the conflictual aspect of historical and clan narratives in the collection of oral heritage instigated by neocustomary and cultural institutions, demonstrate that the internal link between violence and power persists today in Houaïlou.

Conclusion

> [All] political activity is a conflict aimed at deciding what is speech or mere growl; in others words, aimed at retracing the perceptible boundaries by means of which political capacity is demonstrated ... This distribution and this redistribution of space and time, place and identity, speech and noise, the visible and the invisible, form what I call the distribution of the perceptible. Political activity reconfigures the distribution of the perceptible. It introduces new objects and subjects onto the common stage. It makes visible what was invisible, it makes audible as speaking beings those who were previously heard only as noisy animals.
> Jacques Rancière, *The Politics of Literature*, 2011, p. 4

I should like to conclude by returning to the interweaving of the threads I have tied and untied in this book. In this project, Houaïlou has served as an entry point for bringing together various levels of historical and geographical analysis, for grasping the way local social relations are inserted into economy-worlds, imperial projects, state structures, and the diverse points of view of individual and collective actors. It is by recounting the little histories that arise there, weaving them together step by step, that multiple temporalities and overlapping contexts can be articulated, and that I have been able to arrive at a more complex perspective on the use of violence in various historical political mobilisations. Thus, my decision to speak of banal or marginal events, for which there are few documentary sources and which are always neutralised by the epic macrohistorical accounts of colonisation and decolonisation, has led me to individualise violence to a certain extent, taking into account the imbalance between the actors involved, the diversity of their viewpoints and their own forms of subjectivation. My aim has been to describe the connection between violence and politics by means of contextualisation of documents and the heterogeneity of sources, creating a local history.

In tracing thus the history of the Houaïlou region, on the basis of forms of action taken by its inhabitants, I have attempted to combine a number of analytical approaches. On the one hand, I wanted to examine the conventions of the use of physical violence in war, through reference to what information exists regarding a number of cases: the late 18th-century war in Néajië, which involved on one side a complex chiefdom, possibly of Polynesian origin, and on the other families seeking to maintain their autonomy in the face of a hegemonic construction; the repressive operations of 1856, 1863 and 1867 (the Koro war), of 1868 and 1878, which opened up social relations on the regional level between some inhabitants of Houaïlou and the political spaces of the neighbouring regions of Canala, Ponérihouen, Bourail and Poya; the First World War, the repression of the 1917 rebellion, the Second World War; the 'events' of the 1980s; and, finally, present-day village conflicts in Wakaya. In this process, I have tried to focus particularly on practices and their history, sometimes in relation to the circulation of colonial models, sometimes not: thus I have looked at anthropophagy, the destruction of the enemy's means of production, the abduction of women and children, the cutting-off of heads and ears, mobile columns, ambushes, gunfights, brawls and insults, but also forms of psychic preparation and propitiation involving the use of stones or plants and, where it is involved, consumption of alcohol and cannabis by actors involved in warrior violence.

This interest points the way to a second thread of analysis, which I have tried to address at regular intervals, the subjectivation of conflicts. This focus covers everything that relates to the attribution of misfortune and adversity to a contrary and conflictual intentionality: hence the interpretation of the 1912 plague and of leprosy, the witch-hunt of 1955, the political activists' call on a healer in 1999 and, more generally, the overdetermination of current village conflicts (around land, family names or the chiefdom) by the invocation of witchcraft as the source of misfortune. Secondly, I consider all that brings into play techniques of the self – such as the ecstasy required to obtain war stones that support the appeal to ancestral powers – and affects – anger, tension, fear. In my view, moments of violence but also, where appropriate, moments when action is forgone, can be described in this register.

I have focused primarily on the most socialised, collective forms of resort to physical violence. This has led me to examine the modalities and temporality of the formation of collectives, and to address group mobilisations: the assembling of warriors in each of the repressive operations, but also political, economic, association-based and customary mobilisations following the end of the *indigénat* in the 1950s, those that paved the way for the 'events' of the 1980s and, finally, contemporary attempts to invent new forms of communal life in spaces of rural collective habitation, through the investment of the self in political parties (I have used the example of the FCCI (Fédération des comités de coordination indépendantistes (Federation of Pro-Independence Co-operating Committees)), but it applies equally to other groups) and in customary institutions (the Senate or the area council) or cultural activities (led, for example, by the ADCK (Agence pour le développement de la culture kanak, Kanak Cultural Development Agency)). The various forms of collective action I encountered are heterogeneous: sometimes they are based on constructions that draw on the inventiveness and determination of the actors involved, a certain degree of spontaneity, whereas in other cases they appeal to age-old and incorporated, sometimes even institutionalised, ways of structuring the social experience. Thus I have focused particularly on the link between the institution of the chiefdom, in its various, temporally shifting forms, and the ability to gather others around one for specific practical purposes; I have also investigated the existence and meaning of the so-called councils of elders as a way of structuring collective action. Clearly, these considerations cannot be conceived without taking into account the temporality of the various periods of colonial and postcolonial governance (the establishment of the colony's legal framework, the tightening of control under governor Feillet, the end of the *indigénat*, the 'events', the Matignon-Oudinot agreements and the Nouméa Accord), and the interaction between the local issues of rural communal life and their place in broader networks and territories, through the flows of goods and people through them.

Within these processes, the Kanaks of Houaïlou have continued to struggle for their spaces, their times, their places, their identities, and to make their voices heard on shared stages, well before their 'entry into the citadel' (Guiart 1966) following the Second World War, or their 'eruption' (Coulon 1985) at the time of the 'events' of the 1980s. Thus, if I am to do justice to my Kanak interlocutors, I cannot substitute my voice for theirs; they have no need of it. What remains is to understand what kind of historical and anthropological writing then emerges. Jean-Frédéric Schaub recently highlighted an important aspect of this question: 'We have to try to understand the colonial moment of these [colonised] societies as if it were not only external, but also internal' (Schaub 2008, p. 438). This is what I have tried to do, for example, in linking a fragmentary account from the oral tradition, collected orally from Narcisse Kaviyöibanu, with the repressive operation of 1856, or in connecting a range of accounts of the Koro war with the repressive operation of 1867. More broadly, I have engaged throughout the text in historicisation (through the successive periods of colonisation) of the concepts of 'chiefdom' and 'council of elders'. Doing this obviously means stepping beyond the colonial division of knowledges between history and anthropology,[1] which in itself is a denial of the historicity of colonised societies and the shared time that binds us to them.[2]

I have focused on the description of conflicts rather than how they might have been resolved. The moments of peace (sometimes armed), the periods of demobilisation, the acts of contracting more peaceful social relations evoked in the study of ceremonies and the speeches made there have concerned me less than the accumulation of disagreements and the reactivation of past conflicts in contemporary disputes: this reveals starkly that moments of consensus form points of temporary equilibrium in shifting relations of power. Making a history that is not the discourse of power, therefore, means not confining my analysis to the most public forms of action and the most visible actors. The weight of unequal gender and age relations in these forms of mobilisation makes the 'family' a key site for understanding conflict and violence, particularly in terms of the acquisition of repertoires of action, of modes of socialisation in a continuum of domestic violence (by parents against children, older brothers against their younger siblings, men against women), and of construction of habitus in which physical violence, sexual violence and intimidation are not experienced as illegitimate.

My thematic focus on conflict ultimately poses the question of what can be seen of social relations in the sources available, of the ways in which the real is projected onto the documentary spaces (written or interactional) to which empirical ethnographic and historiographic research can give access. Peaceful mornings may not be those that leave the strongest traces in histories and memories.[3] My book can thus also be read as a reflection on a number of documents central to my analysis, around which succeeding chapters are organised: a short extract from

---

1   Wallerstein 1991, 1996 and 1999; Naepels 2010a.
2   Fabian 2002, Thomas 1989a.
3   I sought to develop this point in Naepels 2011.

an interview describing a war on the Houaïlou coast, a well-known text from New Caledonian anthropology entitled 'Jopaipi', the notebook kept by high chief Mèèjâ Néjâ, the Indigenous Affairs Department's *Register of Chiefs*, the 'list of those accused of witchcraft' given to Jean Guiart in late 1955, and some extracts from interviews that I have conducted in the course of my field research since 1991. In this process I have drawn on a multitude of other documents, always seeking to understand as far as possible the social aspects of the production of these materials. It is in their ingrained form that I have attempted never to stop envisioning the richness and complexity of the links that make up the torn fabric of social life, in Houaïlou as elsewhere.

References

'Accord sur la Nouvelle-Calédonie signé à Nouméa le 5 mai 1998' 1998. *Journal officiel*, no. 121, 27 mai, pp. 8039–44

ADRAF 2002. *Foncier et développement en Nouvelle-Calédonie*, proceedings of seminar on 10–12 October 2001, Nouméa, Gouvernement de Nouvelle-Calédonie

—— 2006. 'Projet OGAF de Houaïlou (Nouvelle-Calédonie)', Nouméa

'Affaire de l'*Aurora*': Auditions de la commission d'enquête (Hearings of the Committee of Inquiry). Aix-en-Provence, Centre des Archives d'Outre-Mer (CAOM), SGNC 63

'Affaire des navires *Aurora* et *Lala*': Archives du ministère des Affaires étrangères, série Mémoires & Documents, sous-série Océanie (Archives of the Ministry of Foreign Affairs, Series Memoirs & Documents, Sub-series Oceania), vol. 4

Ageron, Charles Robert 1991 [1979], *Modern Algeria: A History from 1830 to the Present.* London: C. Hurst & Co

Amouroux, Charles and Place, Henri 1881. *L'administration et les maristes en Nouvelle-Calédonie. Insurrection des Kanaks en 1878–1879.* Paris: Périnet

Anonymous 1988 [1853–62], 'Éphémérides de la Nouvelle-Calédonie', in Bernard Brou, Hélène Colombani and Georges Coquilhat (eds), *Six textes anciens sur la Nouvelle-Calédonie.* Nouméa: Publications de la Société d'études historiques de Nouvelle-Calédonie, pp. 277–327

Anscombe, G.E.M. 2002 [1957], *Intention.* Cambridge, MA/London: Harvard University Press

Appadurai, Arjun 1996. *Modernity at Large: Cultural Consequences of Globalization*. Minneapolis: University of Minnesota Press

Aramiou, Sylvain and Euritéin, Jean 2002. *Pèci i Bwêêyöuu Ërijiyi: Cahiers de Boesou Eurijisi, Première série (1915–1920)*. Houaïlou: Fédération de l'enseignement libre protestant

—— 2003. *Pèci i Bwêêyöuu Ërijiyi: Cahiers de Boesoou Eurijisi, Seconde série (1918–1921)*. Houaïlou: Fédération de l'enseignement libre protestant

Aramiou, Sylvain, Euritéin, Jean and Kavivioro, Georges 2001. *Dictionnaire a'jië-français*. Houaïlou: Fédération de l'enseignement libre protestant

Archambault, Marius 1901. 'Les mégalithes néo-calédoniens', *L'anthropologie*, no. 12, pp. 257–68

—— 1902. 'Nouvelles recherches sur les mégalithes néo-calédoniens', *L'anthropologie*, no. 13, pp. 689–712

—— 1909. 'Traces d'une ancienne civilisation en Nouvelle-Calédonie', *La dépêche coloniale illustrée*, 9ᵉ année, no. 11, pp. 143–52

Arens, William 1979. *The Man-Eating Myth: Anthropology and Anthropophagy*. New York: Oxford University Press

—— 2006. 'Review of Obeyesekere, Gananath: *Cannibal Talk*', *The Journal of the Polynesian Society*, vol. 115, no. 3, pp. 295–98

'Assemblée générale de l'AICLF' 1960. Ba, Houaïlou, 10–12 September. Nouméa, Archives de la Nouvelle-Calédonie, 97W18

Astre, Gaston 1947. *La vie de Benjamin Balansa, botaniste explorateur*. Muséum d'histoire naturelle de Toulouse

Augé, Marc 1974. 'Les croyances à la sorcellerie', in Marc Augé (ed.), *La construction du monde: Religion, représentations, idéologie*. Paris: Maspéro (coll. 'Dossiers africains'), pp. 52–74

Backouche, Isabelle and Naepels, Michel 2009. 'Faire la preuve', *Genèses*, no. 74, pp. 2–4

Balansa, Benjamin 1869. 'Lettre sur ses explorations dans la Nouvelle-Calédonie', *Bulletin de la Société botanique de France*, no. 16, p. 323

―― 1872–73. 'Géographie botanique de la Nouvelle-Calédonie et ses dépendances', *Bulletin de la Société d'histoire naturelle de Toulouse*, no. 7, pp. 327–32

―― 1873. 'Nouvelle-Calédonie', *Bulletin de la Société de géographie de Paris*, 6e série, no. 5, pp. 113–32 and pp. 521–34

Balibar, Étienne 2002. *Politics and the Other Scene*, trans. by Christine Jones, James Swenson and Chris Turner. London/New York: Verso

Barbançon, Louis-José 2008. *Il y a vingt-cinq ans: Le gouvernement Tjibaou. 18 juin 1982 – 18 novembre 1984*, text of a lecture given on 21 August 2008. Nouméa, Agence de développement de la culture kanak

Baré, J. 1939. 'Le service de la lutte contre la lèpre en Nouvelle-Calédonie', *Annales de médecine et de pharmacie coloniales*, no. 37, pp. 165–200

Bastide, Roger 1972. *Le rêve, la transe, la folie*. Paris: Flammarion

Baudoux, Georges 1928. *Légendes canaques*. Paris: Rieder

―― 1949. 'Le trou symbolique', in *Légendes canaques*, vol. 2, *Ils avaient vu des hommes blancs*. Paris: Nouvelles Éditions Latines, pp. 47–64

Bazin, Jean 1996. 'Interpréter ou décrire: Notes critiques sur la connaissance anthropologique', in Jacques Revel and Nathan Wachtel (eds), *Une école pour les sciences sociales: De la VIe Section à l'École des hautes études en sciences sociales*. Paris: Éditions du Cerf/Éditions de l'EHESS, pp. 401–20

―― 2000a. 'Science des mœurs et description de l'action', *Le genre humain*, no. 35, *Actualités du contemporain*, pp. 33–58

―― 2000b. 'L'anthropologie en question: altérité ou différence?', in Y. Michaud (ed.), *Qu'est-ce que la société?* Paris: Odile Jacob, pp. 78–88

―― 2003. 'Questions of Meaning', *Anthropological Theory*, vol. 3, no. 4, pp. 416–34

Bensa, Alban 1992. 'Terre kanak: enjeu politique d'hier et d'aujourd'hui. Esquisse d'un modèle comparative', *Études rurales*, nos 127–28, pp. 107–31

―― 1995. *Chroniques kanak: L'ethnologie en marche*. Paris: Peuples autochtones et développement/Survival International

—— 2000. 'Le chef kanak: Les modèles et l'histoire', in Alban Bensa and Isabelle Leblic (eds), *En pays kanak: Ethnologie, linguistique, archéologie, histoire de la Nouvelle-Calédonie*. Paris: Éditions de la Maison des Sciences de l'Homme (MSH), pp. 9–48. doi.org/10.4000/books.editionsmsh.2771

—— 2006. 'Compter les dons: Échanges non marchands et pratiques comptables en Nouvelle-Calédonie kanak contemporaine', in Natacha Coquery, François Menant and Florence Weber (eds), *Écrire, compter, mesurer: Vers une histoire des rationalités pratiques*. Paris: Éditions Rue d'Ulm, pp. 79–112

Bensa, Alban and Goromido, Antoine 1996. 'L'auto-sacrifice du chef dans les sociétés kanak d'autrefois', in Maurice Godelier and Jacques Hassoun (eds), *Meurtre du père, sacrifice de la sexualité: Approches anthropologiques et psychanalytiques*. Paris/Strasbourg: Arcanes, pp. 103–20

—— 1997. 'The Political Order and Corporal Coercion in Kanak Societies of the Past (New Caledonia)', *Oceania*, vol. 68, no. 2, pp. 84–106

—— 1998. 'Contraintes par corps: Ordre politique et violence dans les sociétés kanak d'autrefois', in Maurice Godelier and Michel Panoff (eds), *Le corps humain: Supplicié, possédé, cannibalisé*. Paris: Éditions des archives contemporaines, pp. 169–97

Bensa, Alban and Rivierre, Jean-Claude 1988. 'De l'Histoire des mythes: Narrations et polémiques autour du rocher Até (Nouvelle-Calédonie)', *L'Homme*, vol. 28, nos 106–07, pp. 263–95

Beresford, William E. 1853–54. 'Log Book of the Ship *Louisa*'. Sydney: Mitchell Library A 2596, CY Reel 677

Bergeret, Étienne 1909. 'Un fétiche', *Journal des missions évangéliques*, 4e série, 10e année, mai, 84e année, pp. 409–12

—— 1912. 'Les fétiches du vieux Canaque: Récit retrouvé parmi des notes prises autrefois en Calédonie', *Journal des missions évangéliques*, pp. 134–36

Berman, Judith 1996. '"The culture as it appears to the Indian Himself": Boas, George Hunt and the Methods of Ethnography', in George W. Stocking Jr (ed.), *Volksgeist as Method and Ethic: Essays on Boasian Ethnography and the German Anthropological Tradition*. Madison: University of Wisconsin Press, pp. 215–56

Bernard, Augustin 1894. *L'archipel de la Nouvelle-Calédonie*. Paris: Hachette

Bernier, 1917a. 'Rapport au sujet des opérations effectuées par la colonne des auxiliaires partie avec M.M. Bernier et Martin-Garnand de Poindimié le 14 juillet 1917'. Report to the governor dated 29 July 1917. Nouméa: Archives de la Nouvelle-Calédonie, 1W1

—— 1917b. 'Suite du rapport sur les opérations effectuées par la colonne des auxiliaires ayant quitté Poindimié le 14 juillet avec M.M. Martin et Bernier'. Nouméa: Archives de la Nouvelle-Calédonie, 1W1

Béros and Bocquillon, Drs 1913. 'Épidémie de peste de Nérin et de Gondé (Nouvelle-Calédonie, 1912–1913)', *Annales d'hygiène et de médecine coloniales*, no. 16, pp. 927–31

Bierman, Guy 1992. 'Le recrutement extraordinaire en Nouvelle-Calédonie pendant la grande révolte canaque de 1878'. *Revue française d'histoire d'outre-mer*, no. 297, pp. 517–31. doi.org/10.3406/outre.1992.3051

Blainey, Geoffrey 1963. *The Rush that Never Ended: A History of Australian Mining*. Melbourne University Press

Bougarel 1860. 'Armes des néo-calédoniens', *Revue algérienne et coloniale*, no. 2, pp. 283–86

Boulay, Roger 1986–87. 'La collection Piroutet', *Antiquités nationales*, nos 18–19, pp. 249–55

—— 1990. 'Objets kanak dans les collections européennes', in Roger Boulay (ed.), *De jade et de nacre: Patrimoine artistique kanak* [exhibition]. Paris: Réunion des musées nationaux, pp. 208–43

—— 2000. *Kannibals et vahinés. Imagerie des mers du Sud*. La Tour-d'Aigues: Éditions de l'Aube

—— (ed.) 1990. *De jade et de nacre: Patrimoine artistique kanak* (exhibition). Paris: Réunion des musées nationaux

Bouquet de la Grye, Anatole 1891. *Une exploration en Nouvelle-Calédonie.* Paris: Firmin-Didot

Bourdieu, Pierre 1991. 'Rites of Institution', in *Language and Symbolic Power*, trans. by Gino Raymond and Matthew Adamson. Cambridge: Polity, pp. 117–26

Bourgois, Philippe 2001. 'The Power of Violence in War and Peace: Post-Cold War Lessons from El Salvador', *Ethnography*, vol. 2, no. 1, pp. 5–34. doi.org/10.1177/14661380122230803

—— 2002. *In Search of Respect: Selling Crack in El Barrio.* New York: Cambridge University Press

Bourguignon, Erika 1972. 'Dreams and Altered States of Consciousness in Anthropological Research', in Francis L.K. Hsu (ed.), *Psychological Anthropology*, Cambridge: Schenkman, pp. 403–34

—— 1973. 'Introduction: A Framework for the Comparative Study of Altered States of Consciousness', in Erika Bourguignon (ed.), *Religion, Altered States of Consciousness, and Social Change.* Colombus: Ohio State University Press, pp. 3–38

Bozon-Verduraz, Eugène 1978a [1917]. 'Télégramme du 20 juin au Gouverneur', in *Centenaire Maurice Leenhardt (1878–1954)*, Annexe II, 'Les auxiliaires'. Nouméa: Publications de la Société d'études historiques de la Nouvelle-Calédonie, p. 71

—— 1978b [1917]. 'Télégramme du 28 juin au Gouverneur', in *Centenaire Maurice Leenhardt (1878-1954)*, Annexe II, 'Les auxiliaires'. Nouméa: Publications de la Société d'études historiques de la Nouvelle-Calédonie, p. 77

Bozon-Verduraz, Eugène and Satorek, administrator 1978 [1917]. 'Télégramme du 28 juin au Gouverneur', in *Centenaire Maurice Leenhardt (1878–1954)*, Annexe II, *'Les auxiliaires'*. Nouméa: Publications de la Société d'études historiques de la Nouvelle-Calédonie, p. 76

'Bref rapport sur les origines et le développement de la crise qui ont amené le comité à se séparer d'un de ses missionnaires en Nouvelle-Calédonie: M. Raymond Charlemagne' 1959. Paris: Société des missions, stencil-printed report. Paris: Archives du DEFAP

Brou, Bernard 1988. 'Notes', in Bernard Brou, Hélène Colombani and Georges Coquilhat (eds), *Six textes anciens sur la Nouvelle-Calédonie*. Nouméa: Publications de la Société d'études historiques de Nouvelle-Calédonie

Bullard, Alice 1998. 'The Affective Subject and French Colonial Policy in New Caledonia', *History and Anthropology*, vol. 10, no. 4, pp. 375–405. doi.org/10.1080/02757206.1998.9960904

—— 2000. *Exile to Paradise: Savagery and Civilization in Paris and the South Pacific, 1790–1900*. Stanford University Press

Bulletin du commerce 1917. 23 June

—— 1917. 'L'insurrection canaque dans la région du Nord (Côtes ouest et est)', 30 June

Cacot, Jean 1985. 'Notes sur Houaïlou', *Bulletin de la Société d'études historiques de Nouvelle-Calédonie*, no. 64, pp. 39–43

Chappell, David 2003. 'The Kanak Awakening of 1969–76: Radicalizing Anti-colonialism in New Caledonia'. *Journal de la Société des océanistes*, no. 117, pp. 187–202. doi.org/10.4000/jso.1268

Charlemagne, Raymond 1948a. 'Un choix redoutable: le futur statut indigène calédonien'. Radio Nouméa, *Causerie protestante*, Sunday 11 April. Nouméa: Archives de l'Archevêché 146.3

—— 1948b. 'Parole du missionnaire au communiste indigènes [sic]', *Le Messager. Journal de l'Association des indigènes calédoniens et loyaltiens français*, no. 2, June

—— 1952. Lettre à Schloesing, Dö Nèvâ, Houaïlou, 18 May. Paris: Archives du DEFAP

—— 1956. 'Un seul coup de fusil …', *Journal des missions évangéliques*, no. 10, pp. 283–84

—— 1961. Lettre à Monsieur le Chef du Service de l'Instruction Publique. Nédiva, Houaïlou, 27 July

Chevalier, Auguste 1942. 'L'œuvre d'un grand botaniste colonial méconnu: Benjamin Balansa', *Revue de botanique appliquée et d'agriculture tropicale*, vol. 22, nos 249–50, pp. 241–51

Claverie, Élisabeth, Jamin, Jean and Lenclud, Gérard 1984. 'Une ethnographie de la violence est-elle possible?', *Études rurales*, nos 95–96, pp. 9–21

Clifford, James 1982. *Person and Myth: Maurice Leenhardt in the Melanesian World*. Berkeley/London: University of California Press

—— 1983. 'On Ethnographic Authority', *Representations*, vol. 2, Spring, pp. 118–46

—— 1997. 'Fort Ross Meditation', in *Routes: Travel and Translation in the Late Twentieth Century*. Cambridge, MA: Harvard University Press, pp. 299–344

Cole, Douglas 1995 [1985]. *Captured Heritage: The Scramble for Northwest Coast Artifacts*. Vancouver: University of British Columbia Press

Collecte du patrimoine immatériel de l'aire ajië-arhö, Report 2005, Nouméa, Agence pour le Développement de la Culture Kanak

Collins, Randall 2008. *Violence: A Micro-Sociological Theory*. Princeton University Press. doi.org/10.1515/9781400831753

Colombani, Jean-Marie 1985. *L'utopie calédonienne*. Paris: Denoël

Compton, Robert 1917. 'New Caledonia and the Isle of Pines', *Geographical Journal*, vol. 49, no. 2, pp. 81–106. doi.org/10.2307/1779337

Conseil privé [Privy Council] 1876. 'Au sujet du cantonnement des indigenes', Session of 6 January. Aix-en-Provence: CAOM, SGNC 98

—— 1876. Sessions of 4 and 6 March. Aix-en-Provence: CAOM, SGNC 98

—— 1899. Session of 28 December, '28e cas d'internement administrative'. Aix-en-Provence: CAOM, SGNC 34

Cornet, Claude 2000. *La grande révolte (1878): Comptes-rendus officiels, extraits de presse, lettres et documents inédits*. Nouméa: Éditions de la Boudeuse

Correspondance et pièces diverses 1946. 'Revendications de l'Union des Indigènes Calédoniens Amis de la Liberté dans l'Ordre'. Nouméa: Archives de l'Archevêché 146.1

Correspondance et pièces diverses 1949–1953. 'Sur les élections de 1951'. Nouméa: Archives de l'Archevêché 146.4

Coulon, Marc 1985. *L'irruption kanak: De Calédonie à Kanaky*. Paris: Éditions sociales

Dagneau, Gilles 2008. *Le gendarme Citron*. AAA-ADCK-RFO, 51

Dauphiné, Joël 1987. *Chronologie foncière et agricole de la Nouvelle-Calédonie (1853–1903)*. Paris: L'Harmattan

—— 1989. *Les spoliations foncières en Nouvelle-Calédonie (1853–1913)*. Paris: L'Harmattan

—— 1990a. *Canala et la France (1854–1863)*. Nouméa: Centre territorial de recherche et de documentation pédagogiques

—— 1990b. *Houaïlou: L'implantation du christianisme (1894–1902)*. Nouméa: Centre territorial de recherche et de documentation pédagogiques

—— 1995. *Les débuts d'une colonisation laborieuse: Le Sud calédonien (1853–1860)*, Paris/Nouméa: L'Harmattan/Agence de développement de la culture kanak

—— 1998. *Canaques de la Nouvelle-Calédonie à Paris en 1931: De la case au zoo*, Paris: L'Harmattan

Davis, Mike 2001. *Late Victorian Holocausts: El Niño Famines and the Making of the Third World*. London/New York: Verso

de Heusch, Luc 1971. 'Possession et chamanisme', in *Pourquoi l'épouser? Et autres essais*. Paris: Gallimard, pp. 226–44. doi.org/10.3917/gall.deheu.1971.01

de la Haütière, Ulysse 1869. *Souvenirs de la Nouvelle-Calédonie, voyage sur la côte orientale. Un coup de main chez les Kanacks, Pilou-pilou à Naniouni*. Paris: Challamel aîné

Delord, Philadelphe 1901a, 'Lettre du 2 février 1901', *Journal des missions évangéliques*, no. 1, pp. 329–30

—— 1901b. *Mon voyage d'enquête en Nouvelle-Calédonie, août-septembre 1899*. Paris: Maison des missions évangéliques

Demmer, Christine 2002. 'Les héritiers d'Éloi Machoro (1941–1985): Une génération nationaliste au pouvoir à Amââ et Kûöö, villages du Xârâcûû (Canala), Nouvelle-Calédonie'. Doctoral thesis, EHESS, Paris

—— 2008. '"Les événements" des années 1980: Tremplin pour de nouveaux leaders kanaks en réserve', in Sylvette Boubin-Boyer (ed.), *Révoltes, conflits et guerres mondiales en Nouvelle-Calédonie et sa région*, vol. 1. Paris/Nouméa: L'Harmattan-Cercle du Musée de la ville de Nouméa, pp. 197–214

—— 2009. 'Secrets et organisation politique kanake. Pour sortir des catégories privé/ public', *L'Homme*, no. 190, pp. 79–104

Dening, Greg 1996. 'Possessing Tahiti', in *Performances*. Melbourne University Press, pp. 128–67

Deterts, Dorothea 2000. 'Gabentausch in Neukaledonien zur sozialen Reproduktion der Kanak in der paicî Spracheregion um Koné'. Doctoral thesis, University of Göttingen

Dewerpe, Alain 2006. *Charonne, 8 février 1962: Anthropologie historique d'un massacre d'État*. Paris: Gallimard (coll. 'Folio. Histoire')

Diapea, William 1928. *Cannibal Jack: The True Autobiography of a White Man in the South Seas*. London: Faber and Gwyer

—— 1999. *The Goldfields Journal of William Diaper [sic] (alias 'Cannibal Jack'), 1851–1853*. Carlisle: Hesperian Press

Diaper, William 1951. *The Complete Works of William Diaper*, ed. Dorothy Broughton. London: Routledge and Kegan Paul

Dinnen, Sinclair and Thompson, Edwina 2004. *Gender and Small Arms Violence in Papua New Guinea*. Canberra: State Society and Governance in Melanesia, Australian National University

Djama, Marcel 1999. 'Transformations agraires et systèmes ruraux mélanésiens en Grande Terre de Nouvelle-Calédonie', *JATBA. Revue d'ethnobiologie*, vol. 41, no. 1, pp. 201–24

Dommel, Daniel 1993. *La crise calédonienne, rémission ou guérison?* Paris: L'Harmattan

Dornoy, Myriam 1984. *Politics in New Caledonia*. Sydney University Press

Doucet, Dr, 1913. 'Épidémie de peste en Nouvelle-Calédonie en 1912', *Annales d' hygiène et de médecine coloniales*, no. 16, pp. 891–901

Douglas, Bronwen 1998. 'Apologia on Gender', in *Across the Great Divide: Journeys in History and Anthropology*. Amsterdam: Harwood Academic Publishers, pp. 113–21

Douglas, Bronwen and Ballard, Chris (eds) 2008. *Foreign Bodies: Oceania and the Science of Race (1750–1940)*. Canberra: ANU E Press

Dousset-Leenhardt, Roselène 1970. *Colonialisme et contradictions: Étude sur les causes socio-historiques de l'insurrection de 1878 en Nouvelle-Calédonie*. Paris/The Hague: Mouton

—— 1976. *Terre natale, terre d'exil*. Paris: Maisonneuve et Larose

Du Bouzet, Joseph 1858. 'Note sur la Nouvelle-Calédonie', 25 October. Aix-en-Provence: CAOM, SGNC 231

Dussy, Dorothée 2000. 'La mémoire kanak de Nouméa', in Alban Bensa and Isabelle Leblic (eds), *En pays kanak: Ethnologie, linguistique, archéologie, histoire de la Nouvelle-Calédonie*. Paris: Éditions de la MSH, pp. 147–68. doi.org/10.4000/books.editionsmsh.2779

—— 2012. *Nouméa, ville océanienne? S'approprier la ville*. Paris: Karthala

Erskine, John Elphinstone 1851. 'Proceedings at the South Sea Islands', *Journal of the Royal Geographical Society of London*, vol. 21, pp. 222–40. doi.org/10.2307/1798188

—— 1853. *Journal of a Cruise among the Islands of the Western Pacific … in Her Majesty's Ship Havannah*. London: John Murray

Etemad, Bouda 2007. *Possessing the World: Taking the Measurements of Colonisation from the 18th to the 20th Century*, trans. by Andrene Everson. Oxford: Berghahn Books

'Étude des vœux de l'UICALO' 1947. Nouméa: Archives de la Nouvelle-Calédonie, 97W18

Euritéin, Nissol 1990. 'Kuwa ka baayê rö Wailu', in Sylvain Aramiou and Jean Euritéin (eds), *Gö vârâ mêrê a' jië*. Houaïlou: Fédération de l'enseignement libre protestant, p. 9

Exposition internationale 1889. 'Nouvelle-Calédonie'. Colonies françaises et pays de protectorat. Paris, pp. 167–85

Exposition universelle internationale de 1878 à Paris 1878. 'Nouvelle-Calédonie', vol. 5, Paris, pp. 309–43

Fabian, Johannes 2002. *Time and the Other: How Anthropology Makes its Object*. New York: Columbia University Press

Faugère, Elsa 1998. 'L'argent et la coutume, Maré (Nouvelle-Calédonie)'. Doctoral thesis, EHESS, Paris

—— 2000. 'Transactions monétaires en pays kanak'. *Genèses*, no. 41, pp. 41–62

Feldman, Allen 1991. *Formations of Violence: The Narrative of the Body and Political Terror in Northern Ireland*. University of Chicago Press. doi.org/10.7208/chicago/9780226240800.001.0001

Foucault, Michel 1995 (1977). *Discipline and Punish: The Birth of the Prison*, trans. by Alan Sheridan. New York: Vintage Books

—— 2003. *Society Must Be Defended: Lectures at the Collège de France, 1975–76*, trans. by David Macey. London: Penguin

Foucher, Émile 1988 [1856]. 'Souvenirs des trois moineaux', in Bernard Brou, Hélène Colombani and Georges Coquilhat (eds), *Six textes anciens sur la Nouvelle-Calédonie*. Nouméa: Publications de la Société d'études historiques de Nouvelle-Calédonie, pp. 121–265

France australe (La) 1918. 'Tournée du Gouverneur sur la côte Est', no. 8466, 26 April

Fraysse, Victor 1905. 'Lettre à un scolastique du 10 janvier 1905', *Annales des missions de l'Océanie*, no. 11. Lyon: Librairie E. Vitte, pp. 285–92

Gabriel, Claude and Kermel, Vincent 1985. *Nouvelle-Calédonie, la révolte kanake*. Montreuil: La Brèche

—— 1988. *Nouvelle-Calédonie, les sentiers de l'espoir*. Montreuil: Presse-Édition-Communication

Gauharou, Léon 1882. *Géographie de la Nouvelle-Calédonie et dépendances*. Nouméa: Imprimerie du gouvernement

—— 1892. *Géographie de la Nouvelle-Calédonie*. 2nd edn. Nouméa: Imprimerie nouméenne

Geertz, Clifford 1973. 'Religion as a Cultural System', in *The Interpretation of Cultures*. New York: Basic Books, pp. 87–125

Genevray, J. 1925. 'La lèpre en Nouvelle-Calédonie', *Bulletins de la Société de pathologie exotique et de sa filiale de l'Ouest africain*, vol. 18, no. 1, pp. 78–89; vol. 18, no. 2, pp. 158–71

Geschiere, Peter 1995. *Sorcellerie et politique en Afrique: La viande des autres*, with Cyprian F. Fisiy. Paris: Karthala

Goldberg, Pâquerette, Luce, Danièle, Billon-Galland, Marie-Annick, Quénel, Philippe, Salomon-Nékiriai, Christine et al. 1995. 'Rôle potentiel de l'exposition environnementale et domestique à la trémolite dans le cancer de la plèvre en Nouvelle- Calédonie', *Revue d' épidémiologie et de santé publique*, no. 43, pp. 444–50

González de Reufels, Delia 2003. *Siedler und Filibuster in Sonora: Eine mexikanische Region im Interesse ausländischer Abenteuer une Mächte (1821–1860)*. Cologne/Weimar/Vienna: Böhlau

Goody, Jack 1977. *The Domestication of the Savage Mind*. Cambridge University Press

Grimoult, Jean-Baptiste 1859. *Renseignements nautiques sur la Nouvelle-Calédonie et les îles Loyalty*. Paris: Dépôt des cartes et plans de la marine, Imprimerie administrative de Paul Dupont, extrait des *Annales Hydrographiques,* 2e trimestre

Guiart, Jean 1949. *Les origines de la population d'Ouvéa (Loyalty) et la place des migrations en cause sur le plan général océanien*. Nouméa: Office de la recherche scientifique coloniale, Institut français d'Océanie

—— 1951. 'En marge du "Cargo cult" aux Nouvelles-Hébrides, le mouvement coopératif dit "Malekula Native Company"', *Journal de la Société des océanistes*, no. 7, pp. 242–47

—— 1953. 'Nouvelle-Calédonie et îles Loyalty. Carte du dynamisme de la société indigène à l'arrivée des Européens', *Journal de la Société des océanistes*, no. 9, pp. 93–97

—— 1955. *Structure politique de la société autochtone dans la région de Houaïlou*, stencil-printed report. Paris/Nouméa: Office de la recherche scientifique et technique outre-mer/Institut français d'Océanie

—— 1956a. 'Le mouvement coopératif aux Nouvelles-Hébrides', *Journal de la Société des océanistes*, no. 12, pp. 326–34

—— 1956b. 'Organisation coutumière en Nouvelle-Calédonie et aux Loyalty. Notes à propos de l'organisation intérieure des tribus autochtones en Nouvelle-Calédonie et aux îles Loyalty', printed report. Nouméa: Institut français d'Océanie

—— 1959a. *Développement communautaire et coopération dans le Pacifique Sud*. Paris: Bureau d'études communautaires, Centre de recherches coopératives, extract from *Archives internationales de sociologie de la coopération*, vol. 3, no. 5

—— 1959b. 'Naissance et avortement d'un messianisme. Colonisation et décolonisation en Nouvelle-Calédonie'. *Archives de sociologie des religions*, no. 7, pp. 3–44

—— 1959c. *Destin d'une Église et d'un peuple (1900–1959). Étude monographique d'une œuvre missionnaire protestante*. Paris: Mouvement du christianisme social

—— 1963. *Structure de la chefferie en Mélanésie du Sud*. Paris: Institut d'ethnologie

—— 1966. *L'entrée des Mélanésiens dans la cite*. Paris: Centre de documentation pour l'Océanie

—— 1967. 'De quelques affaires récentes de "voyants" en Nouvelle-Calédonie', *Journal de la Société des océanistes*, no. 23, pp. 135–44

—— 1970. 'Les événements de 1917 en Nouvelle-Calédonie'. *Journal de la Société des océanistes*, no. 26, pp. 265–82

—— 1972. 'Généalogies équivoques en Nouvelle-Calédonie', in Lucien Bernot et Jacqueline M.C. Thomas (eds), *Langues et techniques, nature et société*, vol. 2 *Approche ethnologique, approche naturaliste*. Paris: Klincksieck, pp. 37–51

—— 1987. 'La vallée de Houaïlou, Nouvelle-Calédonie. Une analyse renouvelée', *Journal de la Société des océanistes*, no. 43, pp. 157–79

—— 1993. 'Aventures en recherches sociales appliquées', *Cahiers des sciences humaines* (special issue *Trente ans: 1963–1992*), pp. 51–55

—— 1997. Maurice Leenhardt. *Le lien d'un homme avec un peuple qui ne voulait pas mourir*. Nouméa: Le Rocher-à-la-Voile

—— 1998. *Bwesou Eurijisi. Le premier écrivain canaque*. 2nd revised edn 2003. Nouméa: Le Rocher-à-la-Voile

—— 2004. 'Du nouveau sur "Cannibal Jack"', *Journal de la Société des océanistes,* no. 118, pp. 93–96

Guiart, René 2001. *Le feu sous la marmite*. Nouméa: Le-Rocher-à-la-Voile

Hamayon, Roberte 1995. 'Pour en finir avec la "transe" et l'"extase" dans l'étude du chamanisme', *Études mongoles et sibériennes*, no. 26, pp. 155–90

Hamelin, Christine 2000. '"Les gens de Nouméa": mutations et permanences en milieu urbain', in Alban Bensa and Isabelle Leblic (eds), *En pays kanak. Ethnologie, linguistique, archéologie, histoire de la Nouvelle-Calédonie*. Paris: Éditions de la MSH, pp. 339–54. doi.org/10.4000/books.editionsmsh.2801

Hamelin, Christine and Salomon, Christine 2004. 'Parenté et violences faites aux femmes en Nouvelle-Calédonie. Un éclairage sur l'ethnicité différentiée des violences dans la famille', *Espace, populations et sociétés*, no. 2, pp. 307–23. doi.org/10.4000/eps.195

Hamelin, Christine, Salomon, Christine, Goldberg, Pâquerette, Sitta, Rémi, Cyr, Diane and Goldberg, Marcel 2005. 'Consommation d'alcool et violences à l'encontre des femmes en Nouvelle-Calédonie', *Les Cahiers de l'Ireb*, no. 17, pp. 117–86

—— 2007. 'Violences et familles en Nouvelle-Calédonie. Perspectives ethnographiques et statistiques', in Maryse Jaspard and Natacha Chetcuti (eds), *Violences envers les femmes. Trois pas en avant, deux pas en arrière*. Paris: L'Harmattan, pp. 257–72

Hanoteau, Adolphe and Letourneux, Aristide 1872–73. *La Kabylie et les coutumes kabyles*, 3 vols. Paris: Imprimerie nationale

Harries, Patrick 2000. 'Field Sciences in Scientific Fields: Entomology, Botany and the Early Ethnographic Monograph in the work of H.-A. Junod', in Saul Dubow (ed.), *Science and Society in Southern Africa*. University of Manchester Press, pp. 11–41

—— 2007. *Butterflies and Barbarians: Swiss Missionaries and Systems of Knowledge in South-East Africa*. Oxford/Athens: James Currey/Ohio University Press

Harrison, Simon 1990. *Stealing People's Names: History and Politics in a Sepik River Cosmology*. Cambridge University Press. doi.org/10.1017/CBO9780511521096

—— 1993. *The Mask of War: Violence, Ritual, and the Self in Melanesia*. Manchester University Press

Hau'ofa, Epeli 2008 [1993]. 'Our Sea of Islands', in *We are the Ocean: Selected Works*. Honolulu: University of Hawai'i Press, pp. 27–40

Herle, Anita and Rouse, Sandra (eds) 1998. *Cambridge and the Torres Strait: Centenary Essays on the 1898 Anthropological Expedition*. Cambridge University Press

Hillereau, Father 1878. Letter to R.F. Poupinel, 24 September. Rome: Archives of the Society of Mary

—— 1879. Letter to R.P. Poupinel, 5 February. Rome: Archives of the Society of Mary

Hollyman, Kenneth James 1959. 'A Polynesian Migration Circa 1765', *The Journal of the Polynesian Society*, vol. 68, no. 4, pp. 357–89

Houaïlou Regional Squad (Brigade territoriale de Houaïlou) 1937–1942. 'Registre copie de Correspondance de la Brigade Territoriale de Houaïlou'. Vincennes: Archives de la Gendarmerie, 98E27

Howe, Kerry R. 1974. 'Firearms and Indigenous Warfare: A Case Study', *The Journal of Pacific History*, vol. 9, pp. 21–38

Imbert, Claude 2005. 'Le cadastre des savoirs. Figures de connaissance et prises de réel', in Jean-Claude Passeron and Jacques Revel (eds), *Penser par cas*, Paris: Éditions de l'EHESS, pp. 255–79

ISEE 2009. 'Budget Consommation des Ménages 2008', *Synthèse*, no. 11, June

Jacknis, Ira 1991. 'George Hunt, Collector of Indian Specimens', in Aldona Jonaitis (ed.), *Chiefly Feasts: The Enduring Kwakiutl Potlatch*. American Museum of Natural History/University of Washington Press, pp. 177–224

—— 1996. 'The Ethnographic Object and the Object of Ethnology in the Early Career of Franz Boas', in George W. Stocking Jr (ed.), *Volksgeist as Method and Ethic: Essays on Boasian Ethnography and the German Anthropological Tradition*. Madison: University of Wisconsin Press, pp. 185–14

Jacquemin, Sylviane 1990. 'Une journée en Nouvelle-Calédonie à Paris. Les expositions universelles et colonials', in Roger Boulay (ed.), *De jade et de nacre: Patrimoine artistique kanak* [exhibition]. Paris: Réunion des musées nationaux, pp. 235–37

Jolly, Margaret 1982. 'Birds and Banyans of South Pentecost: Kastom in Anticolonial Struggle', *Mankind*, no. 13, pp. 338–56. doi.org/10.1111/j.1835-9310.1982.tb00999.x

—— 1987. 'The Forgotten Women: A History of Migrant Labour and Gender Relations in Vanuatu', *Oceania*, vol. 58, no. 2, pp. 119–39. doi.org/10.1002/j.1834-4461.1987.tb02265.x

Jouan, Henri 1865. 'Recherches sur l'origine et la provenance de certains végétaux phanérogames observés dans les îles du Grand-Océan', *Mémoires de la société impériale des sciences naturelles de Cherbourg*, no 11, pp. 81–178

Journal officiel de la Nouvelle-Calédonie 1912. 'Décision 396 du 3 avril 1912', and 'Partage des tribus dites de Houaïlou en quatre districts, Arrêté no 353', 15 April

—— 1981. 'Délibération no 351 relative au conseil du clan et au conseil des chefs de clan', 28 December

Juillerat, Bernard 1975. 'Transe et langage en Nouvelle-Guinée', *Journal de la Société des océanistes*, vol. 31, no. 47, pp. 187–212; vol. 31, no. 49, pp. 379–97

Kasarhérou, Christiane 1991 (1988). *Contribution à l'étude de démographie historique de la Nouvelle-Calédonie. 1853–1920*. Nouméa: Centre territorial de recherche et de documentation pédagogiques de Nouvelle-Calédonie

Kaufmann, Christian 1990. 'Fritz Sarasin: un chercheur bâlois en Nouvelle-Calédonie (1911–12)', in Roger Boulay (ed.), *De jade et de nacre: Patrimoine artistique kanak* [exhibition]. Paris: Réunion des musées nationaux, pp. 232–35

Kawharu, Ian H. (ed.) 1989. *Waitangi: Maori and Pakeha Perspectives of the Treaty of Waitangi*. Auckland: Oxford University Press

Keesing, Roger 1982. 'Kastom and Anticolonialism on Malaita: "Culture" as Political Symbol', *Mankind*, no. 13, pp. 357–73

Knauft, Bruce 1990. 'Melanesian Warfare: A Theoretical History', *Oceania*, no. 60, pp. 250–311. doi.org/10.1002/j.1834-4461.1990.tb01557.x

Knoblauch, Ferdinand 1903. '35 Years in New Caledonia'. Sydney: Mitchell Library ZML MSS 969, CY Reel 756

—— 1988. 'Le manuscrit de Ferdinand Knoblauch', in Bernard Brou, Hélène Colombani and Georges Coquilhat (eds), *Six textes anciens sur la Nouvelle-Calédonie*. Nouméa: Publications de la Société d'études historiques de Nouvelle-Calédonie, pp. 19–69

Kurtovitch, Ismet 1997. *Aux origines du FLNKS. L'UICALO et l'AICLF (1946–1953)*. Nouméa: Île de Lumière

—— 2002. 'La vie politique en Nouvelle-Calédonie (1940–1953)'. Doctoral thesis, Université française du Pacifique

Lachapelle, Alfred de (ed.) 1859. *Le comte de Raousset-Boulbon et l'expédition de 'la Sonore': Correspondance, souvenirs et œuvres inédites*. Paris: Dentu

Lacheret, Marc 1951. Letter to M. le Professeur Maurice Leenhardt. Nouméa, 7 July 1951. Paris: DEFAP Archives

Laroche, Marie-Claude 1953. 'Collection d'objets calédoniens du Muséum de Toulouse', *Journal de la Société des océanistes*, no. 9, pp. 307–19

Latham, Linda 1978. *La révolte de 1878: Étude critique des causes de la rébellion de 1878 en Nouvelle-Calédonie*. Nouméa: Publications de la Société d'études historiques de la Nouvelle-Calédonie

Laurent 1857. Extract from a Report, 13 January. Aix-en-Provence: CAOM, SGNC 42

Lavondès, Anne 1990. *Vitrine des objets océaniens. Inventaire des collections du muséum de Grenoble: cultures matérielles et histoire dans le Pacifique au xixe siècle*. Grenoble/Paris: Muséum de Grenoble/ORSTOM

Leblic, Isabelle 1993. *Les Kanak face au développement: La voie étroite*. Grenoble/Nouméa: Presses universitaires de Grenoble/Agence pour le développement de la culture kanak

—— 2000. 'Le dualisme matrimonial paicî en question (Ponérihouen, Nouvelle-Calédonie)', *L'Homme*, nos 154–55, pp. 183–204

Lebœuf, Alexis, Dr 1912a. 'Dossier sanitaire des tribus. Saint-Louis, Conception; Azareux, Ny, Poté, Bouérou (Bourail); Boraré (Houaïlou)', *Journal officiel de la Nouvelle-Calédonie*, 1 April, pp. 130–35

—— 1912b. 'Dossier sanitaire des tribus. Île Ouen, Tribus de Houaïlou', *Journal officiel de la Nouvelle-Calédonie*, 15 October, pp. 347–52

—— 1913. 'Épidémie de peste en Nouvelle-Calédonie en 1912. Travaux de laboratoire', *Annales d'hygiène et de médecine coloniales*, no. 16, pp. 901–10

—— 1914. 'La lèpre en Nouvelle-Calédonie et dépendances', *Annales d'hygiène et de médecine coloniales*, no. 17, pp. 177–97

Le Bris, É. 1856. 'Lettre au ministre de la marine et des colonies', 7 August. Aix-en-Provence: CAOM, SGNC 42

Le Bris, Michel 1988. *La fièvre de l'or*. Paris: Gallimard

—— 1998. *Les flibustiers de la Sonore: A novel*. Paris: Flammarion

—— 1999. *Quand la Californie était française: L'épopée des chercheurs d'or français en Californie (1848–1854) à travers leurs mémoires, journaux, récits et lettres*. Paris: Le Pré aux clercs

Le Cour Grandmaison, Olivier 2005. *Coloniser, exterminer: Sur la guerre et l'État colonial*. Paris: Fayard

Leenhardt, Geneviève and Leenhardt, Raymond 1958. 'Le voyage en Nouvelle-Calédonie', printed memoir. Paris: DEFAP Archives

Leenhardt, Maurice 1902–20. Lettres à ses parents. Aix-en-Provence: CAOM, APOM 54/1

—— 1903. 'Lettre de Houaïlou du 24 novembre 1902', *Journal des missions évangéliques*, no. 1

—— 1907. 'Rapport annuel de la mission en Nouvelle-Calédonie', December 1906, *Journal des missions évangéliques*, no. 1

—— 1909a. 'Note sur quelques pierres-figures rapportées de Nouvelle-Calédonie', *Revue de l'école d'anthropologie de Paris*, 19e année, pp. 292–95

—— 1909b. *La Grande Terre: Mission de Nouvelle-Calédonie*. Paris: Société des missions évangéliques

—— 1910. Letter, 13 February. Archives du musée de Neuchâtel

—— 1910–17. Journal. Aix-en-Provence: CAOM, APOM 54/2

—— 1913. 'À Houaïlou', March letter, *Journal des missions évangéliques*, no. 1

—— n.d. [c. 1914–26]. Notes manuscrites, in one of Élia Mârârhëë's notebooks, including 'Warai. Lignée des Néporo'. Leenhardt private archives

—— 1917–18. Lettres à son épouse Jeanne. Paris: Leenhardt private archives

—— n.d. [c. 1917–19]. 'Recensement ethnologique de la vallée de Houaïlou', microfiche. Paris: Institut d'ethnologie

—— 1922a. *La Grande Terre: Mission de Nouvelle-Calédonie*. 2nd edn. Paris: Société des missions évangéliques

—— 1922b. 'La fête du pilou en Nouvelle-Calédonie', *L'anthropologie*, no. 32, pp. 221–63

—— 1930. *Notes d'ethnologie néo-calédonienne*. Paris: Institut d'ethnologie

—— 1932. *Documents néo-calédoniens*. Paris: Institut d'ethnologie

—— 1935. *Vocabulaire et grammaire de la langue Houaïlou*. Paris: Institut d'ethnologie

—— 1937a. *Gens de la Grande Terre*. Paris: Gallimard

—— 1937b. 'Le temps et la personnalité chez les Canaques de la Nouvelle-Calédonie', *Revue philosophique de la France et de l'étranger*, vol. 124, nos 9–10, pp. 43–58

—— 1953. '1952', in *Gens de la Grande Terre*. 2nd edn. Paris: Gallimard, pp. 213–23

—— 1977. 'Questionnaire pour la connaissance des clans (21 mars 1918)', *Objets et mondes*, vol. 17, no. 2, pp. 89–92

—— 1979 [1947]. *Do kamo: Person and Myth in the Melanesian World*, trans. by Basia Miller Gulati. Chicago/London: Chicago University Press

Leenhardt, Maurice, Sarasin, Fritz and Montague, Paul D. 1998. *Le pilou, moment culminant de la société*, trans. and introd. Raymond Ammann et Bernard Gasser. Nouméa: Grain de Sable

Leenhardt, Raymond 1976. 'Un sociologue canaque: le pasteur Boésoou Erijiyi, 1866–1947', *Cahiers d'histoire du Pacifique*, no. 4, pp. 19–53

Leenhardt, Raymond and Vasseur, Jacques 1987. 'Mindia Wepoe Neja, Grand chef des Houaïlous (1856–1921)', *Journal de la Société des océanistes*, no. 43, pp. 31–47. doi.org/10.3406/jso.1987.2559

Legrand, Maximilien-Albert 1893. *Au pays des Canaques: La Nouvelle-Calédonie et ses habitants en 1890*. Paris: L. Baudoin

Le Meur, Pierre-Yves 2003. *Appui à une politique de sécurisation foncière en Nouvelle-Calédonie*, Report of study visit. Paris: GRET

Lemire, Charles 1877. *La colonisation française en Nouvelle-Calédonie et dépendances*. Paris: Challamel

—— 1884. *Voyage à pied en Nouvelle-Calédonie et description des Nouvelles-Hébrides*. Paris: Challamel

Lenormand, Maurice 1953. 'L'évolution politique des autochtones de la Nouvelle-Calédonie', *Journal de la Société des océanistes*, no. 9, pp. 245–99. doi.org/10.3406/jso.1953.1778

—— 1970. 'Le mariage à Lifou, coutumes et acculturation', *Journal de la Société des océanistes*, no. 26, pp. 39–54

Lercari, Claude 2002. *Dictionnaire ajië-français à l'usage des étudiants. Langue de la région de Houailou, Nouvelle-Calédonie*. Nouméa: Centre de documentation pédagogique de Nouvelle-Calédonie

L'Estoile, Benoît de 2007. 'Une politique de l'âme: Ethnologie et humanisme colonial chez Maurice Leenhardt', in Michel Naepels and Christine Salomon (eds), *Terrains et destins de Maurice Leenhardt*. Paris: Éditions de l'EHESS, pp. 27–49

Lévi-Strauss, Claude 2016. *We Are All Cannibals, and Other Essays*, trans. by Jane Marie Todd. New York: Columbia University Press

Lewis, Ioan M. 1971. *Ecstatic Religion: An Anthropological Study of Spirit Possession and Shamanism*. London: Penguin. doi.org/10.4324/9780203241080

Loraux, Nicole 2006. *The Divided City: On Memory and Forgetting in Ancient Athens*, trans. by Corinne Pache with Jeff Fort. New York: Zone Books

Lucas, Philippe and Vatin, Jean-Claude (eds) 1975. *L'Algérie des anthropologues*. Paris: Maspéro

Luce, Danièle, Brochard, Patrick, Quénel, Philippe, Salomon-Nékiriai Christine et al. 1994. 'Malignant Pleural Mesothelioma Associated with Exposure to Tremolite', *The Lancet*, vol. 344, no. 8939, p. 1777. doi.org/10.1016/S0140-6736(94)92919-X

Luce, Danièle, Bugel, Isabelle, Goldberg, Pâquerette, Goldberg, Marcel, Salomon, Christine et al. 2000. 'Environmental Exposure to Tremolite and Respiratory Cancer in New Caledonia: A Case-Control Study', *American Journal of Epidemiology*, vol. 151, no. 3, pp. 259–65. doi.org/10.1093/oxfordjournals.aje.a010201

Luquet, Georges-Henri 1926. *L'art néo-calédonien*, Marius Archambault (ed.). Paris: Institut d'ethnologie

Mahé, Alain 2001. *Histoire de la Grande Kabylie, xixe-xxe siècles: Anthropologie historique du lien social dans les communautés villageoises*. Saint-Denis: Bouchène

Mamdani, Mahmood 1996. *Citizen and Subject: Contemporary Africa and the Legacy of Late Colonialism*. Princeton University Press

—— 2001. 'Beyond Settler and Native as Political Identities: Overcoming the Political Legacy of Colonialism', *Comparative Studies in Society and History*, vol. 43, no. 4, pp. 651–64

Mandaoué, Paul and Notouo 1978 [1920]. 'Lettre de janvier 1920 au chef du service des affaires indigenes', *Centenaire Maurice Leenhardt (1878–1954)*, Annexe IV, 'Femmes captives'. Nouméa: Publications de la Société d'études historiques de la Nouvelle-Calédonie, p. 91

Mariotti, Jean 1942. *À bord de l'Incertaine*. Paris: Stock

—— 2001 (1953). *Nouvelle-Calédonie: Le livre du centenaire (1853–1953)*, annotated by Bernard Gasser, introduced by Nicolas Kurtovitch. Nouméa: Grain de Sable

Marx, Karl 2005. *The Eighteenth Brumaire of Louis Bonaparte*, trans. by D.D.L. New York/Berlin: Mondial

Maspéro, François 1995 [1993]. *L'honneur de Saint-Arnaud*. Paris: Seuil

Merle, Isabelle 1995. *Expériences colonials: La Nouvelle-Calédonie (1853–1920)*. Paris: Belin

—— 1998. 'La construction d'un droit foncier colonial. De la propriété collective à la constitution des réserves en Nouvelle-Calédonie', *Enquête*, no. 7, pp. 97–126

—— 2002. 'Retour sur le régime de l'indigénat: Genèse et contradictions des principes répressifs dans l'Empire français', *French Politics, Culture and Society*, vol. 20, no. 2, pp. 77–97

—— 2004. 'De la "légalisation" de la violence en contexte colonial: Le régime de l'indigénat en question', *Politix*, vol. 17, no. 66, pp. 137–62. doi.org/10.3406/polix.2004.1019

—— 2005. 'Compte-rendu d'A. Bullard (2000), Exile to Paradise: Savagery and Civilization in Paris and the South Pacific, 1790–1900', *French Politics, Culture and Society*, vol. 23, no. 1, pp. 130–36

Mokaddem, Hamid 2005. *Ce souffle venu des ancêtres … L'œuvre politique de Jean-Marie Tjibaou (1936–1989)*. Nouméa: Expressions-Province Nord

Moncelon, Léon 1885. 'Présentation d'un canaque néo-calédonien', *Bulletins de la Société d'anthropologie de Paris*, 3rd series, vol. 8, pp. 353–65

—— 1886. 'Réponse alinéa par alinéa, pour les Néo-Calédoniens, au questionnaire de sociologie et d'ethnographie de la société', *Bulletins de la Société d'anthropologie de Paris*, 3rd series, vol. 9, pp. 345–80

—— 1887. 'Sauvages et forêts vierges: Une ascension en Nouvelle-Calédonie', *L'Homme*, no. 4, pp. 262–75, pp. 295–310, pp. 335–40

Moniteur (Le) 1951, 'Message du bureau de l'A.I.C.L.F.', no. 7, June.

Moniteur 1863. 'Nouvelles locales', *Moniteur de la Nouvelle-Calédonie*, no. 204, 23 August

—— 1863. 'Quelques mots sur la côte est de la NC. II. De Kanala à Wagap (60 milles)', *Moniteur de la Nouvelle-Calédonie*, no. 205, 30 August

—— 1863. 'Nouvelles locales', *Moniteur de la Nouvelle-Calédonie*, no. 210, 4 October

—— 1864. 'Nouvelles locales', *Moniteur de la Nouvelle-Calédonie*, no. 240, 1 May

—— 1864. 'Nouvelles locales. Expédition de Monéo, Mou et de Pounérihouen', *Moniteur de la Nouvelle-Calédonie*, no. 241, 8 May

—— 1864. 'Projet d'émigration de la Réunion vers la Nouvelle-Calédonie', *Moniteur de la Nouvelle-Calédonie*, no. 267, 6 November

—— 1868. 'De Canala à Bourail et à Houaïlou', *Moniteur de la Nouvelle-Calédonie*, no. 462, 2 August

—— 1868. 'De Canala à Bourail et à Houaïlou', *Moniteur de la Nouvelle-Calédonie*, no. 463, 9 August

—— 1868. 'De Canala à Bourail et à Houaïlou', *Moniteur de la Nouvelle-Calédonie*, no. 466–67, 30 August and 6 September

—— 1878. *Moniteur de la Nouvelle-Calédonie*, no. 989, 4 September

—— 1878. *Moniteur de la Nouvelle-Calédonie*, no. 992, 25 September

—— 1878. *Moniteur de la Nouvelle-Calédonie*, no. 994, 9 October

—— 1878. *Moniteur de la Nouvelle-Calédonie*, no. 995, 16 October

—— 1878. *Moniteur de la Nouvelle-Calédonie*, no. 996, 23 October

—— 1878. *Moniteur de la Nouvelle-Calédonie*, no. 997, 30 October

—— 1878. *Moniteur de la Nouvelle-Calédonie*, no. 998, 6 November

—— 1878. *Moniteur de la Nouvelle-Calédonie*, no. 999, 13 November

—— 1878. *Moniteur de la Nouvelle-Calédonie*, no. 1000, 20 November

—— 1878. *Moniteur de la Nouvelle-Calédonie*, no. 1001, 27 November

—— 1878. *Moniteur de la Nouvelle-Calédonie*, no. 1004, 18 December

—— 1879. *Moniteur de la Nouvelle-Calédonie*, no. 1014, 26 February

Montague, Paul D. n.d. (c. 1914–15). 'Ethnological Notes from the Houaïlou Valley, New Caledonia' (manuscript). Cambridge University Museum of Archaeology and Anthropology

Montrouzier, Xavier 1862. 'Lettre à ses parents', 1 April. Nouméa: Archives de l'Archevêché 9.3

Muckle, Adrian 2006. 'The "Chief without Power"? Téâ Antoine Katélia and the War of 1917–18 in New Caledonia', *Journal of Pacific History*, vol. 41, no. 3, pp. 313–34. doi.org/10.1080/00223340600984810

―― 2008. 'Kanak Experiences of WWI: New Caledonia's Tirailleurs, Auxiliaries, and "Rebels"', *History Compass*, vol. 6, no. 5, pp. 1325–45. doi.org/10.1111/j.1478-0542.2008.00553.x

―― 2010. 'Troublesome Chiefs and Disorderly Subjects: The *Indigénat* and the Internment of Kanak in New Caledonia (1887–1928)', *French Colonial History*, vol. 11, pp. 131–60. doi.org/10.1353/fch.0.0024

―― 2012. *Specters of Violence in a Colonial Context: New Caledonia (1917)*. Honolulu: University of Hawai'i Press

Naepels, Michel 1998. *Histoires de terres kanakes. Conflits fonciers et rapports sociaux dans la région de Houaïlou (Nouvelle-Calédonie)*. Paris: Belin

―― 1999. 'Mobilité et urbanisation kanak: l'exemple du pays ajië', in Gilbert David, Dominique Guillaud and Patrick Pillon (eds), *La Nouvelle-Calédonie à la croisée des chemins (1989-1997)*. Paris: Société des océanistes/Institut de recherche pour le développement, pp. 251–69

―― 2000a. 'Le conflit des interpretations: Récits de l'histoire et relations de pouvoir dans la région de Houaïlou (Nouvelle-Calédonie)', in Bertrand Masquelier and Jean-Louis Siran (eds), *Pour une anthropologie de l'interlocution. Rhétoriques du quotidien*. Paris: L'Harmattan, pp. 337–57

―― 2000b. 'Partir à Nouméa: Remarques sur les migrants originaires de la région ajië', in Alban Bensa and Isabelle Leblic (eds), *En pays kanak: Ethnologie, linguistique, archéologie, histoire de la Nouvelle-Calédonie*. Paris: Éditions de la MSH, pp. 355–65. doi.org/10.4000/books.editionsmsh.2755

―― 2003. 'Savoir, transmettre, enquêter: Quelques remarques sur le "patrimoine oral" et la recherche en sciences sociales', *Mwà véé: Revue culturelle kanak*, no. 40, pp. 13–15

―― 2004. 'Dispositifs disciplinaires: Sur la violence et l'enquête de terrain', *Critique*, nos 680–81, pp. 30–40

―― 2006a. 'Quatre questions sur la violence', *L'Homme*, nos 177–78, pp. 487–95

—— 2006b. 'Réforme foncière et propriété en Nouvelle-Calédonie: L'exemple de la région de Houaïlou', *Études rurales*, no. 177, pp. 43–53

—— 2007a. 'Notion de personne et dynamique missionnaire', in Michel Naepels and Christine Salomon (eds), *Terrains et destins de Maurice Leenhardt*. Paris: Éditions de l'EHESS, pp. 69–91

—— 2007b. 'Les pratiques ethnographiques de Maurice Leenhardt', in Michel Naepels and Christine Salomon (eds), *Terrains et destins de Maurice Leenhardt*. Paris: Éditions de l'EHESS, pp. 95–115

—— 2008. 'La derivazione etnografica: Mobilitazione del sapere e produzione di conoscenze in Nuova-Caledonia', *Quaderni Storici*, vol. 43 (3), no. 129, pp. 653–73

—— 2010a. 'Anthropologie et histoire: de l'autre côté du miroir disciplinaire', *Annales. Histoire, sciences sociales*, vol. 65, no. 4 (themed issue: *L'anthropologie face au temps*), pp. 873–84

—— 2010b. 'Le devenir colonial d'une chefferie kanake (Houaïlou, Nouvelle-Calédonie)', *Annales. Histoire, sciences sociales*, vol. 65, no. 4 (themed issue) *L'anthropologie face au temps*), pp. 913–43

—— 2011. *Ethnographie, pragmatique, histoire: Un parcours de recherche à Houaïlou (Nouvelle-Calédonie)*. Paris: Publications de la Sorbonne

—— 2012. 'Violence segmentaire et construction de l'État post-colonial. Conflictualité et historicité à Wakaya (Houaïlou, Nouvelle-Calédonie)', in Rémy Bazenguissa-Ganga and Sami Makki (eds), *Sociétés en guerres: Ethnographies des mobilisations violentes*. Paris: Éditions de la MSH, pp. 113–27

Nassiet, Michel 2011. *La violence, une histoire sociale. France, xvie-xviiie siècles*. Seyssel: Champ Vallon

Nérhon, Acoma 1969. 'Acoma Nérhon raconte sa vie …', *Le monde non chrétien*, nos 89–90, pp. 38–78

Nicolas, Hélène 2012. 'La fabrique des époux: Approche anthropologique et historique du mariage, de la conjugalité et du genre (Lifou, Nouvelle-Calédonie)'. Doctoral thesis, Aix-Marseille Université

Obeyesekere, Gananath 1998. 'Cannibal Feasts in Nineteenth-Century Fiji: Seamen's Yarns and the Ethnographic Imagination', in Francis Barker, Peter Hulme and Margaret Iversen (eds), *Cannibalism and the Colonial World*. Cambridge University Press, pp. 63–86

—— 2005. *Cannibal Talk: The Man-Eating Myth and Human Sacrifice in the South Seas*. Berkeley: University of California Press

O'Hanlon, Michael and Welsch, Robert (eds) 2000. *Hunting the Gatherers: Ethnographic Collectors, Agents, and Agency in Melanesia 1870s–1930s*. Oxford: Berghahn Books

O'Reilly, Patrick 1953. *Calédoniens. Répertoire bio-bibliographique de la Nouvelle-Calédonie*, illustrated by Jean Lebedeff. Paris: Société des océanistes

Pannetrat, Martin 1993. [*Journal du Havre*, 7, 8 and 10 May 1857]. '1856 au pays des Alikis', *Bulletin de la Société d'études historiques de la Nouvelle-Calédonie*, no. 96, pp. 17–47

Papiers Mindia n.d., microfilm of a notebook that belonged to Mèèjâ Néjâ. Leenhardt private archives

Patouillet, Jules 1872. *Trois ans en Nouvelle-Calédonie*. Paris: Dentu

Pégourier, Paul 1913. *Régime politique et administratif des colonies françaises sous la Restauration et la Monarchie de Juillet*. Brest: Imprimerie commerciale de la Dépêche

—— 1919. *Rapport de Monsieur l'Inspecteur des Colonies Pégourier concernant la vérification du Service de M. Fourcade, Chef du Service des Affaires Indigènes*. CAOM, Affaires politiques 742 (cited from the typescript version, Nouméa: Archives de la Nouvelle-Calédonie 97W11)

'Pensées de base de l'Association des indigènes calédoniens et loyaltiens français' 1946. Nouméa: Archives de la Nouvelle-Calédonie, 97W18

Pierre, Louis-Édouard 1898. 'Rapport sur les conditions dans lesquelles se trouvent actuellement les lépreux en Nouvelle-Calédonie', *Annales d'hygiène et de médecine coloniales*, no. 1, pp. 149–56

Pillon, Patrick 2001. 'En pays Mèa (Nouvelle-Calédonie): Approches ethnologiques des années 1980 et 1990. Lignages et récits lignagers', Professorial thesis for Université Paul-Valéry (typescript)

Piroutet, Maurice 1903. 'Mission géologique en Nouvelle-Calédonie', *Revue coloniale*, pp. 57–85

—— 1917. *Étude stratigraphique sur la Nouvelle-Calédonie*, Mâcon: Protat Frères

Pommé, Christophe 2006. 'La problématique cannabique en Province Nord. Une étude socio-économique'. Master's dissertation, Université de la Nouvelle-Calédonie

Poupinel, Victor, R.F. 1857. 'Letter to Very Reverend Father Colin, Founder of the Society of Mary', 2 December, *Annales des missions de la Société de Marie*, no. 1, pp. 125–26

Priday, H.E. Lewis 1944. *Cannibal Island: The Turbulent Story of New Caledonia's Cannibal Coasts*. Wellington: A.H. and A.W. Reed

—— 1950. 'A Polynesian Migration Circa 1765', *The Journal of the Polynesian Society*, vol. 59, no. 3, pp. 245–60

Rallu, Jean-Louis 1990. *Les populations océaniennes aux xixe et xxe siècles*. Paris: Ined/Puf

Rancière, Jacques 2011 (2006). *The Politics of Literature*, trans. by Julie Rose. Cambridge: Polity

Raousset-Boulbon, Gaston Raoulx (comte de) 1848. *La question des travailleurs résolue par la colonisation de l'Algérie*. Avignon: Fischer

'Rapport sur les opérations militaires' from 28 September to 24 October 1878; from 22 November to 22 December 1878; from 16 January to 5 February 1879. Nouméa: Archives de la Nouvelle-Calédonie, 21J2

Ratzel, Nicolas 2006. *Cahiers de mes souvenirs de géomètre calédonien (1894–1939)*, 2 vols. Nouméa: Publications de la Société d'études historiques de la Nouvelle-Calédonie

Rau, Éric 1944. *Institutions et coutumes canaques*. Paris: Larose

'Recensement général de la population, 5 mars 1911', Nouméa: Archives de la Nouvelle-Calédonie, 441W3

Récompenses accordées aux Auxiliaires Indigènes. Troubles dans les Tribus (1917). Nouméa: Archives de la Nouvelle-Calédonie, 1W1

'Régime des réserves autochtones en Nouvelle-Calédonie et dépendances: projet d'arrêté' 1958. Extraordinary sitting of the territorial assembly, 20 March. Nouméa: Archives de la Nouvelle-Calédonie, 40W14

Registre des tribus et des chefs n.d. Nouméa: Archives de la Nouvelle-Calédonie, 37W313

Repiquet, Jules 1978 [1917]. 'Réponse au président de la commission municipale de Houaïlou'. *Centenaire Maurice Leenhardt (1878–1954)*, Annexe II, 'Les auxiliaires'. Nouméa: Publications de la Société d'Études Historiques de la Nouvelle-Calédonie, p. 77

Retz, Cardinal de 1984. *Œuvres*. Paris: Gallimard

Rey-Lescure, Philippe 1958. 'La sève monte, Souvenirs (1922–1933)'. La Force: Archives de Nouvelle-Calédonie, 21J27

—— 1967. 'Vos racines … Essai d'histoire des débuts de l'évangélisation de la Nouvelle-Calédonie'. Manuscript held by the author, La Force

Rivers, William H.R. 1912. 'A General Account of Method', in *Notes and Queries on Anthropology*. 4th edn. London: British Association for the Advancement of Science, pp. 108–27

—— (ed.) 1922. *Essays on the Depopulation of Melanesia*. Cambridge University Press

Rochas, Victor de 1862. *La Nouvelle-Calédonie et ses habitants. Production-mœurs-cannibalisme*. Paris: Ferdinand Sartorius

Rosaldo, Renato 1989. 'Introduction: Grief and a Headhunter's Rage', in *Culture and Truth: The Remaking of Social Analysis*. Boston: Beacon, pp. 1–21

Rouget, Gilbert 1985 [1980]. *Music and Trance: A Theory of the Relations Between Music and Possession*, trans. Brunhilde Biebuyck. University of Chicago Press

Saada, Emmanuelle 2003. 'Citoyens et sujets de l'Empire français. Les usages du droit en situation colonial', *Genèses*, no. 53, pp. 4–24. doi.org/10.3917/gen.053.0004

—— 2012 [2007]. *Empire's Children: Race, Filiation and Citizenship in the French Colonies*, trans. Arthur Goldhammer. London/Chicago: University of Chicago Press

Sahlins, Marshall 1993. 'Goodbye to *Tristes Tropes*: Ethnography in the Context of Modern World History', in *Culture in Practice: Selected Essays*, New York: Zone Books, 2000, pp. 471–500

—— 2000. *Culture in Practice: Selected Essays*. New York: Zone Books

—— 2003. 'Artificially Maintained Controversies: Global Warming and Fijian Cannibalism', *Anthropology Today*, vol. 19, no. 3, pp. 3–5. doi.org/10.1111/1467-8322.00189

Salomon, Christine 1993. 'Savoirs, savoir-faire et pouvoirs thérapeutiques. Guérisseurs kanaks et relations de guérissage dans la région centre-nord de la Grande Terre'. MPhil thesis, École Pratique des Hautes Études

—— 1999. 'Les femmes face aux violences sexuelles et domestiques: le tournant judiciaire des années 1990', in Gilbert Bladinières (ed.), *Chroniques du pays kanak*, vol. 4. Nouméa: Planète Mémo, pp. 188–96

—— 2000a. *Savoirs et pouvoirs thérapeutiques kanaks*. Paris: Puf/Inserm

—— 2000b. 'Hommes et femmes. Harmonie d'ensemble ou antagonisme sourd?' in Alban Bensa and Isabelle Leblic (eds), *En pays kanak: Ethnologie, linguistique, archéologie, histoire de la Nouvelle-Calédonie*. Paris: Éditions de la MSH, pp. 311–38

Salomon, Christine and Hamelin Christine 2007. 'Les femmes kanakes sont fatiguées de la violence des hommes', *Journal de la Société des océanistes*, no. 125, pp. 284–94

Sand, Christophe 1995. *Le temps d'avant, la préhistoire de la Nouvelle-Calédonie. Contribution à l'étude des modalités d'adaptation et d'évolution des sociétés océaniennes dans un archipel du Sud de la Mélanésie*. Paris: L'Harmattan

Sarasin, Fritz 1913. *La Nouvelle-Calédonie et les îles Loyalty, souvenirs de voyage d'un naturaliste*, trans. by Jean Roux. Paris: Fischbacher

—— 1929. *Atlas zur Ethnologie des Neu-Caledonier und Loyalty-Insulaner*. Munich: C.W. Kreidel's Verlag

Sarasin, Fritz and Roux, Jean 1929. *Nova Caledonia. Forschungen in Neu-Caledonien und auf den Loyalty-Inseln*, vol. D. *Ethnologie*. Munich: C.W. Kreidel's Verlag

Saussol, Alain 1979. *L'héritage. Essai sur le problème foncier mélanésien en Nouvelle-Calédonie*. Paris: Société des océanistes

Savoie, Clovis 1922. *Dans l'Océan Pacifique. Histoire de la Nouvelle-Calédonie et de ses dépendances sous les gouverneurs militaires, 1853–1884*. Nouméa: Imprimerie nationale

Schaub, Jean-Frédéric 2008. 'La catégorie "études coloniales" est-elle indispensable?' *Annales. Histoire, sciences sociales*, vol. 63, no. 3, pp. 625–46

Scheper-Hughes, Nancy and Bourgois, Philippe (eds) 2004. *Violence in War and Peace: An Anthology*. Malden: Blackwell

Schieffelin, Edward L. 1977. 'The Unseen Influence: Tranced Mediums as Historical Innovators', *Journal de la Société des océanistes*, vol. 33, nos 56–57, pp. 169–78. doi.org/10.3406/jso.1977.2954

Schildkrout, Enid and Keim, Curtis A. (eds) 1998. *The Scramble for Art in Central Africa*. Cambridge University Press

Shineberg, Dorothy L. 1967. *They Came for Sandalwood: A Study of the Sandalwood Trade in the South-West Pacific, 1830–1865*. Melbourne University Press

—— 1971. 'Guns and men in Melanesia', *The Journal of Pacific History*, vol. 6, pp. 61–82. doi.org/10.1080/00223347108572183

—— 1983. 'Un nouveau regard sur la démographie historique de la Nouvelle-Calédonie', *Journal de la Société des océanistes*, vol. 39, no. 76, pp. 33–43. doi.org/10.3406/jso.1983.2770

—— 1999. *The People Trade: Pacific Islands Laborers and New Caledonia (1865–1930)*. Honolulu: University of Hawai'i Press

Sofsky, Wolfgang 2003. *Violence: Terrorism, Genocide, War*, trans. by Anthea Bell. London: Granta Books

Soriano, Éric 2000. 'Tisser des liens politiques: Mobilisations électorales et votes mélanésiens (1946–1958)', in Alban Bensa and Isabelle Leblic (eds), *En pays kanak: Ethnologie, linguistique, archéologie, histoire de la Nouvelle-Calédonie*. Paris: Éditions de la MSH, pp. 235–52. doi.org/10.4000/books.editionsmsh.2790

—— 2001. 'Une trajectoire du politique en Mélanésie. Construction identitaire et formation d'un personnel politique. L'exemple Kanak de Nouvelle-Calédonie (1946–1999)'. Doctoral thesis, Université Montpellier 1

Sourisseau, Emmanuelle 2006. 'Les sociétés locales face aux défis du développement économique, Annexe, Les dynamiques économiques et sociales en Province Nord de Nouvelle-Calédonie. Données de cadrage (1989–2005)'. CIRAD-IAC-DDEE-Province Nord Report

Sourisseau, Jean-Michel, Tuyiénon, Raymond, Gambey, Jean-Claude, Djama, Marcel and Mercoiret, Marie-Rose 2006. 'Les sociétés locales face aux défis du développement économique'. CIRAD-IAC-DDEE-Province Nord Report

Stephen, Michele 1979. 'Dreams of Change: The Innovative Role of Altered States of Consciousness in Traditional Melanesian Religion', *Oceania*, vol. 50, no. 1, pp. 3–22. doi.org/10.1002/j.1834-4461.1979.tb01927.x

Stocking, George W., Jr 1995. 'From Armchair to the Field: The Darwinian Zoologist as Ethnographer', in George W. Stocking Jr (ed.), *After Tylor: British Social Anthropology (1888–1951)*. Madison: University of Wisconsin Press, pp. 84–123

Tambiah, Stanley 1985. 'A Performative Approach to Ritual', in *Culture, Thought, and Social Action*. Cambridge, MA/London: Harvard University Press, pp. 123–66. doi.org/10.4159/harvard.9780674433748.c6

Taussig, Michael 1987. *Shamanism, Colonialism, and the Wild Man: A Study of Terror and Healing*. University of Chicago Press. doi.org/10.7208/chicago/9780226790114.001.0001

Testart, Alain 1996–97. 'Pourquoi ici la dot et là son contraire? Exercice de sociologie comparative des institutions', *Droit et cultures*, no. 32, pp. 7–36; no. 33, pp. 117–38; no. 34, pp. 99–134. doi.org/10.4000/lhomme.146

Testart, Alain, Govoroff, Nicolas and Lécrivain Valérie 2002. 'Les prestations matrimoniales', *L'Homme*, no. 161, pp. 165–96

Thomas, Nicholas 1989a. *Out of Time: History and Evolution in Anthropological Discourse*. Cambridge University Press

—— 1989b. 'The Force of Ethnology: Origins and Significance of the Melanesia/Polynesia Division', *Current Anthropology*, vol. 30, no. 1, pp. 27–41. doi.org/10.1086/203707

—— 1989c. 'Material Culture and Colonial Power: Ethnological Collecting and the Establishment of Colonial Rrule in Fiji', *Man*, vol. 24, no. 1, pp. 41–56. doi.org/10.2307/2802546

—— 1990. 'Sanitation and Seeing: The Creation of State Power in Early Colonial Fiji', *Comparative Studies in Society and History*, vol. 32, no. 1, pp. 149–70. doi.org/10.1017/S0010417500016364

Thompson, Anne-Gabrielle 2000. *John Higginson: Un spéculateur-aventurier à l'assaut du Pacifique, Nouvelle-Calédonie, Nouvelles-Hébrides*. Paris: L'Harmattan

Trépied, Benoît 2007. 'Politique et relations coloniales en Nouvelle-Calédonie. Ethnographie historique de la commune de Koné, 1946–1988'. Doctoral thesis, EHESS

—— 2010. *Une mairie dans la France coloniale. Koné, Nouvelle-Calédonie (1853–1977)*. Paris: Karthala

Tuzin, Donald 1988. 'Prospects of Village Death in Ilahita', *Oceania*, vol. 59, no. 2, pp. 81–104. doi.org/10.1002/j.1834-4461.1988.tb02313.x

Vasseur, Jacques 1985. 'Maurice Leenhardt et la rébellion de 1917 en Nouvelle- Calédonie, *Journal de la Société des océanistes*, no. 41, pp. 241–74. doi.org/10.3406/jso.1985.2815

Veyne, Paul 1984 [1971]. *Writing History: Essay on Epistemology*, trans. by Mina Moore-Rinvolucri. Middletown, CT: Wesleyan University Press

Vidal-Naquet, Pierre 1992. 'A Paper Eichmann', in *Assassins of Memory*, trans. by Jeffrey Mehlmann. New York: Columbia University Press, pp. xx

Vieillard, Eugène and Deplanche, Émile 1863. *Essais sur la Nouvelle-Calédonie*. Paris: Challamel

Vigors, Philip Doyne 1850. 'Private Journal of a Four Months Cruise through Some of the South Seas Islands and New Zealand in HMS *Havannah*'. Wellington: Turnbull Library, QMS-2081

Vincent, Jean-Baptiste-Maurice 1895. *Les Canaques de la Nouvelle-Calédonie: Esquisse ethnographique*. Paris, Challamel

'Vœux émis par l'assemblée des délégués de l'UICALO à Paita' 1947. Session of 12–19 March. Nouméa: Archives de la Nouvelle-Calédonie, 97W18

Wahéo, Taï 2008. *Oûguk, le coco vert*. Nouméa: ADCK-Centre culturel Tjibaou

Wallerstein, Immanuel 1980 [1974]. *Le système du monde du xve siècle à nos jours*, vol. 1, *Capitalisme et économie-monde (1450–1640)*. Paris: Flammarion

—— 1983. *Historical Capitalism*. London: Verso

—— 1984 [1980]. *Le système du monde du xve siècle à nos jours*, vol. 2, *Le mercantilisme et la consolidation de l'économie-monde européenne (1600–1750)*, trans. into French by Claude Markovits. Paris: Flammarion

—— 1991. *Unthinking Social Science: The Limits of Nineteenth-Century Paradigms*. Cambridge: Polity

—— (ed.) 1996. *Open the Social Sciences: Report of the Gulbenkian Commission on the Restructuring of the Social Sciences*. Stanford University Press

—— 1999. 'Social sciences in the twenty-first century', in Ali Kazancigil and David Makinson (eds), *World Social Science Report*. Paris: Unesco, pp. 42–49

Westphal, Charles 1957. *Bulletin du commerce*, 30 November

Wittig, Monique 1969. *Les guérillères*. Paris: Éditions de Minuit

Woodin, Edward 1846–53. 'Log Book of the Barque *Eleanor*'. Hobart: State Library of Tasmania, 910.4 ELE

—— 1850. 'Sandalwood Voyage', *Nautical Magazine*, May, pp. 298–302

www.ingramcontent.com/pod-product-compliance
Lightning Source LLC
Chambersburg PA
CBHW061255230426
43664CB00033B/2922